# The Political Economy of Regulation in Turkey

Tamer Çetin · Fuat Oğuz
Editors

# The Political Economy of Regulation in Turkey

Springer

*Editors*
Tamer Çetin
Department of Economics
Yildiz Technical University
Yildiz Kampusu
Yildiz 34349 Besiktas
Istanbul, Turkey
tamer.cetin@yahoo.com

Fuat Oğuz
Baskent University
Baglica Kampusu
Eskisehir Yolu 20
06530 Baglica Ankara
Turkey
foguz@baskent.edu.tr

ISBN 978-1-4419-7749-6 e-ISBN 978-1-4419-7750-2
DOI 10.1007/978-1-4419-7750-2
Springer New York Dordrecht Heidelberg London



Printed on acid-free paper

Springer is part of Springer Science+Business Media (www.springer.com)

# Preface

Turkey, along with many emerging economies, is passing through a transformation in its network and infrastructure industries. While the reform effort has its ups and downs, the trend seems irreversible. We have been watching the transformation since its beginning and wanted to bring together a comprehensive and informative book in order to provide an overview of the major issues from electricity generation to water issues. Seeing the whole picture usually helps to distinguish the institutional aspects more clearly. Our belief that institutional factors play a more prominent role in network industries comes from our readings on other countries' experiences and the regulatory processes in Turkey. In the book, we tried to reflect complexities that surround decision-making in those markets.

This book is the outcome of a collective effort to bring up-to-date information on the regulatory reform in Turkey and provide a general guide to understanding prominent issues. We draw together the main components of the regulatory issues in network industries and the role of competition policy. Regulation and competition policy has to be analyzed together to get a better picture of the nature of regulatory process. We anticipate that the book would be helpful for a wide spectrum of readers, collectively engaged in research, policy, and practice. It is our hope that it will have contributed to the setting of a more relevant research agenda.

We gratefully acknowledge the contributions of the authors. Each of our authors has firsthand experience in the relevant subject both academically and in the field.

We thank our editor Jon Gurstelle and the staff at Springer for bringing this book into publication.

Istanbul, Turkey — Tamer Çetin
Ankara, Turkey — Fuat Oğuz

# Contents

# Contributors

**Sahin Ardiyok**
ACTECON Economic Consultancy, Istanbul, Turkey; The School of Law, Bilgi University, Istanbul, Turkey; The School of Law, Bilkent University, Ankara, Turkey
sahin.ardiyok@actecon.com

**Izak Atiyas**
Faculty of Arts and Social Sciences, Sabanci University, Tuzla 34956, Turkey
izak@sabanciuniv.edu

**Necmiddin Bağdadioğlu**
Department of Public Finance, Hacettepe University, 06800, Beytepe Ankara, Turkey
necbag@hacettepe.edu.tr

**Serkan Benk**
Department of Public Finance, Zonguldak Karaelmas University, 67100, Incivez Zonguldak, Turkey
serkanbenk@yahoo.com

**Tamer Çetin**
Department of Economics, Yildiz Technical University, 34349, Besiktas Istanbul, Turkey
tamer.cetin@yahoo.com

**Erkan Erdoğdu**
Judge Business School, University of Cambridge, Cambridge, UK; Energy Market Regulatory Authority, 06530, Yuzuncuyil Ankara, Turkey
ee243@cam.ac.uk

**Mehmet Cahit Güran**
Department of Public Finance, Hacettepe University, 06800, Beytepe Ankara, Turkey
guran@hacettepe.edu.tr

**Servet Mutlu**
Department of Economics, Baskent University, Baglica Ankara, 06930, Turkey
mservet@baskent.edu.tr

**Fuat Oğuz**
Department of Economics, Baskent University, Baglica Ankara, 06930, Turkey
foguz@baskent.edu.tr

**Isik Ozel**
Faculty of Arts and Social Sciences, Sabanci University, Tuzla 34956, Turkey
ozel@sabanciuniv.edu

**Kerem Cem Sanlı**
Law Faculty, Istanbul Bilgi University, 34440, Dolapdere Istanbul, Turkey
ksanli@bilgi.edu.tr

**Ali Ulusoy**
Faculty of Law, Yasar University, Bornova Izmir, 35040, Turkey
ali.ulusoy@yasar.edu.tr

# Chapter 1
# Introduction: Regulation and Competition in Turkey

**Tamer Çetin and Fuat Oğuz**

This book is a stocktaking on the recent regulatory reform in Turkey. The fast transformation of the institutional structure of network and infrastructure industries has created many issues in the institutional analysis of regulatory and competitive issues.

The World has seen an important change in the institutional framework of regulated industries in the last 3 decades. Globalization and liberalization have pushed many previously state-owned industries towards privatizations and designed markets. Governance through regulation has spread across the world since the 1980s. Not only the developed countries of the European Union but also East Asia, Latin America, and many developing countries have followed the path of liberalization and privatization.

However, after more than 2 decades of liberalization and privatization efforts, the political pendulum around the world has begun to swing back toward more regulation. The financial crisis of 2008, high energy prices, and the recent BP oil spill disaster are three recent examples of the tide against liberalization. There seems to be more reason for government regulation now than the liberal era of Turgut Özal.

What is different about network and infrastructure industries? The produced good is a political good before it is an economic one. So, rules of the game ominate in-market interactions, as opposed to normal goods and services. Governments tend to control these industries and do not leave them up to market.

In this book, we try to bring together papers on the recent developments in the major regulated industries in Turkey. We believe that a good understanding of the general framework is necessary to see what happens and why it happens. For this reason, we have separated the book into two major parts. The first part provides detailed discussions of various aspects of the regulatory reform that influence all regulated industries in one way or another. Then, we turn to specific industries and offer chapters on specific experiences.

---

T. Çetin (✉)
Department of Economics, Yildiz Technical University,
Yildiz Kampusu, Yildiz 34349 Besiktas, Istanbul, Turkey
e-mail: tamer.cetin@yahoo.com

T. Çetin and F. Oğuz (eds.), *The Political Economy of Regulation in Turkey*,
DOI 10.1007/978-1-4419-7750-2_1, © Springer Science+Business Media, LLC 2011

The recent financial crisis was the result of public policy failures and behavioral patterns of private participants in markets. While it is still too early to see the whole picture on the issue of what caused the crisis and what the consequences are likely to be, it is clear that the institutional environment and incentive mechanisms have had key roles. The rush to liberalize has mostly come without due attention to the institutional factors and the apparent rush to regulate still has the same defect of mitigating the importance of the institutional factors. The chapters in this book are particularly relevant with respect to the role of institutional factors on incentive mechanisms in network industries.

In the rest of the chapter, we first discuss briefly the issues of regulatory governance and commitment and then turn to the relationship between competition and regulation in network industries. We conclude with a brief discussion of the recent Turkish experience and the chapters in the book.

## 1.1 Regulatory Governance and Commitment

A major component of a successful regulatory reform is the existence of regulatory commitment, which is possible only when political transaction costs are low. A credible regulatory environment, arbitrary interventions to the system, becomes more costly to implement, and well-defined rules evolve more easily.

If commitment is not credible, the characterization of optimal policy or equilibrium is extremely difficult if not impossible. On the other hand, credible commitment limits the extent to which a party can engage in opportunistic behavior and hence provides a basis for reliance. When commitment is not fully credible, firms have greater difficulty making long-term plans and weaker incentives to make long-term and irreversible investments.

The regulation solves a contracting problem between the government and regulated industry through the regulatory agency (Spiller and Tommasi 2003). When the government tends not to abide by the rules of the regulatory framework because of the available political rents, investment will not be undertaken, or be inefficient. Institutional transaction costs in the industry will rise consequently.

This process creates a vicious circle that supports government ownership and control in the industry. The lack of regulatory commitment reduces foreign investment in the industry. In the absence of a large domestic investment capacity, governments use the issues as an excuse to intervene in the market more aggressively. In this environment, the polity cannot develop regulatory institutions (Spiller and Tommasi 2003).

In Turkey, the regulatory body has changed radically in the last decade, which has brought in the difficulties of transition. A prominent problem of the reform is the inability of independent regulatory agencies (IRAs) to institutionalize their authority and independence in their industries. The lack of constitutional protection and legal ambiguity surrounding IRAs creates a question of legitimacy. However, the feasibility of reform is subject to credible commitment of regulatory institutions.

During the reform process, Turkey has had key steps toward opening markets to competition. These steps have changed the direction of the economy to a more liberal market economy. The changes had begun with the previous government. The incumbent AKP (Adalet ve Kalkinma Partisi, Justice and Development Party) government intended to follow liberalization efforts, by making it a prominent component of the party program. However, it has consistently pushed for a more centralist position in some cases, and a more liberal one in others.

The credibility of a regulatory framework is closely correlated with arbitrary interventions to the system by the government, judiciary, or bureaucracy. Governmental opportunism tends to create holdup problems for investors. Government gives more priority to its political preferences over efficiency or market considerations. Three constraints limit the role of arbitrariness and increase the credibility of the reform: limited discretion of the regulator, continuity of the regulatory system, and the existence of institutional restraints (Holburn and Spiller 2002; Spiller 1996).

The lack of regulatory commitment may easily turn a reform into a failure, while its success depends on the continuous perseverance on the commitment. Regulatory commitment does not work in the same way in all environments. Institutional structure determines the direction of the market. In most cases, there may be a trade-off between flexibility and commitment. While the costs of inflexibility may overweigh the benefits of commitment in well-established markets, newly created market structures, as in the case of Turkey, may require more weight on credible commitment as opposed to the costs of rigidity.

The regulatory reform must include mechanisms to restrain the discretion of executive and legislative agencies so that the legal structure remains intact. Establishing an independent regulatory authority is the usual remedy for credible commitment. Limited empirical work shows that having an independent regulator increases efficiency and output in the generation market. For example, Zhang, Parker, and Kirkpatrick, in their cross-country study on 25 developing countries, found that creating a competitive environment and an independent regulator before privatization increases efficiency and reduces monopolistic restrictions (Zhang et al. 2005: 373). Moreover, starting with privatization and introducing competitive regulatory framework afterward usually fails.

The typical characteristics of utilities create widely known problems of the market mechanism (Spiller and Tomassi 2003). Scope and scale economies, asset specificity, and massive consumption always give way to political interests to take part in the decision making at all stages. For example, widespread use of electricity by households and other industries may give way to holdup problems in a free contracting system, among other issues, limiting the role of markets, which is a legitimate excuse for government intervention. However, it also becomes part of political maneuvering and election politics. In this environment, there is no easy way to separate "political" from "economic" or purely "technical" considerations.

The necessity of large-scale investments, absence of any efficiency criterion, and politicization make utilities a major victim to rent-seeking activities. As the domain of rent seeking looms, profit seeking takes a less significant place. Entrepreneurs take smaller market risks and may not spend their resources for specific investments. In Turkey, the limited amount of private investments in utilities is related to this additional risk. In a vicious circle, governments keep controlling the market, even though they want to privatize it (Ercan and Öniş 2001).

An important proposition of the institutional analysis of regulation is that regulatory incentives work only if regulatory governance is working (Spiller 1996: 427). The recent administrative intervention aims to push for regulatory incentives without institutionalizing regulatory governance. The evidence from other countries shows that it is very hard to establish regulatory commitment by increasing executive discretion.

Entrepreneurs try to maximize their yields, without any distinction between productive profit and unproductive rents. A credible regulatory framework closes the doors to rent seeking and forces utilities to productive profit-seeking activities. In the absence of commitment, firms choose underinvestment and expect higher returns from their investments, which include the risk premium of regulatory uncertainty. Poor performance becomes part of the market structure. This environment creates conditions for active government involvement. In Spiller's words (1996: 426), "government ownership, then, reflects the inability of the polity to develop regulatory institutions that limit the potential for government opportunistic behavior."

## 1.2 Competition or Regulation?

The new institutional emphasis on commitment and transaction costs brings the political dimension to the forefront. The relative efficiency of competition policy or regulation takes a new shape in this framework. On their connection this is what Stigler writes in 1975: "regulation and competition are rhetorical friends and deadly enemies: over the doorway of every regulatory agency … should be carved: Competition Not Admitted" (Stigler 1975: 183).

The interaction between competition law and regulation becomes prominent in network industries where interconnection and third party access issues create discrepancies between regulatory preferences and competition policy. To a lesser extent, as in the case of banking, regulators may have overriding political goals rather than the goal of creating a competitive environment.

Why do we regulate network industries instead of putting them under the jurisdiction of competition policy? The answer takes us to their natural monopoly characteristics. The economic justification of regulation is based on the coexistence of natural monopoly and network externalities. For example, if more than one firm can provide long-distance phone service efficiently, the economic justification for regulation becomes very weak.

Economides (2006: 97) puts forward three reasons for choosing regulation rather than relying on competition policy only. To begin with, market failures may make it impossible to reach competition in the industry. Second, social goals do not fit well with economic efficiency. And finally, social and private benefits may differ. This description takes an economic approach.

While economic arguments are used extensively to justify the existence of regulatory institutions, in some cases, there is no strong "economic" argument in favor of regulation. Instead, political considerations take the lead in establishing IRAs.

A fundamental issue is whether competition policy and regulation can be complements rather than substitutes. While theoretical considerations would favor complementarity to increase efficiency and social welfare, reality makes them rivals.

Complementarity arises from a number of issues. To begin with, a competition authority does not have adequate capabilities to solve price-setting and descriptive issues in regulated industries. Industry-specific IRAs are better equipped to know the structure of the market. Second, competition policy can be used as a tool to control regulations in the industry. This feature restricts the role of political action in the industry. This use of competition policy as a check on regulatory agencies is crucial in deregulating network industries.

Competition policy works only if it is institutionalized. There are important impediments to implementing competition policy in regulated industries (Spiller and Tomassi 2005). In cases where competition authorities are under political pressure, there is no noticeable difference between them and IRAs.

Another important issue is the relative speed of decision making in competition authorities and IRAs. On sector-specific issues of tariffs and pricing, competition authorities take, usually, more time to resolve the issue. IRAs have a comparative advantage here, under the assumption that the industry or politicians do not capture them.[1]

Banking, telecommunications, and energy markets may require speedy decisions in cases of crises. Competition authorities may not be sensitive to crises as much as regulators. Even regulators can be very slow in managing crises, as the Californian energy crisis shows. The same was true of the Turkish financial crisis of 2001, where the banking regulatory authority was too slow to understand the apparent signs of the crisis and lacked the ability to intervene.

It is necessary to distinguish "economic" and "political" reasons for regulation. In many cases, they can be in conflict. It may be economically reasonable to have a regulatory authority; yet, strong lobbying power may weaken its implementation. Thus, a preference of a competition authority over IRA or vice versa should be based on comparative analysis of alternative methods of increasing social welfare.

In regulated industries, competition does not take the first place in Turkey. IRAs prefer protection of consumers, and other political goals. Competition is seen as a tool to reach other goals. So, it is supported as long as it helps.

[1] In Turkey, Telecommunications Authority was slow in resolving roaming issues and some other cases. Neither CA uses its time and resources efficiently. It usually takes more than a year to reach a conclusion in most cases.

There are fundamental tensions between competition and regulation in regulated industries. For example, power outages may become a rational option in some cases. However, it is never a politically feasible option. Governments try to provide electricity at any costs. Institutional factors that shape competition policy of CA and IRAs make the implementation of competition more difficult in regulated industries.

In this book, the tension between competition policy and regulation is addressed in the context of a number of industries. The Turkish regulatory reform provides important insights on potential problems and tension when jurisdictional ambiguity dominates agenda in many industries.

## 1.3 The Turkish Experience

In the last two decades, Turkey has experienced a regulatory reform. Transition to the institutions of capitalism has been one of the most important issues of political agenda in Turkey. In a sense, this book scrutinizes the evolution of the traditional patrimonialism into the regulatory state in Turkey. Since the establishment of IRAs and the enactment of new laws concerning regulation of network industries, Turkey has reshaped its own regulatory institutional structure. The process has brought about political clashes and high transaction costs in some cases. Governments have not desired to delegate the political property rights to IRAs. The lack of constitutional protection and legal ambiguity surrounding IRAs creates a question of legitimacy. The dispute between government and IRAs feeds the rent-seeking activities. Although IRAs is de jure established, such conflicts de facto impede the institutionalization of IRAs. In some cases, the reform was not able to establish competition. The reason was obvious. Yet, the legal and institutional structure in the country was not ready for the transition to IRAs. The transition has been kept in force by the pressure of international antigovernment mood or the so-called neoliberal discourse.

But, each country has a distinctive regulatory institutional endowment. For this reason, all countries, especially developing countries, should establish the regulatory institutional structure by taking into account this feature of regulation. One of the problems of Turkish experience is that the transition process assumed the primacy of the market and neglected the institutional structure and developmental objectives of Turkish economy as a rapidly developing economy.

This book deals with the regulatory reform and especially regulation of network industries in Turkey. In doing so, this book aims to understand the nature of transition to regulatory state in Turkey and to reveal the regulatory issues occurring during the transition with lessons from the markets. In this context, the book consists of two parts. However, it begins with an introduction that consists of this chapter. Part I includes a general outlook that analyzes the institutional environment of regulation and competition in Turkey. Lastly, part II observes the regulatory process in many industries. The focus of this part is particularly on regulation of network industries.

### 1.3.1 A General Outlook

Including the distinctive features of regulation and competition in Turkey, Part I brings together conceptual and general issues. The part consists of four chapters. In Chap. 2, Ali Ulusoy addresses the constitutional status of IRAs in Turkey. The regulatory reform has been around only since the last decade. Regulatory agencies do not have constitutional protection, and their legal statuses are still not well defined. This issue is fundamental in evaluating the nature of the reform process. Many legal setbacks in liberalization efforts in network industries find their origins in the ambiguity over objectives of regulatory reform. Decisions by the Constitutional Court and Danı tay, the Council of State, reflect the tension between alternative viewpoints on the constitutional nature of network industries and public service.

Chapter 3, by Mehmet Cahit Güran, presents a political economic analysis of the privatization movement in Turkey. Güran examines the privatization experience in two different periods. During the period 1985–2003, privatization amounted to only 8.2 billion dollar, while it reached approximately 36.4 billion dollar during the period 2004–2009. The radical transformation in the privatization policies of Turkey is worth analyzing from the perspective of a political economy. With this purpose, the chapter first examines the historical background to privatization in Turkey and the circumstances leading to liberalization and privatization policies. Second, it discusses the factors influencing the privatization process such as objectives, strategies, and the effects of economic, legal, institutional, and political conditions. Analysis of the privatization experience in Turkey reveals that factors such as legal and institutional structure, political will, unstable macroeconomic conditions, ideological resistance, and rent-seeking activities shaped the privatization movement and its consequences.

Güran states that after the organizational and legal substructure for privatization was formed in the 1990s and after macroeconomic stability was achieved in 2002, the conditions conducive to privatization were created. The presence of a politically powerful and determined government during this period increased privatization. The Turkey experience of privatization illustrates that privatization policy making is a necessary but insufficient condition for privatization to take place in countries where this is desired because, although virtually all governments that came into power after 1980 favored privatization, no success was achieved in the field. Hence, for privatization policies to be successfully implemented, the legal and organizational substructure should first be formed, and macroeconomic stability should be achieved.

In Chap. 4, Işık Özel and İzak Atiyas examine the diffusion and actual operation of regulatory reforms since the 1990s in Turkey, focusing on national regulatory agencies (NRAs) in various sectors. The chapter takes a step further from the mere initiation of regulatory reforms along with de jure institutional design of the NRAs and explores the actual processes through which NRAs function. It, then, finds out a considerable discrepancy between de jure design and de facto operation of the NRAs in terms of independence, accountability, and capacity to enforce; the extent of such discrepancy varies across sectors. Özel and Atiyas specifically investigate the Competition Authority and NRAs in banking, telecommunications, energy, sugar, tobacco, and alcohol markets. They suggest that the operation of NRAs in practice may create new forms of rents, giving rise to significant distributive consequences.

In Chap. 5, Şahin Ardıyok ve Kerem Cem Sanlı focus on the legal structure of competition policy in Turkey. Ardıyok and Sanlı introduce readers to the basics of Turkish antitrust law and its enforcement practices. They first analyze the background and the sources of Turkish Antitrust Law. After mentioning the legislative background, they specify the main legal sources of the Law. Then, the chapter is devoted to the main concepts prescribed in the Act such as the relevant market and the concept of undertaking. The chapter explains substantive provisions. Restrictive agreements are expounded along with the exemption rule. Subsequently, they observe the monopoly provision with some examples of abuse. And, finally, they explain the provision and the secondary legislation governing the concentrations. In this chapter, the procedural issues are given importance. For this reason, enforcement authorities and sanctions are discussed at the end of the chapter.

Ardıyok and Sanlı observe that as Turkey has been implementing market system for the past 20 years, the national laws regulating trade and economy have been steadily altered and new laws have been enacted to cope with the dynamics of this system. The Act of Protection of Competition, which was adopted in 1994, can be regarded as a product of this process of forming a legal framework. By enacting the Act, Turkish government endorsed the "competition" as a social value and also fulfilled its legal obligations stemming from the Constitutional mandate (art. 167) and the acquis of the European Union.

### *1.3.2 Lessons from the Markets*

Part 2 presents lessons regarding the regulatory issues in the markets. This part consists of five chapters. In Chap. 6, Necmiddin Bağdadioğlu focuses upon the envisaged regulatory framework to be applied after the transition period in the Turkish Electricity Industry ceases at the end of 2012, and then, evaluates the performance of the electricity distribution companies under the envisaged incentive regulation scheme in 2006 when the transition period commenced. The chapter states that the electricity transmission and distribution will be regulated by the revenue cap and the mixture of price/revenue cap, respectively. The retail supply to captive customers will also be regulated by the price cap. The Energy Market Regulatory Authority has already announced measures to incentivize the distribution companies to behave cost and quality consciously. An illustrative application of the Data Envelopment Analysis on the distribution companies shows that only 8 out of 20 distribution companies were operating efficiently in 2006. With that application, the chapter analyzes that had the envisaged incentive regulation framework been implemented for the transition period, these inefficient companies would have been allowed to benefit from any additional improvement they could achieve after they met their set targets during the 6-year transitory period. Although the necessary institutional, legal, and market arrangements were made, until the end of 2008, the reform did not progress as fast as it was planned. Accordingly, the real test of the full-scale implementation of the cost-based tariff mechanism under the new electricity market structure will be in the new regulatory period commencing in 2013. Hence, whether the new framework will manage to bring more reliable, secure, high-quality, and less costly electricity supply to customers is yet to be seen.

Chapter 7 by Erkan Erdoğdu observes regulation of natural gas industry in Turkey in detail. Located between natural gas rich countries of Asia and Middle East on the one hand and European countries with rapidly increasing demand on the other, Turkey is situated at a geography where natural gas demand and supply intersect. With an annual average gas demand growth rate of 10.4% during last decade and a consumption of more than 32 billion $m^3$ in 2009 (which was just 12.5 billion $m^3$ in 1999), Turkey is gradually turning out to be an important gas market in its own right. This trend is reinforced by the fact that Turkish natural gas consumption is projected to further increase in the coming years. To transform the Turkish gas market into a competitive one and to make sure that it develops in the lines of the European Union (EU), a reform process has been initiated in 2001, which involves privatization, liberalization, as well as a radical restructuring of the gas industry in Turkey.

Erdoğdu particularly focuses on the reform process. First of all, the chapter provides a short summary of the developments that have been taking place in Turkish gas market since 1980s. Then, it attempts to evaluate the regulatory framework created as a result of the reform process. The next two subsections are devoted to two important issues in the Turkish gas market, namely, theTurkish gas release programme and the auctions in the gas distribution market. Another subsection deals with the issue of compatibility between Turkish reforms and EU norms. In the last part, the chapter touches upon some regulatory issues and provides some policy guidelines for both improvement and filling what is called "expectations-capabilities gap" in the Turkish natural gas market. Erdoğdu concludes that in spite of a relatively good legislative framework and some encouraging developments in practice, the reforms in Turkey are far from ideal and that a significant amount of work still lies ahead of Turkey to set up a full fledged liberal natural gas market.

In Chap. 8, İzak Atiyas provides an overview of the state of liberalization, competition, and regulation of major segments of the telecommunications industry in Turkey. The chapter shows the competitive stance of the regulatory authority and observes that the development of actual competition has been uneven across segments. Specifically, the degree of competition has been higher in the mobile segment relative to fixed telephony or broadband. The chapter also discusses the new Electronic Communications Law and argues that although not perfect, it provides a coherent basis on which the regulatory authority can pursue competitive objectives in a more even manner. However, the actual development of competition will depend a lot on how the law and the ensuing legislation are actually implemented.

Atiyas concludes the new Electronic Communications Law, even though not perfect, provides a major improvement over the previous regime and establishes a coherent basis on which to push for the development of competition in the industry. Lack or incoherence of legal instruments did play a role in the delays in the development of competition especially in the fixed telephony and broadband segments, but unwillingness or incomplete ownership of the liberalization agenda by the Ministry and Information Technology and Communications Authority (ITCA) also played a role. It remains to be seen whether the duality apparent in ITCA's approach to fixed vs. mobile segments will continue in the near future or give place to a more consistently procompetitive approach.

In Chap. 9, focusing on the effects of regulation, deregulation, and competition in the Turkish airline industry, Tamer Çetin and Serkan Benk analyze the pre- and postreform structure of the industry. In doing so, they reveal the effects of deregulation over development of competition and service quality. Before 2003, the industry was not open to competition. The necessary legal environment had not been established to ensure that private airline firms other than Turkish Airlines might also operate, especially in the scheduled domestic flights and cargo transport. Thirteen firms along with Turkish Airlines that operated in the unscheduled flights were inadequate to trigger competition, to increase demand, and to attract investments in the industry. Turkish Airlines was a Turkey's state-owned airline company. However, the airline deregulation movement of 2003 opened the market to competition. The movement released entry into the industry. Fares have begun to be determined by competition. In this context, by analyzing developments in the industry, they aim to present how the postreform structure of the industry has been reshaped.

Çetin and Benk conclude that the deregulation movement of 2003 has brought about the significant positive impacts over the industry. The deregulation movement has succeeded in terms of the establishment and institutionalization of competition in the industry in comparison with the pre-deregulation industry structure, although Turkish Airlines has continued to dominate the industry.

Lastly, in Chap. 10, Servet Mutlu discusses the water issues in Turkey at length. Environmental issues are dealt with only insofar as they affect and are affected by water use. The chapter starts with a brief description and analysis of the water endowments and water demands by competing users in different regions and in the country as a whole. Mutlu also analyzes the climatic cycle and the level of regional water scarcity. He discusses the institutions and organizations that are responsible for the management and regulation of water and for the environment. The chapter analyzes how these institutions and their functions evolved in response to changing demands and pressures emanating from competing uses and perception of issues, especially as regards the environment. It takes up current management, regulation, allocation, and pricing of water, both surface and underground. In the chapter, a subsection is devoted to the Southeastern Anatolia Project (GAP; acronym in Turkish) and the problems it faces with the riparian states, Syria and Iraq, regarding the allocation of the waters of the Euphrates and Tigris. In the end, Mutlu discusses environmental problems arising from water use, such as water pollution by agricultural uses, soil salinity, changes in water levels of lakes arising from excessive withdrawal from underground water reserves and destruction of natural habitat of flora and fauna.

## References

Economides, N. (2006) 'Competition policy in network industries: an introduction', in D. Jansen (ed.), *New Economy and Beyond*, New York: Texas A&M University, 96–121.

Ercan, M.R. and Z. Öniş (2001) 'Turkish Privatization: Institutions and Dilemmas', *Turkish Studies*, 2: 109–134.

Holburn, G. and P. Spiller (2002) 'Institutional or structural: lessons from international electricity sector reforms', in E. Brousseau and J.-M. Glachant (eds.), *The Economics of contracts: Theories and Applications*, Cambridge: Cambridge University Press.

Spiller, P. (1996) 'Institutions and Commitment', *Industrial and corporate change*, 5 (2): 421–452.

Spiller, P. and M. Tomassi (2003) 'The Institutional Foundations of Public Policy: A Transactions Approach with Application to Argentina', *Journal of Law, Economics and Organization*, 19, 281–306.

Spiller, P. and M. Tomassi (2005) 'The institutions of regulation: an application to public utilities', in C. Menard and M. Shirley (eds.), *Handbook of New Institutional Economics*, Netherland: Springer, 515–543.

Stigler, G. (1975) *Citizen and the State*: *Essays on Regulation*, Chicago: University of Chicago Press.

Zhang, Y., D. Parker and C. Kirkpatrick (2005) 'Competition, regulation and privatization of electricity generation in developing countries: does the sequencing of the reforms matter?' *The Quarterly Review of Economics and Finance*, 45: 358–379.

# Part I
# A General Outlook

# Chapter 2
# The Place of Regulation Within the Public Law in Turkey

**Ali Ulusoy**

## 2.1 Introduction

From a general perspective, Turkish public law has not really been coherent with the economic notions. The majority of public lawyers, including administrative tribunal judges, have usually had a tendency to disregard the economic aspects of legal conflicts. Thus, economic analysis in public law works and judgments is extremely uncommon. *Regulation* is a part of the economy-based notions that have generally been neglected by Turkish public law doctrine and jurisprudence. However, things have begun to change since the last few decades as a result of globalization, locating the economy and even the public law disputes at the "centrum" of politics.

## 2.2 How Does the Turkish Public Economic Law Perceive the Regulation?

The Turkish public law doctrine had not been using the term "regulation" until the 1990s, when the concept of regulation penetrated into Turkish law via French law despite the fact that the notion is of Anglo-Saxon origin.[1] We can explain this indirect penetration by the fact that the Turkish administrative system had adopted the French style "unitary" system instead of a "federal" system and embraced the "civil law" system instead of "common law." Thereby, Turkish legal doctrine has preferred to grant to French legal doctrine the honor of "facing" this "American invention" of regulation. Since adapting that unfamiliar notion of common law to the civil law system is an important issue.

[1] The first academic works about regulation and regulatory agencies in Turkish legal doctrine directly refer to the French legal doctrine (Duran 1998; Tan 1996; Erkut 1998; Ulusoy 2003).

A. Ulusoy (✉)
Department of Law, Yasar University, Izmir, Turkey
e-mail: ali.ulusoy@yasar.edu.tr

T. Çetin and F. Oğuz (eds.), *The Political Economy of Regulation in Turkey*,
DOI 10.1007/978-1-4419-7750-2_2, 

In this context, regulation is perceived in Turkish law as the establishment of rules concerning a specific field, and ensuring their compliance by applying sanctions if necessary.

The Turkish legal doctrine seems to apprehend the regulation in a broader sense than the economic theory. Lawyers talk about regulation in the following three situations:

- Subordinating to public rules and control a former legal monopoly subject to open competition (e.g., fix telephone operating service).
- Subordinating to public rules and control a natural monopoly (e.g., electricity transmission and distribution activities).
- Realizing a public control mechanism toward an economic activity in order to ensure fair competition and protect the public interest (e.g., electricity generation and mobile telephone operating service).

Regulation has actually become a key notion in public economic law because of the transformation of the role of the state as a result of globalization. In this recent paradigm, the fundamental mission of the state is not the direct undertaking of responsibility for the main public necessities but the performance of the duty of referee and organizer of public life. In lieu of being an armed deterrent force, the state acts in its new role to show a conciliatory, moderate, and guiding moral authority.

Establishing rules and sanctions for "regulating" does not constitute a primary objective but just an instrument to be used in case of emergency. Before applying a sanction, the general tendency is warning and using persuasive methods toward economic actors. Reducing the legal norms or at least rendering the rules more flexible, as called "deregulation," is also being accepted. In the process, economic actors gain a broader margin of action.

The essential aim of regulation is to secure efficiently the common needs of humanity through a public control mechanism. In this context, a connection similar to socialism and social democracy seems to be created between liberalism and regulation. Considering that social democracy assumed the mission of rationalizing socialism by "taming" it, regulation could probably perform the same mission with regard to liberalism.

Regulation is understood, in the Turkish public law, as rulemaking and control activity performed by independent regulatory agencies (IRA) that stay out of conventional administrative bureaucracy and are independent of the political power.[2] Despite the several privatizations realized during the last decade in Turkey, the state still operates many economic activities that bear a public service character. Thus, the state functions as a direct producer of goods and services. Moreover, it competes with the private sector with regard to several public utilities, e.g., the generation, wholesale and retail of electricity, banking, internet service providing, radio–TV broadcasting, postal service, etc.

Referring to the idea that the state cannot be a fair referee if it is a player in the same game, the Turkish public opinion is convinced that the regulation of the main

---

[2] Regulation has also been conceived as the same manner in French public law (Rapp 2001; Guedon 1991; Gazier and Cannac 1984; Hubac and Pisier 1988; Teitgen-Colly 1988; Chevallier 1986).

public economic activities should be done by IRA, being more autonomous and neutral institutions vis-à-vis the government.

Concerning d*eregulation*, this notion has not been used to mean a total withdrawal of the regulations but rather as rendering them "softer." Therefore, deregulation requires the loosening and, occasionally, the annulment of the rules applicable to economic actors (Turkkan 2001: 12).

## 2.3 The Constitutional Framework of the Regulation in Turkey

The Turkish Constitution does not contain any general provision about the economic regulation. Nevertheless, the Constitution requires an administrative control over any type of public entities including public economic entities and activities. This mandatory administrative control over public economic entities and activities results from the principle of the unity of the public administration having the constitutional authority. The principle of the unity of the public administration is formulated by the article 123/1-2 of the Constitution which states "*The administration forms a whole with regard to its structure and functions… The organisation and functions of the administration are based on the principles of centralization and local administration…*"[3]

Furthermore, "The central administration has the power of administrative trusteeship over the local governments in the framework of principles and procedures set forth by law with the objective of ensuring the functioning of local services in conformity with the principle of the integral unity of the administration, securing uniform public service, safeguarding the public interest, and meeting local needs, in an appropriate manner," in accordance with the Article 127/5 of the Constitution.

Those constitutional provisions expose that a regulation over the economic activities of the state and the public enterprises is made mandatory in the name of the constitutional principle of unity of the public administration. This type of regulation should be effectuated by the administrative agencies under the hierarchical structure of the administration and the principle of administrative tutelage.[4]

On the other hand, Article 167/1 of the Constitution imposes an obligation on the public authorities to take proper measures in order to ensure and promote a

[3] "*IV. Administration/A. Fundamentals of the Administration/1. Integral Unity and Public Legal Personality of the Administration/ARTICLE 123.* The administration forms a whole with regard to its structure and functions, and shall be regulated by law. The organization and functions of the administration are based on the principles of centralization and local administration. Public corporate bodies shall be established only by law or by the authority expressly granted by law."

[4] Under the principle of administrative tutelage, the central government has the power of control over the local authorities and the public enterprises. Contrary to the hierarchical control, the administrative tutelage involves a limited and exceptional power of control (Gozubuyuk and Tan 2008; Gozler 2009).

better functioning of the money, credit, capital, goods, and services markets. They shall also prevent the formation of monopolies and cartels in the markets.[5]

Besides, Article 172 empowers the public authorities to take measures to protect and inform consumers and to encourage their initiatives to protect themselves.[6]

There is, finally, no doubt that regulating the public economic activities is a constitutional obligation with regard to Articles 123/1-2 and 127/5. However, whether Articles 167/1 and 172 of the Constitution could form a legal basis for raising the issue that regulation of all kinds of economic activities is a constitutional necessity under Turkish public law is an open-ended question.

Nevertheless, the delegation, on the constitutional level, of duty toward the public authorities for ensuring "orderly functioning of the money, credit, capital, goods, and services markets" is in our view an undeniable legal necessity of regulation.[7] Otherwise, we cannot see how the consumers could be protected without the regulation of the economic activities and the provision of competition in the markets. In fact, the Turkish Constitutional Court has, referring to Article 167/1 of the Constitution, affirmed the constitutionality of the power of "regulation" of the *Tobacco and Alcohol Market Regulatory Body* in the foregoing market.[8]

However, the constitutional obligation of regulation with regard to the public and private economic activities does not mean that regulation should be effectuated by IRA. Actually, the legislator has discretionary power to implement regulations via IRAs or conventional administrative agencies (Ulusoy 2003: 140–141). The Constitution does not reveal any preference concerning the "origin" of regulation. The question of "who shall regulate?" does not constitute a problem of the Constitution.

## 2.4 The IRA in Turkey

### *2.4.1 The Appearance of IRA in the Legal Environment*

The main reason of the appearance of IRA in the Turkish legal environment is certainly the necessity for an independent and reliable regulation. The sensible

[5] "*II. Supervision of Markets and Regulation of Foreign Trade/ARTICLE 167.* The state shall take measures to ensure and promote the sound, orderly functioning of the money, credit, capital, goods, and services markets; and shall prevent the formation, in practice or by agreement, of monopolies and cartels in the markets. In order to regulate foreign trade for the benefit of the economy of the country, the Council of Ministers may be empowered by law to introduce or lift additional financial impositions on imports, exports, and other foreign transactions in addition to tax and similar impositions."

[6] "*VI. Protection of Consumers, Small Traders and Craftsmen/A. Protection of Consumers/ ARTICLE 172.* The state shall take measures to protect and inform consumers; shall encourage their initiatives to protect themselves."

[7] Turkish legal doctrine has disregarded to discuss this matter.

[8] Constitutional Court, November 20, 2003, E.2002/32, K.2003/100, *Official Gazette*, August 11, 2004.

fields in common everyday life such as energy, telecom, banking, stock market, public procurement, broadcasting, and economic competition should be free from the influence of politics and politicians, and also from the "capture" of the economic actors. The best way of such regulation seems to be to perform it via IRA, as "councils of sages" (Sabourin 1983: 292).

In addition, we can describe two more reasons that confirm the appearance of IRA in Turkey. First, the inefficiency of the conventional administrative structure in preventing the widespread corruption, especially in some key sectors such as banking and energy, provoked the lawmakers to call upon IRA as "corruption rescuers." In this context, the creation of BDDK (Banking Regulation Authority) following a huge corruption wave in the banking sector in the early 2000s, and also the founding of the EPDK (Energy Market Regulatory Agency) after several corruption operations, in which the personnel of the Ministry of Energy had been involved at the end of the 1990s, confirm this thesis.

On the other hand, some IRA seemed to be created under the influence of international economic public opinion and international economic organizations in order to attract more international investment. In this context, we could mention, as examples, the creation of the Telecommunication Authority, the Tobacco and Alcohol Market Regulatory Authority, and Sugar Market Authority (Ulusoy 2003: 7).

The influence of the international economic organizations such as IMF or World Bank in creating some IRA had also been sensed by a section of Turkish public opinion as an example of the exploitation and domination of the emerging countries' markets by the international or "supranational" economic powers.

IRA depart from the conventional administrative agencies on two points:

- The lack of the typical administrative control mechanisms, as hierarchy and administrative tutelage, of the central government over board members and their decision power.
- The mission of regulation, rather than management, of public services or other sensible private activities.

Indeed, IRA do not undertake any public service or other activities as operators. Their competence is limited by regulating a designated field. On the other hand, IRA benefit from a much broader administrative autonomy compared with conventional administrative agencies.

### *2.4.2 The Reactionary Points of the Conventional Administrative Structure Toward IRA*

The surprising and sudden appearance of IRA in the Turkish administrative structure has attracted a lot of criticism, which could be classified into two groups.

The first preoccupation is about the erosion of the centralist and also unitary character of the state via IRA.

The Turkish Constitution imposes a unitary state system. The Constitution literally gives a discretional power to lawmakers for upholding a centralized or decentralized administration.[9] However, The Constitutional Court seems to smell a rat in the decentralization of the state in the name of its unitary character. In this context, the Court invalidated a recent law that had been giving more power to local authorities.[10]

Taking inspiration from this jurisprudence, a number of doctrines allege that the presence of IRA is a different way of decentralization, by transferring the power of central administration to atypical administrative agencies, which benefit from more administrative autonomy without the control of tutelage.

The second concern about the presence of IRA is more theoretical. By the proliferation of IRA, bureaucracy acquires more ground and decision making powers in the public life to the detriment of politicians. This effect causes a democracy problem. Elected people lose ground against appointed bureaucrats as IRA use more important powers than the other administrative agencies. The big part of those powers should normally be used by the legislative agencies. The main concern is whether IRA's "coup d'Etat" concerning the essential competence in the context of weakened political power poses a democracy problem.

## 2.5 Conclusion

The regulation has become actually a key notion in the Turkish public economic law because of the transformation of the role of the public authority as a result of globalization. For the public law doctrine, the objective of regulation is to secure efficiently the common needs of society through a public control mechanism. In the Turkish public law, the regulation of the main public utilities has been generally performed by IRA.

The Turkish Constitution requires an administrative control over any type of public entities including public economic entities and activities under the Articles 123/1-2 and 127/5. The necessity for an independent and reliable regulation of the public utilities and the other key public services has obliged the appearance of IRA in the Turkish legal environment. However, the Turkish legal doctrine discusses whether IRA erode the centralist and unitary character of the state and IRA "pamper" the bureaucracy to the detriment of politicians.

---

[9] Article 123 of the Constitution: "The administration forms a whole with regard to its structure and functions, and shall be regulated by law. The organization and functions of the administration are based on the principles of centralization and local administration. Public corporate bodies shall be established only by law, or by the authority expressly granted by law."

[10] Constitutional Court, February 4, 2010, E.2008/27, K.2010/29; E.2008/28, K.2010/30, *Official Gazette*, June 21, 2010.

## References


Chevallier, J. (1986). Reflexions sur l'institution des autorités administratives indépendantes. *JCP.I.1986*, no 3254.

Duran, L. (1998). Turkiyede Bagimsiz Idari Otoriteler. In I. Kaboglu (Ed.), *Autorités Administratives Indépendantes-Bagimsiz Idari Otoriteler* (p. 24). Istanbul: Institut Français d'Istanbul.

Erkut, C. (1998). Bagimsiz Idari Makamlar Muessesesi Acisindan Sermaye Piyasası Kurulu. In I. Kaboglu (Ed.), *Autorités Administratives Indépendantes-Bagimsiz Idari Otoriteler* (p. 129). Istanbul: Institut Français d'Istanbul.

Gazier, F., Cannac, Y. (1984). Etudes sur les autorités administratives indépendantes. *EDCE*, 1984/13.

Gozler, K. (2009). *Idare Hukuku Dersleri*. Bursa: Ekin Publication.

Gozubuyuk, S., Tan, T. (2008). *Idare Hukuku, C.1 Genel Esaslar*. Ankara: Turhan Publication.

Guedon, M.-J. (1991). *Les Autorités Administratives Indépendantes*. Paris: LGDJ.

Hubac, S., Pisier, E. (1988). Les Autorités Face au Pouvoir. In C.A. Colliard & G. Timsit (Eds.), *Les Autorités Administratives Indépendantes* (p. 117). Paris: PUF.

Rapp, L. (2001). Les nouvelles régulations économiques. *AJDA*, 2001/561.

Sabourin, P. (1983). Les autorités administratives indépendantes, une catégorie nouvelle. *AJDA*, 1983/275.

Tan, T. (1996). Bagimsiz idari otorite olarak Sermaye Piyasasi Kurulu. In Ismail Turk'e Armagan (p. 3). Istanbul: SPK Publication.

Teitgen-Colly, C. (1988). Les Autorités Administratives Indépendantes. In C.A. Colliard & G. Timsit (Eds.), *Les Autorités Administratives Indépendantes* (p. 21). Paris: PUF.

Turkkan, E. (2001). Rekabet Teorisi ve Endustri Iktisadi. Ankara: Turhan Publication.

Ulusoy, A. (2003). *Bagimsiz Idari Otoriteler*. Ankara: Turhan Publication.

# Chapter 3
# The Political Economy of Privatization in Turkey: An Evaluation

**Mehmet Cahit Güran**

## 3.1 Introduction

Although Turkey started liberalization and privatization policies in 1980, it has a low performance when compared with other countries with similar policies. While in the period 1977–2002, the total privatization to GDP ratios were approximately 25% in Portugal, 24% in New Zealand, 18% in Australia, 11% in Spain and in the UK, and 7% in Greece, this ratio was only 0.2% in Turkey. Similarly, while in 1985–2002 privatization implementation reached 65 billion dollar in the UK, 74 billion in Italy, 40 billion in Brazil, 38 billion in Spain, 23 billion in Argentina, and 20 billion in Mexico, it reached only 8 billion dollar in Turkey. Moreover, 2.7 billion dollar of this privatization income was obtained in 2000 only. However, this negative picture of privatization in Turkey changed starting from 2004 and implementation of Turkey's privatization reached 36.4 billion dollar in the period 2004–2009. That is, while annual privatization implementation was 380 million dollar before 2003, after 2003 it reached 6 billion dollar annually. This change is rather radical. Therefore, an examination of the dynamics underlying this change may provide insight into the privatization policies in Turkey and the potential experiences of other countries with similar structure.

Apart from the introduction, this chapter consists of three parts, the second of which focuses on the economy, in general, in Turkey and the historical development of policies of public entrepreneurship and its periodical breaking points. This part will be divided into two periods: the first of which covers the étatist interventionist period in which state enterprises were established and the second of which covers the period when liberal economic policies were followed and privatization policies were implemented. Part three of this chapter, the outcome of privatization policy and its structure will be examined. In this framework, the dynamics underlying

M.C. Güran (✉)
Department of Public Finance, Hacettepe University, Ankara, Turkey
e-mail: guran@hacettepe.edu.tr

T. Çetin and F. Oğuz (eds.), *The Political Economy of Regulation in Turkey*,
DOI 10.1007/978-1-4419-7750-2_3, 

privatization in Turkey, and the legal, institutional, economic, and political factors that affect the pace of privatization will be investigated. The conclusion with a discussion of the findings will complete the study.

## 3.2 Historical Background

The rise of state ownership in Western Europe can be correlated particularly to three waves of nationalizations that occurred: after the Great Depression of 1929–1933, during the post-World War II period, and after the oil crises in the 1970s (Bortolotti and Milella 2008). Therefore, in the sound evaluation of State Economic Enterprises (SEEs), the privatization movement in a country requires comprehension of the historical and economic conditions under which public enterprises were established and continued to exist. To this purpose, economic views on the role of the state in the economy over different periods of time and the public financial conditions and needs that led to the establishment of SEEs will be treated in the following section. Then, the developments that changed this view and that led to the liberalization and the privatization movement will be illustrated. That is, the historical, political, and economic characteristics of the periods that witnessed the rise and fall of SEEs will be presented.

In terms of the nature of the economic policies followed, the economic development of Turkey can be divided into five periods (Kepenek and Yentürk 2001; Öniş 1998; Öniş 2003): (1) 1923–1929, the period of liberal policies, (2) 1930–1945, the period of étatist and import substitution economic policies, (3) 1946–1959, the period of an open economy and that relies on an economic growth strategy prioritizing agriculture, (4) 1961–1979, the planned period that is based on import substitution and the high protection of domestic sectors, and (5) the post-1980 neoliberal period that is based on open economic development and economic liberalization. However, in terms of state entrepreneurship and SEEs, these five periods can be reduced to two: (a) 1923–1979 period that witnessed the initiation and development of state entrepreneurship in a predominantly interventionist state and (b) the post-1980 period during which the privatization of SEEs was aimed and liberal economic policies were applied.

### *3.2.1 Interventionist State Policy and Establishment of SEEs*

There are different economic theories that attempt to explain the growth of a state. While the neoclassical theory explains growth of the state with the increase in demand for services that the state provides based on consumer sovereignty, public choice theoreticians see this increase in growth as a result of politicians', bureaucrats', and state officials' behavior aimed at benefit maximization. Marxist theory explains public growth as the outcome of the laws of motion of capitalism

(Pitelis 1991; Clarke and Pitelis 1993). Another dimension of the growth of the state relates to its involvement in economic life as an entrepreneur and manufacturer of goods and commodities of certain quality.

In general, SEEs in developing countries were established as a result of development policies. These countries thought that targets set for total investment, investment pace, and the spread of investment over different sectors and regions could not be reached through operating market forces. Consequently, in these countries, SEEs were considered more effective than private enterprises in reaching targeted growth rates and distributional equity (Ramanadham 1991).

Although it might be over generalized, the motives behind the establishment of SEEs can be classified into three main categories: political-ideological, social, and economic motives. Political-ideological motives are mainly related to the formation of conditions conducive to the establishment of SEEs in developing and developed countries that were affected by the policies of communist countries. Social motives basically involve targets related to the reduction of unemployment, improvement of working conditions, and development of local entrepreneurship. Economic motives are more diverse. The first is the existence of market failures. When market failures, such as the lack of information, economic and social externalities, and natural monopolies are the case, the establishment of SEEs is not only justified but also necessary. The second economic motive involves support to the economic and social transformation in less developed countries and regions. The third economic motive involves the rescue of private enterprises negatively affected by economic and financial crises (Toninelli 2000). According to Ramanadham (1991), who studied countries' rationale behind the establishment of public enterprises from 1950 onward, the motives behind the establishment of SEEs are plan strategy and social gain, the status of private entrepreneurship, aid to private enterprises, control of the economy, antimonopoly, indigenization of ownership and social restructuring, distributional justice, raising surpluses for investment, meeting the ravages of serious occurrences such as war, and promoting economic development.

Before presenting the motivation and rationale behind the establishment of SEEs in Turkey, the economic and political conditions and the mentality of politicians, especially in the years when SEEs were systematically established, need to be discussed. The Republic of Turkey was founded on the economic and social heritage of the Ottoman Empire in 1923. Apart from the wars in the last years of the decline of the Ottoman Empire, World War I (1914–1918) and the War of Independence (1919–1922) had ravaging effects, and this negatively affected the economic and social heritage that the new Republic took over in both quantitative and qualitative terms. In addition to the social and economic capital of the Ottoman Empire, the Republic of Turkey took over its institutional structure, which is an important factor in a country's development performance.[1] One of the most important elements of this structure is that of the organization of the state. The Ottoman

[1] North (1990) and other related literature present the crucial effects of institutional factors and/or economic structure on the economic development of countries.

Empire had a rather centralized political system and in this centralized structure, political power was in the hands of the bureaucracy and the army (Mardin 1980; Heper 1985; Lewis 1961; Frey 1975).

In studies of Turkish economic history, the division of the period between the establishment of the Republic of Turkey and end of the World War II (1923–1945) into the "liberal period" (1923–1929) and "étatist period" (1930–1945) is very common. In Izmir, an Economic Conference was gathered to determine the fundamental principles of the economic policies to be followed after the War of Independence in 1923. "Nationalism" and "étatism" are considered to be the most fundamental principles among the principles agreed on in this conference. However, it was also agreed that foreign capital would be allowed to operate under certain conditions and that support would be extended to develop private entrepreneurship (Kepenek and Yentürk 2001). In the period from the establishment of the republic to the beginning of the 1930s, three policies followed for the development of state entrepreneurship can be identified. The first is the establishment of the Sanayi ve Maadin Bankası (Industrial and Mines Bank-1925) to operate the state enterprises taken over from the Ottoman Empire. The second is the nationalization of the railways that were in the hands of foreign countries,[2] and the third is the establishment of state monopolies for the import and/or manufacturing of basic commodities such as tobacco, sugar, salt, alcoholic drinks, petroleum, ethyl alcohol, matches, gunpowder, mail, telegraph, and telephone services[3] (Kepenek and Yentürk 2001; Cillov 1970).

Even though the 1923–1929 period is called the "liberal era," defining this period as "liberal" may be wrong[4] or difficult as the characteristics of the policies followed during this period conflict with the fundamental elements of a liberal structure (Beriş 2009; Boratav 2006). In this period, the state sometimes supported private enterprises and sometimes acted as an economic actor in the market. A model in which the state determines the investor and also acts as the greatest actor in the market obviously cannot be called a "liberal model" (Takim and Yilmaz 2010). In this era, a society worn out through several wars, the existence of a centralized and étatist economic structure taken over from the Ottoman Empire, the absence of a well-functioning market economy, the absence of a social class of capital owners and investors to take the role of entrepreneurs, the absence of a developed money and capital market, and insufficient intellectual knowledge accumulation on the operation of a market economy and on the role of the state in this system made it impossible to enforce the rules of a market economy and make

[2] For the nationalization practices in the first years of the Republic, see Akalın (2008: 101–118).

[3] The total share of income obtained from state monopolies in the total budget in 1924–1930 was 18.3% on average (Ministry of Finance 1992). For detailed information about the étatism and state monopolies in the Ottoman Empire and the founding years of the Republic of Turkey, see Derin (1940).

[4] For a study argues that the étatist mentality was adopted at the establishment of the Republic of Turkey in order to achieve the legitimacy of the new state and to hold the economic power so that authority was created over the public, see Beriş (2009).

progress in a short time. Moreover, due to their basic professional experience and life perceptions, the political elite governing the country had a more interventionist, planned, nationalist, and activist approach to economic policy than the civil politicians who appeared from democratic political struggle, which was expectable. Moreover, it should be expectable that the political elite governing the country had a more interventionist, planned, nationalist, and activist approach to economic policy due to their basic professional experience and life perceptions than the civil politicians who appeared from democratic political struggle.

The fact that by the 1929 crisis no significant developmental moves had been made in the economy by private entrepreneurs in Turkey created among political authorities the view that the state should intervene. The basic reasons for this view and the domination of étatist policies after 1929 are (a) social expectations,[5] insufficiencies of capital accumulation, technology and qualified labor force of the private sector, (b) authorities' belief that industrialization would occur faster and more easily when initiated by the state, (c) reduction of foreign dependency through the manufacturing of basic consumption goods within the country, (d) the fact that the 1929 crisis had a more devastating effect on capitalist countries than on the more controlled Russian economy (Tekeli and İlkin 1977). According to Okyar (1965), three basic factors played a role in the birth of étatism in Turkey. These are the 1929 crisis, Russia's success in the field of industrialization, and the effect of the Kadro Movement.[6] The 1929 crisis made Turkey reduce imports drastically to achieve foreign trade balance.[7] Thus, manufactured goods that could not be imported had to be manufactured within the country and since private entrepreneurship was not developed, they inevitably had to be manufactured by the state. The second factor involves the good relationships between Russia and Turkey after WWI and Russia's success in industrialization achieved through planning. This success affected the Turkish public and authorities. In addition, the fact that Russia promised to provide support in the form of loans and technical personnel for capital goods facilitated the adoption of étatism. The last factor is the intellectual climate created by the elitist and reformist Kadro Movement which started to publish a

[5] These words by K. Atatürk, founding leader of the Republic of Turkey, clearly illustrate this view: "Our community is completely étatist. In fact, it views demanding all types of needs from the state as a right."

[6] The Kadro Movement is a movement that, under the influence of the 1929 crisis that capitalism went through, defends the industrialization of Turkey through a noncapitalist approach. The group consisting of Şevket Süreyya Aydemir, İsmail Hüsrev Tökin, Vedat Nedim Tör, Burhan Asaf Belge, and Yakup Kadri Karaosmanoğlu published a journal titled the Kadro Journal in 1932–1934. While there are those who define the Kadro Movement as a communist propaganda instrument (Harris 1967; Tuncay 2009), there are those who define it as a movement that blocked the Turkey socialist movement (Şişmanov 1990; Küçük 1985). A group consisting of Şevket Süreyya Aydemir, İsmail Hüsrev Tökin, Vedat Nedim Tör, Burhan Asaf Belge, and Yakup Kadri Karaosmanoğlu published a journal titled the Kadro Journal in 1932–1934.

[7] While the total import of Turkey in 1929 was 256 million TL, this figure dropped to 85 million TL in 1932 (Okyar 1965: 99).

monthly journal in 1932 and which advocated planning in all areas of life. It needs to be noted that although the étatist industrialization policy applied in Turkey partly satisfied the expectations of the Kadro Movement, it is different in that it is of a more pragmatic rather than ideological character. This can be understood directly from the words that Atatürk, the founder of the Republic of Turkey, said in 1932 (Okyar 1965):

> The principle of étatism that we have chosen to follow is not in any way the same as in Collectivism or in Communism which aims at removing all instruments of production and distribution from individuals, thus organizing society on a completely different basis and leaving no room for private and individual enterprise and action in the economic field. The end of Étatist policy, while it recognizes private initiative and action as the main basis of the economy, is to bring the Nation in the shortest time possible to an adequate level of prosperity and material welfare, and in order to achieve this, to ask the State to concern itself with those affairs where this is required by the high interests of the Nation, especially in the economic field.

As was with other countries, the 1929 crisis led to significant changes in economic policies in Turkey as well. Moreover, the "étatist development policy" resulting from these changes was of such a nature that it influenced the economic policies of Turkey in the periods to follow and that it played a role in the formation of today's economic structure. As a result of étatist policies, the start was made to the further development of étatism in the following periods and the steering of the market by the market actors was restricted. Rather than an investor seeking novelty in a competitive environment, a rent seeking investor was born[8] and thus, development and institutionalization of a market economy was hindered (Uzun 2005).

The 5-year industry plans have been the basic instrument of the étatist and import substitution approach to industrialization. Within the framework of The First Five Year Industrial Plan (I.FIP) carried out in 1934–1938, many state enterprises were established in the field of basic commodities. Although II.FIP to be carried out in 1938–1943 was prepared during this plan period, it was not implemented due to WWII. In the Turkish economy, the establishment of state enterprises outside the plan is observed in both the industrial sector and services and agricultural sectors (Şahin 2006). Thus, an étatist approach to entrepreneurship has dominated the economy.

It was not until WWII and the switch to the multiparty period[9] in 1946 that some breaks occurred in this étatist policy that emphasized the entrepreneurship of the state. Domestic and international factors influenced major political and economic changes in Turkey after WW-II. Domestically, many social groups had become dissatisfied with the single-party regime. They now preferred greater emphasis on private enterprise and less government interventionism. In addition, the emergence

---

[8] For this also, see Buğra (1994) and Keyder (1987).

[9] From the establishment of the Republic of Turkey in 1923 until 1946, the Republican People's Party founded by Atatürk was the only political party in the country. This sense of democracy practiced could be called plebiscite in nature. For the concept of "Plebiscite Democracy," see Hayek (2007: 100–111).

of the USA as the dominant power after the war shifted the balance toward a more liberal and open economic model (Pamuk 2007). The Democratic Party (DP), which voiced different social groups' demand for democratic rights and which defended more liberal economic policies, played a major role in this shift. The establishment of the DP both moved the Republican People's Party (CHP) more to the center of the political spectrum and when DP came to power in 1950, led to the implementation of economic policies that emphasized an outward-oriented market economy. However, paradoxically, in the years the DP was in power, the effectiveness of SEEs in the economy was increased through renewal and capacity increase investments in existing SEEs and through the establishment of new SEEs, in contradiction the party's discourse (Aktan 1972). For example, the Turkey Petroleum Corporation, the Meat and Fish Corporation, the Turkey Iron and Steel Factory, the Turkey Cellulose and Paper Industry, the Tourism Bank, Karabük Iron and Steel Factory, and Turkey Coal Corporation were all established in this period.

Although after 1946 no change appears in the expansion of state enterprises, differences in the approach to state entrepreneurship were observed in the functions attributed to these enterprises. During the étatist era of the 1930s, the state had established the SEEs to substitute for the absence of a private entrepreneurial class. In the post-1946 period, however, the role of SEEs became increasingly complementary of the private sector in a mixed economy (Öniş 1998, 2003).

With the military coup of 1960, the DP was removed from power, and in the same year the State Planning Organization was established. Those who realized the 1960 coup had similar economic, political, and social views as those who played a role in the establishment of the Republic and the implementation of étatist policies. Thus, it can be said that one of the basic aims of the coup was to end the liberal, outward- and market-oriented policies that became dominant in the 1946–1960 period and to return to the interventionist-étatist policies. From 1963 onward, 5-year development plans were carried out and in a sense, a second phase of étatism, interventionist economic policy and state entrepreneurship started. Unlike the earlier sector-based industrialization plans, the development plans implemented in this period aimed at planning the whole economy and functioned as guides to the private sector and as commands to the public sector. Especially, these plans can be said to have been prepared based on the idea to shift the economy to a higher phase of import substitution in order to achieve high growth rates. In this sense, as import substitution was thought to be realized in the basic commodity industries, the realization of import substitution in the field of intermediate and investment good industries was aimed. To this purpose, economic policies that protected local production through high import tariffs and import bans, and supported it through subsidies and incentive policies. Another important element of these policies is policies related to income transfers to the private sector through SEE goods that are offered at a price below their cost of production.

To sum up, from the years that the Republic was established until 1980s, the scope, size, and importance of SEEs in the economy continuously expanded. Although initially this policy was claimed to be temporary, continuous state intervention and state entrepreneurship prevailed until the1980s. This structuring was influence by social expectations, political preferences, authorities' worldviews, periodical and country-related conditions, and external economic developments. Moreover, this structuring has determined the economic growth performance of Turkey in subsequent periods and the structural problems it experiences. In fact, the Turkey experience illustrates how initially temporary policies of state interventionism and state entrepreneurship ultimately transformed into permanent institutional structures. A discussion of the place of state interventionism and SEEs in the Turkish economy before 1980 will shed light on this issue.

Table 3.1 presents the contribution of the public sector in the manufacturing industry in terms of production, value added, and employment. The table shows that in some sectors, production, value added, and employment are virtually completely controlled by the state. Moreover, economic activities of the state in the electricity, transportation, and communication sectors are not included. The initially temporary étatism and state entrepreneurship policies at the end of the 1970s, resulted in a structure where virtually one-third of the total manufacturing industry was controlled by the state. The fact that neither leftist nor rightist parties took concrete steps to change the situation when they came into power played a role in this outcome. The activity of the state in the economy as well as the number and influence of SEEs continued to increase in the DP period (1950–1960) and in the Justice Party (AP) period (1961–1980), which can be seen as an extension of the DP.

**Table 3.1** The contributions of public sector in manufacturing industry (1979, %)

| Industry | Production | Value added | Employment |
|---|---|---|---|
| Processed food | 37 | 39 | 50 |
| Beverages | 40 | 43 | 46 |
| Tobacco | 91 | 93 | 94 |
| Textiles | 12 | 13 | 20 |
| Wearing apparel | 15 | 22 | 15 |
| Fur and leather products | 20 | – | 24 |
| Wood and cork | 31 | 34 | 41 |
| Furniture and fixtures | 12 | 17 | 16 |
| Paper and paper products | 60 | 43 | 69 |
| Printing and publishing | 10 | 17 | 23 |
| Chemicals | 28 | 25 | 25 |
| Petroleum | 97 | 75 | 76 |
| Rubber and rubber products | 1 | 1 | 0 |
| Nonmetallic minerals | 18 | 15 | 20 |
| Basic metals | 46 | 46 | 67 |
| Metal products | 11 | 16 | 7 |
| Machinery | 21 | 26 | 28 |
| Electrical machinery | 2 | 3 | 7 |
| Transport equipment | 14 | 29 | 41 |
| Miscellaneous | 8 | 10 | 12 |
| *Total* | *32* | *30* | *36* |

*Source*: World Bank (1982), A World Bank Country Study, pp. 249

### 3.2.2 Liberal Economic Applications and Privatization Policies

Another milestone in the political economy history of the Turkey is the military coup of 1980. The negative economic conditions had contributed to the political instability Turkey moved towards and to the following interruption of democracy. After the effects of the oil shocks starting from the second half of the 1970s the vulnerabilities of the economy emerged, especially huge shocks were experienced in the balance of payments, and the problems continued and aggravated from 1975 onward (Öniş and Riedel 1993). The economic factors that caused a continuous crisis atmosphere in the country can be listed as follows (Şahin 2006; Öniş and Riedel 1993).

The planned import substitution development strategy did not reduce the demand for foreign currency and dependence on foreign countries; on the contrary, it led to the withdrawal of productive sources from the production and services sector that earned foreign currency, which resulted in a foreign currency bottleneck that made the import of petroleum, investment goods and intermediate goods impossible.

Another factor, which can be related to the above factor, was the oil shocks that increased the petroleum prices. This increase in petroleum prices brought a heavy load in the balance of payments of Turkey, which was totally dependent on foreign countries in terms of oil. The petroleum import to total import ratio that was 10% in 1972 had risen to 47% in 1980.

Public finance became unbalanced and budget deficits became constantly. While the need for public borrowing was 2% in 1972–1973, it rose to 10.5% in 1980. This imbalance was caused more by SEEs than by public expenditure, as can be seen in Table 3.2.

As the public borrowing need was high in subsequent years, the debt stock of the state increased and the country's external borrowing became difficult and the interest cost of total public debt increased.

The economic repercussions of all these negative developments include the increase of inflationary pressure, the increase in unemployment, in balance of payment deficits, and in foreign currency deficits, and the repeated shrinking of the

**Table 3.2** The contribution of SEEs to the public borrowing before the 1980s (%)

| Years | Public borrowing need/GDP | SEEs budget deficits/GDP | Share of SEEs budget deficits in the public borrowing need |
|---|---|---|---|
| 1975 | 6.1 | 5.2 | 85.2 |
| 1976 | 8.7 | 7.1 | 81.6 |
| 1977 | 10.4 | 5.0 | 48.1 |
| 1978 | 4.1 | 2.0 | 48.8 |
| 1979 | 9.4 | 5.2 | 55.3 |
| 1980 | 10.5 | 5.8 | 55.2 |
| 1975–1980 | 8.2 | 5.1 | 62.4 |

*Source*: State Planning Organization

economy due to the decrease in capacity use and production. The resulting crisis was not only of economic nature, but also had political and social features. In 1970–1980, the average lifetime of governments in Turkey was 10.5 months. Moreover, the social agenda of this period was marked with the armed and unarmed activities of radical political elements in the country. Almost every day, tens of people died as a result of these violent actions. Thus rather than economic problems and solutions, it was through the political conflict and the desire to seize political power in whichever possible manner that the country's future was shaped. These negative developments led to the military coup on September 12, 1980, which was followed by a junta government that stayed in power until 1983.

The foundations of the post-1980 were laid with the January 24, 1980 stability program that was implemented during the office of the 43rd Government of the Republic formed by the AP and headed by Prime Minister Süleyman Demirel. The army can be said to have had no direct influence on the formation of economic policy in the post-1980 period. However, the suspension of democracy and the junta's adoption of the economic package made it possible to implement the stability program without any opposition and reaction from the society (Öniş 1992). The architect of these policies was Turgut Özal who held the position of Deputy Under-Secretary of the Prime Minister and the Head of the State Planning Organization during this government. After the Motherland Party (ANAP), which he established in 1983 for the first elections held to restore democracy, came into power on its own, he found the opportunity to implement economic policies that overlapped with the philosophy of January 24 stability program and which aimed at liberalization and the introduction of market economy regulations.[10]

In addition to the short-term goals to create stability, the Neoliberal January 24 stability program also included long-term goals to transform the economic structure. The short-term goals were (a) to solve the foreign currency bottleneck and balance of payment problems, (b) to achieve price stability, and (c) to activate idle capacity and increase the growth rate. Among the long-term goals to transform the economic structure were (a) to minimize state intervention and develop a market economy and (b) to shift from import substitution policies to industrialization policies aimed at export.

In the course of the 1980s, Turkey's economy went through a step-by-step liberalization. Liberalization of market interest rates to encourage private savings and of the foreign trade regime, removal of exchange rate controls, adoption of encouraging policies for foreign capital, privatization of SEEs, and shifting to income transfers through public spending instead of price mechanisms were some of the components of the new economic program (Öniş 1998; Celasun 1990). Within this framework, the measures taken of the stability program can be summarized as follows: Foreign currency control was abandoned, the Turkish Lira was devalued and the foreign currency rates were determined daily and based on

[10] For a study on the positive and negative effects of Özal's post-1980 economic transformation, see Öniş (2004: 113–134).

the market. The prices of commodities produced by the public sector were raised substantially. Efforts started to end the state monopoly on the tobacco market and to start the privatization of SEEs. In addition, autonomy was given to SEEs to determine the price of the goods they produced. In order for the price mechanism to operate, the prices of goods and services on the market were allowed to be determined freely. To create price competition, import was liberalized. To allow interest and foreign currency rates to form in a free market, institutional substructure was developed. The scope of the minimum prices and support purchases were narrowed in the agricultural sector and determined prices started to approximate market prices. The foreign trade regime was liberalized, the number of goods that were quota bound was reduced, and from 1984 onward, the average customs tax/tariff rate was reduced from 76 to 49%. Regulations were made to encourage and facilitate the entry of foreign capital to the country.

The structural features of the economy at the end of the 1970s and the increasing trend in the applications of neoliberal theory in the same period, facilitated the acceptance of liberalization in general and privatization in specific terms. One of the most important areas where the January 24 stability policies were applied involved the SEEs and public entrepreneurship. While the stability program aimed at the transfer of SEEs to the private sector on the one hand, it aimed at the reduction of the state's activities in the economy and thus allow the functioning of the institutions of a free market economy, on the other. In this context, several policies that have been implemented in Turkey since the beginning of 1980 can be included in the narrow or broadest definitions of privatization.[11] Some of these are deregulation, imposition of user charges for public goods and services, the selling of SEEs, contracting-out and joint venture policies.

## 3.3 Privatization Policy in Practice

As is the case with all public policy, privatization policies in a country result in gains and losses by different groups in the society. Although privatization policies are perceived to increase the social welfare in economic terms and are therefore efficient, the political costs of these policies sometimes may cause difficulties in their application. As the losses of especially the losing parties in privatization policies are considerable and visible, and as the winning parties are not aware or do not care about their gains, the reform process may be paralyzed. Therefore, the factors that

[11] The term privatization can be used to cover a range of policies from those of governmental disengagement and deregulation to the sale of publicly owned assets (Hemming and Mansoor 1988: 1). In its broadest definition, privatization represents a counter movement to the growth of government and means reducing all forms of state control over resource allocation. Its narrow definition refers to the sale or leasing of assets in which the state has a majority interest, and the contracting out of publicly provided services (Bienen and Waterbury 1989: 617).

trigger the start or application of privatization policies and the question of with what motive politicians start the reform process are important. It is not possible to make a certain judgment; however, factors such as the experiences of other countries, the pressure of international organizations and loan extending countries, financial needs, political authorities' ideological view that adopts a free market economy, the increase in financial globalization, and the demand for more democratic government have an effect on the start of the reform process (Bangura 2000; Bienen and Waterbury 1989). It is possible to evaluate the factors that drove privatization in Turkey within the same framework. International institutions and creditor countries played a role in the January 24 stability program and the liberalization and privatization process in Turkey (Öniş 2004). Additionally, it is known that the fact that politicians and the political authorities, especially Özal, had great faith in the success of the private sector and the institutions of the market economy was of influence on the liberalization and privatization policies.[12] Thus, it can be said that in Turkey, Özal represented a similar ideology and leadership function to that of Reagan in the USA and Thatcher in the UK. However, it needs to be conceded that Özal's weak attachment to democracy, institutions, and rule of law in his government style separates him from the mentioned leaders (Yayla 2001; Öniş 2004).

The most basic document that shaped the privatization applications in Turkey was the "Privatization Main Plan" that was prepared in 1986 by Morgan Guaranty Trust Company of New York, the Turkish Industrial Development Bank, the Industrial Investment and Credit Bank, Investment Finance, Inc., and PricewaterhouseCoopers. In this plan, the following privatization aims pertaining to Turkey's conditions were included: to allow market forces to drive the economy, to increase productivity, to increase the number, quality, and diversity of products, to encourage joint ventures and capital markets, to reduce the burden of SEEs on the Treasury, to reduce the monopolist prices of SEEs, and indirect taxes, to use modern technology and management techniques, to increase productivity by giving company shares to the workers, to change the balance between the public and private sector institutions, to develop international economic and political relationships through foreign investment, to increase the internal profitability of current capital investments, and to create revenue for the state. At present, the privatization aims of Turkey are expressed as follows: to reduce the industrial and economic activity of the state to a minimum, to form a competitive market economy, to decrease the financial burden of SEEs on the state budget, to develop the capital market and to transfer idle savings to the economy, and to channelize sources obtained from privatization to substructure investments (PA 2010). When these aims are grouped, they can be observed to fall into four categories: the transformation and development of the economic structure, the increase of productivity of SEEs, the improvement of public finance, and the development of capital markets.

[12] See Bienen and Waterbury (1989: 623) for the effects of the pressure exerted by international organizations and credit providing countries during the implementation of reform processes and privatization policies in developing countries.

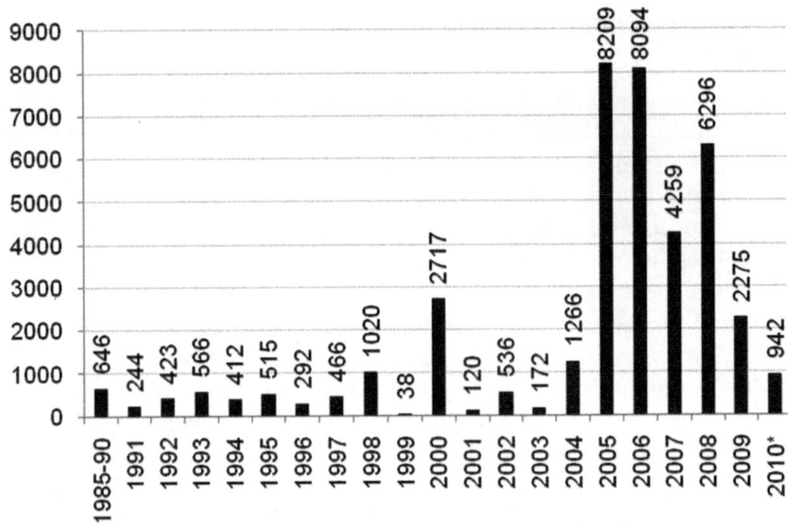


* *For the first half of year.*
*Source:* Republic of Turkey Prime Ministry Privatization Administration.

**Fig. 3.1** Privatization implementations by years (million $)

Although in Turkey the first steps toward privatization of SEEs in political terms were made with January 24 stability program in 1980, the realization of this political will has been a painful and slow process, which can be observed in the size of privatization sales over the years presented in Fig. 3.1. The first element to note in Fig. 3.1 is the sharp increase in privatization sales revenues starting from 2004.[13] In the period between the first privatization sale in 1986 and 2004, the privatization movement proceeded very slowly, which was due to defects in privatization practices and political, social, and legal factors.

There are different factors of different degrees of importance that affected the privatization process in practice by slowing down policymaking or interrupting it. Bienen and Waterbury (1989) lists these factors as (a) ideological factors, (b) public deficits, (c) the resistance by those who had interests in the continuation of the status-quo, (d) authorities' views on the control of economic resources and patronage. In this framework, the factors that were of influence on the privatization pace and scope in Turkey will be grouped and discussed in three categories: institutional and legal factors, economic factors, and political factors.

[13] In the period 2000–2007, Turkey ranked fifth among OECD countries in terms of absolute size of privatization and seventh in terms of the privatization to GDP ratio and is among the leading countries in the field of privatization (OECD 2009: Chap.1, Table 1).

### 3.3.1 Institutional and Legal Factors

It is not possible to say that during the implementation of privatization policies in Turkey a legally and administratively well-defined framework was formed. The legal and institutional defects that appeared over time were amended as the process continued, which caused problems in the pace and the effectiveness of privatization practices. Basically, a legal framework for privatization is necessary to regulate and define the government's objectives, to establish commitment to the privatization process, to make amendments to existing laws which otherwise would be an obstacle to privatization, for example, laws preventing private sector participation in what were previously considered "strategic" activities, to create institutions with the authority to implement privatization, to avoid spontaneous or unauthorized privatization, to allow for the financial restructuring of enterprises prior to sale, deferred or swapped for equity, to define the methods of privatization and any limitations on potential bidders, and to provide for the allocation of sale proceeds (UNESCAP 2001). However, the legal and administrative tools of privatization policies in Turkey did not have such broadly defined sets of objectives at the beginning. In the course of time, the legal and administrative regulations were improved and insufficiencies were made up for substantially. These improvements can be summarized as follows (PA 2010):

- With Law Nr. 2983 enacted on 29.2.1984, privatization methods that consisted of revenue sharing bonds, stocks, and transfer of operating rights were defined, and the Housing and Public Participation Council (HPPC), the Housing and Public Participation Administration (HPPA), and the Public Participation Fund (PPF) were established, and the privatization-related decision-making authorization was given to the HPPC.
- With Law Nr. 2985 enacted on 02.03.1984, the Housing Development Fund (HDF) was established and its relationships with the HPPC and the HPPA were defined.
- With Article 38 of Statutory Decree Nr. 233 enacted on 08.06.1984, the privatization-related decision-making authorization initially given to the HPPC was transferred to the Economic Affairs High Coordination Council (EAHCC) and the implementation remained with the HPPA.
- With Law Nr. 3291 enacted on 28.5.1986, it was ruled that Article 38 of Statutory Decree Nr. 233 could not be applied, and new regulations were made related to decision-making and implementation stages in privatization. The most important regulation that Law Nr. 3291 brought was that the scope and inclusion process of privatization was defined and that the responsibilities and authorizations initially given to the EAHCC were given back to the HPPC.
- With Statutory Decree Nr. 304 enacted on 28.12.1987, the HPPC and the EAHCC were abolished, and their responsibilities and duties transferred to the High Planning Council (HPC).
- With Statutory Decrees Nr. 412 and 414 enacted on 09.04.1990, the HPPA was divided into two entities: the Housing Development Administration (HDA) and

the Public Participation Administration (PPA), and all privatization-related responsibilities and authorizations were given to the PPA.

- With Law Nr. 3701 enacted on 6.3.1991, the decision authorization of the PPA was given to the HPC again. Later, with Statutory Decree Nr. 473 enacted on 20.12.1991, the Public Participation High Council (PPHC) was established and was authorized to make decisions related to privatization implementations and the PPF.
- As legal gaps in privatization regulations became apparent and as general competence laws and the Statutory Decrees based on these laws were revoked by the Constitutional Court (CC), the need arose to formulate regulations that encompassed privatization regulations and that addressed the issues in the revocation grounds of the CC. Accordingly, with Law Nr. 3987 enacted on 5.5.1994, the government was authorized for 3 months to pass Statutory Decrees pertaining to privatization. With Statutory Decrees Nr. 530, 531, and 532 that were enacted on 30.5.1994 after this authorization, important regulations that were aimed at privatization and at the solution of employment problems after privatization were made.
- However, when Competence Law Nr. 3987 was revoked by the Constitutional Court on 07.07.1994, a plea for the revocation and motion of stay of execution of Statutory Decrees Nr. 530, 531, 532, 533 and 546, which were based on this Law, was submitted to the Constitutional Court. Consequently, the Statutory Decrees in question were revoked by the Constitutional Court on 21.07.1994 with Decree of Court Nr. 1994/63.
- With Law Nr. 4046 enacted on 24.11.1994, the Privatization High Council (PHC), the Privatization Administration (PA), and the Privatization Fund (PF) were established. In addition, the scope of privatization was expanded and the principles and procedures of the privatization implementation of enterprises to be privatized were determined. The Law also provided that the personnel contracted in enterprises within the scope of privatization that might become redundant during or after privatization were paid "Redundancy Compensation" in addition to other indemnities foreseen in the collective bargaining agreements and/or in the existing laws in relation with potential employment reductions that may occur. Furthermore, to encourage early retirement, the Law provided that of the personnel in enterprises to be privatized those who were entitled to retirement as of the period of service under the Turkish Pension Fund Law, would be paid post-retirement gratuity with a 30% increment, if they asked to be retired within 2 months. Additionally, the Law included regulations through which permanent and contracted personnel in enterprises within the scope of privatization who became redundant could be transferred and assigned to vacant positions in other enterprises. Other provisions were that the proceeds of privatization would not be used for general budget expenditures and/or investments and that privileged state shares for strategic enterprises would be created. Law Nr. 4046 was amended with Law Nr. 4105 enacted on 27.04.1995, Law Nr. 4108 enacted on 25.05.1995, Law Nr. 4232 enacted on 03.04.1997, Law Nr. 4568 enacted on 26.05.2000, Law Nr. 4971 enacted on 01.08.2003, Law Nr. 5148 enacted on

27.4.2004, Law Nr. 5189 enacted on 16.6.2004, Law Nr. 5234 enacted on 17.9.2004, and lastly Law Nr. 5398 enacted on 03.07.2005. These amendments were aimed at solving the social problems caused by privatization, reducing legal conflicts, decreasing bureaucracy, and achieving transparency.

- With Law Nr. 4446 enacted on 13.8.1999, Article 47 of the Constitution was changed and it was decided that the rules and regulations for the privatization of SEEs and other public-owned businesses and assets would be determined by Law. Thus, the concept of privatization entered the Constitution of Turkey for the first time.

When the mentioned developments of legal framework in Turkey are analyzed, it is seen that the legal framework lacks in several perspectives and that there are factors which slow down the process. To begin with, there is no consistency between the regulations. It is clear that as long as there are inconsistencies on even issues such as the authority to decide on privatization, it is not possible to make progress in more detailed issues of privatization. Secondly, privatization policies and legal regulations were not formed from a holistic perspective from the very beginning. Yet, it is recommended that the legal requirements of privatization be considered in three respects: (a) The legal requirements for the formulation of privatization procedures, (b) The legal requirements for the implementation of privatization, and (c) The legal requirements for monitoring and control after privatization (UNESCAP 1996). This lack in the legal framework was only amended with Law Nr. 4046 in 1994, and with the establishment of the "Privatization Administration" with this law, privatization reached an effective administrative structure. In addition, with Law Nr. 4054 on the "The Act on The Protection of Competition" (1994), Law Nr. 4077 on the "Consumer Protection Law" (1995), and Law Nr. 4501 on the "Principles That Shall be Complied with When There is an Access to Arbitration for Disputes Arising From Concession Contracts" (2000), the legal gaps that were important in terms of the effects of privatization were also filled. The third involves the influence of the CC on the privatization process. Although this may be perceived as a negative and slowing effect on the privatization process at first glance, it has enhanced the proper functioning of the privatization mechanism and reduced political resistance by partly compensating for the losses of those negatively affected by privatization. Finally, it can be said that politicians and the implementers of privatization policies were not able to interpret the legal framework and take the necessary steps. A country that explicitly treats concepts such as expropriation and nationalization in its constitution, but does not treat the concept of privatization, will experience difficulty in implementing privatization policies without violation of the Constitution at some point in the process. The concept of privatization entered the Constitution of the Republic of Turkey only in 1999, with a delay of 18–19 years.

Another issue, which is ignored in parallel to the gaps in the legal framework in Turkey, is that a framework for regulatory institutions was not formulated for many years. Although in theory, privatization is associated with positive aspects, such as competition, increase in productivity, and improvement in product quality, in the absence of a regulatory framework, these positive aspects are not likely to be observed in the privatization of public monopolies (Öniş 1991a). The gains of privatization arise when privatized firms operate in a competitive environment and encounter serious threats of takeover and potential risk of bankruptcies (Vickers and Yarrow 1988; Yarrow 1986). The absence of a competitive environment would mean that privatization could change firm ownership without changing firm behavior (UNESCAP 2001). In Turkey, the Turkish Competition Authority that regulates competition started to act in 1997. Regulatory authorities in natural monopoly sectors, such as electricity and telecommunication, were established in 2000 and 2001, respectively. Thus, the institutions to regulate the natural monopoly sector after privatization were established and these filled the gaps in operational procedures.

To sum up, privatization in the 1980s was practiced without proper attention to administrative and legal requirements. It proceeded very slowly and was also interrupted due to revocations by legal authorities and social reactions. It was not until the 2000s that privatization started to be practiced faster and on a legally and administratively sound basis.

### 3.3.2 *Economic Factors*

The shocks experienced in the Turkish economy and cyclical developments have played a role in the applicability of privatization policies. Although the transformation period after the January 24 stability program changed the structural character of the economy, the vulnerability of the economy continued due to wrong economic policies followed. The structural transformation and macroeconomic situation of the Turkish economy can be summarized through the data presented in Table 3.3.

After the post-1980 liberalization policies, Turkey underwent an important change in structural terms. As can be seen in Table 3.3, this structural change is significant in terms of variables such as the composition of GNP, the share of public expenditure in GNP, and the change in foreign trade volume. However, the macroeconomic performance of the postliberalization economy of Turkey was too poor to successfully implement privatization policies.[14] The growth rate of the Turkish economy was negative in 1994 (−6.1%), 1999 (−6.1%), and 2001 (−9.4%). After 1987, the political competition in Turkey rose gradually. As a result, the populist political attitudes of political parties and governments were not directed by economic needs and economic rationality, but by vote maximization and political rationality. Therefore, the "populist democracy"[15] approach prevalent in Turkey

---

[14] For an analysis of postliberalization macroeconomic performance of the Turkish economy, see Güran and Tosun (2008), which state that Turkey exhibits an unstable economic structure after liberalization.

[15] For a detailed evaluation of the populist mentality differences of the political parties and/or party leaders and of the interaction between politics and economic policies in Turkey, see Türkkan (1996).

**Table 3.3** Selected economic indicators of the Turkish economy (average yearly)

| Indicators | 1980 | 1981–1990 | 1991–2002 | 2003–2008 |
|---|---|---|---|---|
| Reel economic growth rate (%) | −2.8 | 5.3 | 2.9 | 7.0 |
| Unemployment ratio (15+ age) (%) | – | 2.5 | 7.9 | 10.6 |
| Consumer price index changes (%) | – | 53.2 | 63.8 | 10.2[a] |
| Current account deficit/GNP (%) | −5 | −1.3 | −0.8 | −5.7 |
| Public sector borrowing requirement (%) | 8.8 | 4.9 | 10.4 | 2.3 |
| Total public expenditure/GNP (%) | 20.3 | 16.7 | 29.5 | 34.1 |
| Industrial production/GNP (%) | 19.3 | 24 | 25 | 25.8[a] |
| Agricultural production/GNP (%) | 26.1 | 19.7 | 14.9 | 10.2 |
| Export/GNP (%) | 4.2 | 10.2 | 13.6 | 20.7 |
| Import/GNP (%) | 11.4 | 15.2 | 21.8 | 32.2[a] |
| Industry export/total export (%) | 36.6 | 71.1 | 88.2 | 94.1[a] |
| Foreign direct investment (billion $) | 18 | 235 | 999 | 10,105 |

*Source*: State Planning Organization, Economic and Social Indicators, http://www.dpt.gov.tr/DPT.portal; Turkish Statistical Institute, http://www.tuik.gov.tr; Turkish Treasury, http://www.treasury.gov.tr

[a]For 2003–2006 periods

after 1987 has hindered liberalization in general and privatization implementations in specific (Öniş and Aysan 2000). The monetary and fiscal policy that can be summarized as "borrow and print money, rather than collect tax" and that was followed in the 1990s when the economy was unstable, completely destroyed economic balance increased economic instability. Under these conditions, both foreign and domestic capital avoided investment in the economy, and high real profit yielding government securities and speculative stock market and foreign currency investment became attractive. Thus, in a period of high economic instability and uncertainty and when speculative financial assets were more popular than real assets, the sale of SEEs in the form of private placement or public offer was not possible. Moreover, the increase in the vulnerability of the Turkish economy made that it was negatively affected not only by shocks resulting from its own internal dynamics but also from external shocks. The Turkish economy was negatively affected by the 1995 Mexico, 1997 Asia, 1998 Russia, and 1999 Brazil crises, which reduced the applicability of privatization policies. On the other hand, in these years of high economic volatility, privatization lost its priority for government policy. When instability rose during the 1990s and at the beginning of the 2000s, governments prioritized economic variables such as unemployment, inflation, and growth, and problems of political and social nature. Yet, they were unsuccessful in improving these variables because of irrational economic policies. Hence, increasing and persistent instability made it impossible to privatize by selling SEEs through private placement or public offer. This picture changed especially after 2002 when measures taken for financial discipline and inflation control proved successful and both small and corporate investors' interest was attracted to privatization.

As Table 3.3 shows, the public financial balance in Turkey is characterized by negative developments throughout the 1990s. Under these conditions, it was impossible to obtain the financial sources required to rehabilitate and prepare enterprises to be privatized for sale. Moreover, this situation was a vicious cycle. While on the one hand, the need for borrowing brought high interest costs, on the other, the state owned assets to be privatized the interest burden of which it could not rid itself of through sale. The cost of this vicious cycle has been high for Turkey. From 1995 onward, Turkey has been indebted with 18% real interest. If the 36.4 billion dollar income Turkey obtained from privatization in the period 2004–2009 had been spread over the period after the 1994 stability program in the same manner as was the case between 2004 and 2009, the saving on interest that Turkey would have obtained through this income would have been 130 billion dollar. In other words, by obtaining this privatization income with a 10 years' delay, Turkey actually has had to shoulder a cost equivalent to four times the value of the assets privatized. Another loss caused by the delay of privatization has been the decrease in the value of the assets in the privatization portfolio due to the changes in the market conditions and technological changes. The privatization of Turkish telecommunication constitutes an interesting example to this. This enterprise, which would be privatized after the April 4, 1994 stability program, was not privatized until 2005. At the beginning of 1993, the market value of Turkish telecommunication was estimated at 25–30 billion dollar. Yet, the 10-year delay resulted in a decrease in the market value of this enterprise due to technological changes, and the income obtained for 55% of its shares and a GSM operator license was limited to 6.5 billion dollar.

Another economic factor at play in the slow progress of privatization procedures in Turkey was the low level of savings, the insufficient development of security markets and the great role that the public sector played on the securities market as demander of funds (Bortolotti and Milella 2008; Bortolotti and Pinotti 2003; Öniş 1991a). The low per capita income, the increase in the consumption trend in an inflationary environment, and the insufficient depth of the securities market blocked the sale of SEEs through popular capitalism. On the other hand, this situation was also stifled by the implementation of privatization due to public sensitivity against privatization through block sale practices.

### *3.3.3 Political Factors*

Many studies in the literature stress the effects of political structure and its components such as leadership, political incentives, political division, interest groups, political patronage, and rent seeking activities on the pace and success of privatization (Vickers and Yarrow 1988; Haggard and Webb 1994; Shleifer and Vishny 1994; World Bank 1995; Shirley and Walsh 2000; Bortolotti and Pinotti 2003; Börner 2004).

Under the planned and import substitution policies before 1980, entrepreneurs became increasingly dependent on the subsidies provided by the state than seeking the opportunities created by the market. As a result of these economic policies, serious moral hazard problems and rent-seeking behaviors were generated on a systematic basis in both public and private sectors (Balkan and Yeldan 1998; Öniş and Riedel 1993).

Although from a political perspective the existence and performance of SEEs has continuously been debated in Turkey and although the need for reform has always been recognized (Öniş and Riedel 1993), the question of why the necessary steps were not taken needs to be answered. Atatürk's opening speeches in the Turkish Great National Assembly and the government programs of the İnönü Governments (1923–1924 and 1925–1937), the Cemal Gürsel Governments (1960–1961), the I. Erim (1971), and the Melen Governments (1972) include recurrent suggestions for the restructuring of SEEs. The most important of these suggestions for reform are aimed at the empowerment of SEEs through restructuring and their privatization (Babüroğlu 1982). These demands reflect the problems experienced by SEEs, the most important of which is the problem of unproductivity (YDK 1973). When the output of public enterprises per unit input is compared with that of private enterprises for the years 1963 and 1976, this significant difference in productivity is observed. The italicized figures in Table 3.4 show where public sector output productivity per unit input is lower than that of the private sector,

**Table 3.4** Ratio of public-to-private output per unit of input

| | 1963 | | | 1976 | | |
|---|---|---|---|---|---|---|
| Sector | Output per capital | Output per labor | Output per weighted inputs[a] | Output per capital | Output per labor | Output per weighted inputs[a] |
| Food | *0.212* | *0.642* | *0.264* | *0.828* | *0.592* | *0.729* |
| Beverages | **3,509** | **1,577** | **2,762** | **3,030** | **1,876** | **2,525** |
| Tobacco | **1,709** | *0.684* | **1,221** | *0.842* | *0.923* | *0.857* |
| Textiles, wearing, apparel, and footwear[b] | *0.741* | *0.805* | *0.762* | **1,712** | *0.641* | **1,080** |
| Wood and cork products | **1,199** | *0.893* | **1,068** | *0.815* | *0.536* | *0.700* |
| Paper and products | *0.50* | **1,005** | *0.597* | *0.495* | *0.759* | *0.55* |
| Chemicals | *0.315* | *0.715* | *0.369* | *0.496* | *0.773* | *0.446* |
| Nonmetallic minerals | *0.978* | **1,550** | **1,129** | *0.812* | *0.909* | *0.848* |
| Petroleum and coal | – | – | – | *0.630* | **8,000** | *0.781* |
| Basic metals | *0.605* | **1,284** | *0.710* | *0.220* | *0.358* | *0.251* |
| Metal products | *0.218* | *0.818* | *0.300* | *0.122* | *0.733* | *0.182* |
| Machinery | **1,887** | **1,170** | **1,631** | **1,616** | *0.711* | **1,063** |
| Electrical machinery | *0.670* | *0.428* | *0.587* | *0.318* | *0.181* | *0.248* |
| Transport equipment | *0.372* | *0.227* | *0.313* | *0.394* | *0.205* | *0.313* |

*Source*: Krueger and Tuncer (1980), p. 43

[a] Weights are factor shares in the private sector as of the years in question

[b] Because capital stock data were available jointly for textiles and wearing apparel and footwear, any separate estimation of efficiency was biased by the split used, and it was deemed preferable to aggregate the two sectors

whereas the bold figures show where public sector productivity is relatively higher than that of the private sector. As can be observed from Table 3.4, the factor productivity of public enterprises is lower than that of private enterprises, with the exception of five sectors in 1963 and three sectors in 1976 (Krueger and Tuncer 1980). Similarly, in the period 2001–2006, while average labor productivity growth in public firms decreased 5.5 annually, it increased 29.7 in private firms (World Bank 2008). Thus, it can be said that, in general, the factor productivity of public enterprises is low and that it follows a worsening trend. This low productivity has been mainly due to advanced technology-dependent investment decisions for SEEs and over employment resulting from political interventions. The basic reasons why the required measures to solve the problems that SEEs have experienced for many years were not taken can be said to be ideological and political in nature.

Although privatization policies have been a global trend in the last 20 years, the extent of divestiture varies greatly across countries. In some countries, governments have pursued a consistent and sustained privatization policy as a part of wider reform packages, while in others ambitious programs have been blocked on their way by adverse interest groups, so that privatization has been irregular and small scaled (Bortolotti and Pinotti 2003). In that sense, Turkey constitutes an example to the second group. As mentioned above, SEEs have a long history and hold an important place due to their large share in the economy. Hence, the privatization of SEEs means economic gains or losses for different interest groups in the society. In Turkey, the different interest groups profiting from SEEs are public workers and unions, politicians and bureaucrats, and consumers among others.[16] It is known that before 1980, public workers earned 1.33 times more, on average, than private sector workers. This difference reaches 1.83 times in some sectors such as Tobacco Processing (Krueger and Tuncer 1980). Similarly, when workers who became redundant after privatization found new jobs their loss of earnings was determined to be 66% on average (Tansel 2002). These figures indicate that losses due to privatization experienced by the losing parties are substantial and that they are substantial enough to create resistance to privatization. Unions are important actors in the struggle against privatization, as they do not only defend worker rights, but also their own positions, and economic and political power. A second interest group profiting from SEEs are politicians and bureaucrats. Starting from the beginning of the multiparty period in 1946, politics has been a determining factor in state economic policies in Turkey. The dominant position of SEEs in the economy has rendered them an instrument for political patronage and rent distribution by governments (Sunar 1990). One dimension of these policies involves politicians' manipulation of prices, wages, and employment in SEEs to remain or come in power, while another involves employment of political partisans and promoting them to administrative or supervisory and executive levels. Thus, SEEs historically have been

[16] Therefore, "privatization" concept should be defined in broader terms as to include the "privatization of the private sector" (Öniş 1998: 506).

**Table 3.5** Top management turnover in the privatization administration

| | 1986–1993 | 1994 | 1995 | 1996 | 1997 | 1998 |
|---|---|---|---|---|---|---|
| Number of presidents | 6 | 2 | 3 | 4 | 3 | 1 |
| Number of vice-presidents | 18 | 3 | 9 | 10 | 11 | 7 |

*Source*: Ercan and Öniş (2001)

instruments used for political purposes to indirectly redistribute income to preferred groups. Moreover, this structure has been of influence on also the PA, which was established to manage the privatization process. The recruitment system of the PA was based on political and personal connections. Ad hoc and arbitrary selection criteria have rendered the agency increasingly vulnerable to political pressures and external intervention. Heavy political involvement in the recruitment process is also reflected in the high turnover of top management. The PA has undergone major changes too frequently at the top management level. Between 1993 and 1997, acting presidents have been able to serve only for 5.25 months on average. It is rather striking that the PA has had more than three presidents and ten vice-presidents, on average, for each year between 1997 and 1999 as seen in Table 3.5 (Ercan and Öniş 2001). In 1998 and onward, the turnover in top management decreased and a more stable structure in the management appeared. To illustrate, the present Director of the PA has been in office for 7 years since June 2003.

Consumers form the last interest group. It can be said that the median voter in Turkey consisting of farmers, small tradesman, and wageworkers, demands transfer of income through subsidized SEEs prices. While in Turkey the number of tax declaration submitting taxpayers was 5 million as of 2009, the number of voters is 48 million. This illustrates the imbalance between the political power of those who contribute to public finance and those who direct spending policies. As mentioned in the above sections, although SEEs continuously experienced problems, the privatization of SEEs was not thought of by the CHP governments during the single-party period because of their mentality, and during the multiparty period after 1950, SEEs continued their existence due to populism. Privatization practices mostly started after the 1980 coup when elections and political pressure were not on the agenda. However, after the restoration of democracy, increasing political competition and the fear of losing votes made it impossible to ignore the demands of the median voter. Especially after the elections in 1987, political concerns take precedence over economic rationality in both economic policy in general and privatization policies in specific. That is, the populist democracy approach foiled economic priorities and requirements (Türkkan 1996; Öniş 1991b, 1998; Sayarı 1992). Recently, an important change in the political approach has been observed in Turkey. The anchor function of the standby agreement signed with the IMF (2001) and the policies of the AKP governments (2002, 2007) that are sensitive to economics, requirements and priorities have contributed significantly to this change.

Another political factor, which has had a negative effect on the privatization process in Turkey, is the negative picture of the determination and power of governments. Due to the increasing political tension and competition in Turkey, especially in the 1990s, political fragmentation increased and the country was governed by coalitions. Between 1990 and 2000, nine different governments were formed, two of which were a coalition of three parties and six of which were a coalition of two parties. Moreover, two of these were minority governments. In addition, five of these governments consisted of a coalition formed by one leftist and one rightist party. This shows that in the period after 1990, political fragmentation increased, and political determination behind policies and political power decreased. Especially in coalition governments with left and right wing parties, privatizations were pushed to the background as they were perceived to be an issue of conflict between the coalition partners and thus a threat to the unity of the government. At times, issues of controversy, such as privatization, led to conflicts and resulted in the breakup of the coalition partners. However, after the 2002 elections, this politically fragmented picture changed. The Justice and Development Party (AKP) came to power on its own with 66% of the seats in the legislative assembly in the 2002 elections and with 62% of the seats in the 2007 elections. Thus, a politically more powerful and stable environment can be said to have appeared after 2002.

## 3.4 Conclusion

An étatist, nationalist, and autocratic management approach dominated the period of the establishment of the Republic of Turkey. This approach is reflected in not only the organization of social life but also the policies that allow the state to develop and control economic life. As a result of this approach, SEEs started to be established with the establishment of the Republic in 1923 and after the 1929 crisis, the development of SEEs gradually increased. Even in periods when more liberal oriented governments were in power, as was the case with the Democrat Party in 1950–1960, no changes were observed in policies involving SEEs until the 1980s. Although after the liberalization policies in 1980 privatization policies were started to be implemented, privatization was implemented very slowly and the process was accompanied by problems. This low performance in privatization can be attributed to political, economic, legal, and institutional factors.

In Turkey, from the establishment of the Republic onward, policy can be said to have been shaped and directed by a political and bureaucratic elite with Jacobin, autocratic, and leftist ideology. These political and bureaucratic elites considered state intervention, economic planning, and public entrepreneurship the basic instruments for economic development and formed the opposition in times when liberalization and privatization policies were practiced. This opposition blocked privatization practices sometimes by using state bureaucracy or the legal system, or sometimes through the support of the military forces in the form of coups or warnings. In fact, liberalization and privatization policies were viewed as a counterrevolution in response to Atatürk's revolutions that aimed to wipe out the political, social, and economic traces of the Ottoman Empire as an Islamic state. Within this point of view, privatization policy debates were detached from economic rationality and conducted within a totally political and ideological framework, and privatization was interrupted and hindered. Another political dimension involves the understanding of democracy in Turkey and the activities of certain interest groups. There has been a rent seeking median voter group consisting of farmers, small tradesmen, workers, and civil servants in Turkey. Due to vote maximization concerns, politicians have widely applied populist policies. As a result of these policies, the investment and production decisions as well as employment policies of SEEs were distorted and these enterprises were used as instruments for political patronage. Therefore, due to both the features of political demand and supply, it was not possible to eliminate the political control over SEEs through privatizations. Especially, politically weak coalition governments did not receive the required political support and could not take the politically costly steps toward privatization. The corruption that occurred due to the lack of transparency in privatization procedures also reduced the political and social support to privatization.

Another factor that caused the slow progress in privatization policies in Turkey involves the legal and organizational structures. As stressed earlier, the economy of Turkey for many years followed an étatist trend. Hence, both organizational and legal substructures were not conducive to the privatization of SEEs and reform process took time. In Turkey, the stock market was established only in 1994, the Competition Authority in 1993, and sectoral regulatory institutions after the second half of the 2000s (for example; the Telecommunication Higher Council in 2000 and the Energy Market High Council in 2001). Privatization legislations satisfying all economic-, judicial-, and social-related parties were not passed until 1994, and the term "privatization" entered the Constitution only in 1999. Thus, in Turkey, the organizational and legal structures required for privatization were formed only at the beginning of the 2000s.

Economic factors also affected the privatization policies in Turkey. The Turkish economy exhibited an extremely unstable character until 2002 due to wrong economic policies based on the liberalization policies after 1980 and populist democracy. Consequently, prices instability, budget deficits, and debt stocks increased, which affected growth negatively. The country became unattractive to both foreign investors and domestic investors. The vulnerability of the economy combined with internal and external triggering factors resulted in the economic crises of 1994, 1995, 1997, 1998, 1999, and 2001. The unfavorable economic conditions made privatization policies lose their priority and applicability. However, since the Transformation to a Powerful Economy Stability Program was started in 2002 and due to the favorable international economic conditions, a new economic environment conducive to privatization has been formed. Although the 2009 crisis cast a shadow over this picture, privatizations in the year 2009 yielded 2.3 billion dollar of privatization income.

To conclude, after the organizational and legal substructures for privatization were formed in the 1990s and after macroeconomic stability was achieved in 2002, the conditions conducive to privatization were created. The presence of a politically powerful and determined government during this period increased privatization.

The Turkey experience of privatization illustrates that privatization policy-making is a necessary but insufficient condition for privatization to take place in countries where this is desired because although virtually all governments that came in power after 1980 favored privatization, no success was achieved in the field of privatization. Hence, for privatization policies to be successfully implemented, first of all the legal and organizational substructure should be formed and macroeconomic stability should be achieved.

## References


Akalın, G. (2008). *Atatürk dönemi maliye politikaları (The fiscal policies in Atatürk period)*. Ankara: Maliye Bakanlığı Yayınları.

Aktan, R. (1972). *Türkiye iktisadı (Turkish economy)*. Ankara: Sevinç Matbaası.

Babüroğlu, B. (1982). Atatürk dönemi ve sonrası kamu iktisadi teşebbüsleri (*State economic enterprises in Atatürk period and after)*. In *Atatürk dönemi ekonomi politikası ve Türkiye'nin ekonomik gelişmesi semineri (The economy policies of Atatürk period and economic development symposium)* (pp. 151–184). Ankara: Üniversitesi Siyasal Bilgiler Fakültesi Yayınları.

Balkan, E. & Yeldan, A. E. (1998). Financial liberalization in developing countries: The Turkish experience. In R. Medhara & J. Fanelli (Eds.), *Financial liberalization in developing countries* (pp. 129–155). London: Macmillan.

Bangura, Y. (2000). *Public sector restructuring: The institutional and social effects of fiscal, managerial and capacity-building reforms*. Geneva: The United Nations Research Institute for Social Development.

Beriş, H. E. (2009). *Tek parti döneminde devletçilik: Türkiye'de otoritarizmin siyasal ve ekonomik kökenleri (Étatism in the singal-party period: The economic and polical roots of authoritarianism in Turkey)*. Ankara: Liberte Yayınları.

Bienen, H. & Waterbury, J. (1989). The political economy of privatization in developing countries. *World Development*, 17(5), 617–632.

Boratav, K. (2006). *Türkiye'de devletçilik (Étatism in Turkey)*. Ankara: İmge Kitabevi.

Börner, K. (2004). The political economy of privatization: Why do governments want reforms? Discussion Paper No. 2004-1. Department of Economics University of Munich. http://epub.ub.uni-muenchen.de/296/1/PrivatizationPaperDiskussionJan04.pdf. Accessed 25 May 2010.

Bortolotti, B. & Pinotti, P. (2003). The political economy of privatization. Research Paper Series No. 45.2003. Fondazione Eni Enrico Mattei. http://papers.ssrn.com/sol3/papers.cfm?abstract_id=418020. Accessed 25 May 2010.

Bortolotti, B. & Milella, V. (2008). Privatization in Western Europe: Stylized facts, outcomes, and open issues. In G. Roland (Ed.), *Privatization: Success and failures* (pp. 32–75). New York: Columbia University Press.

Buğra, A. (1994). *State and business in modern Turkey: A comparative study*. Albany: State University of New York Press.

Celasun, M. (1990). Fiscal aspects of adjustment in the 1980s. In T. Arıcanlı & D. Rodrik (Eds.), *The political economy of Turkey* (pp. 37–59). New York: St. Martin's Press.

Cillov, H. (1970). *Türkiye ekonomisi (Turkish economy)*. İstanbul: İktisat Fakültesi Yayınları.

Clarke, T. & Pitelis, C. (1993). Introduction: The political economy of privatization. In T. Clarke & C. Pitelis (Eds.), *The political economy of privatization* (pp. 1–28). London: Routledge.

Derin, H. (1940). *Türkiye'de devletçilik (Étatism in Turkey)*. İstanbul: Çituri Biraderler Basımevi.

Ercan, M. & Öniş Z. (2001). Turkish privatization: Institutions and dilemmas. *Turkish Studies*, 2(1), 109–134.

Frey, F. W. (1975). Patterns of elite politics in Turkey. In G. Lenczowski (Ed.), *Political elites in the Middle East* (pp. 41–82). Washington, DC: American Enterprise Institute for Public Policy Research.

Güran, M. C. & Tosun, U. (2008). The macroeconomic performance of Turkish economy after 1980's liberalization. *Asian-African Journal of Economics and Econometrics*, 8(1), 67–82.

Haggard, S. & Webb, S. B. (1994). Introduction. In S. Haggard, & S. B. Webb (Eds.), *Voting for reform: democracy, political liberalization, and economic adjustment* (pp. 1–32). New York: Oxford University Press.

Harris, G. (1967). *The origins of communism in Turkey*. Stanford: Hoover Institution Publications.

Hayek, F. V. (2007). *The Road to Serfdom: Text and Documents*. (The Collected Works of F. A. Hayek-Volume 2). London: The Chicago University Press.

Hemming, R. & Mansoor, A. M. (1988). Privatization and public enterprises. IMF. http://ssrn.com/abstract=884559. Accessed 25 May 2010.

Heper, M. (1985). *The state tradition in Turkey*. Walkington: The Eothen Press.

Kepenek, Y. & Yentürk, N. (2001). *Türkiye ekonomisi (Turkish economy)*. İstanbul: Remzi Kitabevi.

Keyder, Ç. (1987). *State and class in Turkey: A study in capitalist development*. London: Verso.

Krueger, A. & Tuncer, B. (1980). *Estimating total factor productivity growth in a developing country*. World Bank Staff Working Paper No: 422. Washington, DC: World Bank.

Küçük, Y. (1985). *Planlı kalkınma ve Türkiye (Planned development and Turkey)*. İstanbul: Tekin Yayınevi.

Lewis, B. (1961). *The emergence of modern Turkey*. London: Oxford University Press.

Ministry of Finance. (1992). *Bütçe kesin hesap kanunları 1924-1941 (Budget final account laws 1924-1941)*. Ankara: Maliye Bakanlığı Yayınları.

Mardin, S. (1980). Turkey: The transformation of an economic code. In E. Özbudun, & A. Ulusan (Eds.), *The political economy of income distribution in Turkey* (pp. 12–54). New York: Holmes & Meier.

North, D. (1990). *Institutions, institutional change and economic performance*. Cambridge: Cambridge University Press.

OECD. (2009). *Privatisation in the 21st century: Recent experiences of OECD countries*. Paris: OECD Publication.

Okyar, O. (1965). The concept of étatism. *The Economic Journal*, 75(297), 98–111.

Öniş, Z. (1991a). The evolution of privatization in Turkey: The institutional context of public-enterprise. *International Journal of Middle East Studies*, 23(1991), 163–176.

Öniş, Z. (1991b). The political economy of Turkey in the 1980s: The anatomy of unorthodox liberalism. In M. Heper (Ed.), *The strong state and economic interest groups: The post-1980 Turkish experience* (pp. 27–39). New York & London: Walter de Gruyter.

Öniş, Z. (1992). Redemocratization and economic liberalization in Turkey: The limits of state autonomy. *Studies in Comparative International Development*, 27(2), 3–23.

Öniş, Z. (1998). *State and market: The political economy of Turkey in comparative perspective*. İstanbul: Boğaziçi University Press.

Öniş, Z. (2003). The post-war development performance of the Turkish economy: A political economy perspective. In C. Kollias & G. G. Şenesen (Ed.), *Greece and Turkey in the 21st century: Conflict or cooperation?* (pp. 67–87). New York: Nova Science Publishers.

Öniş, Z. (2004). Turgut Özal and his economic legacy: Turkish neo-liberalism in critical perspective. *Middle Eastern Studies*, 40(4), 113–134.

Öniş, Z. & Aysan, A. F. (2000). Neoliberal globalization, the nation state and financial crises in the semi-periphery: A comparative analysis. *Third World Quarterly*, 21(1), 119–139.

Öniş, Z. & Riedel, J. (1993). *Economic crises and long-term growth in Turkey*. Washington, DC: The World Bank.

PA. (2010). Privatization endeavor in Turkey. Republic of Turkey Prime Ministry Privatization Administration. http://www.oib.gov.tr/yayinlar/publications.htm. Accessed 25 May 2010.

Pamuk, O. (2007). Economic change in twentieth century Turkey: Is the glass more than half full? Working Paper No. 41. The American University of Paris. http://www.aup.edu/pdf/WPSeries/AUP_wp41-Pamuk.pdf. Accessed 25 May 2010.

Pitelis, C. (1991). Market failure and the existence of the state: A restatement and critique. *International Review of Applied Economics*, 5(3), 325–340.

Ramanadham, V. (1991). *The economics of public enterprise*. London: Routledge.

Şahin, H. (2006). *Türkiye ekonomisi (Turkish economy)*. Bursa: Ezgi Kitabevi.

Sayarı, S. (1992). Politics and economic policy-making in Turkey, 1980–1988. In T. F. Nas & M. Odekon (Eds.), *Economics and politics of Turkish liberalization* (pp. 26–43). Bethlehem: Lehigh University Press.

Shirley, M. M. & Walsh, P. (2000). Public versus private ownership: The current state of the debate. Working Papers No. 2420. World Bank. http://www-wds.worldbank.org/servlet/WDSContentServer/WDSP/IB/2000/09/15/000094946_00090605460293/Rendered/PDF/multi_page.pdf. Accessed 25 May 2010.

Shleifer, A. & Vishny, R. (1994). Politicians and firms. *Quarterly Journal of Economics,* 109(4), 995–1025.

Şişmanov, D. (1990). *Türkiye işçi ve sosyalist hareketi (1908-1965) (The Movement of worker and socialist in Turkey (1908–1965))*. Istanbul: Belge Yayınları

Sunar, İ. (1990). Populism and patronage: The Demokrat Party and its legacy in Turkey. *Il Politico*, LV(4), 745–757.

Takim, A. & Yilmaz, E. (2010). Economic policy during Ataturk's era in Turkey (1923 1938). *African Journal of Business Management,* 4(4), 549–554.

Tansel, A. (2002). The effects of privatization on labor in Turkey. Working Paper No. 2002-5. METU Economic Research Center. http://papers.ssrn.com/sol3/papers.cfm?abstract_id=303440. Accessed 25 May 2010.

Tekeli, İ. & İlkin S. (1977). *1929 dünya buhranında Türkiye'nin iktisadi politika arayışları (The economic policy quests of Turkey in the 1929 World Crisis)*. Ankara: ODTÜ İdari İlimler Fakültesi Yayını.

Toninelli, P. A. (2000). The rise and fall public enterprise. In P. A. Toninelli (Ed.), *The rise and fall of state-owned enterprise in the western world* (pp. 3–24). Cambridge: Cambridge University Press.

Tuncay, M. (2009). *Türkiye'de sol akımlar (1908-1925) (Left movements in Turkey (1908 1925))*. Ankara: İletişim Yayınevi.

Türkkan, E. (1996). *Ekonomi ve demokrasi (Economy and democracy)*. Ankara: Turhan Kitabevi.

UNESCAP. (1996). *The role of the private sector and privatization for industrial and technological development in South Asian Economies*. Bangkok: The United Nations Economic and Social Commission for Asia and the Pacific Publications.

UNESCAP. (2001). Privatization: A panacea or a palliative. Development Papers No. 22. The United Nations Economic and Social Commission for Asia and the Pacific. http://www.unescap.org/drpad/publication/toc/dp22con.htm. Accessed 25 May 2010.

Uzun, A. (2005). Tek parti döneminde iktisadi devletçilik ve piyasa ekonomisi kültürü (1923-1946) (Economic étatism and market economy culture in the single-party period (1923-1946)). *Piyasa Dergisi*, 14, 109–135.

Vickers, J. & Yarrow G. (1988). *Privatization: An economic analysis*. Cambridge: MIT University Press.

World Bank. (1982). *Turkey industrialization and trade strategy*. Washington, DC: World Bank Publication.

World Bank. (1995). *Bureaucrats in business: The economics and politics of government ownership*. New York: Oxford University Press.

World Bank. (2008). Turkey country economic memorandum-Volume II. World Bank Publication. http://siteresources.worldbank.org/TURKEYEXTN/Resources/361711-1209153236622/Volume_II_Final.pdf. Accessed 25 May 2010.

Yarrow, G. (1986). Privatization in theory and practice. *Economic Policy*, 2, 324–377.
Yayla, A. (2001). Liberal siyaset-liberal iktisat Özal çizgisi (Liberal Politics-liberal economics the line of Özal). In İ. Sezal & İ. Dağı (Eds.), *Kim bu Özal? Siyaset-iktisat-zihniyet (Who is Özal? Politics-economics-mentality)* (pp. 425–442). Istanbul: Boyut Kitapları.
YDK. (1973). *Yüksek denetleme kurulunun denetimine giren kamu iktisadi teşebbüsleri 1971 yılı genel raporu (1971 general report for state economic enterprises included the Supreme Audit Board control)*. Ankara: TC Başbakanlık Yüksek Denetleme Kurulu.

# Chapter 4
# Regulatory Diffusion in Turkey: A Cross-sectoral Assessment

**Isik Ozel and İzak Atiyas**

## 4.1 Introduction

Diffusion of regulation and the accompanying independent regulatory agencies is now a worldwide phenomenon, commonly referred to as "the rise of regulatory capitalism" (Levi-Faur and Jordana 2005). The current global crisis has further intensified discussions regarding the need for more and better regulation within the realm of economic governance both in the North and the South (OECD 2010; Stiglitz 2008). Economic crises are considered major drivers of regulatory reform, and they "allow politicians to justify the necessity and cost of change" (OECD 2010: 259). Many developing countries have implemented regulatory reforms in the context of severe economic crises since the 1990s, where instabilities and uncertainties abound. Given the relatively weaker institutional endowments of these countries (with respect to rule of law, courts, markets, stock exchange, etc.), yielding credible signals to the potential investors in the sectors to be privatized became crucial, and those signals could be facilitated by carrying out regulatory reforms (Levy and Spiller 1996; Gilardi 2002; Majone 2003). Hence, following a process of extensive deregulation accompanied by market transitions launched since the 1980s, many of these countries have gone through coupled processes of deregulation and reregulation. Nevertheless, studies on regulation in the developing world are still scarce, and they mostly explore the initiation of regulatory reforms, rather than the regulatory outcomes shaped by the complex interplay between the regulatory reconfiguration and the existing institutional frameworks (Jacobs 1999; Gilardi 2005a).

Turkey provides an interesting case with respect to regulatory reforms and their outcomes, as it is a latecomer in regulatory reforms, but it went through a so-called "regulatory inflation" over the course of a decade between the 1990s and 2000s. As a result of such accelerated regulatory reform process, regulatory agencies were not only established in key network sectors, where market failures that call for regulatory

I. Ozel (✉)
Sabancı University, Istanbul, Turkey
e-mail: ozel@sabanciuniv.edu

T. Çetin and F. Oğuz (eds.), *The Political Economy of Regulation in Turkey*,
DOI 10.1007/978-1-4419-7750-2_4, © Springer Science+Business Media, LLC 2011

intervention are easy to identify, but also in unusual sectors such as agriculture which did not necessarily suffer from standard forms of market failures. In the network sectors, on the other hand, presence of sunk cost generates a particular necessity for regulatory frameworks, which would then facilitate credible commitments, central for investment behavior (Gilardi 2002).

This chapter explores the diffusion of regulatory reforms in Turkey by means of the emergence of national regulatory agencies (NRAs). It, first, provides a theoretical background for the simultaneous diffusion of regulation in many parts of the world in the last few decades. Second, it examines the context in which the NRAs were established in Turkey through a complex interplay between international, supranational, and domestic actors at the time of a severe economic crisis. By doing so, it analyzes the cross-sectoral variation regarding the diffusion. Third, it provides a general performance analysis for the NRAs in their respective sectors. A full-fledged evaluation of the performance of regulatory agencies would have required a regulatory impact analysis for each of the agencies covered in this chapter. Even though such an analysis is beyond the scope of this chapter, we would like to take a few initial steps in that direction. By doing so, we would also like to suggest a number of varying factors that have likely affected the performance of NRAs in Turkey. The regulatory practices in Turkey show that emergence of the NRAs does not necessarily thwart rent-seeking processes, but, indeed, new forms of rents may be created by the regulatory agencies. In addition, competition may be distorted further in certain sectors depending on the de facto operation of the regulatory agencies, although the initial goal of these agencies was to improve it. Thus, regulatory reforms in general and the mere emergence and functioning of the NRAs in particular do not necessarily insulate these industries from influence activities with significant distributive implications.

## 4.2 Varying Perspectives on the Diffusion of Regulatory Reforms

Independent regulatory agencies (NRAs) operate outside the hierarchical control or oversight by the central governments and bureaucracies, giving rise to a new mode of public administration (Majone 1996, 2001; Maggetti 2007; Ulusoy 2003). NRAs are considered to enhance credibility and economic efficiency, by depoliticizing the regulatory process, thus contributing to aggregate social welfare (Gilardi 2002). Majone (2003) argues that independent regulatory agencies facilitate credible commitments by governments which would not easily commit due to their high discount rates. Drawing from the literature linking credible commitments to democracy, Majone (2003) further suggests that the NRAs would contribute to democracy by facilitating credible commitments. Respective literature usually regards governments' delegation of authority to independent regulatory agencies as a solution to credible commitments in securing property rights. By means of delegation, governments provide guarantees for private investors that the rules of the game are preestablished, so that the investors would not be subject to arbitrary interventions in the market, given that the governments' hands are tied (Gilardi 2002; Levy and Spiller 1996). (Levi-Faur and Jordana 2005) suggests that the NRAs are established to pursue maximization of welfare, enhance accountability, and correct market failures.

In the standard "public interest" theory of regulation, government interventions in markets are justified on the basis of market failures. One set of such failures has to do with the existence of extensive economies of scale and scope. Under scale and scope economies, markets can sustain only one firm or a small number of firms. This is the case, for example, in network industries such as telecommunications and electricity, where often a single firm enjoys the position of a natural monopoly over the network, and competition in downstream markets requires competing actors to have access to the network. Absence of competition justifies regulation of key retail and wholesale prices and other variables such as entry and quality. In addition, investment in such industries is often sunk, providing governments with an incentive to appropriate profits ex post. This raises a problem of regulatory commitment and credibility, which may deter investments in the first place. Moreover, direct intervention by the government may politicize the regulatory process and induce governments to protect political interest rather than efficiency or long-term productivity.

Besides economies of scale and scope, other market failures also may require various forms of government intervention. Hence, financial markets and the banking industry suffer from imperfect information and contagion effects, giving rise to adverse selection, moral hazard, and financial fragility, justifying in turn the creation of regulatory agencies to prevent excessive risk-taking, ensure proper disclosure of financial information, and intervene under situations of financial distress to prevent bank runs. The independence of the regulatory agency from the government would ensure that interventions are rule-based, welfare-maximizing, and not distorted by short-term political interests.

Scholarship on regulation also offers critical perspectives which questions if the NRAs are truly independent of the regulated interests and claims that NRAs would indeed hazard public interest by empowering certain groups (mainly regulated business interests) over others, most importantly consumers (Moran 2002; Stigler 1971; Sezen 2005). Moran (2002) asserts that the regulatory state may not necessarily serve public interests, as it usually furthers "sectional interests" of certain groups such as politicians, businessmen, and bureaucrats. According to Stigler (1971), the regulatory state is the outcome of the strategic pursuit of interests by rational actors, notably big firms and regulators in big agencies. According to this perspective, NRAs enhance mechanisms that would facilitate incorporation of regulated interests' into decision making while excluding the public interests which would be directly affected by those decisions. Thus, these agencies are easily "captured" by regulated interests. Implicit in these arguments is that NRAs might endanger democracy, rather than contributing to it, given the privileges they provide to some groups at the expense of the others.

Independent of such diverging analyses regarding the impact of regulation on public interest, establishment of regulatory agencies is commonly considered an important institutional reform through which power is delegated (Gilardi 2002; Levi-Faur 2005; Vogel 1996). Such institutional reforms bear particular importance during the processes of market transitions where liberalization and privatization are simultaneously implemented, thus governments' need to yield credible signals to investors intensifies. These new institutions lead to significant outcomes with respect to restructuring the state and altering state–society relations, as regulation shapes the ways in which state controls private sector behavior (Levi-Faur 2005; Ayres and Braithware 1992; Vogel 1996). This is particularly striking in developing countries most of which have long legacies of state interventionism brought about by the state-led development strategies implemented well into the 1980s and 1990s along with their institutional arrangements. Therefore, it is the complex interactions between old institutions as well as legacies and the new ones, which determine the regulatory outcomes in different institutional settings (Sancho and Jordana 2004).

The process of reregulation then, has not necessarily brought about convergence, but, indeed, resulted in considerable cross-national divergence, since existing institutions filter and determine the ways in which these new agencies are institutionalized, and function in practice (Vogel 1996). As Jordana and Levi-Faur (2004) suggest, "the new transplants are being adapted to their new homes and in the process may acquire new meanings and uses." Cross-national divergence is particularly striking in cases where the central impetus of regulatory reforms comes from identical international and supranational organizations, such as the IMF and the EU. Tenbucken and Schneider (2004: 263) stress out the cross-national divergence with respect to NRAs' operation in the same sectors. This chapter additionally suggests that the divergence is not only limited to the cross-national level but also prevails at the cross-sectoral level, as the variation among different sectors in Turkey regarding de jure design and de facto practice exemplifies.

Recent diffusion of the NRAs in developing countries is explained by bottom-up, horizontal, and top-down approaches (Gilardi 2005a; Levi-Faur 2005). The bottom-up approach offers a functional explanation that these agencies were established to improve credible commitment capacity particularly in the context of liberalization and privatization, intertwined processes where uncertainties abound (Scott 2006). Importance of credible signals yielded by individual economies increased within the context of globalization process, which intensified the competition for international investment (Franchino 2002; Majone 1999; Gilardi 2002). Such signals are considered crucial particularly for developing countries that are dependent on capital inflows (Gilardi 2003; Majone 1996, 1997).

The horizontal approach focuses on policy learning through emulation across countries in explaining the emergence of NRAs (Meseguer 2005; Dolowitz and Marsh 2000). Such voluntary emulation of regulatory reforms takes place particularly in the context of severe crises, in an attempt to emulate the institutions of the better-performing countries (Dolowitz and Marsh (2000). Policy learning was a common mechanism of NRAs' diffusion in Latin America throughout the 1990s (Levi-Faur and Jordana 2005).

The top-down approach, on the other hand, explains the emergence of NRAs by formal and informal pressures exerted through international and supranational organizations such as the IMF, World Bank, European Union, and the OECD (DiMaggio and Powell 1991; Gilardi 2005a). These pressures over regulatory reforms may take the form of conditionalities such as in the case of the IMF and the EU, signifying "coercive isomorphism" (DiMaggio and Powell 1991: 67) or "soft methods of influence and coordination" as in the case of OECD (2010). Recent harmonization or regulatory policies within the EU and in accession countries have led to a major institutional change in terms of building of NRAs, bolstering the overall "Europeanization process" (Cowles et al. 2001). Nevertheless, even the EU's strict conditionalities have not resulted in "institutional isomorphism" or convergence across the members and accession countries, as there is significant cross-country divergence, caused by the interaction between the old and the new institutions and the resistance stemming from the former. The concern caused by conditionalities is that institutions are imposed on a top-down basis without building support from domestic constituencies, endangering legitimacy. Without such domestic constituencies entrenched in bureaucracy, legislature and/or the executive, regulatory reforms can hit a deadlock in practice. Thus, top-down emergence of NRAs can be limited to a symbolic move to comply with the international and supranational organizations' conditionalities and/or harmonization requirements without proper implementation, and Turkey makes a good case for this.

## 4.3 Regulatory Reforms in Turkey

Emergence of NRAs in Turkey can be partially explained by each of the three aforementioned approaches. Turkey is one of the latecomers where most of the NRAs were established in the late 1990s and early 2000s, when credibility was urgently needed given the severity of the economic and political instabilities the country suffered.[1] Nevertheless, there was no strong domestic support for regulation particularly in the earlier phases of regulatory reforms in Turkey. Political commitment to regulatory reforms was considerably weak in the beginning, indicated by sluggish implementation of regulatory reforms between 1999 and 2001, including, for example, significant time lags in the appointment of board members of Banking Regulation and Supervision Agency (Bakır and Öniş 2010: 85). Initially, the major demand for regulation mostly arose from international and supranational organizations, namely, the IMF, the World Bank, OECD, and the EU, which became the key actors in launching regulatory reforms in Turkey. IMF's letters of intent played a significant role in the establishment of the NRAs in energy and finance, while the EU's effect was central in the establishment of the Competition Agency – a

[1] Currently, there are nine NRAs in Turkey: Capital Markets Board (date of establishment: 1982), The Higher Board for Radio and TV (1994), Competition Agency (1994 and 1999), Banking Regulation and Supervision Agency (1999), Telecommunications Agency (2000), Energy Markets Regulatory Agency (2001), Sugar Agency (2001), Tobacco and Alcohol Market Regulatory Agency (2002), and Public Procurement Agency (2002).

conditionality for Turkey's entry to the Customs Union in 1996 – both the EU and the IMF played important roles in the establishment of the public procurement agency, and the World Bank was the leading actor in creating international coercion in the establishment of the IRA in telecommunications – that are explained further in the respective sections below. The interesting cases which emerged out of the regulatory reforms are the NRAs in the agricultural sector, namely, in sugar and tobacco, indicating an aberration from the common practices of regulation. Although the IMF and the World Bank were critical of price supports in these sectors, it seems the NRAs emerged based on a common understanding between international organizations and a contingent of Turkish bureaucrats especially in the Treasury. These agencies were established with an on-the-surface-agenda to regulate and retreat government intervention; however, they eventually have expanded opportunities for politicization, which is usually justified as "mitigating the effects of liberalization promoted by the IMF and the World Bank" (Sosay and Zenginobuz 2005: 35).

Although domestic drivers of regulatory reforms existed in Turkey since the 1980s, the constituency of regulatory reforms was rather small. Brought about by the country's embarking on a process of market orientation and liberalization since the early 1980s, there was a drive to attract private investment into infrastructure industries such as electricity and telecommunications by the end of the 1990s. Such private sector orientation was reinforced by the persistent macroeconomic instability and fiscal constraints which precluded the governments from raising adequate public funds to undertake the necessary infrastructure industries. In addition, there was a constant effort to privatize state-owned assets in infrastructure industries, and these efforts were often blocked by legal challenges posed by the Constitutional Court and the Council of State, inter alia, on the grounds that natural monopolies were being privatized without adequate measures to ensure that they would behave in the public interest. Hence, the prospect of privatizing state monopolies and opening imperfectly competitive industries to new entry clearly called for the establishment of a regulatory framework. With respect to regulation in finance sector, the financial crisis of 1982 was already a reminder to governments that unregulated banking was prone to financial stability.

While all these factors necessitated credible regulatory institutions in various industries, efforts to establish such institutions were not effective until the end of 1990s because, among other reasons, most politicians were not willing to delegate regulatory power at the expense of losing control over administrative agencies. This understanding of the need for NRAs was relatively more prevalent among parts of the bureaucracy.[2]

Political and bureaucratic commitment for regulatory reforms strengthened when the crisis deepened in 2001. Starting with Derviş' appointment as the Minister of Economy, a team of bureaucrats led by Derviş steered the process of regulatory

[2] For example, the first reports emphasizing the necessity of establishing independent regulatory agencies in telecommunications and electricity industries came out from the State Planning Organization, the Treasury, and the Scientific and Technological Research Council of Turkey.

reforms through maintaining coordination among the key agencies of bureaucracy. Bakır and Öniş (2010: 86) also suggest that Derviş "played an important policy entrepreneurship and mediation role between domestic and transnational policy communities." Therefore, the Turkish reform process makes a good case to show the importance of the presence of domestic will, even as a thin coalition of bureaucrats and politicians. Indeed, as discussed in more detail below, this thin coalition was not enough to guarantee that regulatory reforms would be implemented effectively in time.

The financial crisis of 2001 created an opportune environment to pass the necessary legislation on regulatory reforms, as well as strengthening the domestic support for reforms. Respective legislation had already been recommended by the World Bank and the IMF, particularly in the context of the disinflation program of 1999. The 2001 crisis, which further endangered the country's credibility, weakened the resistance against regulatory reforms, fostering a proreform coalition.

Legislation on Turkish regulatory reforms has gone through successive amendments altering various rules such as the level of independence, authority, and NRAs' interaction with public and private actors – mostly dependent on the executive's discretion. Besides such modification of the formal structure of the NRAs, their de facto operation and effectiveness have been subject to continuous change, since each incumbent has interacted differently with these agencies. Hence, some NRAs have suffered from loosely defined institutional structures and accompanying uncertainties, along with persistent government control.[3] Nevertheless, there are striking differences across sectors both in terms of de jure design and de facto operation of these agencies. Ambiguity in institutional design and the government control over the regulatory agencies are particularly prevalent in sectors such as telecommunications, sugar, and tobacco and alcoholic products. State Audit Board's subsequent reports on individual agencies and those analyzing all agencies generally point out the absence of a "framing law," which would apply to all agencies across sectors (DDK 2010/2-2010/11). Hence, harmonization and coordination between the agencies appear as a pressing issue with respect to the operation of the regulatory agencies. The coordination problems are particularly prevalent between the Competition Authority and authorities responsible for sector-specific regulation.[4]

In general, independency of the Turkish NRAs is at stake, as there is still considerable discretion of political authority over these agencies, in varying levels across different sectors. In spite of the formal independence along with full financial and administrative autonomy of most NRAs, de facto operation deviates from the formal structures, as, in some cases, they are subject to capture by various actors: politicians, bureaucrats, and private interests (Sezen 2005). Interestingly,

[3] State Audit Board, "Düzenleyici ve Denetleyici Kurumların Oluşumu, Teşkilatı, Yetki ve Görevleri, Denetlenmeleri ve Kurul Üyeleri ile Çalışanlarının Statüsüne İlişkin Hususların İrdelenmesi," [An Analysis of the Emergence of Regulatory and Auditing Agencies, their Organization, Authority and Duties, their Auditing, the Status of Their Board Members and Employees], May 14, 2010, No. 2010/11.

[4] Güler, M. (2003) "Düzenleyici Kurullar Ekseninde Üst Kurullar ve Yargısal denetimi," Yüksek Lisans Tezi, Ankara: TODAIE.

Turkish NRAs seem to have considerably high levels of formal independence, compared to their counterparts in several other countries (Tenbucken and Schneider 2004; Şanlısoy and Özcan 2006). Using independence indices designed by Gilardi (2002, 2005b), Şanlısoy and Özcan (2006) assert that Turkey has the highest values in terms of formal independence of the NRAs (a composite value of 0.76), when compared with 16 European countries, the independence index values of which vary between 0.36 and 0.63.[5] According to the authors, Turkey has even the highest values of independence in Europe in finance, competition, and telecommunications. Using the Gilardi (2002) methodology as well, Çetin et al. (2010) find significant cross-sectoral differences among NRAs in Turkey, with BRSA appearing as the most independent and the Tobacco and Alcohol Market Regulatory Agency as the least independent.

Although the independence of the regulatory agencies is considered crucial for good regulatory outcomes, formal independence itself does not necessarily lead to "good" outcomes. Thus, Turkey makes a good case to show the discrepancy between formal structure and de facto operation. For example in telecommunications, according to Tenbucken and Schneider (2004: 257–258) the independence of the ICTA in Turkey is nearly as high as those in Ireland and the U.S., a remarkable outcome for a "latecomer" in regulatory reforms. However, there is a considerable cross-sectoral variation among the NRAs in terms of de facto independence and performance (DDK 2010/11). Some NRAs in Turkey suffer from high levels of government intervention: Information Technology and Communications Authority (ICTA), Sugar Agency (SA), and the Agency for Tobacco and Alcohol Markets (TAMRA) are good examples for this. In the case of ICTA, the Ministry of Transport, under the influence of Turk Telekom, was instrumental in delaying a number of liberalization measures such as giving out licenses to new operators. In the case of SA and TAMRA, the mere institutional design of the agencies facilitated high levels of government intervention: at these agencies, some of the board members are still state employees and work under the initiative of the respective governments.

### 4.3.1 Competition Authority

The Competition Authority was established by the enactment of the Law on the Protection of Competition in 1994, the substance of which was closely harmonized with the relevant legislation in the EU. The appointment of the management of the Authority was delayed for 2 years, and the Authority became operational in 1997.

---

[5] Gilardi (2005b) designs the independence-index-based five indicators that would determine independence: the status of the Chair of the NRA, the status of the board members of the NRAs, NRAs' relations with the executive and legislature, financial and organizational autonomy, and regulatory authority. These indicators have equal weights (20%) in the overall independence value.

The overall evaluation of a peer-review report on the Competition Authority prepared by the OECD (2005) was positive, underscoring that "most members of the legal and academic communities in Turkey compliment the quality of the Board's decisions, particularly in comparison to those issued by other agencies" (p. 38). Generally, the Competition Authority is praised for its professionalism and objective and nondiscriminatory treatment of most of cases it handles. Similarly, the recent Progress Report of the European Commission (2009) commends the Authority for "satisfactory level of administrative and operational independence," "high administrative capacity," and "clear track record on the implementation of competition rules." Hence, overall international observers' evaluation of the institutional characteristics of the Competition Authority is quite positive.[6]

There is an additional component of the institutional characteristics of the Competition Authority that may deserve attention. Until recently, the Competition Authority was the only regulatory agency in Turkey where the decisions of the Board have to be published in the Official Gazette with justifications. In addition, the law also requires that the published decision contains a summary of the view/recommendation of the team that handles the case (the "rapporteurs") and carries out the investigation. This has acted as an important source of discipline, reduced the degree of arbitrariness in the decisions and very likely increased their quality.

Of course, the performance of the agency should be evaluated not only on the basis of its institutional characteristics but also by the actual quality of its decisions, including in particular the scope and sophistication of economic analysis contained therein. Thorough evaluations of the quality of decisions of the CA Board are scarce but gradually emerging. The OECD (2005) report has stated that "the sophistication of the Board's economic analysis varies considerably from decision to decision". Sanlı (2010) has reviewed decisions regarding vertical restraints and has concluded that decisions are formalistic and show a degree of tolerance. "Formalism" here is a measure of the extent to which decisions identify violations of competition law merely on the basis of existence of a form of behavior. A less formalistic approach would base decisions on an economic analysis of the competitive impact of the behavior in question. Atiyas et al. (2010) have also reviewed decisions regarding vertical restraints and have concluded that the degree of formalism has been declining recently.[7] The advantage of a less formalistic approach is that it would increase the accuracy with which decisions identify true competitive harm, and this is indeed the trend in the US and the EU. The disadvantage is that it reduces legal certainty and requires a higher degree of capacity to undertake economic analysis. The Competition Board has shown an increasing willingness to undertake economic analysis; this is a commendable intention and will take some time to reach maturity.

[6] "Turkey 2009 Progress Report", Commission of the European Communities, Commission Staff Working Document, SEC (2009) 1334, Chapter 4.8. Chapter 9: Competition Policy, p. 49.

[7] For example, in a number of recent decisions, the mere existence of a clause restricting resale prices is not seen as sufficient to condemn a vertical agreement, but it is inquired whether the restriction is implemented in practice. See Atiyas et al. (2010) for details.

Indeed, the studies mentioned above reveal inconsistencies across decisions regarding standards about what type of restrictions are allowed under the competition law and what type of restrictions are penalized. Ekdi (2010) has analyzed Board decisions on cases that involve product bundling and tie-in sales. His conclusion is somewhat similar: the Board has consistently (and correctly) undertaken a dominance test as a condition of liability under the law and then has examined the economic effects of bundling and tying behavior. At the same time, inconsistencies were found in the conditions under which such behavior is found in violation of the law. To summarize, the Board is facing up the challenge of increasing the level of economic analysis in its decisions, and one would expect that such inconsistencies decline over time as the Authority increases its capacity to undertake more sophisticated economic analysis.

### 4.3.2 The Banking Regulation and Supervision Agency

Banking Regulation and Supervision Agency (BRSA) was established in 1999 by the new banking law (#4389) in the midst of an IMF-supported disinflation program. This was a crucial element of the program because the exchange-rate based disinflation strategy was likely to result in overvaluation of the exchange rate, which in turn would generate incentives for banks to increase their exchange rate risk to profit from interest rate arbitrage. Hence, a solid regulatory system was crucial to monitor banks and prevent excessive accumulation of foreign liabilities. However, infighting within the coalition government delayed the appointment of the management of the BRSA. By the time the BRSA was operational, it was too late, and the banking system was slated for one of the biggest financial crisis of Turkish history. The crisis created a context conducive to strengthening the regulatory framework: A new stabilization program was launched under the auspices of the IMF, with a strong focus on the financial system.

In terms of formal institutional structure, the BRSA is one of the most strictly designed agencies regarding the safeguards for its independence, accountability, and transparency. For instance, it is the only agency whose board members cannot be reappointed, a rule established by the amendment of the banking law in 2005. All decisions taken by the BRSA Board require justifications. According to Şanlısoy and Özcan (2006), formal independence of BRSA is generally higher than the European average.

The BRSA was equipped with sufficient regulatory tools at its disposal. The banking legislation determined capital adequacy requirements so as to incorporate market risk; connected lending was defined so as to consolidate the balance sheets of capital groups, and international accounting standards were established. In addition, banks were required to set up their own inspections and risk management systems. Caps were placed on foreign exchange, interest rate, and liquidity risks. A major restructuring took place in the banking system, and 14 banks were taken over in 2000–2003. Banks were capitalized, and foreign liabilities were restructured.

Over time, capital structures of banks improved significantly, and nonperforming loans declined (Bakır and Öniş 2010). Recent resilience and outstanding performance of Turkish banking in the context of the global crisis is generally explained by "good regulation" (OECD 2010) that has been established over the 2000s.

There were also shortcomings, however (Bakır and Öniş 2010). The regulatory measures became too protective of the banking system, and perhaps the balance shifted toward excessive prudency. There was a significant increase in banking concentration accompanied by excessively high bank profitability, even during the global crisis. Intermediation toward investments did not increase, and small and medium enterprises have suffered most from lack of credit. Instead, consumer credits have increased substantially. Consumer protection has been extremely low in the credit cards market, where banks have made very high returns through overpricing of their products. So, while the regulatory framework has been very successful in maintaining financial stability, it has been less successful in protecting the interests of the consumers and promoting competition.

Given that there is no data about the de facto independence of the BRSA, State Audit Board reports can provide some evidence for it, as they evaluate the BRSA based on the criteria of transparency, independence, and accountability and provide recommendations accordingly. According to these reports, independence of the regulatory agency is consistent with its de jure status, and the principle of accountability is respected. However, the State Audit Board points out certain concerns about the effectiveness of the BRSA such as reappointment and lack of enforcement. According to these reports, the most important institutional weakness that impairs the independence of the BRSA is the reappointment opportunity provided for the board members which might affect the members' capacity to make independent and impartial decisions. Reappointment does not comply with the BRSA's administrative and fiscal independence.[8] According to the report, another issue which hazards BRSA's effectiveness is that monetary fines are found to have insufficient deterrent effect, and it is recommended that rules about monetary fines be reformulated.[9]

### 4.3.3 Information Technology and Communications Authority[10]

The Information Technology and Communications Authority (ICTA, previously TA) was established through the enactment of Law No. 4502 in 2000, as the regulatory agency in the sector; however, the licensing authority remained in the Ministry of

[8] The Audit Report by the State Audit Board "Bankacılık Düzenleme ve Denetleme Kurumunun 2006, 2007 ve 2008 Yılları Faaliyet ve İşlemlerinin Denetlenmesi" p. 281. http://cankaya.gov.tr/sayfa/cumhurbaskanligi/ddk/ddk36.pdf.

[9] Ibid.

[10] Formerly "the Telecommunications Authority".

Transport for a while. Although the licensing authority was eventually transferred to the agency, the Ministry of Transport still persists as a prominent player. More specifically, the Cabinet retains authority to determine the minimum fees for certain authorizations, which in practice may be (and has been) used to delay entry. ICTA is a striking example for the discrepancy between the de jure and de facto independence of the regulatory agencies (Atiyas and Doğan 2010). ECTA reports[11] on the Turkish ICTA suggest that the agency is not effective with respect to improving the conditions of competition, and it acts under the influence of the Ministry of Transport, which still maintains significant discretionary power on the sector and ICTA.[12]

The legal framework of regulation and liberalization in the telecommunications industry in Turkey is effectively based on the recent developments in the EU with respect to regulation in telecommunications. The first liberalizing law was enacted in 2001, and the monopoly rights of Turk Telekom were abolished in 2003. While initially there were some discrepancies between Turkey and the EU, especially in specific areas such as licensing, such discrepancies have been eliminated over time, and the recent Electronic Communications law (2008) pretty much includes the most essential components of the 2003 Framework of the EU. Furthermore, the methodology through which operators with significant market power are identified and specific regulatory obligations are imposed on operators conforms to the rules and procedures established by the EU Directives.

However, the implementation of the regulatory framework has not been uniform across the different segments of the industry. In the mobile industry, the regulatory authority has adopted a strongly procompetitive stance, and this has been most importantly reflected in interconnection charges that have declined rapidly over time and are now among the lowest in Europe. As a result of this stance, while the degree of concentration in the mobile industry is among the highest in the OECD, the market share of the dominant firm has declined from 69% in 2000 to 56% in 2010.[13] The regulatory authority has also been active in implementing number portability, which reduces costs subscribers suffer when they switch operators, and this is also widely seen as a reflection of its competitive stance. Finally, the authority has gone out of its way to implement floors and caps on the dominant operators' tariffs to prevent it from using its large subscriber base as an additional source of competitive advantage and as a barrier to the growth of the market share of the other operators.

By contrast, ICTA authority has acted in a much more conservative manner in the fixed line segments. The interconnection rates have been higher than EU averages for a long time and have declined slowly over time. Liberalization has proceeded slowly, new entry into long distance and international call markets was delayed significantly, and entry into the local calls market has been liberalized only

---

[11] ECTA Scores are calculated based on the surveys conducted with the ECTA members and national regulatory agencies.

[12] http://www.ectaportal.com/en/basic651.html.

[13] See Atiyas (Chap. 8).

in November 2008 and first licenses issued in May 2009. Methods widely used in the EU to promote new entry into the broadband internet markets, such as bit stream and unbundled access to the local loop, have become effectively available only in 2009–2010. This conservative attitude has been reflected in main indicators of the degree of competition: Turk Telekom's market share in fixed line telephony is still 93%. Its share in broadband internet is even more dramatic, 89% in March 2010 (ICTA 2010).

The general assessment is that the degree of independence of the authority, despite its de jure existence, is in fact quite limited. It is generally believed that Turk Telekom has had undue influence on the Ministry, and this has in turn slowed the process of liberalization and the implementation of procompetitive regulation (Atiyas and Doğan 2010). In fact, it is likely that it is the influence of Turk Telekom that explains the differing attitudes of the regulatory authority in the fixed and mobile segments: Turk Telekom's subsidiary in the mobile segment, Aycell, is a new entrant and favors a more competitive stance by the regulator, and the opposite is true in the fixed industry, where Turk Telekom is the incumbent operator. In summary, the evolution of competition in the telecommunications industry has suffered from problems that are familiar for network industries, namely, the incumbent operator has done its best to hinder and delay the development of competition and exert influence on the regulatory process with that objective.

ICTA's institutional design provides opportunities for capture both from the politicians and the private players. The Ministry of Transportation has substantial influence in the composition of the Board because it nominates two candidates for each of the following posts: Chairman of the Board, representative of telecommunication services, and representative of wireless services. The representative of telecommunication services are nominated by each of the private companies with more than 10% nationwide market share. Representative of consumers is selected from among four candidates, nominated by the Ministry of Industry and Union of Chambers and Commodity Exchanges of Turkey (TOBB), each nominating two candidates.

### *4.3.4 Energy Market Regulatory Authority*

Energy Market Regulatory Authority (EMRA) of Turkey was established in 2001, based on the Laws 4628 (electricity) and 4646 (natural gas) in charge of both network and nonnetwork segments such as electricity, natural gas, petroleum, and LPG. The major functions of the EMRA are licensing (provision/renewal/cancellation), service pricing, and determining performance standards and their auditing. Regulations in the petroleum and LPG markets were later incorporated in 2003 by the laws 5015 (petroleum) and 5307 (LPG). A prevalent issue about the EMRA is the mere regulation in the petroleum and LPG sectors, which are not network industries.[14]

[14] Interview with PETDER, May 17, 2010, Istanbul.

The EMRA has nine board members, unlike seven in all other agencies, and these members are nominated by the cabinet directly, while other institutions and stakeholders are excluded from the nomination of the board members. Reappoint ment of the board chairman is possible according to the legal design of the EMRA, which is subject to severe critiques of the State Audit Board (DDK, 2010/10). Between 2001 and 2008, the votes within and resulting decisions of EMRA did not require justification, but since 2008, both consenting and dissenting votes necessitate justification. Although the legal framework is fairly well designed, there is no perfect compliance to this framework in practice.

The resistance of the state to retreat has been an outstanding issue in electricity distribution, indicated by the privatization process and government's reluctance to allow regulated retail prices to reflect costs (European Commission Progress Report 2009). A pressing issue underlined by the private players in this sector is that there is considerable resistance by the public players against the private players and they justify their positions by serving the "public good."[15] Private players, such as the Electricity Producers' Union are never invited for ex ante consultations during the preparation of draft regulations, but they are asked for ex post comments. The privatization of distribution companies in 2007 was cancelled right before the elections, exemplifying political capture out of electoral concerns.

#### 4.3.4.1 Regulation of the Electricity Industry

Success with liberalization and competition has also been limited in the electricity industry, but the causes are somewhat different from the telecommunications industry. There were attempts to attract private investment into the industry without creating a competitive environment over the 1990s, but many such efforts were met with legal challenges from higher courts (Atiyas and Dutz 2005; Ulusoy and Oğuz 2007). Finally, the restructuring process in electricity was launched through the enactment of the Electricity market Law in 2001, which also established the Energy Market Regulatory Authority (EMRA). The restructuring model was inspired by the New Electricity Trading Arrangements (NETA) of the UK. At the end of the day, the market share of the incumbent state-owned generator does remain high (46% as of 2009),[16] but the story is not one of direct entry deterrence and foreclosure by an incumbent enterprise. This is important because foreclosure by vertically integrated incumbents has been a common problem of liberalization in many jurisdictions, especially in the European Union, and this risk has been identified by the European Commission (2007) as one of the most important barriers to the

[15] Interview with the Chairman of Electricity Producers' Union.

[16] An additional 32% of output is produced by private enterprises under take or pay contracts with the government. Clearly, this production is sheltered from competitive pressures. Hence, the share of the production of genuinely independent private power producers is a mere 22%. See EMRA (2010).

development of competition in the EU electricity markets. In the Turkish case, this risk was already reduced significantly with the vertical separation of the transmission operator from the other activities of the industry. The real weakness of the restructuring process in the Turkish case is one of incoherent market design and continuation of political influence in the pricing of retail electricity.

There were a number of weaknesses in the design of the restructuring process. There was a heavy emphasis on privatization rather than competition, and constitutional and legal hurdles have resulted in delays in privatization, creating in turn delays in the whole restructuring process (Ulusoy and Oğuz 2007). The initial design did not include a spot/wholesale market. Similar to NETA, the market was envisaged to consist of bilateral contracts and a balancing market that would address last-minute discrepancies between supply and demand. However, the balancing market was severely delayed. At the same time, despite the formation of an independent regulatory authority, the government retained effective control over retail prices. It used this control to suppress retail prices, possibly below average costs and most likely due to political reasons. Since private sector producers were effectively competing with government-controlled retail prices, private generators were squeezed between rising gas costs and suppressed retail prices and started to make losses. This eliminated any incentives to invest, and the country was faced with insufficient capacity and possibility of blackouts in 2008–2009 (blackouts did not happen because demand was reduced as a result of the crisis). Absence of private investment until after 2008–2009 was a major disappointment because mobilizing private investment was identified as one of the most important objectives of the restructuring process (Atiyas 2010).[17]

Hence, regulatory reform in electricity was characterized not necessarily by capture by incumbent enterprises but by a lack of willingness by the political authorities to delegate regulatory powers to the regulatory authority and lose political control of consumer prices. In fact, disagreements between the Ministry and the regulatory authority were a major source of regulatory uncertainty and credibility in the electricity industry (Çetin and Oğuz 2007).

#### 4.3.4.2 Regulation in the Gas Industry

The weakness of the EMRA relative to the Ministry – and relative to the state-owned players in the market – is perhaps even better reflected in the gas industry. As discussed by Erdoğdu (Chap. 7), while the Natural Gas Market Law of 2001 envisaged that the market share of the vertically integrated state-owned incumbent BOTAŞ would be reduced from 100 to 20% by 2009, as of 2010 the share of BOTAŞ in total imports was 90%. BOTAŞ has vehemently opposed any measures that would reduce its market share and "inability of EMRA in enforcing the articles of

---

[17] Private investment did respond positively after the balancing market was launched in 2006, thereby providing an outlet to private generation at market-clearing prices.

the law that aim at reducing BOTAS' influence in the market. Although the law gives EMRA the right to impose large amounts of fines on market participants violating the regulations, EMRA in practice has never applied any fines to BOTAS for violating articles of the law" (Erdoğdu, Chap. 7). The unwillingness of EMRA to carry out its prerogatives, in turn, reflects the unwillingness of the government in general, and the Ministry of Energy in particular regarding the effective operation of regulatory rules.

The evolution of liberalization and regulatory reform in the electricity and gas industries underlines a misgiving of reform undertaken with IMF pressure and with insufficient ownership of state actors. Unlike, for example, trade liberalization, success in regulatory reform in network industries critically depends on the persistence of the procompetitive stance and welfare-enhancing interventions by agents of the state. It seems that the problem with reform in energy was that the principles behind reform were widely shared neither in the bureaucracy nor in the political parties, and the initiating laws, though exemplary for their content, were enacted as conditionality for and under the pressure of emergency financing obtained from the IMF. Alternatively, the evidence suggests that without continued political ownership delegation is likely to be incomplete.

The Consumers' Association sued the agency several times, based on the concern that the EMRA harms public interest. In its final report about the EMRA, the Association claims that "public interest is endangered because of high prices brought about by the unlawful actions of the EMRA, which impose penalties only on the small firms, providing concessions for particular firms, and causing oligopolies in the market at the expense of violating the law."[18] Among other things, the concerns raised by the Consumers' Associations particularly about the prices reflect the inability of the reformers to engage the general public in the reform program and its potential consequences, epitomizing the weakness of the domestic coalitions endorsing the reform process.

### *4.3.5 Anomalies in Regulation: Turkish NRAs in Unusual Sectors*

Turkish excursion toward the establishment of regulatory agencies has gone far from what was initially envisaged by the literature in terms of regulatory diffusion across sectors, as the NRAs were also established in unusual sectors such as sugar, tobacco, and alcohol. What explains, then, the emergence of NRAs in such sectors in Turkey as an anomaly in the context of regulatory reforms? There are competing explanations for such anomalous emergence: According to Sosay and Zenginobuz (2005: 35), these NRAs were not imposed by international actors, but they were established through domestic will "to mitigate the effects of liberalization promoted by the IMF

[18] Anadolu Ajansı, March 24, 2010.

and the World Bank," which had opposed Turkish government's distortive price support for these sectors. Another perspective analyzes these agencies merely based on the impositions of the international and supranational actors. IMF and the World Bank were highly critical of the state subsidies provided for sugar and tobacco production in Turkey, considered inefficient in world standards. According to this view, the establishment of independent agencies in sugar and tobacco industries was part of the project to reduce state intervention and government subsidies in these sectors, and increase commercialization.[19] Our understanding is that the establishment of the agencies emerged as a solution shared both by the international organizations and parts of the bureaucracy, especially in the Treasury. Both sectors which had benefited from price supports suffered from accumulated inventories. Thus, one of the central objectives of the agencies was to limit subsidies, establish production quotas, eliminate inventories, and eventually create the conditions through which state-owned enterprises in industries of sugar, tobacco, and alcoholic beverages could be privatized. Expectedly, these objectives have major distributive implications, and it was thought that they could be more easily achieved through independent agencies insulated from political pressures. As such, establishment of these agencies and the eventual privatization of production facilities became important components of the IMF program that followed the financial crisis in 2000–2001. Nevertheless, while the IMF Program targeted to eliminate politicization in these sectors, the operation of these agencies, particularly Sugar Agency, enhanced politicization further and created new forms of rents in this process.

#### 4.3.5.1 Sugar Agency

Sugar Agency (SA) was established in 2001 in close affiliation with the Ministry of Industry and Trade, based on the Sugar Law (#4634), which has been subject to frequent changes.[20] The manipulations about the Sugar Agency reached the extent of the Agency's closing down in 2004 based on the MIT's demand. The Şeker-İş Union (Sugar Beet Trade Union) brought the closure before the Council of the State, which then cancelled the closure. The central function of the SA is to determine production quotas for beet sugar and starch-based sugar. Nevertheless, the Cabinet still holds the right to increase/decrease the amount determined by the SA up to 50%, epitomizing the extent of government intervention in the agency and its functions. Government intervention in Sugar Agency is not limited to the quotas through which the Agency distributes substantial rents to certain private players through their connections. Government also intervenes in the Agency through the board members it nominates, hazarding the independence of the Agency. The SA Board is composed of seven members, and three ministries have significant power in the nomination process, namely, the Ministry of Industry and Trade, the Ministry of Agriculture, and the

[19] See, for example, Undersecretariat of the Treasury (n.d.).

[20] http://www.sekerkurumu.gov.tr/icerik.aspx?id=70.

Ministry of State.[21] Pankobirlik (The Association of Sugar Beet Cooperations) and Türkşeker (the state-owned enterprise for saccharose-based sugar production) hold authority to nominate as well. The nomination which is subject to severe critiques is that of the private companies (saccharose and starch-based sugar business) with the highest nominal production of past 3 years. The CEOs of these companies are authorized to nominate four people (two appointed by the Cabinet). The board faces serious accusations of capture due to the fact that not only large private companies are represented in the Board, but also these companies have significant power over the board. This issue is exemplified by the largest players' power over the Cabinet, as well as the SA, such as Cargill and Ulker, having 60% of the market in the starch-based sugar segment, have imposed pressure on the Cabinet and the SA over quotas.[22]

The problems about the legal design of the Sugar Agency are not limited to nomination which provides an available ground for capture. In addition, the Sugar Law and the by-law establishing the working principles of the SA do not set any clear limitations about the board members' status such as association membership, engagement in the sector, ownership of assets in the sector, relationship of members' relatives to the sector, whereas there are strict limitations concerning other NRAs' Board Members in their respective legal documents. This type of loose institutionalization provides the government and the private players with tools to have major influence on the Agency, bolstering rent distribution.

A major function of the Sugar Agency is the quota distribution for the production of beet sugar and starch-based sugar. However, the use of this function by the Agency resulted in many court cases – 90 cases in 2009 only. Despite such authority of the SA, the Cabinet also holds the authority to change the amount determined by the SA up to 50%, an authority which has been used for the starch-based sugar production (SBSP) on a yearly basis. The existence of the state as a producer in the market complicates the picture further because Türkşeker, a state-owned company, produces about half of the beet sugar as of 2010. The Cabinet's right to increase quotas for starch-based sugar on an annual basis caused serious tensions between the sugar beet producers and the SA. The Sugar Beet Union (Şeker-İş) has taken these Cabinet decisions to court each year because it has been argued that the increase in the starch-based sugar production causes a reduction in sugar beet sales, thus leading to unfair competition.[23] The Council of State has repeatedly found the Cabinet decision to increase SBS quotas against the law.[24] However, despite the court rulings, the Cabinet decisions in favor of quota increase have been implemented.

[21] The respective law refers to the Ministry of State as "the state ministry that the Undersecretariat of Foreign Trade is associated with."

[22] http://hurarsiv.hurriyet.com.tr/goster/haber.aspx?id=3520879&yazarid=8.

[23] The disagreements over quotas with the SBSP is based on the Şeker-İş Union claims that if the beet sugar production capacity fell to 40%, there is excess supply and consequent price increases. Interviews with the Şeker-İş Union, June 8, 2010.

[24] "NBŞ Kotalarının %50 Arttırılmasına Karşı Açılan Davalar" [Cases against the increases on starch-based sugar quotas] http://www.sekeris.org.tr/index2.asp?sayfa=28, Accessed on July 15, 2010.

Such was the case in 2008, when the quotas were increased by 35% in spite of the court decision.

The process of quota distribution indicates a good example of the extent to which politicians and the private sector can capture regulatory agencies. While sugar production necessitates the Agency's permission and the quota provision, a domestic company, which had close ties with the incumbent party, produced sugar to be used as input for its own coke production facility, and this was brought to the Court by the other coke producers but left without concrete sanctions.[25] This was followed by a sudden decision of closing down the Agency, a decision interpreted as the result of lobbying conducted by the favored coke producers. Hence, rather than improving efficiency in the sugar sector, the Sugar Agency ended up limiting competition through its decisions favoring certain producers over the others, sustaining the long-lasting legacy of Turkish bureaucracy's distributing patronage through public instruments. SA makes a good example of politicization of regulation and capture by both public and private actors in different dimensions. In this process of politicization, new rents have been created, and competition is distorted further.

#### 4.3.5.2 Tobacco and Alcohol Market Regulatory Agency

The other regulatory agency in the agricultural sector is the Tobacco and Alcohol Market Regulatory Agency (TAMRA), which was established in 2008 (Law #4733), and has also been subject to multiple changes regarding its institutional configuration, authority structures, and the level of autonomy. TAMRA is authorized to regulate and supervise tobacco production; grant permits for tobacco processing, and importation of tobacco seeds; and issue authorization to tobacco trade by public auctions. It is also authorized to regulate the markets of ethyl alcohol, methanol, distilled alcoholic drinks, and fermented alcoholic drinks, and maintain harmonization with the EU regulations.[26] The Board of the TAMRA is also highly controlled by the politicians. Board members are nominated by the Ministries of Economy, Health, Agriculture and the Ministry of State, as well as the Undersecretariat of Foreign Trade, Undersecretariat of Treasury and the Association of Agricultural Chambers. Each nominates two people, out of which the Cabinet appoints seven.

The State Audit Board (DDK)'s report on the activities of TAMRA between 2006 and 2008 states that the aforementioned ministries manipulate the board decisions by exercising influence on the board members they nominated.[27] The DDK report is also critical of the reappointment rule for the board members and suggests

[25] http://hurarsiv.hurriyet.com.tr/goster/haber.aspx?id=3520879&yazarid=8.

[26] http://www.invest.gov.tr/enUS/investmentguide/investorsguide/Pages/BusinessEnvironment.aspx, retrieved from www.tapdk.gov.tr.

[27] DDK report (oversight of TAMRB activities 2006–2008), http://www.tccb.gov.tr/ddk/ddk39.pdf, p.434.

that both factors endanger the autonomy of the Board. Underlining the need for consultation with the private players in the sector, the report emphasizes that these players need to be represented on the Board.[28]

The State Audit Board report[29] on the TAMRA provides quite a negative picture on both the institutional aspects and the performance of the Authority. Regarding the institutional design, the report states that the possibility of the Cabinet of Ministers to reappoint board members at the end of their terms hurts the indepen dence of the Authority. It mentions that procedures for appointments to the Board allow ministries to influence the activities of the Board through the appointed board members. According to the report, the decision-making rules within the Board often results in stalemates. Moreover, the Board has failed to issue a number of secondary legislation, a situation that "even prevents the implementation of some of the provisions of the law" (p. 435). The report suggests that the fact that the Board decisions are not published on the Board's web site impairs transparency. It also states that the Authority does not have the capacity for data collection that is required for the effective execution of its regulatory and audit functions. In summary, the report concludes that the Authority has failed in developing a management style that would conform to the principles of good governance and that it has not executed its regulatory and audit tasks in an effective manner.

## 4.4 Conclusion

The recent diffusion of regulatory reforms led to the emergence of new institutions and new modes of governance in many parts of the world. Although these new regulatory institutions represent a new mode of governance, existing institutional constellations affect the ways in which these new institutions are designed and adopted in different national settings. Existing institutions act as domestic filters for widespread regulatory reforms, which are promoted by various international and supranational actors. Hence, the outcome of such interaction between the existing and new institutions has been a considerable variation in the design and actual operation of regulatory agencies. In addition to cross-national variation brought about by the existing institutions resistance, cross-sectoral variation also prevails within the same national institutional settings.

This chapter examined the diffusion of regulatory reforms in several sectors in Turkey, focusing on the emergence and operation of national regulatory agencies. The chapter specifically investigates the Competition Authority and NRAs in banking, telecommunications, energy, sugar, tobacco, and alcohol markets. As regulatory impact analyses in different sectors are lacking in the Turkish case, this chapter's

[28] DDK report (oversight of TAMRB activities 2006–2008), http://www.tccb.gov.tr/ddk/ddk39.pdf, p. 434.

[29] A summary of the report is available at http://cankaya.gov.tr/ddk/ddk39.pdf.

undertaking is a rather limited one including a general assessment of the NRAs. The chapter finds that varying factors have led to the emergence of NRAs across sectors, and even the conditionalities imposed by international and supranational actors were not adequate for an effective operation of the NRAs. One of the findings of this chapter is that effective operation of the NRAs could not be attained without building a domestic constituency for regulatory reforms. In the Turkish case, the severe crisis of 2000–2001 facilitated the building of such constituency for regulatory reforms.

The chapter also pointsout the discrepancies between de jure institutional design and de facto operation of the NRAs in Turkey. In spite of having been designed as highly independent entities through the influence of multifarious international, supranational, and domestic actors, most agencies in Turkey lose some of their independence during their operations, deviating from their de jure designs. Discrepancy between de jure design and de facto operations is not only limited to concerns about independence of the NRAs but also applies to the overall enforcement of the regulatory rules which tends to be weak in many sectors. One of the major emphases of the chapter is the cross-sectoral differences in terms of such discrepancy between de jure design and de facto operation of the agencies. The Turkish experience in regulation shows that the discrepancy is greater in some sectors than in the others.

The chapter underlines that implanting regulatory agencies particularly in developing countries with weak institutional endowments (such as the rule of law, courts, etc.) brought about new forms of rent seeking with significant distributive implications. It provides some empirical examples of rent-seeking processes generated by the operation of NRAs in sectors such as telecommunications and sugar. Thus, the chapter pinpoints the importance of analyzing regulatory processes to understand the complex interplays between the existing institutional configurations along with public and private actors involved in these processes.

**Acknowledgement** The authors would like to thank Asli Kadriye Suel for her assistance in this project.

## References

Atiyas, I. (2010) "Türkiye Elektrik Sektöründe Yeniden Yapılanma Sürecinin Hikâyesi Nasıl Anlatılmalı," paper presented at the Fourth Law and Economics Forum, Hacettepe University.

Atiyas, I. and Doğan, P. (2010). Glass Half Empty? Politics and Institutions in the Liberalization of the Fixed Line Telecommunications Industry in Turkey. In T. Çetin and F. Yilmaz (Eds.) *Understanding the Process of Economic Change in Turkey* (pp. 261–284). New York: Nova Science Publishers.

Atiyas, I. and Dutz. M. (2005) Competition and Regulatory Reform in the Turkish Electricity Industry. In B. M Hoekman and S. Togan (Eds.) *Turkey: Economic Reforms and Accession to the European Union* (pp. 187–208). Washington, DC: The World Bank and the CEPR.

Atiyas, I., Doğanoğlu, T., Gürkaynak, G., Öz, G. and İnceoğlu, F. (2010) "The Vertical Restraints Regime in Turkish Competition Law," work in progress.

Ayres, I. and Braithware, J. (1992) *Responsive Regulation: Transcending the Deregulation Debate*, Oxford: Oxford University Press.

Bakır, C. and Öniş, Z. (2010) The Regulatory State and Turkish Banking Reforms in the Age of Post-Washington Consensus, *Development and Change*, *41* 77–160.

Çetin, T. and Oğuz, F. (2007) The Politics of Regulation in the Turkish Electricity Market, *Energy Policy*, *35* 1761–1770.

Çetin, T., Sobaci, M. Z., Nargeleçekenler, M. and Abdülhakimoğullari, E. (2010). The Political Economy of Independent Regulatory Agencies in Turkey. In T. Çetin and F. Yilmaz (Eds.) *Understanding the Process of Economic Change in Turkey* (pp. 239–260). New York: Nova Science Publishers.

Cowles, M. G., Carporaso, J. and Risse, T. (2001) *Transforming Europe: Europeanization and Domestic Change*, Ithaca: Cornell University Press.

DiMaggio, P. and Powell, W. (1991) *The New Institutionalism in Organizational Analysis*, Chicago: The University of Chicago Press.

Dolowitz, D. P. and Marsh, D. (2000) Learning from Abroad: The Role of Policy Transfer in Contemporary Policy-Making, *Governance*, *13* 5–24.

Ekdi, B. (2010) "Ürün Bağlama Ve Paket Satışlar Yoluyla Hakim Durumun Kötüye Kullanılması", paper presented at conference on Hakim Durumun Kötüye Kullanılması: Sorunlar ve Çözüm Önerileri, İstanbul Bilgi University June 22, 2010.

Energy Market Regulatory Authority (EMRA). (2010) *2009 Faaliyet Raporu*, Ankara: EMRA.

European Commission. (2007) DG Competition report on energy sector inquiry SEC(2006)1724.

Franchino, F. (2002) Efficiency or Credibility? Testing the Two Logics of Delegation to the European Commission, *Journal of European Public Policy*, *9* 1–18.

Gilardi, F. (2002). Policy Credibility and Delegation to IRAs: A Comparative Empirical Analysis, *Journal of European Public Policy*, *9* 873–893.

Gilardi, F. (2005a) The Institutional Foundations of Regulatory Capitalism: The Diffusion of IRAs in Western Europe, *The Annals of the American Academy of Political and Social Science*, *598* 84–101.

Gilardi, F. (2005b) The Formal Independence of Regulators: A Comparison of 17 Countries and 7 Sectors, *Swiss Political Science Review*, *11* 139–167.

Information and Communications Technology Authority (ICTA). (2010) Üç Aylık Pazar Verileri Raporu, 2010 Yılı 1. Çeyrek, http://www.btk.gov.tr/Yayin/pv/ucaylik10_1.pdf Accessed July 8, 2010.

Jacobs, S. (1999) "The Second Generation of Regulatory Reforms", paper presented at the IMF Conference on Second Generation Reforms, 8–9 November, Washington, DC.

Jordana, J. and ve Levi-Faur, D. (2004) "The Politics of Regulation in the Age of Governance, in, Jordana, Jacint and David Levi-Faur eds. The Politics of Regulation, Institutions and Regulatory Reforms in the Age of Governance. Glasgow: Edwar Elgar.

Levi-Faur, D. and Jordana, J. (2005) The Making of a New Regulatory Order, *The Annals of the American Academy of Political and Social Science*, *598* 6–9.

Levy, B. and Spiller, P. (Eds.) (1996) *Regulation, Institutions and Commitment*, Cambridge: Cambridge University Press.

Maggetti, M. (2007) De Facto Independence After Delegation: A Fuzzy-Set Analysis, *Regulation and Governance*, *1* 271–294.

Majone, G. (1996) *Regulating Europe*, London: Routledge.

Majone, G. (1997), "From Positive to the Regulatory State. Cuses and Consequences of Changes in the Mode of Governance", *Journal of Public Policy*, *17*(2) 139–167.

Majone, G. (1999) The Regulatory State and Its Legitimacy Problems, *West European Politics*, *22* 1–24.

Majone, G. (2001) Two Logics of Delegation. Agency and Fiduciary Relations in EU Governance, *European Union Politics*, *2* 103–122.

Majone, G. (2003) "The Internationalization of Regulation: Implications for Developing Countries," paper presented at International Conference on 'Innovation and Change in Regulation and Competition'" 13–15 October 2003, Mandaluyong City, Philippines.

Meseguer, C. (2005) Policy Learning, Policy Diffusion, and the Making of a New Order, *The Annals of the American Academy of Political and Social Science*, *598* 67–82.

Moran, M. (2002) Understanding the Regulatory State, Review Article, *British Journal of Political Science, 32* 391–413.
OECD. (2005) *Competition Law and Policy in Turkey*, Paris: OECD.
OECD. (2010) *Making Reform Happen, Lessons from OECD Countries,* Paris: OECD.
Sancho R. D. and Jordana, J. (2004) Institutional Constellations and Regulatory Policy. In D. Levy-Faur and J. Jordana (Eds.) *The Politics of Regulation* (pp. 296–321). Glasgow: Edwar Elgar.
Sanlı, K. C. (2010) Rekabet Kurulu'nun Kararları Işığında Eşik Sisteminde Dikey Anlaşmalara Olası Yaklaşım. In K. C. Sanlı (Ed.) *Rekabet Hukuku ve Dikey Anlaşmalar*. İstanbul: Oniki Levha Yayincilik.
Şanlısoy, S. and Özcan, A. (2006) Türkiye'de Bağımsız Düzenleyici Kurumların Bağımsızlığı, *Siyasa, 2* 99–132.
Scott, C. (2006) Privatization and Regulatory Regimes. In M. Moran, M. Rein, and R. E. Goodin (Eds.) *The Oxford Handbook of Public Policy* (pp. 651–668). Oxford, UK: Oxford University Press.
Sezen, S. (2005) Türkiye'de Düzenleyici Kurulları Kimler, Nasıl Yönetiyor? *Amme İdaresi Dergisi, 38* 85–115.
Sosay, G. and Zenginobuz, E. U. (2005) "Independent Regulatory Agencies in Emerging Economies," paper presented at the 2005 Annual Conference of the ECPR, Budapest, September 8–10, 2005.
Stigler, G. J. (1971). "The Theory of Economic Regulation," *Bell Journal of Economics*, *2*(1) 3–21.
Stiglitz, J. (2008). "A Crisis of Confidence", The Guardian, October 22.
Tenbucken, M. and Schneider, V. (2004) Divergent Convergence: Structures and Functions of National Regulatory Authorities in the Telecommunications Sector. In D. Levy-Faur and J. Jordana (Eds.) *The Politics of Regulation*. Glasgow: Edwar Elgar.
"Turkey 2009 Progress Report", Commission Staff Working Document, SEC(2009)1334, Commission of the European Communities. http://ec.europa.eu/enlargement/pdf/key_documents/2009/tr_rapport_2009_en.pdf
Ulusoy, A. (2003) Bağımsız İdari Otoriteler, Ankara: Turhan Kitabevi.
Ulusoy, A. and Oğuz, F. (2007) The Privatization of Electricity Distribution in Turkey: A Legal and Economic Analysis, *Energy Policy, 35* 5021–5034.
Undersecretariat of Treasury. (n.d.) Tarım Sektöründe Reform: Tarım Sektöründe Reform Nedir – Niçin Gereklidir? www.hazine.gov.tr Accessed July 1, 2002.
Vogel, S. (1996) *Freer Markets, More Rules: Regulatory Reform in Advanced Industrial Countries*, Ithaca: Cornell University Press.

# Chapter 5
# The Legal Structure of Competition Policy in Turkey

**Kerem Cem Sanli and Sahin Ardiyok***

## 5.1 Introduction

In the last 20 years, states across the globe have relied increasingly on market economy as a way of allocating resources, in the hope that markets would produce the most desirable outcomes. However, to attain these outcomes, markets require a strong and solid legal framework. Antitrust laws are considered to be the main components of this legal framework.

As Turkey has been implementing market system for the past 20 years, the national laws regulating trade and economy have been steadily altered, and new laws have been enacted to cope with the dynamics of this system. The Act of Protection of Competition, which was adopted in 1994, can be regarded as a product of the process of forming the legal framework. By enacting the Act, Turkish government endorsed "competition" as a social value and also fulfilled its legal obligations stemming from the Constitutional mandate (art. 167) and the acquis of the European Union.

Despite having some unique provisions, the Act is modeled on European competition law (the art. 101-102 of the Rome Treaty), which renders the judgments and the policies of the European authorities very relevant to Turkish practice. The Act established the Competition Authority as the main enforcement body equipped

---

*Former official of Turkish Competition Authority, present partner of ACTECON Economic Consulting, and lecturer of "Economic Regulation and Law," "Telecommunications Law," "Energy Law and Policy," and "Pharmaceutical Law" at Istanbul Bilgi and Ankara Bilkent Universities.
Special thanks to ACTECON partners and all consultants for their contribution to this study.

S. Ardiyok (✉)
Actecon Economic Consultancy, Istanbul, Turkey
and
The School of Law, Bilgi University, Istanbul, Turkey
and
The School of Law, Bilkent University, Ankara, Turkey
e-mail: sahin.ardiyok@actecon.com

K.C. Sanli
Assistant Professor and Director of the Competition Law and Policy Research Center at Istanbul Bilgi University Faculty of Law and Adjunct Professor at Bilkent University LL.M. Program

T. Çetin and F. Oğuz (eds.), *The Political Economy of Regulation in Turkey*,
DOI 10.1007/978-1-4419-7750-2_5, 

with executive as well as rule-making powers. For the past 13 years, the Authority and the Board, the decision-making body, have been very active, especially with respect to legislative functions.

The purpose of this study is to introduce readers to the basics of Turkish Antitrust Law and its enforcement practices. In this respect, the chapter is categorized into four parts. The first part covers the background and the sources of the Turkish Antitrust Law. After the legislative background is mentioned, the main legal sources of the law are specified. The second part is devoted to the main concepts prescribed in the Act such as the relevant market and the concept of undertaking. Substantive provisions are explained in the third part, and this part is organized under three headings. First, restrictive agreements are expounded along with the exemption rule. Subsequently, the abuse of dominant position is illustrated with some examples of abuse. And finally, the provision and the secondary legislation governing the concentrations are explained. Here, the procedural issues are of importance. Enforcement authorities and sanctions are discussed in the final part.

## 5.2 Background and the Sources of the Antitrust Law

The main legal source of the Turkish Antitrust Law is the Act on the Protection of Competition numbered 4054 (herein referred to as the Antitrust Act).[1] The Antitrust Act was enacted in 1994, and prior to this date, Turkey did not have an antitrust legislation despite the legal mandate in the Article 167 of the Turkish Constitution dated 1982, which obliges the government to prevent cartelization and monopolization in the economy.[2] However, it should be mentioned that there were several attempts to make antitrust legislation in the late-1970s and early-1980s, but the drafts that were prepared upon these initiatives were not finalized in the legislative process. So, the Antitrust Act, which was drafted during the years 1992–1994, filled an important loophole in the Turkish legal system.

Because of the late establishment of the Competition Authority, the main enforcement body vested with investigative and rule-making powers, the effective enforcement of the Antitrust Act was initiated in 1997, 3 years after the adoption of the Act.[3] Since then, it has been subjected to several amendments,[4] which mainly aimed at strengthening and rationalizing the operational efficiency of the Competition

---

[1] The Act on the Protection of Competition No: 4054. Date of Adoption: 7/12/1994. OG. Date: 13/12/1994, Number: 22140.

[2] The first paragraph of the Article 167 provides that "*the state shall take measures to ensure and promote the sound, orderly functioning money, credit, capital, goods and services markets; and shall prevent the formation, in practice or by agreement, of monopolies and cartels in the markets.*"

[3] The Communiqué on the Conclusion of the Organization of the Competition Authority, No: 1997/5 OG. Date: 9.12.1998, Number: 23461.

[4] The Acts that have amended the Antitrust Act can be listed as follows: the Act numbered 4971, dated 01.08.2003; the Act numbered 5234, dated 17.9.2004; the Act numbered 5388, dated 2.7.2005, and the Act numbered 5728, dated 23.1.2008.

Authority and the enforcement system. Substantive rules have been intact since the enactment of the Antitrust Act.

Most of the 63 provisions of the Antitrust Act are related to the institutional structure and legal powers of the Competition Authority. Few substantive rules are found in section 2 between Articles 4 and 7 and in section 5 between Articles 56 and 59. When one considers the nature of these rules, it is easily observed that the Antitrust Act is modeled on the European Community Antitrust Law (herein referred to as European Antitrust Law). In particular, substantive rules prohibiting restrictive agreements and abuse of dominant position are almost identical to the Articles 101 and 102 of the TFEU. This is a natural consequence of the fact that Turkey has an obligation to harmonize its laws with those of the European Union. Hence, the Turkish Antitrust Law including secondary legislation is congruent with the European Antitrust law.

The secondary legislation consisting of regulations, communiqués and guidelines, and the Turkish Competition Board Decisions are other sources of the Antitrust Law. Among these resources, probably the most important ones are block exemption communiqués, given the extensive coverage of these rules. The Turkish Competition Board has issued various block exemption communiqués, which are based on European Antitrust Law, covering vertical restraints,[5] insurance sector,[6] R & D agreements,[7] and technology transfer agreements.[8] Merger Communiqué, numbered 1997/1,[9] which lays down principles of merger analysis, has an important function in merger control. Also, to strengthen the cartel enforcement policy, two regulations have recently been enacted, one being the Leniency[10] and the other being the Fine Regulation,[11] and these regulations have become vital in enforcement practice. The vagueness of the substantive provisions of the Antitrust Act amplifies the importance of these legal sources. In particular, the decisions of the Turkish Competition Board, the decision-making body of the Competition Authority, provide useful guidance in the interpretation of the Antitrust Act, which is unique for the Turkish legal system given that the Turkish Competition Board is not a judiciary organ.

Apart from these legal sources, there are various provisions in other Acts that also aim at protection of competition. These provisions are mainly found in the

---

[5] The Block Exemption Communiqué on Vertical Agreements, No: 2002/2, OG. Date: 7.14.2002, Number: 24815.

[6] The Block Exemption Communiqué in Relation to Insurance Sector, No: 2008/3, OG. Date: 2.1.2008, Number: 26774.

[7] The Block Exemption Communiqué on Research and Development Agreements, No: 2003/2, OG. Date: 8.27.2003, Number: 25212.

[8] The Block Exemption Communiqué on Technology Transfer Agreements, No: 2008/2, OG. Date: 1.23.2008, Number: 26765.

[9] The Communiqué on the Mergers and Acquisitions, No: 1997/1, OG. Date: 8.12.1997, Number: 23078.

[10] The Regulation on Active Cooperation for Detecting Cartels, OG. Date: 15.2.2009, Number: 27142.

[11] The Regulation on Fines to Apply in Cases of Agreements, Concerted Practices, and Decisions Limiting Competition and Abuse of Dominant Position, OG. Date: 15.2.2009, Number: 27142.

Acts regulating special industries such as banking, energy, and telecommunication. Therefore, they cannot be qualified as antitrust law. Also, there are few provisions in the Criminal Code that can be concurrently applied to an antitrust infringement. For example, Article 235 of the Turkish Criminal Code prohibits collusive practices in public bids. Arguably, the first paragraph of Article 237 can also be applied against price-fixing cartels.

## 5.3 Main Concepts

The Turkish Antitrust Law deals with three major problems, which may endanger the functioning of the market economy. Rules remedying these problems consist of (a) the prohibition of agreements, concerted practices, and decisions regarding firms restricting competition (Article 4), (b) the prohibition of abuse of dominant position (Article 6), and (c) mergers and acquisitions (Article 7).

The Competition Board is the sole administrative body that can apply these rules to undertakings covered by the scope of the Antitrust Act. In each of these rules, there are three main points that the Turkish Competition Board takes into consideration:

- *The relevant market*, including both product and geographical markets in which the undertaking operates
- *Territorial reach*, which determines whether the geography of the activity is caught by the Antitrust Act
- *Exemptions* related to the industry that the undertaking in question falls under

Below, the applicability of the Antitrust Act is examined in terms of relevant markets, territorial reach, and special industries.

### *5.3.1 Scope of Application*

The scope of the Antitrust Act is set forth in Article 2. Basically, the provision describes the dimensions of application in terms of the transactions between undertakings, geographic territory, and effects of the transactions on competition. Article 2 provides a clear explanation as follows:

> Agreements, decisions and practices which prevent, distort, or restrict competition between any undertakings operating in or affecting markets for goods and services within the boundaries of the Republic of Turkey, and the abuse of dominance by the undertakings dominant in the market, and any kind of legal transactions and behavior having the nature of mergers and acquisitions which shall decrease competition to a significant extent, and transactions related to the measures, establishments, regulations and supervisions aimed at the protection of competition fall under this Act.

Under further subtitles, the scope is observed in detail by elucidating the method of defining the relevant market, the Antitrust Act's territorial reach, and special industries that are subject to special rules or not subject to the Antitrust Act.

#### 5.3.1.1 Relevant Market

The purpose of defining the relevant market is to identify which products and services are close substitutes for one another so that they operate as a competitive constraint on the behavior of the suppliers of those products or services (Jones and Sufrin 2004, p. 48). Thus, to decide whether there is an anticompetitive conduct in the market, defining the market is the priority subject on the to-do list of the Turkish Competition Board.

Although the definition of the relevant market does not appear explicitly in the Antitrust Act, a clause containing product and geographical market definitions was set forth in the previous Merger Communiqué. The Article 4 of the previous Merger Communiqué states the following:

> The geographic market which comprises a substantial part of the country within the meaning of paragraph 1, are areas in which undertakings operate in the supply and demand of their goods and services, in which the conditions of competition are sufficiently homogenous, and which can easily be distinguished from neighboring areas, as the conditions of competition are appreciably different from these areas.
>
> In determining the relevant product market within the meaning of paragraph 1, the market comprising the goods or services which are the subject of a merger or an acquisition, and the goods or services which are deemed identical in the eye of consumers in terms of their prices, intended use and characteristics is taken into account; other factors that may affect the market determined shall also be assessed.

Moreover, there is a Guideline[12] enacted by the Turkish Competition Board to provide a framework based on economic principles. This Guideline is aimed at ascertaining which competitors have the power to restrict the behavior of the undertakings under examination, and preventing these from behaving independently of an efficient competitive pressure. This guideline explains technically the methods and objective criteria that the Turkish Competition Board applies in its decisions.

In its many decisions, the Turkish Competition Board follows the rules set by the Guideline. The Guideline lists the basic principles of market definition as demand substitution, supply substitution, and potential competition. Demand substitution, determining other products that consumers deem substitutable for the relevant product, and supply substitution, where suppliers could be able to switch their production to other products when faced with small and nontransitory increases in relative prices, are the main consideration points for the Turkish Competition Board. As an instance, in its case dated 25.9.2008 and numbered

[12] Guidelines on the Definition of Relevant Market (http://www.rekabet.gov.tr/dosyalar/kilavuz/kilavuz5.pdf).

08-56/891-352 , in which a fruit yogurt license agreement was signed between Pinar and Sodima SAS, the Turkish Competition Board compared yogurt types, namely, fruit yogurt and fruit cheese to determine the relevant product market. The Turkish Competition Board observed that these are not substitutes to each other in either demand or supply level while stating the reasons as follows:

> Therefore fruit cheese is not a substitute to fruit yogurt regarding its consumer group (mostly children) in terms of demand. Moreover, from the supply substitution point, any yogurt producer cannot easily produce fruit cheese, similar to fruit yogurt, depending on its additional investment and know-how requirements.

In the course of the assessment on defining the relevant market by either the Turkish Competition Board or the European Commission, a three-dimensional method consisting of the "product market," "geographical market," and "temporal market" is generally used (Sanlı 2000a, p. 246). However, "temporal market" dimension is stated neither in the Merger Communiqué nor in the Guideline published by the Turkish Competition Board, while it can be considered in several cases depending on its relevance with time.[13]

Many of the Turkish Competition Board decisions involve market definitions, determination of both the product market and geographical market. The Turkish Competition Board defines market especially in application of Article 6, abuse of dominant position, and Article 7, mergers and acquisitions, as these provisions require a given market.

#### 5.3.1.2 Territorial Reach

As mentioned in the Article 2 of the Antitrust Act regarding scope, the Act covers "agreements, decisions and practices which prevent, distort or restrict competition between any undertakings operating in or affecting markets for goods and services within the boundaries of the Republic of Turkey."

In accordance with this rule, an anticompetitive practice exercised by an undertaking within the boundaries of Turkey or an undertaking operating or residing in Turkey will not make any difference in terms of the application of the Antitrust Act. What matters is whether the outcomes of the conduct exercised by the undertaking residing in Turkey or in abroad negatively affect the competition in a Turkish market. This rule holds the undertakings that reside or operate abroad liable for their conduct if they infringe competition rules in Turkey (Sanlı 2000a, p. 246).

Scholars have named this approach as "*effects doctrine,*" a common principle stating that competition rules shall be applied to any undertaking, irrespective of its nationality or residence, upon the effects of its practices or transactions on the

[13] In the 25.8.2009 dated and 09-38/925-218 numbered decision of the Turkish Competition Board, the Board stated that beer sales should display the differences upon the winter and summer seasons, and, therefore, this factor should be taken into account while considering the dominant position in the relevant market.

competition conditions in that country.[14] The resulting effect within domestic territory is the sole condition for the application of this doctrine,[15] and even its negative or positive feature is no matter (Erol 2000, p. 161). The "effects doctrine" was embraced by the Court of First Instance in the Gencor Case when stating that the application of the Merger Regulation to a merger between companies located outside EU territory "is justified under public international law when it is foreseeable that a proposed concentration will have an immediate and substantial effect in the Community."

When it is considered that the object of the Antitrust Act is the protection of competition in the markets within domestic territory, then it should be admitted that any restrictive behavior affecting the Turkish market, irrespective of where it is realized, shall be sanctioned in the scope of the Antitrust Act.

#### 5.3.1.3 Special Industries

Normally, the Antitrust Act covers all portions of the economy. Exceptionally, there are some special industries that have some permanent market failures and thus require special provisions to correct them by regulation. This portion of the economy is normally out of the scope of the Antitrust Act. There are some other industries without serious market failures but immune from the application of Antitrust Law.

In EU, until 2002 coal and steel industries were governed by the European Coal and Steel Community Treaty, and as a result, these industries were not subject to the TFEU (Treaty on the Functioning of the European Union). European Coal and Steel Community Treaty set special competition provisions similar to the ones in TFEU. Upon the expiry of the European Coal and Steel Community Treaty, coal and steel industries passed into the normal regime laid down by TFEU. Nonetheless, in Turkey, there has never been such a distinction for the coal and steel industry.

In 1962, the European Commission adopted Regulation 26,[16] which modified the competition rules in agriculture, as there was some tension between the objectives of the common agriculture and competition policies (Monti 2003). In Turkey, the Turkish Competition Board exhibited its attitude with respect to agriculture through the opinion given for many markets within agriculture, such as tea, sugar, and tobacco. Supporting policies, purchases by agricultural governmental institutions,

---

[14] Explanation is taken from Dictionary of Competition Terms published by the Turkish Competition Board.

[15] Turkish Competition Board has accepted this principle and used it in various decisions, such as 15.12.1999 dated and 99-59/639-406 numbered decision, 15.7.2009 dated and 09-33/763-183 numbered decision, 29.4.2009 dated and 09-20/404-99 numbered decision.

[16] http://eur-lex.europa.eu/LexUriServ/LexUriServ.do?uri=CELEX:31962R0026:EN:HTML (no longer in force).

stock costs, and privileges granted to governmental undertakings operating in this industry created anticompetitive effects and necessitated market reforms. The Turkish Competition Board expressed its opinion that the Board should keep its eye on these markets and streamline its approach with the reforms.

EU's Regulation No. 4056/86 was a separate implementing legislation in terms of application of competition rules to maritime transport. However, the block exemption required by this Regulation to liner shipping services has recently been repealed, while tramp vessel services are still benefiting from the exemption. Although Turkey closely follows the rules and precedents of the EU Antitrust Law, Turkey has not adopted a secondary legislation regarding a block exemption for liner conferences. The reason might be that Turkey is located in the Mediterranean Sea and is not neighboring to an ocean that can necessitate special treatment for liner shipping.

On the other hand, the Turkish Competition Board closed two investigations related to the maritime industry, as this industry is exempted in the EU by the Regulation No. 4056/86. In a meeting, it was declared that Turkey is watching the course of reviewing the Regulation No. 4056/86 in the EU and will move upon the latest decisions of the Commission. As the Commission revoked the block exemption for this sector, Turkey is not expected to adopt a relevant legislation lately.

According to the European Antitrust Law, atomic energy, noneconomic aspects linked to the specific nature of sport, trade in arms, ammunitions, and war material are/were subject to special provisions besides the Antitrust Law. Nevertheless, the Turkish Competition Board has not applied or adopted special provisions for these industries to date. They are treated in the same way as any other area of economy and have been applied the Antitrust Act.

Due to many reasons, such as late appointment of the Turkish Competition Board almost three years after the enactment weak public awareness about the welfare advantages of market economy and particularly competition rules, has not been constituted properly. Crucially, the independence of the Turkish Competition Board has not been digested sufficiently by legislative authorities. Thus, much legislation enacted before the Antitrust Act was enacted obstructs or precludes the Antitrust Act's application to the industries that are regulated by the said legislation. Worse than that, even though requesting the Turkish Competition Board's opinion by prime ministry mandate is a must by law for any rule-making activity, almost never has the opinion been requested or even taken into consideration on the several occasions that it has been obtained. As a result, the competition law enforcement appears to be weak with respect to certain industries.

This factual situation leads to a general lack of approach to the special industries. The Turkish Competition Board has many exemplary decisions in this regard. In these decisions, the Turkish Competition Board expresses that it cannot apply the competition rules to the industry in question owing to the special rules prescribed by related laws, and it leaves the dispute to the authority that is competent to apply the related laws to the industry.

One of the prominent examples of this issue is the approach of the Turkish Competition Board toward football-broadcasting rights. In its previous decisions on football-broadcasting rights, the Turkish Competition Board had ruled in detail that the scope and duration of exclusive broadcasting rights should be determined in a manner that would impede market foreclosure. However, in the tender realized in January 2010, the Turkish Football Federation has granted exclusive broadcasting rights of the Turkish Super League without dividing the rights concerned into competitive live packages and for 4 years (plus a year of extension right). Although the scope and the duration of exclusive rights could lead to market foreclosure, the Turkish Competition Board opted not to intervene in the tender process. The only reason for the Turkish Competition Board to change its settled enforcement is the new law on the Establishment and Duties of the Turkish Football Federation (TFF).[17] Article 13 of the law concerned states the exclusive authority of TFF on broadcasting rights as follows:

> Article 13 – (1) The TFF Executive Board shall be exclusively entitled to broadcast all the football matches in the territory of the Republic of Turkey on TV, radio, the Internet and via all other similar sound and data carriers, and to organize and plan such broadcasts.
>
> (2) The above-said power particularly encompasses the marketing of the TFF's broadcasting rights centrally and the distribution of the proceeds derived from such rights to Member clubs in such manner as may be decided by the relevant bodies of the TFF.

Because of the authority given to TFF by Article 13 of the Law, the Turkish Competition Board did not monitor the tender process, even though it conflictingly pointed out that "the possibility of obtaining other packages by the broadcaster of Turkish Super League and the 4-year (plus a year of extension right) duration of exclusive rights could lead to prevention of competition."

Moreover, Attorneys Act numbered 1136 and the Law of Independent Accountancy, Independent Accountant Financial Advisorship and Sworn in Financial Advisorship numbered 3568 grant the associations of undertakings the authority to fix the minimum prices and force the undertakings to adhere to a minimum price list, which constitutes a practical infringement of Article 4 of the Antitrust Act. As a concrete example, the decision of the Turkish Competition Board dated 13.11.2003 and numbered 03-73/876(a)-374 ruled that the Attorneys Act is in conflict with the Antitrust Act and shall be adapted and amended in accordance with the competition rules. Unfortunately this advise had been never adopted.

Another contradiction is concerned with municipal laws numbered 5393 and 5216, which provide the municipalities with the power to determine and apply the route, timing, and ticket prices of public transport means. As a matter of fact, public transportation prices are subject to the regulation of municipalities and consequently the supply and demand conditions in the market has no effect on prices. The 26.05.2005 dated, 05-36/458-108 numbered decision and 22.11.2007 dated, 07-87/1103-428 numbered decision of The Turkish Competition Board are relevant examples of the fact that the Turkish Competition Board cannot interfere with the price-fixing actions of municipalities.

---

[17] The relevant Act numbered 5894 was enacted on 05.5.2009, OG. Date:16.5.2009, Number: 27230.

Additionally, Article 19 of Banking Law numbered 5411 states the following:

> Article 19 – (…) In mergers, disintegrations and transfers of banks to be carried out pursuant to the provisions of this Law, the provisions of Turkish Commercial Code No. 6762 and, on the condition that the industrial share of the total assets of the banks subject to merger or integration does not exceed twenty percent, the provisions of Articles 7, 10 and 11 of the The Antitrust Act shall not be applied.

Thereby, an exception to the Articles 7, 10, and 11 of the Antitrust Act has been created by another sector-specific law. This controversy has been criticized by EU in its latest progress report about Turkey's accession to the Union.

### *5.3.2 Undertakings and the Associations of Undertakings*

Competition rules apply to the behaviors of undertakings and associations of undertakings. Hence, the subject of Turkish Antitrust Law is "undertakings." Prior to the enactment of the Antitrust Act, the term "undertaking" was an unfamiliar concept for the Turkish Legal System. So, the Antitrust Act brought a new legal term into the Turkish Law and defined this term in Article 3. According to this definition "an undertaking is a natural or legal person who produces and sells goods or services in the market, and units which can decide independently and do constitute an economic whole." This definition in fact has two elements: "*economic activity*" and "*independence.*" Explaining these elements will help us understand the concept.

The meaning of economic activity seems self-evident. When one provides goods or services in exchange for economic benefit, i.e., money, then he/she is engaged in an economic activity. Apparently, corporations, firms, and other commercial entities operating with profit-maximizing incentives are economic entities. However, a profit-making motive is not a condition for economic activity. Natural or legal persons, especially government bodies that lack profit-maximizing motives can be qualified as undertakings provided that they offer goods and services in markets. In that regard, foundations and cooperatives conduct economic activity as well. The Turkish Competition Board endorsed this view in its several decisions including TSE[18] and ASKI.[19]

The second element, independence, means that the economic unit should determine its own economic and commercial policies without interference or decisive influence of any other natural or legal person. So, independence is an economic, not a legal, concept. For example, if the commercial policies of a company "S" (i.e., subsidiary) are determined by another company "H" (i.e., holding company), then despite having a legal independence, company "S" is not considered as an undertaking, as it lacks economic independence. For competition law purposes, these two companies are treated as a single "economic unit" and therefore as single

---

[18] Decision of the Turkish Competition Board dated 8.3.2002, numbered 02-13/126-53.

[19] Decision of the Turkish Competition Board dated 8.8.2002 and numbered 02-47/587-240.

undertaking. The question of when and under what conditions an economic unit is controlled by another person or firm could only be determined in specific cases by taking into account all relevant legal and economic factors.

There are two main consequences of this "independence" element. One is that economic relations within the economic unit are beyond the scope of competition law. Accordingly, Article 4 is not applied to commercial agreements between "S" and "H," and the merger between "S" and "H" is not covered in Article 7 of the Antitrust Act. There are many illustrations of this application in the Board's decisions, particularly with respect to merger cases.[20] The second result is concerned with the imputation of the subsidiary's behavior with regard to its parent. As the subsidiary is controlled by the parent company, the subsidiary's legal personality is disregarded, and the parent company is held responsible for the competition law infringement. The practical consequence is that the aggregate turnover figures of the two companies are taken into account when calculating substantive monetary fines.[21] In its several decisions, the Turkish Competition Board has applied this criterion and, for example, treated a group of companies as a single economic whole as they were controlled by a family.[22] Also, group exemption regulations explicitly adopt the independence element, and in calculating turnover and/or market share, all "connected" economic units are taken into account.[23]

As seen from these explanations, an undertaking is a very broad concept, and it encompasses every entity engaged in an economic activity regardless of the legal status. It is evident that an undertaking can be a natural person[24] as well as a legal person. Also, a group of persons, whether legal or natural, may well constitute an undertaking.[25] The Turkish Competition Board adopts a functional and economic approach just as that adopted by the European Commission.

It should be noted that the ownership structure is not important either. So, state-owned companies are also considered as undertakings and subjected to competition rules unless their acts are purely regulatory in nature.[26] In fact, given the extensive involvement of government in Turkish economy, decisions concerning state-owned undertakings loom large in the Competition Board's practice. In particular, Article 6, which governs abuse of dominant position, is frequently applied to state-owned undertakings.[27]

[20] Decision of the Turkish Competition Board dated 4.3.2010 and numbered 10-21/264-97.

[21] Although it should be said that economic unit criterion has been occasionally applied inconsistently, especially with regard to the imposition of fines. In some decision, Turkish Competition Board took the turnover figure of the subsidiary, whereas in others, all economic unit. Although there are explicit provisions in the Fine Regulation, recent decisions also indicate inconsistent application.

[22] Decision of the Turkish Competition Board dated 16.1.2001 and numbered 01-04/21-04.

[23] Decision of the Turkish Competition Board dated 25.12.2001 and numbered 01-63/652-174.

[24] Decision of the Turkish Competition Board dated 9.2.2006 and numbered 06-11/130-32.

[25] Decision of the Turkish Competition Board dated 17.7.2000 and numbered 00-26/291-161.

[26] Decision of the Turkish Competition Board dated 13.3.2001 and numbered 01-12/114-29.

[27] Approximately 30% of all Article 6 decisions involve state-owned undertakings.

The Turkish Antitrust Law also applies to behaviors of associations of undertakings. The Antitrust Act defines the concept in Article 3 and according to that definition, "any kind of associations with or without a legal personality, which are formed by undertakings to accomplish particular goals are considered as associations of undertakings." Here again, the legal form and the purpose of association are irrelevant for competition law purposes. However, it is imperative that the association should not itself conduct economic activity, because in that case, it will be characterized as an undertaking. As a consequence of being subject to competition law, associations and their directors could be held responsible for the competition law infringements (Article 16). Given that associations generally play vital roles in the formation and the sustainability of cartels, imposition of fines on associations might have major deterrent effects on cartels.

## 5.4 Overview of Substantive Provisions

Similar to other jurisdictions that have adopted competition rules, Turkish practice has three pillars of substantive provisions: (a) Restrictive agreements, (b) Abuse of dominant position, and (c) Concentrations.

### *5.4.1 Restrictive Agreements*

#### 5.4.1.1 Collusive Behavior

According to Article 4 of the Antitrust Act, agreements and concerted practices between undertakings, and decisions and practices of associations of undertakings that have as their object or effect or likely effect the prevention, distortion, or restriction of competition directly or indirectly in a particular market for goods or services are illegal and prohibited.

The article mentions half a dozen possible examples of restriction of competition. However, these examples are not *numerus clausus*, and so the Turkish Competition Board is not limited by these listed examples of restriction. Because the Turkish Competition regime is set up to protect the competitive environment in the market, every action of the undertakings that falls into the scope of restrictive agreements, concerted practices, and decisions and practices of associations of undertakings will be considered illegal, regardless of whether the particular action is listed under Article 4 or not. The examples that are listed under the mentioned article are as follows:

(a) Fixing the purchase or sale price of goods or services, elements such as cost and profit which form the price, and any terms of purchase or sale.
(b) Partitioning markets for goods or services, and sharing or controlling all kinds of market resources or elements.

(c) Controlling the amount of supply or demand in relation to goods or services, or determining them outside the market.
(d) Complicating and restricting the activities of competing undertakings, or excluding firms operating in the market by boycotts or other behavior, or preventing potential new entrants to the market.
(e) Except for exclusive dealing, applying different terms to persons with equal status for equal rights, obligations, and acts.
(f) Contrary to the nature of the agreement or commercial usages, obliging to purchase other goods or services together with a good or service, or tying a good or service demanded by purchasers acting as intermediary undertakings to the condition of displaying another good or service by the purchaser, or putting forward terms as to the resupply of a good or service supplied.

### The Agreement

An "Agreement" in the Turkish Antitrust Law practice has a broader meaning, and the Turkish Competition Board attributes a wider scope to it, if it is compared to contracts law, in its decisions. The most important perquisite for an agreement in competition law is the intention of the parties to take actions as mutually agreed. As a matter of fact, there are no adjective requirements for the Turkish Competition Board to decide whether there is an agreement or not. If the parties somehow feel themselves as if they are bounded with the terms of agreement, it is enough to state that there is an agreement.

The agreements restricting competition are also broadly discussed in the Turkish Competition Board. In its recent decision on *Poultry Cartel*,[28] the Turkish Competition Board clarified the notion of agreement with following words "rationale of the Article 4 of no. 4054 expressly states that, agreement should not carry all the requirement arise from contract law. The concept of agreement in competition law is used to define any mutual consent among the parties."

### Concerted Practices

It is quite easy to assert that the common approach in the Turkish Antitrust Law on concerted practices is very similar to the European Antitrust Law enforcement. However, there is one very unique difference in Turkish legislation, which is "the presumption of concerted practice". Article 4/III and 4/IV of the Antitrust Act define this presumption and grant the Turkish Competition Board a very strong weapon. The mentioned provision is as follows:

> Cases where the existence of an agreement cannot be proved, or that the price changes in the market, or the balance of demand and supply, or the operational areas of undertakings

---

[28] Decision of Turkish Competition Board dated 25.11.2009 and numbered 09-57/1393-362, para. 2460.

> are similar to those markets where competition is prevented, distorted, or restricted constitute a presumption that the undertakings are engaged in concerted practice.
> Each of the parties may relieve itself of the responsibility by proving not to engage in concerted practice, provided that it is based on economic and rational facts.

At a glance, the presumption of concerted practice seems to be different from the EU practice. However, if we look at the Woodpulp[29] and Dyestuffs[30] cases, we can see that the practices of both jurisdictions are parallel. The main difference is that in Turkey, the presumption is explicitly codified under the Antitrust Act. Consequently, the presumption of concerted practice shows its affects mostly for the burden of proof. The application of the presumption shifts the burden on the alleged party, and it is often hard to prove innocence. Thus, to prevent the unfair consequences that might arise from exploitation of the presumption of concerted practice, the Turkish Competition Board set forth its approach explicitly in various decisions. For instance the concerted practice are clearly defined in the Turkish Competition Board's *Newspaper*[31] decision:

1. There must have been positive contacts between the parties such as meetings, discussions, exchanges of information, which are generally expressed orally or in writing,
2. Such contacts must have been aimed at influencing the market behavior and especially eliminating the uncertainty of an undertaking's future competitive behavior in advance,
3. They must have influenced or changed the commercial behavior of the undertaking concerned in a manner that cannot fully be explained with reference to competitive effects.

### Decisions of Associations of Undertakings

Article 4 of the Antitrust Act also prohibits the behaviors of undertakings that restrict competition, through associations of undertakings. Associations of undertakings are defined in Article 3 of the Antitrust Act: "any kind of associations with or without a legal personality, which are formed by undertakings to accomplish particular goals."

As Sanlı stated, "associations of undertakings are also a subject of the Antitrust Act under the scope of Article 4. Thus, (…) it is possible to open an investigation against a conduct of a decision of associations of undertakings" (Sanlı 2000a, p. 83). Moreover, it makes no difference whether the association in question has a legal entity or not. The Turkish Competition Board stated this point so clearly in its

---

[29] "Woodpulp II" Cases C-89, 114, 116 to 117, 125 to 129/85, A. Ahlstroem Osakeyhtiö and others v. Commission, (1984) ECR 1679.

[30] "Dyestuffs", Case 48/69, ICI v. Commission (1972) ECR 619.

[31] Decision of Turkish Competition Board dated 17.07.2000 and numbered 00-26/291-161.

*Press Monitoring*[32] decision that the Board applied an injunction decision to BIAK, which is a joint industrial committee for monitoring the circulation of printed press in Turkey,

> BIAK is a committee, which does not have a legal entity, and that is formed by representatives of advertising agencies, advertisers, channel organizations that came together in order to carry out and finance investigations (...) run and coordinate the projects.

#### 5.4.1.2 Test of Illegality: Restriction of Competition

##### Horizontal and Vertical Restraints

The business relations between the undertakings may be either horizontal or vertical. Restrictions of competition, horizontally or vertically, by undertakings fall under the scope of Article 4 of the Antitrust Act. Similar to practices of other jurisdictions, the approach of the Turkish Antitrust Law regime is different from horizontal and vertical restraints. The main rationale behind this approach is the basic fact that generally the horizontal restraints create benefit for the society in limited circumstances, whereas vertical restraints may give rise to economic efficiency under certain conditions. Thus, the Turkish Competition Board uses a much more per se approach to the horizontal restraints of competition.

On the other hand, vertical restrictions of competition may create positive effects and heighten the social welfare. This characteristic of the vertical agreements makes the assessment under Article 4 much more broad and complex. To clarify this approach to the vertical agreements, the Turkish Competition Board has published numerous communiqués and guidelines on vertical relations.

The common vertical agreements that restrict competition in practice are exclusive distribution agreements, non-compete obligations, and market sharing agreements between the undertakings that operate in different levels of the supply chain. The Turkish Competition Board makes a case-by-case analysis to reveal whether the efficiency gained by the agreement is greater than the loss due to the restriction of competition. However, if a vertical agreement fulfills the conditions on block exemption, the agreement is automatically exempted from the application of Article 4 of the Antitrust Act, and it is not necessary for that agreement to make a notification to the Turkish Competition Authority. Horizontal agreements on the contrary are usually subject to individual exemption scrutiny.

##### Per Se Prohibitions and *Rule of Reason*

Most of the horizontal restrictions listed in Article 4 are subject to per se analysis and directly considered void and illegal. Also, vertical restraints such as resale price

[32] Decision of Turkish Competition Board dated 04.03.1999 and numbered 99-13/99-40.

maintenance (RPM) and other hard-core restrictions are prohibited by law per se. Contrary to Article 101 of TFEU, Article 4 of the Antitrust Act does not contain any de minimis provisions. Hence, the Turkish Competition Board is authorized to investigate any kind of agreements between undertakings and to impose fines, even though the stated agreement does affect a minor portion of the economy. Such a per se approach is used in many of the investigations of the Turkish Competition Board, such as its *Marmara Region Cement*[33] decision.

> If an anticompetitive aim is clearly observed in an agreement, the agreement itself or the provisions that distort competition would form a "per se" competition infringement. In such case, there is no need to examine the effect of the agreement on competition. Restrictive agreements would form a structural case that parties would discard their own independent competitive activities on behalf of their common interests. Because of such reason, only being a part of a restrictive agreement is prohibited as well, even if the agreement had not showed effect.

Other important point to notice is Article 4/I, which also prohibits agreements that "likely effect the prevention, distortion or restriction of competition directly or indirectly." If an agreement does not affect competition but there is a chance that it might affect competition in the future, then the stated agreement is also prohibited. So, the Turkish Competition Board has a broad discretion to decide whether an agreement is anticompetitive or not.

If Article 4 is assessed from a per se point of view, it can be said that the examples listed in the second paragraph of the article set a situation that make per se analysis nearly impossible, as it has listed nearly all possible (at least the most common ones) per se restrictions. In other words, if an agreement falls under the scope of one of the listed examples, the agreement in question will be deemed to restrict competition, prima facie. However, if Article 4 is assessed together with Article 5 (exemption provision), we can say that there is a form of rule-of-reason analysis for every case. Also, the exemption analysis is made for every investigation (Sanlı 2000a, p. 99).

Also, if the investigation that the Turkish Competition Board relies on the grounds of concerted practice, then the Turkish Competition Board is bound to make a rule-of-reason analysis. This situation occurs from the above-mentioned presumption of concerted practice. Consequently, making a per se analysis and using the presumption of concerted practice would not give any chance to the undertaking to defend itself. As a result, the Turkish Competition Board uses a rule-of-reason analysis in cases where the allegation is based on concerted practices.

Another important point to mention is that even in the cases where a horizontal relation is founded to realize some higher causes, such as protecting environment, and even if a governmental institution has an encouraging effect on a cartel, a fine

[33] Decision of Turkish Competition Board dated 5.12.2005 and numbered 05-81/1118-320.

may be imposed by the Turkish Competition Board. *Accumulator*[34] Decision is a good example for this situation:

> None of the actions that are admitted as infringement would be grounded by the APAK Regulation[35] or incentives of the Ministry of Environment and Forest. Incentives of the Ministry is for providing the management compatible with environment, of waste accumulators and for forming a system about this matter and supporting formation of associations. Enterprises claiming that they have to comply the APAK Regulation are also obliged to comply with the Antitrust Act on the Protection of Competition.

### Leniency

On February 2009, the Turkish Competition Board introduced two regulations on leniency and monetary fines. The aim of the new leniency regime is to help the Turkish Competition Board to detect cartels and also deter them from the very beginning. Leniency is simply, giving immunity from sanctions, mainly fines, to the undertaking which has revealed evidence concerning the cartel of which it was a member. Another implication of these Regulations is that the undertaking's managers and employees having active participation to the violation can also be fined up to 5% of the fine that is imposed on the employer undertaking.

In order to apply the Leniency regulation effectively, the scope and the magnitude of fines should be foreseeable, and the undertakings should be able to assess the consequences of their actions.[36] So, the Regulation on Monetary Fines (the Fine Regulation) also came into effect on the same day as the Leniency Regulation.

For leniency applications, first undertaking that submits the information and evidence independently from its competitors, shall be granted immunity from fines on condition that the Authority does not have, at the time of the submission, sufficient evidence to find the violation of Article 4 of the Antitrust Act. So, the first undertaking that applied for the leniency will be granted a full immunity, but undertakings that could not take the first place can also apply for the leniency to get a reduction from their fines. The reduction scheme is given below:

(a) The fine to be imposed on the first undertaking shall be reduced by one third to half.
(b) The fine to be imposed on the second undertaking shall be reduced by one fourth to one third.
(c) The fines to be imposed on other undertakings shall be reduced by one sixth to one fourth.

---

[34] Decision of Turkish Competition Board dated 20.5.2008 and numbered 08-34/456-161, p. 79.

[35] An industry-specific regulation found by the Turkish Competition Board to facilitate an environment that makes it easy to form a cartel.

[36] The system before the adoption of the Fine Regulation granted the Turkish Competition Board a broad discretionary power to impose a fine ranging from 0 to 10% of the annual turnover.

#### 5.4.1.3 Exemption

Article 5 of the Antitrust Act and the Communiqué Regarding Vertical Agreements No. 2002/2 (Communiqué No. 2002/2) published by the Turkish Competition Board regulates the exemption procedure in general. Article 5 of the Antitrust Act is very similar to Article 101/3 of the TFEU, and it assesses the impact of an agreement on the general public. If the net effect of the agreement in question is positive despite restricting competition, the agreement in question will be individually exempted from the application of Article 4 of the Antitrust Act. The test used to assess whether an agreement fulfills the requisitions to acquire an exemption is stated in Article 5.

(a) Ensuring new developments and improvements, or economic or technical development in the production or distribution of goods and in the provision of services
(b) Benefitting the consumer from the above-mentioned
(c) Not eliminating competition in a significant part of the relevant market
(d) Not limiting competition to more than what is compulsory for achieving the goals set out in subparagraphs (a) and (b)

In addition to the provisions of the Antitrust Act, the Communiqué No. 2002/2 exempts the vertical agreements that fulfill the conditions set in the Communiqué. The block exemption will be applied if the market share of the supplier in the relevant market to which it supplied the goods and services in a vertical agreement does not exceed 40%.[37] The block exemption is also applied if the market share of the buyer does not exceed 40% in an exclusive supply agreement. However, the agreement must not include the hard-core restrictions, which are stated in Article 4 of the Communiqué no. 2002/2.

Also, the Vertical Guidelines published by the Turkish Competition Board make a detailed assessment of the vertical agreements, and it is very instructive for the undertakings. Finally, it is notable that the assessment of both individual and block exemption is made by the parties of an agreement, and it is not necessary to make a notification to the Turkish Competition Board. Provided that an agreement does not fulfill the conditions of exemption or in order to avoid legal ambiguity, the parties are free to make a negative clearance and/or exemption notification to the Turkish Competition Board.

### *5.4.2 Abuse of Dominant Position*

Article 6 of the Antitrust Act prohibits abusive behavior of dominant undertakings. According to the first paragraph, "the abuse, by one or more undertakings, of their

[37] This threshold is determined as 30% in EU Regulation.

dominant position in a market for goods or services within the whole or a part of the country on their own or through agreements with others or through concerted practices is illegal and prohibited." As it can be observed, the wording of the paragraph seems quite complex as it refers to agreements and concerted practices between undertakings. However, the logic of Article 6 is very simple: it controls the unilateral behavior of dominant undertakings. Holding a dominant position in the market is not unlawful, but it is the behavior that is proscribed provided that it impairs the competition in the market. The nature of abusive behavior whether implemented through agreements or concerted practices is irrelevant.

The second paragraph lists some examples of abusive behavior, and this list is not an exhaustive catalogue of what kinds of behavior are regarded as abusive. According to the second paragraph, some examples of abusive behaviors are as follows:

(a) Preventing, directly or indirectly, another undertaking from entering into the area of commercial activity, or actions aimed at complicating activities of competitors in the market.
(b) Making direct or indirect discrimination by offering different terms to purchasers with equal status for the same and equal rights, obligations, and acts.
(c) Purchasing another good or service together with a good or service, or tying a good or service demanded by purchasers acting as intermediary undertakings to the condition of displaying another good or service by the purchaser, or imposing limitations with regard to the terms of purchase and sale in case of resale, such as not selling a purchased good below a particular price.
(d) Actions that aim at distorting competitive conditions in another market for goods or services by means of exploiting financial, technological, and commercial advantages created by dominance in a particular market.
(e) Restricting production, marketing, or technical development to the prejudice of consumers.

In order to apply Article 6, at least two conditions must hold: "*dominance in the relevant market*" and "*abusive behavior.*" There is no exemption provision in Article 6; therefore, dominant undertakings' efficiency defenses (objective justification) may be recognized under the concept of abuse. These two conditions are analyzed in detail below.

#### 5.4.2.1 Dominant Position

Article 6 deals with the behavior of monopolies and dominant undertakings. To be caught by the Article 6, one should first establish dominance in the relevant market. Market dominance is an economic concept, and it merely refers to a high degree of economic power. Article 3 of the Antitrust Act defines the following concept: "The power of one or more undertakings in a particular market to determine economic parameters such as price, supply, the amount of production and distribution, by acting independently of their competitors and customers." The legal definition seems to be in accordance with the economic theory, which basically demotes the description to "*power over price.*"

However, neither legal nor economic definition solves the problem of determining dominance in a particular case. Probably, the main question that the competition law seeks to answer is the degree of economic power that is is necessary for dominance in the market or the conditions under which an undertaking has a power over price.

One way to deal with this problem is looking directly at the performance, i.e., profit levels of the undertakings at hand. However, there are a variety of causes that may complicate this analysis, and therefore, just as other competition authorities tend to prefer, the Competition Board measures the dominance by looking at two factors: "market shares" and "entry barriers."

The preliminary filter to determine the dominance is the "market share" of the undertaking. To determine the market share, first the relevant market is defined, which is not unique to dominance analysis. After determining the relevant market, the shares of undertakings and their rivals are calculated. Although market share values in the Turkish Competition Board's decisions are generally omitted due to trade secrecy concerns, it is still possible to infer some implications from the decisions. According to the Turkish Competition Board's case law, shares above 40% create risk of dominance, and shares beyond 60% can give rise to a presumption of dominance. It is interesting to note that, although in theory, low market shares may trigger the risk of dominance, when one looks at the actual practice of the Turkish Competition Board, the dominant undertaking has held market shares in excess of 70 or even 80% in the majority of cases. So, it would not be an overstatement to say that the Turkish Competition Board generally requires higher market shares when establishing dominance. Mere existence of high market shares is not deemed sufficient. High market shares should last for some time and market shares of the rivals of the undertaking should be significantly smaller.

The second factor in determining dominance is entry conditions in the market. It is well established that dominance does not exist without high entry barriers because if entry is easy, other firms will be able to exert competitive pressure on the undertaking by holding high market shares. There is no common understanding on the definition of "*entry barrier*" in economic theory; however, in competition law practice, the issue seems to be settled. The concept is broadly defined, and any impediment/barrier challenging the entrant is regarded as an entry barrier. Apparently, with this definition one could not think of any market without entry barriers. So, the concept is a relative one.

What are entry barriers? Case law provides an extensive list of factors that are recognized as entry barriers. Of course, primary examples are legal ones. Licenses, other intellectual property rights, and entry and exit regulations are considered as significant, if not absolute, entry barriers.[38] Market conditions could also help the undertaking to protect its position in the market and deter entry. In this regard,

[38] Decision of the Turkish Competition Board dated 6.11.2000 and numbered 00-44/472-257.

economies of scale and scope, network externalities, and high proportion of sunk costs also indicate high entry barriers. The behavior and performance of the undertaking could also make entry more difficult for newcomers. For example, a well-organized distribution system, idle capacity, advertising and brand recognition, limit pricing, product differentiation, high quality of the product, innovation, and deep pockets are also deemed to contribute to the dominant position.[39] As seen from the examples, there are many factors that may indicate dominance, and the Turkish Competition Board shows no reluctance to characterize any other factor as barrier to entry.

Article 6 applies not only to single dominance, which is usually the case, but also to joint/collective dominance situations. The wording of the article explicitly refers to an abuse "*by one or more undertakings,*" and the definition of dominance in article 3 mentions "*one or more undertaking's dominance.*" Joint dominance used to be a controversial topic in the European Antitrust Law; however, the recent case law seems to have put an end to that controversy.[40] Joint dominance refers to situations where due to the economic links among them, two or more undertakings can act independently from their competitors and customers. It is necessary that joint dominant undertakings should act as a single entity. The economic link could be established by agreements or by market conditions. Especially in tight oligopoly markets where characteristics of the market are prone to tacit collusion, it is assumed that such links may exist without an agreement.

The Turkish Competition Board has embraced the principles of European case law and surprisingly has been very enthusiastic to apply collective dominance. Out of 23 Article 6 infringements decided by the Turkish Competition Board, four cases involve joint dominance. In its early years of enforcement, two leading media companies and the joint venture that was established to undertake their distribution operations in the daily newspaper market were found to be collectively dominant and they abused their position by refusing to deal with a competitor.[41] Just a year after, the Turkish Competition Board reached a very similar verdict involving the same undertakings and imposed penalties.[42] In both of the decisions, the economic links were said to be established by agreements, the joint venture company. In fact, it was doubtful whether resorting to the concept of joint dominance was necessary as these two undertakings were also found to have violated Article 4 of the Antitrust Act. In 2003, the Turkish Competition Board has imposed harsh penalties to two leading mobile phone operators due to collective refusal to deal practices implemented through 22 consecutive months.[43] Here, there was no evidence of an agreement or a concerted practice. With this decision,

[39] Decision of the Turkish Competition Board dated 29.12.2005 and numbered 05-88/1221-353.

[40] Compaigne Maritime Belge NV v. Commission (1996) ECR II 1201 (1997) 4 CMLR. 273.

[41] Decision of the Turkish Competition Board dated 17.7.2000 and numbered 00-26/292-162.

[42] Decision of the Turkish Competition Board dated 14.12.2000 and numbered 00-49/529-291.

[43] Decision of the Turkish Competition Board dated 9.6.2003 and numbered 03 -40/432-186.

the Turkish Competition Board has endorsed the view that economic links can be established solely by market conditions and that joint dominance can be used as a weapon to combat the oligopoly problem.[44]

#### 5.4.2.2 The Concept of Abuse

It is not illegal to hold a dominant position in the relevant market, but what is prohibited by the Antitrust Act is the abuse of this position. The Antitrust Act imposes special responsibility on dominant undertakings not to allow their conduct to impair the competition on the market. The problem with this proposition is that the scope of the responsibility is not entirely clear. Abuse is an elusive concept, and despite the nonexhaustive list of abusive behavior enumerated under Article 6/2, it requires interpretation. In that regard, the European case law and the doctrine are primary resources in understanding the concept and the Turkish Competition Board frequently refers to the European case law.

Abuse is an objective concept.[45] It is irrelevant whether the dominant undertaking has an intention of infringing Article 6. Conduct could be abusive, even if, for instance, it harms the competitive structure in the downstream markets where the dominant undertaking has no operations and does not have a potential to do so.[46] Accordingly, it is not necessary that the dominant undertaking should have benefited from the consequence of its abusive behavior. What matters is the harmful effect of the conduct on the market. This understanding of abuse is endorsed by the Turkish Competition Board in several cases. However, it should also be noted that in certain types of abuses, such as predatory or selective pricing, intention is generally the essential part of the infringement.

Abuse can take a variety of forms. An agreement, contract, or purely unilateral decision, or even inaction can be characterized as abusive behavior. Therefore, it is not possible to exhaustively enumerate the types of abusive behavior. Taking into account its effects on the competitive process, abuse is generally analyzed under two main categories: "*exploitative*" and "*exclusionary*" abuses. This classical categorization is helpful in understanding the concept; therefore, the main types of abusive behavior are analyzed under two categories below. It should be mentioned

[44] In this decision, the Turkish Competition Board listed some nonexhaustive conditions, which may amount to finding of economic links. These conditions are: few market players, mature market structure, stagnant and moderate increase in demand, low demand elasticity, homogenous products, similar cost structures, similar market shares, transparent market conditions, low rate of innovation, idle capacity, high entry barriers, no market power on the buyer side, no potential competition, some sort of connection between relevant undertakings, possibility of retaliation, and lack of price competition.

[45] Decision of the Turkish Competition Board dated 23.8.2002 and numbered 02-49/634-257, p.54.

[46] Decision of the Turkish Competition Board dated 20.4.2009 and numbered 09-16/374-88.

that there is no rigid demarcation between these categories; the same behavior may fit in with both categories depending on the circumstances of the case.

#### Exploitative Abuses

The term abuse in fact evokes exploitation, and that is normally what one expects from dominant undertakings. A dominant undertaking exploits its customers by charging high prices and/or by supplying poor-quality products and/or by dictating unfair terms and impairing innovation. These behaviors result in inefficiency and directly harm consumers. Given that this is the public harm that the competition law intends to prevent, it is natural that Article 6 explicitly prohibits exploitative abuse. By prohibiting these behaviors, inefficient practices will be deterred, and social/consumer welfare will be ensured. Article 6 explicitly confirms this logic; all these practices are proscribed by the examples of abuse set out in the second paragraph. Article 6/2 (b) prohibits discriminatory practices, 6/2 (c) bans tying, and 6/2 (e) forbids impairing innovation and restricting the output.

Nevertheless, the actual practice of the Turkish Competition Board has not been entirely compatible with this theoretical logic. Compared to exclusionary abuses, the Turkish Competition Board has not been keen to apply Article 6 to exploitative abuses. 34% of all (205) Article 6 decisions involve exploitative abuses, and only in four cases of 23, abuse was established.[47] So, the majority of exploitative abuse allegations were denied by the Turkish Competition Board, and the verdict of those four cases generated a lot of controversy.

Not surprisingly, this practice is in line with the European Commission's attitude. One would then wonder why the theoretical logic contradicts the practice. The explanation lies in the economic thinking. If an undertaking charges high prices and/or offers poor-quality goods, this will provoke entry into the market and increase competition. So, the market will itself correct this failure without costly and imperfect government interference. Besides, there are practical problems associated with enforcing competition law to exploitative practices. To be more specific, it is difficult to identify the parameters of intervention, and even if this could be done, there is a problem of remedy. Therefore, perhaps the (second best) solution is not to interfere at all (Sanlı 2000b, p. 87 et. seq.).

This line of thinking has affected the Turkish Competition Board, and despite the existence of a few infringement decisions, enforcement policy toward exploitative abuses seems reluctant. For example, there are almost no cases about dictating unfair conditions and impairing innovation. Unfair pricing and price discrimination have been the main types of exploitative practices that the Turkish Competition Board has dealt with, and there are only four decisions where the behavior was

[47] Considering that there are in twenty-three cases the Turkish Competition Board determined that the Article 6 was violated, overwhelming majority (%83) of infringement decisions involve exclusionary abuse.

found abusive within the meaning of Article 6. Among the four infringement decisions, three cases concern price discrimination and one case relates to unfair pricing. However, that ratio is reversed when it comes to the percentage values involving all cases decided by the Turkish Competition Board: 24% of all cases relate to unfair pricing. This is surprisingly high given the general tendency toward these practices. One probable reason is that state-owned monopolies still have significant influence on the Turkish economy, and a large fraction (30%) of Article 6 cases relate to practices of state-owned monopolies.

The cases involving price discrimination exhibit interesting features as different legal standards have been applied. In the first case, the CINE 5, besides two conventional conditions, the Turkish Competition Board required that the discrimination should put at least one customer in a competitive disadvantage vis-a-vis its competitors.[48] So, there should be a negative effect in the competitive conditions of downstream markets to label the conduct as abusive. However, in the two subsequent cases, the IBOIAŞ[49] and IZOTAŞ,[50] both of which involved bus-station operators holding monopoly positions in their markets, the Turkish Competition Board, after deliberating the issue, did not insist on this condition and applied Article 6, even though there was no competitive harm caused. One should note that these two cases closely resemble the practice of the European Commission in a case where bus and airport monopolies' discriminatory prices were found to be abusive despite the fact that the competitive disadvantage condition was missing.[51] Another point that further complicates the issue of discrimination is that in appeal, the Council of State, appeal court for the decision of Turkish Competition Board quashed the first decision on the ground that pricing policies adopted by dominant undertakings were lawful as it was objectively determined, was not beyond the regulatory cap, and enabled the small and medium-sized TV stations to enter the market. So the pricing policy was, in fact, perceived as a discount. After this decision of reversal, it is unclear whether exploitative discrimination will fall within Article 6.

The sole unfair pricing case involves a state-owned undertaking, the BELKO, operating in coal distribution and sales in Ankara.[52] The coal was used for residential heating; accordingly, it was consumed by a large fraction of the inhabitants, and the demand was inelastic as at that time substitutes were limited. The undertaking had a legal monopoly, and therefore, there was no prospect of entry. The Turkish Competition Board determined that the BELKO was charging very high prices for coal when compared to the prices of coal sold in other cities, and was abusing its dominance by unfair pricing. Benchmarking method indicated that the price of coal was almost 60–70% higher than the prices in neighboring markets. The unusual

[48] Decision of the Turkish Competition Board dated 11.10.1999 and numbered 99-46/500-316.

[49] Decision of the Turkish Competition Board dated 23.9.2005 and numbered 05-60/893-242.

[50] Decision of the Turkish Competition Board dated 11.1.2007 and numbered 07-01/1-1.

[51] OJ (1999) L 69/31, (1999) 5 CMLR 103, upheld on appeal Case 163/99, Portugal v. Commission, 29.3.2001; also see Zaventem decision OJ, dated 12.9.1995, L 216.

[52] Decision of the Turkish Competition Board dated 8.7.2009 and numbered 09-32/703-163.

thing about the case was that the BELKO was making losses due to operational inefficiency and it was obvious that Belko was subsidizing other municipality firms and activities. So, the BELKO argued that the pricing could not be considered abusive, given that it was not making profit. The Turkish Competition Board analyzed this argument and determined that it was true. Nevertheless, the Turkish Competition Board rejected the defence on the grounds that profit is not required for unfair (excessive) pricing. In effect, BELKO was punished because of its inefficiency. With this formulation, it is accepted that Article 6 can be used to control the performance of the dominant undertakings.

### Exclusionary Abuses

There is no doubt that Article 6 covers exclusionary abuse as the second paragraph explicitly lists exclusionary practices as examples of abusive behavior. In fact, Article 6 has been more frequently applied to the anticompetitive practices of dominant undertakings. To be more precise, 65% of all Article 6 decisions involve anticompetitive abuses and, as mentioned above, the proportion of anticompetitive abuses in infringement decisions is much higher. These figures are in conformity with the general tendency in the EU and in the US case law. Given the problems associated with applying competition law to exploitative abusive behavior, competition authorities are seemed to be less reluctant to combat with anticompetitive abuses.

Anticompetitive abuse simply refers to exclusionary practices aimed at actual and potential rivals. Here, the motivation of the dominant undertaking is clear: to exclude the actual and the potential rival from the market, and thereby maintaining and increasing its market share. The main concern of the competition law is protecting the rivals to preserve the competitive structure of the market. So, the anticompetitive behavior does not actually directly harm the competitive parameters (or the performance) of the market. However, if the competition authorities do not interfere in time, there is a probability that the market concentration may increase, which in turn could negatively affect the performance of the market.

Application of Article 6 to anticompetitive abuses is not without problems. As seen from the definition, the behavior appears competitive on the face of it, and it does not produce harmful results per se. There is a likelihood that the dominant undertaking is actually competing on the merits despite the fact that its rivals are injured and are even excluded from the market as a result of its practices. For instance, the dominant undertaking, due to economies of scale or productivity, may well drive its competitors out of business by lowering its prices. Are we going to characterize this as anticompetitive abuse? So, the main question here is the merits on which dominant undertakings are allowed to compete. The jurisprudence and case law on anticompetitive abuse seek to answer this question by demarcating exclusionary practices from efficient but aggressive commercial policies.

When we look at the case law of the Turkish Competition Board, we observe that a variety of practices fall within the category of exclusionary abuses. The pricing practices probably constitute the main subcategory as they comprise a range of pricing schemes such as "*predatory pricing,*" "*selective pricing,*" "*price squeeze,*" and "*discriminatory pricing.*" Almost half of the infringement decisions and more than two third of all cases involve a pricing behavior. Among them, price discrimination and predatory pricing cases are very common. An interesting observation is the proportion of "refusal to deal" cases. The Turkish Competition Board dealt with too many "*refusal to deal*" cases, and in five out of 23 infringement decisions, the refusal was found to be abusive.

To have a better understanding of the current practice on exclusionary abuse, it would be useful to take a look at some of the leading case laws of the Turkish Competition Board. As just mentioned, there are several pricing policies that are proscribed as abusive. Among them predatory and discriminatory pricing cases loom large. Exclusionary type of discriminatory pricing can take very different forms, and for this reason, it is problematic to recapitulate the Turkish Competition Board's practice on this matter. Besides, the case law concerning discrimination seems unsettled as there have been contradictory judgments.[53] In contrast, the practice about predatory pricing appears to be more predictable. Although the Turkish Competition Board found abusive behavior only in two predatory pricing cases, there have been many cases illuminating the attitude of the Turkish Competition Board.[54] For instance, upon a complaint made against the Coca Cola Company, the Turkish Competition Board denied the allegations after carefully analyzing the facts of the case, though it gave a comprehensive verdict articulating the legal test of predatory pricing.[55] According to the decision, to establish a successful case on predatory pricing, three conditions must be satisfied: Dominance, extraordinarily low prices, and exclusionary intent. The Turkish Competition Board has also explained the meaning of extraordinarily low prices. Referring to European case law, prices below average variable costs were in principle regarded as predatory; however, in some cases, prices above average variable costs but below average total costs might be deemed as predatory. This could especially be the case when the economic investment requires high fixed costs, and in this case, there is a special emphasis on the intent requirement. Another condition that is indirectly stipulated is that the low pricing should last for a certain period. Short-term low pricing indicates that the dominant undertaking acted with a motive other than exclusion. Hence, according to the Turkish Antitrust Law, recoupment is not deemed necessary for establishing a case on predatory pricing.

Both infringement decisions on predatory pricing were committed by the Turk Telecom; Turkish fixed-line telephony incumbent and pricing scheme have the characteristics of (vertical-predatory) price squeeze. In recent years, there have

[53] For an interesting judgment on discrimination see Decision of the Turkish Competition Board dated 20.4.2009 and numbered 09-16/374-88.

[54] Decision of the Turkish Competition Board dated 2.10.2002 and numbered 02-60/755-305; Decision of the Turkish Competition Board dated 19.11.2008 and numbered 08-65/1055-411.

[55] Decision of the Turkish Competition Board dated 23.1.2004 and numbered 04-07/75-18.

been numerous complaints[56] about the price squeezing behavior, especially in the telecommunications industry. So, the latest decision, which was rendered in 2008, is important in the sense that the Turkish Competition Board set the legal standard and clarified the controversy surrounding the predatory price squeeze. According to this decision, to establish a successful case on price squeeze, six conditions must hold: the undertaking must be vertically integrated; it should have a super dominant position in the upstream wholesale market; the input produced in the upstream wholesale market should be an essential facility for the undertakings operating at the retail level including both the dominant undertaking and its rivals; the price demanded for the essential facility should be so high that it is not possible for an equally efficient competitor in the downstream retail market to operate profitably given the level of retail prices; as a result of the pricing behavior, competition should be negatively affected in the downstream retail market; and finally, there should be no objective justification for the pricing behavior. These conditions indicate that the Turkish Competition Board followed the precedents of the European case law[57] and secondary legal documents[58] were explicitly referred in the decision.

Another pricing practice that was found abusive was selective pricing. The decision[59] involved the pricing behavior of a glass manufacturer, Anadolu Cam, in a bidding process that was alleged to have exclusionary effect on the sole rival, Marmara Cam. Anadolu Cam had a dominant position with 90% market share, and throughout the bidding process of the major glass purchaser, it implemented a selective pricing scheme. According to the facts of the case, Anadolu Cam lowered its prices in bids where it had the rival, Marmara Cam, and increased its prices where it faced no competition. Even though its lowest prices were not below its costs, the Turkish Competition Board found the pricing scheme illegal under Article 6. According to the Turkish Competition Board, four conditions of selective pricing were met in the present case. These conditions are as follows: the undertaking in question should be evidently dominant; there should be only one rival in the market; clear evidences should indicate that the dominant undertaking has acted with exclusionary motive. As it is well known, selective pricing is a matter of controversy in European Antitrust Law; however, this did not prevent the Turkish Competition Board from labeling this kind of profitable pricing as abusive. However, there have been no other cases of selective pricing, and it is unclear whether this precedent will be followed in the future.

As mentioned, there have been several refusal-to-deal cases, and in five of them, dominant undertakings were held responsible and subjected to monetary fines. In

[56] Decision of the Turkish Competition Board dated 4.7.2007 and numbered 07-56/634-216.

[57] Case COMP/38.784 – Wanadoo España vs. Telefónica, 4.7.2007.

[58] Notice on the Application of the Competition Rules to Access Agreements in the Telecommunications Sector, Framework, Relevant Markets and Principles, 98/C 262/02, O.J. C 265/2.

[59] Decision of the Turkish Competition Board dated 6.8.2009 and numbered 09-35/877-206.

these decisions, the Turkish Competition Board developed and applied consistent legal standards for a successful refusal-to-deal case. In the leading case, the Roaming,[60] the Turkish Competition Board held that refusal to deal will be regarded abusive provided that five conditions are met. These conditions are as follows: access to facility by the undertakings competing in the relevant market should be indispensable, and it should be impossible to supply the product or service without access to the network; there should be sufficient capacity to meet demand; the undertaking controlling the essential facility should deny the access to the facility and hinder the supply of a new substitute product or a service; the undertaking demanding access should be ready to pay a reasonable and nondiscriminatory price for the access; there should not be an objective justification for refusal. The Turkish Competition Board also explained what it meant by the first condition and, among other things, emphasized the importance of the nonduplicative feature of the facility. In the case at hand, building infrastructure for mobile communication was not feasable. Board had no difficulty in labeling the service as essential and nonduplicative.

Although quite common in the Turkish retail sector, exclusive agreements and practices have been occasionally analyzed under Article 6. There are only few infringements on this matter, and in the leading case, Karbogaz, the Turkish Competition Board explicitly stated that the exclusive contracts amounted to foreclosure of the market and therefore were abusive.[61] Karbogaz was a dominant undertaking in the liquid carbon dioxide market, and in response to the prospect of the entry of a competitor, the Barit, it extended the duration of its 1-year exclusive supply contracts with major buyers (the Coca Cola Co., Pepsi Co., etc.) to 5 years. This policy was apparently aimed at the rival, and the purpose was to exclude the latter from the market. Upon a complaint by the rival, the Turkish Competition Board after analyzing the facts of the cases determined that even though the customers agreed with the extension of the contracts, there was no business purpose other than excluding the rival. The Turkish Competition Board did not discuss the efficiencies of the conduct and merely focused on the intention of the dominant undertaking. This is quite an unusual case, not only because very high penalties were imposed and the importance of intention was amplified but also because there was deviation from the general tendency of the Turkish Competition Board. When we look at the legal policy toward vertical exclusive agreements concluded by dominant undertakings, it is generally the case that the Turkish Competition Board has tended to base its analysis on Article 4 and has refrained from imposing fines.[62] Since those agreements were covered by the Block Exemption Communiqué, withdrawal of the Block Exemption was deemed sufficient.

[60] Decision of the Turkish Competition Board dated 9.6.2003 and numbered 04-40/432-186.

[61] Decision of the Turkish Competition Board dated 23.8.2002 and numbered 02-49/634-257.

[62] See for example the Decision of the Turkish Competition Board dated 4.5.2004 and numbered 04-32/377-95; the Decision of the Turkish Competition Board dated 22.4.2005 and numbered 05-27/317-80; Decision of the Turkish Competition Board dated 10.9.2007 and numbered 07-70/864-327.

## Concentrations

### *The Concept of Concentration*

For a transaction to fall within the scope of the Turkish merger control regime, it should qualify as a concentration. And, parallel to the EU merger regime if there is no change of control on a lasting basis according to Article 5 (1) of the recently enacted Merger Communiqué No. 2010/4 (Merger Communiqué or recently enacted Merger Communiqué), mergers or acquisitions are not assessed as concentrations.

The control of a firm or entity may be acquired by a single undertaking, leading to sole control, or jointly by two or more undertakings, leading to joint control. An acquisition of sole control would mean that there is a concentration in the form of a merger, while an acquisition of joint control means that the concentration is in the form of a joint venture. A concentration will also arise if there is a change from sole control to joint control or from joint control to sole control, including where this is a return to an earlier situation. Transactions in which there is a change in the structure of joint control (such as an increase in the number of shareholders exercising joint control) are also considered as a concentration.

Article 7 of the Antitrust Act has counted some means of transfer of control for acquisitions. Moreover, as in the definition of undertaking, the legal basis of the change of control is not important as competition law is concerned with the economic impact rather than the legal form. As a result, when there is no change of control, mergers or acquisitions are not assessed as concentrations in the Turkish Antitrust Law. The Turkish Competition Board has made this clear in its *Uludag Erbag Decision*[63] as follows:

> (...) when the essence of the acquisition transaction is dealt with, it is clear that both the partnership structures and The Turkish Competition Boards of management of the parties consist of the same persons, therefore, even though they are legally independent from each other these undertakings are dependent from the economic perspective and should be evaluated as a single economic unit.

While the Antitrust Act does not define the concept of control that is so vital for the merger regime, the Merger Communiqué provides the following definition in its Article 5(2):

> For the purposes of this Communiqué, control may be acquired through rights, contracts or other instruments which, separately or together, allow de facto or de jure exercise of decisive influence over an undertaking. In particular, these instruments consist of ownership right or operating right over all or part of the assets of an undertaking, and those rights or contracts granting decisive influence over the structure or decisions of the bodies of an undertaking.

The essence of the definition lies in the words "decisive influence on an undertaking" as in the European Community Merger Regulation No 139/2004 since the

[63] Decision of Turkish Competition Board dated 03.03.1999 and numbered 99-12/93-35.

means that bring control are not important in merger reviews. The existence of decisive influence cannot be established with certainty. The Merger Communiqué, thus, refers to the major forms of corporations.

The Merger Communiqué also provides the possibility for the consideration of occurrences with indirect control instead of direct control, in the third paragraph of Article 5(2), by stating that control can be acquired either by holders of rights or those "persons or undertakings who, while lacking such rights and powers, have de facto strength to exercise such rights." What matters here is where the decision-making capacity and commercial matters lies.

*Mergers and acquisitions.* In the Turkish Antitrust Law, the definition of concentration can be simplified to mean an act by an undertaking to take over exclusive or joint control of another undertaking. The defining characteristic of these operations is the requirement of a permanent or lasting change in the control structures of the undertakings resulting from the concentration process. In this sense, it is possible to classify two types of concentration: (a) the merger of two or more previously independent undertakings or (b) the acquisition of direct or indirect control of the whole or part of one or more other undertakings by one or more undertakings (or one or more persons already controlling at least one undertaking), whether by purchase of securities or assets, by contract, or by any other means. In the latter case, the legal personality of the acquired enterprise is terminated.

*Joint ventures.* Even if it is not a "merger" within the narrow meaning of the concept, the assembly of activities of undertakings under a single economic unit is also considered as a merger. This situation is generated particularly when two or more undertakings create a joint economic unit – a joint venture while maintaining their economic freedom and their seperate legal entities.

Joint ventures create further difficulty in merger control, since they are deemed to be concentrations only when they are autonomous. Such autonomous joint ventures are called full-functional in merger terminology. To qualify as autonomous, a joint venture should have the capacity to carry out all its functions by itself. These functions include, but are not limited to, management, production, and sales.

As a benchmark, a joint venture is expected to fulfill all the functions of a competing undertaking carried out in the relevant market. Thus, joint ventures that are formed for the purpose of outsourcing some of the tasks of the parent companies do not qualify as full-functional. If a joint venture is not full-functional, its anticompetitive effects, if there are any, can be examined under Article 4 of the Antitrust Act, which prohibits anticompetitive agreements.

*Exceptions.* The Merger Communiqué enumerates cases that are not considered as mergers or an acquisitions; thus, it is not required to obtain the authorization of the Turkish Competition Board for such mergers and acquisitions. The first exception is applied to undertakings whose ordinary activities are to transact with securities for their own account or for the account of others, temporarily hold the securities acquired with a view to reselling them, provided that the voting rights arising from such securities are not exercised by them in such a way that the competition policies of the undertaking issuing the securities are affected.

Another exception arises where the acquisition is carried out by a public institution and an organization with the aim or reason of liquidation, winding up, insolvency, cessation of payments, composition, and privatization or by a similar reason, and as required by law. The exemption also applies to the cases provided that they take place via inheritance.

*Thresholds for notification of mergers.* According to Article 7(1) of the Merger Communiqué, a merger must be notified and clearance must be obtained in the event of the following:

- Total turnovers of the transaction parties in Turkey exceed one hundred million TL, and turnovers of at least two of the transaction parties in Turkey each exceed thirty million TL, or
- Global turnover of one of the transaction parties exceed five hundred million TL, and at least one of the remaining transaction parties have a turnover in Turkey exceeding five million TL.

When looking at the high turnovers stated by the first threshold, it could be thought that the Authority opts to pay attention only to transactions which significantly affect Turkish markets. However, considering the second threshold that 500 million TL and 5 million TL are quite low thresholds for world-wide and Turkey turnovers, respectively, global transactions will be the main work load of the Authority. The Merger Communiqué thus adopts a dual or twin-track approach, that is, two different turnover criteria for determining the scope of merger control. Even if the thresholds listed above are exceeded, authorization of the Board shall not be required for transactions without any affected market according to Article 7 (2). However, this Article also states that this exception is not applied in cases of joint ventures. However, because the term "affected market" is brought into Turkish merger control regime by recently enacted Merger Communique, parties may not take the risk of being fined and notify their transactions in cases where it is not certain whether there is an affected market or not.

The calculation of turnover is a matter of accountancy, where, according to Article 8(6) of the Merger Communiqué, turnover "shall consist of the net sales generated as of the end of the financial year preceding the date of the notification, or, if this can not be calculated, of those generated as of the end of the financial year closest to the date of notification" excluding the sales of the relevant undertakings between themselves. If the concentration is the result of a partial acquisition, only the turnover of the transferred part is excluded from the turnover base.

*Merger Test: Creating or Strengthening Dominance and Thereby Lessening Competition*

The Turkish Competition Board assesses the competitive environment to be created after the transaction. This is an *ex ante* control mechanism. Once it is established that a concentration falls within the scope of Article 7 of the Antitrust Act, the

Turkish Competition Board is required to carry out an examination that involves the execution of a dominance test and, if the outcome is positive, checking whether or not the concentration significantly decreases competition, i.e., applying what is called the SLC (Significant lessening of competition) test. Accordingly, the Antitrust Act defines the determination of the dominant position as a prerequisite for the assessment of whether the competition is significantly lessened through this dominant position. This approach is, a carbon copy of the previous EU legislation that implemented the European perception of merger control for 15 years.

The same goes also for the case of strengthening of a dominant position, a phenomenon that covers a wide range of transactions since it is possible for a dominant undertaking to acquire a small firm in the relevant market without altering the competitive conditions.[64]

The basic element of the dominance test is the market structure that can be determined by an examination of the market shares in the relevant market, the supply and demand elasticity of the relevant product, the market concentration (as usually measured by HHI Tests), the barriers to entry and exit, and also the developmental stage of the market. In other words, the Authority should determine the level of competitiveness in the relevant market and also study the factors that will have a bearing on the actual and potential competitive behavior of the concentration including the efficiencies.[65]

Although competition authorities of the US and EU adopted "*competition test*" (also called as SLC test) in assessing the merger cases, The Turkish Competition Board has not changed its old style "dominance test" yet. As such a change requires amendment in the Turkish Antitrust Law, recently enacted Merger Communiqué also follows the dominance test.

On the other hand, the Antitrust Act defines dominant position as the power of one or more undertakings to determine economic parameters by acting independently of their competitors and customers. Together with the provisions of the Article 6, it is clear that the Antitrust Act refers to cases where more than one undertaking may be in abusive conduct through the market power they hold which may classify both undertakings as being collectively in dominant position. Accordingly, the collective dominance is included in the definition of dominant position. Therefore, since mergers that create dominant position are prohibited, this prohibition should normally be expected to prohibit the cases of collective dominance as well. Although the Turkish Competition Board seems to depend on this approach implicitly when blocking mergers that cannot pass the SLC test at the background, the Appeal Court rejected the Turkish Competition Board's decisions

---

[64]Decision of Turkish Competition Board dated 02.05.2000 and numbered 00-16/160-82 (Cisco/IBM) in which Cisco is market leader in switch market in terms of market shares and the transaction is found not to strengthen dominant position. See also Decision of Turkish Competition Board dated 10.02.2000 and numbered 00-6/51-23.

[65]According to the OECD this policy is an application of the standard multifactor analysis to concentrations. (OECD 2002), (OECD 2005).

based on this approach in 2005. These are Ladik Cement[66] and Şanlıurfa Cement[67] decisions, and they were the first prohibition decisions on collective dominance. The focus point was the questioned ability of the Turkish regime to prohibit a transaction where there is no creation of a single dominance but a collective dominance.

Ladik Cement decision has been brought to appeal before the Council of State, and it has been granted a stay of execution[68] on the grounds that the Turkish merger control regime cannot prohibit a transaction that leads to collective dominance but the creation of single dominant position. Nevertheless, the controversy whether the Turkish merger regime allows the prohibition of a transaction leading to collective dominance has not been finalized as the plaintiff has withdrawn the case and the High Council of State has not reached its final judgment.

Recent decisions demonstrate that the Turkish Competition Board follows its approach that the concept of collective dominance is subject to evaluation within Article 7 of the Antitrust Act and the Merger Communiqué. In one of these decisions concerning the acquisition of Lipman Electronics by Verifone Inc,[69] the Turkish Competition Board ruled that Verifone does not hold a dominant position in postmerger POS devices market due to the strong presence of Ingenico, even though Verifone has a market share of over 50%. However, the Turkish Competition Board stated that due to the oligopolistic and concentrated market structure, the transaction concerned has to be analyzed within the concept of collective dominance likely to be created by Verifone and Ingenico. It pointed out the following facts:

(a) POS devices market is a constantly growing, technology-based market and is prevailed by buyer power as the demand varies according to the the needs of customers.
(b) Nontransparency in the market arises from the sealed-bid tender processes enforced by the buyer banks of POS devices.
(c) Import facilities and tendency of buyer banks to work with more than one supplier make the coordination between competitors difficult.

Therefore, the Turkish Competition Board concluded that collective dominance cannot be created in such market conditions.

*Procedural Issues*

(a) Is the Final Agreement Between the Parties Required for the *Assessment?*

To start assessing a transaction, Article 7 of the Antitrust Act practice appraises the final consent of the parties for a proposed transaction as a prerequisite for the

---

[66] Decision of Turkish Competition Board dated 20.12.2005 and numbered 05-86/1188-340 dated 20.12.2005.

[67] Decision of Turkish Competition Board dated 20.12.2005 and numbered 05-86/1191-343.

[68] Decision of 13th Chamber of High State Council No. 2005/10038.

[69] Decision of Turkish Competition Board dated 13.04.2009 and numbered 09-14/300-73.

initiation of competitive assessment. This mutual consent is usually present via a Sale Purchase Agreement, Memorandum of Understanding, binding offers signed by the parties. However, the established enforcement of the Turkish Competition Board demonstrates that it also evaluates and clears transactions that are notified with framework agreements or binding consensus of the parties with no final agreements. This may show that the Turkish Competition Board also follows the practice of the Commission in cases where the parties present their binding consent for the realization of the proposed transaction. It has to be emphasized that the Notification Form of the recently enacted M&A Communiqué indicates that the final agreement between the parties is not required for the assessment of the Competition Authority since it demands the copy of final or draft agreement.

Even though the recently enacted Merger Communiqué remain silent on the issue, the Turkish Competition Board, in its decision dated 06.01.2010, numbered 10-01/13-8, also cleared the hostile takeover (Gürtler and Kräkel 2009, pp. 3–4) of Cadbury by Kraft Foods. In this case, the Turkish Competition Board accepted the notification made right after the public announcement of intention to make an offer in accordance with EU enforcement. However, it obliged Kraft to submit the final offer to the Turkish Competition Board.

(b) What Is the Time Table for the Clearance?

*Preliminary Investigation (Phase I)* As long as the transaction concerned does not pose a competitive concern, the Turkish Competition Board has to decide on a concentration transaction notified to it in 15 days starting from the date of receiving the notification file completely and accurately. However, the Turkish Competition Board is entitled to ask for additional information and documents which resets the 15 days.

Accordingly, a time table of 15 days for the first evaluation, 15 days for the submission of a possible additional information requested by the Turkish Competition Board, 15 days for reevaluation, 10 days for its decision, plus 10 days for notification of short decision is needed. So, if there is no unforeseen situation to clear the transaction, a maximum of 65 days is needed.

*Final Investigation (Phase II)* If the Turkish Competition Board decides to deal with the transaction under final investigation after Phase I procedure due to the competitive concerns, it is obliged to duly notify the parties, with its preliminary objection letter, that the merger or acquisition transaction is suspended and cannot be put into practice until the final decision, together with other measures deemed necessary by it. During this final investigation period, the Turkish Competition Board has 6 months to grant a final decision. If deemed necessary, this period may be extended once by up to 6 months by the Board.

(c) Does Failure of Notification/Closing Before Authorization Require Fines?

Where a merger and acquisition transaction whose notification to the Turkish Competition Board is compulsory is not notified to the Turkish Competition Board, the Board shall deal with the merger or acquisition under examination on its own initiative. As a result of this examination, the Board either authorizes or rejects the completion of the transaction; both undertakings in a merger or the purchaser in an acquisition are imposed fines up to 0.1% of the turnover of the undertakings concerned due to failure to notify. Aside from this administrative penalty, transactions leading to concentration are void.

If the Turkish Competition Board establishes that the transaction shall be prohibited, it terminates the transaction together with fines up to 10% and removes all de facto legal consequences of every action that has been taken.

## 5.5 Consequences of Violations and Enforcement Institutions

### *5.5.1 Administrative Enforcement*

The Turkish Competition Board is the only administrative institution legally authorized to implement the Antitrust Act. As an independent regulatory agency, the Turkish Competition Board has the power to impose administrative sanctions under following articles:

- Article 10 – Notification of Mergers and Acquisitions to the Turkish Competition Board
- Article 13 – Revocation of Exemption and Negative Clearance Decisions
- Article 16 – Administrative Fine
- Article 17 – Proportional Administrative Fine

These provisions mainly set forth an enforcement system for the Turkish Competition Board to take administrative decisions and impose administrative fines against anticompetitive conduct.

In this section of our study, we start our analysis of consequences of violations and enforcement institutions with the Turkish Competition Board and its sanctions. Later on, we cover civil enforcement.

#### 5.5.1.1 The Turkish Competition Board

Formation and Composition

The Turkish Competition Board is actually composed of the Turkish Competition Authority and its decision making body, the Competition Board. The Turkish Competition Board commenced its function 3 years after the enactment of the Antitrust Act in 1994. The Turkish Competition Board is headquartered in Ankara but has only a liaison office in Istanbul.

The Turkish Competition Board is autonomous, and thus it is independent when discharging its duties. No organ, authority, or person may give commands and orders to influence the final decision of the Board. The Board's decisions can be considered as semijudicial decisions granted by an administrative agency.

The Turkish Competition Board consists of the Board, the Office of the President, Main Service Units, Auxiliary Service Units, and Advisory Units of a total of seven members, including the Chairman and the Deputy Chairman. The Presidency is formed of the Chairman of the Turkish Competition Board/President of the Authority, Deputy Chairman/President, and Vice Presidents. The Chairman is the highest ranking official of the Authority and is responsible for the overall management and representation.

The Main Service Units carry out the cases by competition experts and assistant experts. They are organized as departmental Head Offices, where each department is in charge of particular industries assigned to them.

The Turkish Competition Board gives decisions for each case reported by the Main Service Unit departments. According to Article 23 of the Antitrust Act, the Chairman and members shall be appointed from those who have had a 4-year higher education in one of the departments of law, economics, engineering, management, or finance. And finally The Competition Board has 7 members coming from different institutions. The selection process of the Board Members are outlined in the Article 22 as follow:

> The Council of Ministers elects and appoints the members from among the two candidates apiece, to be nominated from inside or outside the following institutions for each vacant membership: two members from the Competition Board, one member from the Ministry of Industry and Trade, one member from the Ministry of State with which the Undersecretariat of State Planning Organization is affiliated, and one member apiece from the Supreme Court of Appeal, Council of State, and Turkish Union of Chambers and Commodity Exchanges.
>
> The Council of Ministers shall commission one of the three candidates to be nominated by the Board as the President/Chairman. The Deputy President/Chairman is elected by the members of the Board.

## Investigative Powers

In accordance with the Antitrust Act, an investigation may be commenced on a complaint, information or a notification, or the Authority may initiate the procedure ex officio. The investigation shall be concluded within 6 months, and where it is deemed necessary, the Turkish Competition Board may grant an additional period of 6 months only once. In Turkey, the Turkish Competition Board is competent with respect to the investigative measures including "*Request for Information*" and "*On-the-Spot Inspection.*"

First, request for information is cited in Article 14 of the Antitrust Act as follows:

> In carrying out the duties assigned to it by this Act, the Board may request any information it deems necessary from all public institutions and organizations, undertakings, and associations of undertakings.
>
> Officials of these authorities, undertakings, and associations of undertakings are obliged to provide the requested information within the period to be determined by The Board.

Accordingly, the article states that the Turkish Competition Board may be in need of detailed information to perform its duties. It shall obtain such information primarily from the concerned undertakings and associations of undertakings. In addition to this, it might need to obtain some information from several public organizations and private undertakings. Organizations other than the concerned parties may not deny the request of the Turkish Competition Board for information and document, either.[70]

But main flow of evidence comes from another mechanism, which is outlined in Article 15 of the Antitrust Act. This article sets forth the specifics of the on-the-spot inspection:

> In carrying out the duties assigned to it by this Act, the Board may perform examinations at undertakings and associations of undertakings in cases it deems necessary. To this end, it is entitled to:
>
> (a) Examine the books, any paperwork and documents of undertakings and associations of undertakings, and take their copies if needed
> (b) Request written or oral statement on particular issues
> (c) Perform examinations on the spot with regard to any assets of undertakings
>
> Examination is performed by experts employed at the disposal of the Board. While going for an examination, experts carry with them an authorization certificate showing the subject matter and purpose of the examination, and that an administrative fine shall be imposed should incorrect information be provided. Those concerned are obliged with providing the copies of information, documents, books and other instruments requested. In case an on-the-spot inspection is hindered or likely to be hindered, the on-the-spot inspection is performed with the decision of a criminal magistrate.

Both of the articles involve the terms of "*in carrying out the duties assigned to it by this Act*"; as it is seen, the Turkish Competition Board's discretion on using the investigative powers is defined very widely. Although the inspection does not cover "searching," the authorization to search is used in practice. *"The books, any paperwork and documents"* expressions stated in the Antitrust Act may stand for "books and other business records" in EU legislation (Yolcu 2003, pp. 49–50). However, differently from search, any power to use force or search of the person is not within the authorities of the Turkish Competition Board. In this framework, inspection can be performed on any kind of assets of an undertaking where it operates in terms of commercial activities (rooms, warehouses, garages, vehicles of buildings, safes, cabinets, drawers, bags located in rooms; computers, CDs, floppy disks, cassettes involving audio and image records, etc.) (The Seminar 2005). Finally, evidence not falling under the scope of the authorization allowing the inspection may be used as evidence in another case (ICN 2009).

---

[70] Grounds for the Article 14 of the Antitrust Act.

#### 5.5.1.2 Administrative Fines

The Antitrust Act foresees a strict investigation procedure to impose fine on undertakings up to 10% of the annual gross revenue. Article 16 and article 17 set forth the conditions for imposing fines.

Article 16 states the authorization to impose fines for the following cases: (a) false or misleading information or documents is provided in exemption and negative clearance applications and in authorization applications for mergers and acquisitions, (b) mergers and acquisitions that are subject to authorization are realized without the authorization of the Turkish Competition Board, (c) in implementation of Articles 14 and 15 of the Antitrust Act, incomplete, false, or misleading information or document is provided, or information or document is not provided within the determined duration or at all, and (d) on-the-spot inspection is hindered or complicated. For instance, the Turkish Competition Board has imposed a 11200 TL fine on Reysaş on the grounds that on-the-spot inspection was hindered and complicated.[71]

Provided that penalties mentioned in Article 16 paragraph 1 are reserved, according to Article 17, the Turkish Competition Board shall, for each day, impose on undertakings and associations of undertakings an administrative fine by five in ten thousand of annual gross revenues in the event that (a) obligations introduced or commitments made by a final decision or interim measure decision are not complied with, (b) on-the-spot inspection is hindered or complicated, (c) in implementation of Articles 14 and 15 of the Antitrust Act, information or document requested is not provided within the duration determined. Besides, Article 16 also specifies that

> issues taken into consideration in fixing administrative fines to be imposed pursuant to this article, terms for immunity from or reduction of fines in case of cooperation, and procedures and principles in relation to cooperation shall be determined by communiqués to be issued by the Board.

From this point of view, the Turkish Competition Board introduced “Regulation on Active Cooperation for Detecting Cartels” and “Regulation on Fines to Apply in Cases of Agreements, Concerted Practices and Decisions Limiting Competition, and Abuse of Dominant Position” in 2009. Under the new regime, the fines begin from (a) 2–4%, for cartels and (b) 0.5–3%, for abuse of dominance. The Turkish Competition Board will apply aggravating and extenuating factors to the above-stated base fines.

As a result of these two regulations aiming at increasing transparency, objectivity, and consistency and ensuring deterrence of anticompetitive practices, the fines applied in this legal framework increased significantly in 2009 (Directorate for Financial and Enterprise Affairs Competition Committee 2010). The highest fine on a single undertaking up to now is TL 36,072,230, which was imposed on Turkcell.[72]

---

[71] Decision of Turkish Competition Board dated 11.11.2009 and numbered 09-54/1320-M.

[72] Mobile Marketing Decision dated 23.12.2009 and numbered 09-60/1490-379.

#### 5.5.1.3 Administrative Injunctions

In general, the Turkish Competition Board's tendency is to give injunctions to the relevant parties involved in a competition infringement. For instance, in its decision regarding Audit Bureau of Circulation (ABC)'s discriminatory anticompetitive practices against a newspaper (Zaman), the Board decided that an investigation was not required to be opened in accordance with Article 41 of the Antitrust Act. But the Turkish Competition Board concluded that ABC's practices resulted in harming the market mechanism and invalidated its inspection results. In the decision, the Turkish Competition Board rejected the inspection results provided by ABC and gave an additional 90 days period to set new standards that may enable all media and press institutions to be represented equally and prevent any privileges to newspapers working on a subscription basis, and it withdrew the exemption granted to ABC Corporation Agreement.[73]

#### 5.5.1.4 Interim Measures

In the case of urgency due to the risk of serious and irreparable damage to competition, the Turkish Competition Board may order interim measures prior to taking a decision on the merits of the case. Article 9 of the Antitrust Act states the following:

> where the occurrence of serious and irreparable damages is likely until the final decision, the Board may take interim measures, which have a nature of maintaining the situation before the infringement and which shall not exceed the scope of the final decision.

The article provides the methods that the Turkish Competition Board shall follow, in case of infringements of the Articles 4, 6, and 7, to terminate the infringements and states that the Turkish Competition Board can take interim measures if there are strong signs that show that serious and irreparable damages may occur before the final decision is made.[74] For instance, the Turkish Competition Board, in TTNET Decision,[75] had taken an interim measure to terminate price squeeze practices, before the final decision was given. Türk Telekom and TTNET terminated the relevant practices in compliance with the interim measure.[76]

### 5.5.2 *Civil Enforcement*

The Antitrust Act adopted a dual enforcement system. Besides the Turkish Competition Board, the civil courts also have the jurisdiction to apply the Turkish Antitrust Law. To this end, Articles 56–59 set out specific provisions about the civil

---

[73] Decision of Turkish Competition Board dated 24.4.2007 and numbered 07-34/347-127.

[74] Grounds for the Article 9 of the Antitrust Act. No. 4054.

[75] Decision of Turkish Competition Board dated 19.11.2008 and numbered 08-65/1055-411.

[76] Decision of Turkish Competition Board dated 11.7.2007 and numbered 07-59/676-235.

law consequences of antitrust violations. According to these provisions, civil enforcement is based on two pillars: "*nullity*" and "*tortious liability.*" It is clear that by drafting specific provisions, the lawmaker intended to increase the effectiveness of the enforcement of the Antitrust Act. However, currently, the civil enforcement seems underdeveloped, and reconsideration of the relevant provisions of the Antitrust Act might be necessary to increase the deterrence of the civil enforcement.[77] Below, the application of civil law consequences is explained in detail.

#### 5.5.2.1 Nullity

According to Article 56 of the Antitrust Act, any agreement contrary to Article 4 of the Antitrust Act is void and unenforceable before the courts. The provision does not set out the nature of the nullity. However, as Article 4 is a mandatory provision, which aims to protect public interest, its violation should lead to ab initio and *automatic* nullity. Nullity occurs without a need for any proceeding or legal action; the court will take nullity into account on its own initiative. However, nullity is not absolute because if Article 5 applies to the case, then the agreement restricting the competition becomes lawful. So, the probability of application of Article 5 transforms this nullity into a "*provisional*" one. Absolute nullity exists only if the conditions of Article 5 are not satisfied (Sanlı 2007, p. 18; Gürzumar 2002, p. 53; Özdemir 2002, p. 177; (Aslan 2007, p. 770).[78] Both types of exemptions validate the agreement restricting competition; however, in the case of individual exemption, a decision of the Turkish Competition Board is required. This complicates the application of nullity by courts as the Turkish Competition Board has monopoly over granting an exemption decision. This is one of the factors that impede the effectiveness of civil enforcement system.

The Antitrust Act does not contain any specific rule on the nullity of agreements contrary to Article 6, but given the wording and the purpose of Article 6, legal transactions contrary to that article should lead to some sort of nullity. As there is no exemption provision for Article 6, one may first think that absolute nullity applies in this case. However, considering the types of abusive behavior, this does not seem like an appropriate solution. In some cases, it is highly likely that invalidity of an agreement or a decision would be contrary to the end that the competition law seeks to achieve. For instance, applying absolute nullity in the case of predatory pricing will lead to absurd results. First, voidness of legal transactions with low prices will victimize third parties who are completely alien to the conflict, and punishing them does not serve a meaningful end. Second, many transactions will

---

[77] The Draft of Proposed Law has numerous new provisions on the civil law consequences of the Antitrust Act. For a detailed analysis of this matter, see (Sanlı 2007).

[78] However, there are conflicting views about the nature of the nullity. See for example (Aksoy 2004, p. 45).

become void, and this will impose huge transaction costs on the legal system and seriously impair the principle of legal certainty. So, applying absolute nullity across the board is not a good solution. However, in some cases, such as exclusive dealing, invalidating contracts appears to be a fitting sanction. In those cases, by invalidating these contracts, parties will be free to make a contract with third parties, and the foreclosure effect will be diminished. Thus, with respect to Article 6, it seems that nullity should be applied based upon the discretion of the judge analyzing the case (Sanlı 2007, p. 16; also see Aslan 2007, p. 783). This type of nullity exists in Turkish private law and is named "*discretionary nullity.*"

The Antitrust Act does not have any explicit provision with respect to the civil law consequences of the mergers and acquisitions that are contrary to Article 7. However, considering the nature of Article 7 and some other rules (Article 10, 11) in the Antitrust Act, there is no doubt that the legal sanction of Article 7 is "*absolute nullity*"(Sanlı 2000a, p. 445). Here, nullity applies as a consequence of not only substantial infringements but also procedural violation. According to the second paragraph of Article 7, "The Board shall declare, via communiqués to be issued by it, the types of mergers and acquisitions which have to be notified to The Turkish Competition Board and for which permission has to be obtained, in order them to become legally valid." The Turkish Competition Board has issued the communiqué, and this rule is repeated in Article 1 of that legal document. So, mergers and acquisitions falling within the Communiqué are not valid, until an explicit or implicit decision is granted by the Turkish Competition Board. In that time frame, the nullity of transactions is provisional in nature (Sanlı 2000a, p. 446; Aksoy 2004, p. 41).

#### 5.5.2.2 Damages

The main component of the civil enforcement is obviously tort liability of antitrust offenders.[79] The Antitrust Act explicitly grants rights to third parties to claim damages and provides some unique provisions with an aim to increase the effectiveness of the civil enforcement. According to Article 57, "Anyone who prevents, distorts, or restricts competition via practices, decisions, contracts, or agreements contrary to this Act, or abuses his dominant position in a particular market for goods or services, is obliged to compensate for any damages of the injured. If the damage has resulted from the behavior of more than one people, they are responsible for the damage jointly." From the wording of this rule, it appears that infringing Article 7 does not lead to a damage action. This proposition makes sense since concentrations are controlled *ex ante* and infringing Article 7 rarely causes any recoverable damage. So, it is possible to argue that losses resulting from infringement of Article 7 are not within the protective sphere of Article 7 (Sanlı 2003, pp. 230–231; Gürzumar

[79] For a detailed analysis of tort liability in Turkish Antitrust Law see (Sanlı 2003).

2005, pp. 150–151; İnan 2002, pp. 609–610). However, this matter is controversial in Turkish law, and there are opposite views (Aslan 2007, p. 784; Güven 2005, p. 515; Topçuoğlu 2001, p. 310).

The first paragraph of Article 58 provides a provision on the calculation of damages. According to the article: "Those who suffer as a result of the prevention, distortion, or restriction of competition may claim as a damage the difference between the cost they paid and the cost they would have paid if competition had not been limited. Competing undertakings affected by the limitation of competition may request that all of their damages are compensated by the undertaking or undertakings which limited competition. In determining the damage, all profits expected to be gained by the injured undertakings are calculated by taking into account the balance sheets of the previous years as well." There are two things worth mentioning about this article. The first is that it does not provide a unique principle about calculating damages. Should there be no explicit provision, general principles of damage calculation would govern the matter in the same way. Second, the article expresses that the competitors have a standing, but it does not limit the scope of litigants. Therefore, in the light of expansive wording, it seems that both consumer and nonrival undertakings have a standing.

The second paragraph of Article 58 sets out an interesting and problematical provision. According to the article, "If the resulting damage arises from an agreement or decision of the parties, or from cases involving gross negligence of them, the judge may, upon the request of the injured, award compensation by threefold of the material damage incurred or of the profits gained or likely to be gained by those who caused the damage." This is a unique provision for Turkish law as it enables the injured parties to claim three times their damages. The general principle in Turkish private law is that the compensation is limited to the amount of damages. So, by allowing victims to ask for three times their damages, the compensatory nature of the damage action becomes punitive in the Turkish Antitrust Law. The rationale of this rule, which probably was inspired by the Clayton Act of the USA, is to facilitate private actions by creating financial incentives to antitrust victims (Sanlı 2003, p. 270; Gürzumar 2005, p. 169). Although currently there is not much private antitrust litigation, this rule, if correctly interpreted, will no doubt increase the enforcement of private competition law.

An important error in the wording of the provision is that, it mentions "agreement or decision" as if these concepts are related to the state of mind of an antitrust offender or faultiness. Such wording is interpreted theologically and understood as "intentional" (Sanlı 2003, p. 270; Aksoy 2004, p. 58).[80] So, the judge may award three times compensation, if the resulting damage arises from intentional or gross negligent behavior of the antitrust offenders. It should also be mentioned that, unlike the US practice, the judge may, based upon his/her discretion, award one or twofold damages (Sanlı 2003, p. 271). The factors affecting discretion will be determined according to the general principles in Turkish private law (Articles 43–44 of the Code of Obligation).

---

[80] That wording has been corrected in the Draft Law see (Sanlı 2007, pp. 47–48).

Article 59 provides a provision that shifts the burden of proof to the defendant in cartel cases. According to the article: "Should the injured submit to the jurisdictional bodies proofs such as, particularly, actual partitioning of markets, stability observed in the market price for quite a long time, the price increase within close intervals by the undertakings operating in the market, which give the impression of the existence of an agreement, or the distortion of competition in the market, then the burden of proof is for the defendants that the undertakings are not engaged in concerted practice. The existence of agreements, decisions and practices limiting competition may be proved by any kind of evidence." This rule is in line with presumption of concerted practice, which is governed by Article 4/3. So, the Antitrust Act seeks to ease the burden of proof not only for the Turkish Competition Board but also for private plaintiffs.

The principles regarding antitrust damages in the Antitrust Act are limited to these articles. So, other conditions of tort liability are governed by general principles of private law. In this regard, apart from sustaining damages and illegal behavior, fault and causality will be required to recover damages. Issues regarding limitation, competent courts, and evidence are also regulated under general principles of private and procedural law. However, there are certain unique matters of competition law litigation for which general principles of Turkish law may not produce adequate solutions: for instance, issue of "passing-on defence." According to this defense rule, which was borne in the US litigation practice, the defendant argues that the plaintiff did not sustain whole or part of the damage (price increase) because by reflecting the price increase to its customers, the burden of price increase is dispersed in the different levels of the economic chain. So, to recover damages, the plaintiff should prove that as a customer, it not only paid a monopoly price, but also absorbed the premium and did not pass on the premium to its customers. The Turkish law seems silent on this issue, and it would be useful to unambiguously address this matter in the Antitrust Act (Sanlı 2007, p. 68).

Similarly, it is not clear whether the customers in downstream markets, who may sustain damages as a result of the passing on of the price premium, have a standing to sue for their damages. In the US litigation, the Supreme Court solved the problem by denying the indirect purchaser's claims in a famous case of Illinois Brick Co. v. Illinois,[81] and the principle is known as "Illinois Brick rule." Despite the fact that indirect purchasers might have been genuinely injured by the antitrust violation, it seems likely that the "relational economic loss rule" of Turkish private law would bar their claim. Besides, allowing indirect buyers to sue for their damages would significantly burden the enforcement system. However, that matter is controversial (Sanlı 2003, p. 240; Topçuoğlu 2001, p. 303).

The Antitrust Act does not contain any provision regarding the relation between the courts and the Turkish Competition Board either. It is unambiguous that both institutions have jurisdiction regarding the application of the Antitrust Act. As a general matter, when that is the case, there is a risk of contradictory judgments and

[81] Illinois Brick Co. v. Illinois, 431 U.S. 720 (1977).

it seems difficult to deal with this risk under Turkish law. Similar to this risk, the legal effect of an earlier decision granted by an institution, i.e., the Turkish Competition Board, on the other institution's decision-making process, i.e., of courts, is not clear. Unfortunately, the recent judgments of the Court of Appeals on the matter further complicate the issue. Accordingly, in the majority of the cases decided by the Court of Appeals, the Turkish Competition Board has the sole authority on the determination of infringement, and the courts have a jurisdiction only after the Turkish Competition Board has given a verdict on the conflict.[82] Should there be no verdict of the Turkish Competition Board, the courts have to refer the matter to the Turkish Competition Board and postpone the judgment until the Board makes a decision. This view apparently diminishes the effectiveness of private enforcement and frustrates the purpose of the dual enforcement system. However, in a minority of decisions, the Court of Appeals accepted the view that courts can decide on the infringement of the Antitrust Act without referring the case to the Turkish Competition Board.[83] This is a crucial matter for efficient operation of the system, and especially for follow-on cases, we are of the opinion that there should be clarity about legal effects.[84]

## 5.6 Conclusion

Turkish Antitrust Act, being a relatively new law, not surprisingly various problems occurred during its 13 years of enforcement. For instance, almost all of the final decisions of the Turkish Competition Board have been quashed by the Council of the State on procedural grounds, and therefore, hundreds of repetitive decisions have been taken by the Turkish Competition Board. This legal setback not only diminished the effectiveness of the competition law but also created a lot of burden on the Turkish Competition Board, and for a long period, a fraction of its resources has been allocated to deal with this problem. Thankfully, the Turkish Competition Board reconsidered its methods of decision making and issued several regulations, which basically aim to increase the quality of the internal legal processes.

Another drawback that we notice when we look back is the tolerant and sometimes inconsistent enforcement policy pursued by the Turkish Competition Board. Despite the fact that substantive law was very well developed during the 13 years

[82] The Court of Appeals, 19. HD 1.11.1999 Date., File no: E 99/3350, K.99/6364; The Court of Appeals 19. HD 3.1.2003 Date., File no: E.2002/2827, K.2002/7580; The Court of Appeals 19 HD. 29.11.2002 Date. File no: 2002/2827 E. and 2002/7580 K.., The Court of Appeals 19. HD. 6.11.2006 date and File no 2006/2809 K., 2006/10346 E.

[83] The Court of Appeals 13. HD. 25.12.2002 date and file no: 2002/12626 E. 2002/14028; The Court of Appeals, 19. HD. 21.4.2005 date and file no: 2004/9634E. and 2005/4463 K.

[84] For a detailed examination of relations between courts and the Turkish Competition Authority, see (Sanlı 2003, pp. 255–265; also İnan 2002, pp. 590–628).

of implementation, for some reason, the Turkish Competition Board followed a weak enforcement policy. We have observed this not only for vertical restraints and mergers but also for cartels. That attitude has been changing in a positive direction as well. In early 2009, the Turkish Competition Board has issued two important regulations that aim to increase the deterrence and to attain consistency in its enforcement policy. Application of the Fine Regulation increased the amount of fines substantially. This development together with the Leniency Regulation totally changed the enforcement policy toward cartels. It is also observed that the level of investigations has been increasing for the past 3 years, which should be considered as an improvement.

Finally, a few words should be expressed about the legislative endeavors of the Turkish Competition Board and the prospects of the competition law. As just mentioned, it is likely that more vigorous enforcement policy will be implemented, and thanks to new regulations about decision-making processes, the quality of decisions will be improved, which will in turn decrease the amount of reversal decisions of the State Council. It is also probable that the Turkish Competition Board will continue its efforts on legislative activities, which have been already very intensive in the past. There is a Draft of the Antitrust Act waiting in the legislative process, and should that be adopted by the Parliament, there will be major changes in competition law including exemption, mergers, and investigation methods. This law will also drastically alter and improve the current system. Another important development should be expected in the private enforcement system. The Draft already contains new provisions regarding the private law consequences of the competition law, which might enhance the effectiveness of the civil enforcement. Besides, the Turkish Competition Board has given many infringement decisions, and one should expect "follow-on cases" brought by antitrust victims.

## References

Aksoy, N. (2004). Rekabetin Korunması Hakkında Kanun'a Aykırılığın Özel Hukuk Alanındaki Sonuçları. Ankara.

Aslan, Y. (2007). Rekabet Hukuku. Bursa.

Directorate for Financial and Enterprise Affairs Competition Committee. (2010). Annual Report on Competition Policy Developments in Turkey.

Erol, K. (2000). Rekabet Kurallarının Ülke Dışı Uygulanması. Rekabet Kurumu Yayını.

Gürtler, O., Kräkel, M. (2009). HostileTakeover and Costly Merger Control.

Gürzumar, O. B. (2002). 4054 Sayılı Rekabetin Korunması Hakkında Kanun'un 4. Maddesine Aykırı Sözleşmelerin Tabi Olduğu Geçersizlik Rejimi. Rekabet Dergisi, S.12, pp. 3–76.

Gürzumar, O. B. (2005). Özel Hukuk Açısından 4054 Sayılı Kanun. 4054 Sayılı Rekabetin Korunması Hakkında Kanun ve Bu Kanun'da Değişiklik Yapılmasına İlişkin Taslak, Sempozyum, 7-8 Ekim 2005; Banka ve Ticaret Hukuku Araştırma Enstitüsü Yayın No 426; Ankara, pp. 117–184.

Güven, P. (2005). Rekabet Hukuku. Ankara.

İnan, N. (2002). Rekabet Hukuku Uygulamasında Adliye Mahkemelerinin Rolü. Ankara Barosu Uluslar arası Hukuk Kurultayı, pp. 590–628.

International Competition Network (ICN). (2009). Anti-Cartel Enforcement Template. Subgroup 2: Enforcement Techniques: Turkey.
Jones, A., Sufrin, B. (2004). EC Competition Law: Text, Cases and Materials, New York: Oxford University Press.
Monti, M. (2003). The Relationship Between CAP and Competition Policy. Does EU Competition Law Apply to Agriculture? COGECA Conference Helsinki Fair Trade.
OECD. (2002). Competition Law and Policy in Turkey.
OECD. (2005). Competition Law and Policy in Turkey.
Özdemir, O. S. (2002). Sınai Haklara İlişkin Lisans Sözleşmeleri ve Rekabet Hukuku Düzenlemelerinin Lisans Sözleşmelerine Uygulanması. Istanbul.
Sanlı, K. C. (2000). Rekabetin Korunması Hakkındaki Kanun'da Öngörülen Yasaklayıcı Hükümler ve Bu Hükümlere Aykırı Sözleşme ve Teşebbüs Birliği Kararlarının Geçersizliği.
Sanlı, K. C. (2000b). Relabet Hukukunda Tekelci Fiyatlandırma, Perşembe Konferansları, S.10, Rekabet Kurumu Yayını Ankara, pp. 75–165.
Sanlı, K. C. (2003). Rekabet Hukukunda Haksız Fiil Sorumluluğu. Rekabet Hukukunda Güncel Gelişmeler Sempozyumu I. Konferans Kitabı (editör Ayşe Odman Boztosun), Rekabet Kurumu Yayını, Ankara, pp. 211–277.
Sanlı, K. C. (2007). Rekabetin Koruması Hakkında Kanun Tasarısı Taslağı'nın Özel Hukuk Hükümlerinin Değerlendirilmesi, pp. 30–72.
Topçuoğlu, M. (2001). Rekabeti Kısıtlayan Teşebbüsler Arası İşbirliği Davranışları ve Hukuki Sonuçları. Ankara.
Yolcu, İ. (2003). Assessment of the Investigation Procedures in the Act No. 4054 on the Protection of Competition and the Procedural Problems Arising from their Implementation in Comparison with the EC Law.

# Part II
# Lessons from the Markets

# Chapter 6
# Regulation in the Turkish Electricity Industry

**Necmiddin Bağdadioğlu**

## 6.1 Introduction

This chapter focuses on the envisaged regulatory framework to be applied after the predefined transition period, which started in 2006, in the Turkish Electricity Industry ceases by the end of 2012. Then, it evaluates the performance of the Turkish electricity distribution companies under the envisaged incentive regulation scheme.

As in many countries undergoing reformation, the electricity reform in Turkey was largely motivated by the rising costs sustained as a result of the two major oil crises of 1970s, the fast-growing demand, and the lagging investments (Dubash 2003). Before 1980, the impact of these issues on the Turkish electricity industry was observed as frequently occurring blackouts. The situation was aggravated due to the overall financial burden imposed on the central budget for the new, renewal and maintenance investments needed in the electricity industry, as well as the poor performance of the integrated utility of the Turkish Electricity Board (TEK) under public ownership (World Bank 2005).

These issues required a change in the way in which the electricity industry was financed and managed in Turkey. This need was responded by the initiation of an ambitious electricity reform in the mid-1980s. The reform envisaged a market-oriented solution to end the blackouts, by both liberalizing the electricity market and inviting the private sector not only to invest in but also to run the electricity facilities. Although the necessary institutional, legal, and market arrangements were made, until the end of 2008 the reform did not progress as fast as it was planned.

In any case, the reform has brought a fundamental shift in the regulatory power over electricity market activities from the Ministry of Energy and Natural Resources (MENR) to the newly created sector regulator, the Energy Market Regulatory Authority (EMRA). Since then, EMRA has been responsible, among other issues, for ensuring that competition prevails in the electricity generation and supply parts of the electricity market, the electricity companies have equal and fair access to the

N. Bağdadioğlu (✉)
Department of Public Finance, Hacettepe University, Ankara, Turkey
e-mail: necbag@hacettepe.edu.tr

T. Çetin and F. Oğuz (eds.), *The Political Economy of Regulation in Turkey*,
DOI 10.1007/978-1-4419-7750-2_6, © Springer Science+Business Media, LLC 2011

naturally monopolistic transmission and distribution networks, and the tariff is reflective of the costs of electricity provision.

All these issues are accounted for in this chapter in three main sections. The following section tells the story of Turkish electricity industry reform briefly, since it is well covered elsewhere, for instance, in Bagdadioglu and Odyakmaz (2009). The third section outlines the regulatory framework which will be imposed on the activities of naturally monopolistic networks and captive customers after the end of transition period in 2012. The privatization process has started at the distribution side of the Turkish electricity industry, where the end-user tariff is designed to reflect costs, while meeting certain service quality measures. EMRA has already announced measures to incentivize the distribution companies that are cost conscious and quality conscious. Using the data of 2006, the starting year of transition period, published by TEDAS, the fourth section shows how EMRA could use the methodology of data envelopment analysis (DEA) as a tool for incentive regulation of the electricity distribution companies. The chapter concludes with an evaluation of these developments.

## 6.2 Reform in the Turkish Electricity Industry

The latest information on the progress of Turkish electricity reform is available in the "Teaser: Privatization of Turkey's Electricity Distribution Industry" published by Privatization Administration (2010). Hence, we utilize from this report as appropriate in this section.

### *6.2.1 Historical Development of Market Structure*

The reform in the Turkish electricity industry can be analyzed under three main periods as the pre-1993 period, the period between 1993 and 2003, and the period from 2003 to date as shown in Fig. 6.1.

From the establishment of TEK in 1970 to 1993, the Turkish electricity industry was run essentially as an integrated public monopoly, handling all four core production steps of electricity provision, namely, generation, transmission, distribution and supply, in one company. This is the traditional structure purportedly originated from the benefits of economies of vertical integration (Michaels 2004).

The reform in the Turkish electricity industry, commenced in the mid-1980s, has followed the sequences of liberalization, restructuring, creation of sector regulator, and privatization. These sequences are consistent with many applications in the reforming countries (Zhang et al. 2005).

Accordingly, first, the private investors were offered various financial schemes, namely, the transfer of operational rights (TOR) in 1984 with the Law No: 3096,

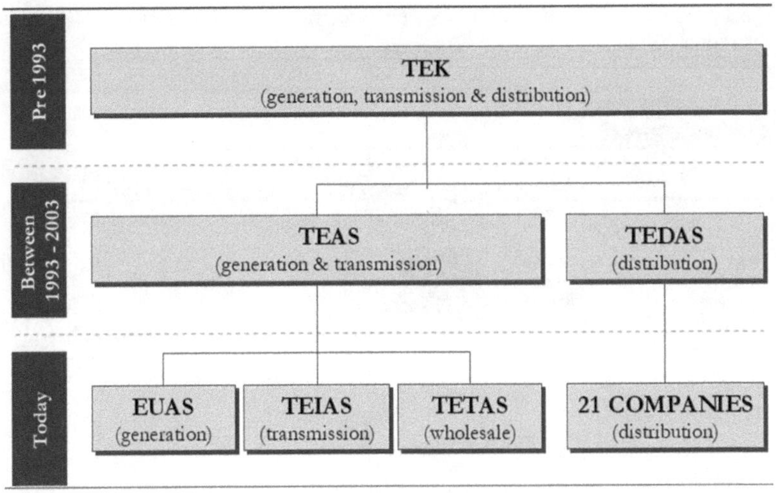


**Fig. 6.1** Historical development of market structure (Privatization Administration 2010)

the build–operate–transfer (BOT) in 1994 with the Law No: 3996, and the build–operate (BO) in 1997 with the Law No: 4283, to guarantee their participation in the Turkish electricity market. Meanwhile, at the beginning of the second period in 1993, TEK was divided into two public companies, as TEAS (generation and transmission) and TEDAS (distribution).

Despite these arrangements, the private participation in the electricity industry remained limited until the legal and institutional framework were completed by the announcement of the Electricity Market Law and the creation of EMRA in 2001 with the Law No: 4628. By the same Law, to ease privatization, TEAS was divided further into three companies, as EUAS (generation), TEIAS (transmission) and TETAS (wholesale), while TEDAS was reorganized so as to create 20 new publicly owned distribution companies. All companies were unbundled legally, as well.

Finally, as illustrated in Table 6.1, the timetable for the privatization of public electricity companies and the transition to the market-oriented electricity activities until the end of 2012 was determined by the Electricity Sector Reform and Privatization Strategy Paper (hereafter, the Strategy Paper) published in March 2004. The privatization of distribution companies were planned to commence at the beginning of 2005 to end by the end of 2006. Then, the generation companies were planned to be transferred to private sector between the mid-2006 and the end of 2009.

Nevertheless, the reform has not followed this timetable largely due to the unfavorable political climate derived from the strong opposition to privatization and the disagreement and power struggle among related public institutions over energy issues in Turkey (Cetin and Oguz 2007). Therefore, as discussed in the next section, only since the end of 2008 the privatization of distribution companies, and more recently of the power plants, has speeded up. However, today the electricity industry is still dominated by the public electricity companies.

**Table 6.1** Timetable for transition to new electricity market structure (Privatization Administration 2004)

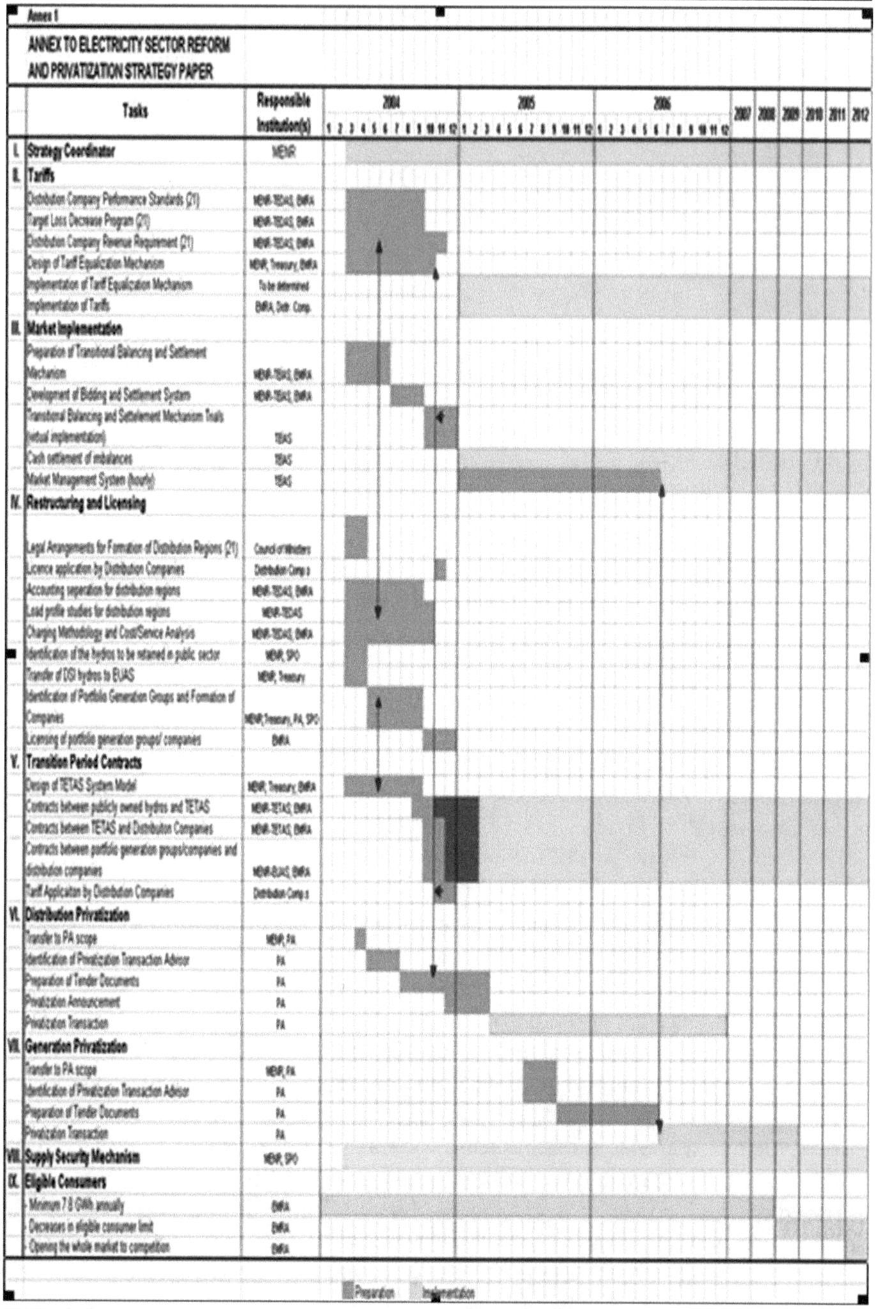

### 6.2.2 *Present Structure of the Turkish Electricity Industry*

Under the new industry structure, according to the most recent data of 2008 available from MENR, EUAS, which inherited the thermal power plants of TEAS and the hydroelectric power plants of the State Water Works, had 57% of the total installed generation capacity and generated 49% of electricity produced in Turkey. Meanwhile, the private producers (TOR, BOT, BO, and mobile power plants) and the auto-producers were generated 43 and 8% of the remaining electricity production, respectively.

The public company TEIAS, which was established by the transfer of all transmission networks from TEAS, was assigned with both the administration of transmission system operations and the operation of market financial reconciliation center. TETAS was particularly created to handle a number of important issues during the transition period, such as, to administer the wholesale operations, to take over the existing energy sale and purchase agreements from TEAS and TEDAS, and to manage the stranded costs related to TOR, BOT, and BO generation contracts. Lastly, as before, TEDAS was assigned with the task of electricity distribution and supply to end users.

As can be seen from Fig. 6.2, Turkey was almost self-sufficient in electricity in 2008. If the small amount of export and import of electricity was ignored, the total electricity generation was almost equal to the total electricity consumption in Turkey, which was around 200 TWh. However, considering that the average electricity demand has been increasing about 8% per year, the current installed generation capacity (41.987 MW) and the generation was expected at least to double by 2010.

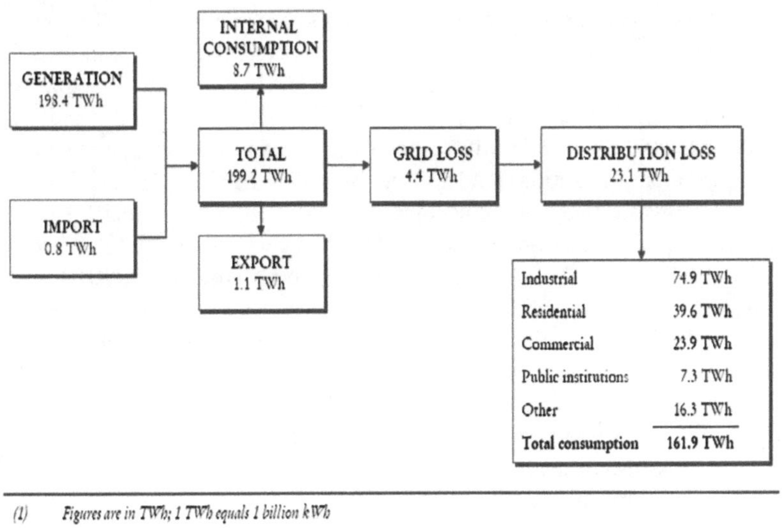


**Fig. 6.2** Generation and consumption, 2008 (Privatization Administration 2010)

However, this has not been materialized probably due to the impact of financial crisis, started in the USA in 2007, and then, spread worldwide (International Monetary Fund 2008), which brought with it a significant drop in electricity demand in Turkey. Moreover, a noticeable share of generated electricity, about 14%, was lost during the electricity delivery. The largest amount of losses (23.1 TWh) was in the distribution networks. Perhaps because of this reason, the electricity distribution companies (EDAŞs) were singled out as the primary privatization candidates in the Strategy Paper.

### *6.2.3 Current State of Privatization in Distribution Companies*

The distribution network was divided into 21 distribution areas in 2001, based on geographical closeness, energy demand, managerial structure, legal, and other technical and financial features. A separate distribution company was created in each distribution area, making 21 companies in total, 20 public and one private, which has been serving in and around Kayseri Province. The purchased electricity, the sold electricity, and the loss and theft values for each distribution area are given in Table 6.2. Kayseri has been the longest surviving private distribution company founded in 1926. However, the aforementioned values for Kayseri were not available, and thus, not included in Table 6.2.

The geographical location of the distribution companies is given in Map 6.1, where Kayseri EDAŞ is shown as Kcetas. TEDAS was included into the privatization portfolio of the Privatization Administration in 2005, but only since the last quarter of 2008 it has started to give up its shares in electricity distribution market. The Privatization Administration has privatized Başkent EDAŞ, Sakarya EDAŞ, and Meram EDAŞ in 2009. For Aras EDAŞ, Çoruh EDAŞ, Osmangazi EDAŞ, Yeşilirmak EDAŞ, Uludağ EDAŞ, Camlıbel EDAŞ, Fırat EDAŞ, and Vangölü EDAŞ, the privatization tenders have been completed and the transfer process is continuing. The privatization tenders for Boğazici EDAŞ, Dicle EDAŞ, Gediz EDAŞ, and Trakya EDAŞ will be accepted until the end of July 2010. Meanwhile, 52 hydroelectricity generation plants of EUAŞ has been divided into 19 groups and opened for tender in 2009, expected to be privatized by the end of 2010.

All aforementioned privatizations of distribution companies have been handled according to the Law No: 4826, while for Menderes EDAŞ and Göksu EDAŞ, the transfer procedure has been implemented according to the Law No: 3096. Nonetheless, TEDAS still has the largest share in electricity supply as only around 30% customers was eligible to obtain electricity through sources other than TEDAS in 2008.

All these privatization implementations have been executed under the TOR scheme supported by the share sale model. According to this model, the private investor will be the sole owner of the distribution company but not the electricity equipments. That is, the current assets and the new assets arising from investments carried out by the private investors will stay with TEDAS. Meanwhile, all investments approved by EMRA will be carried out by the private investor.

**Table 6.2** Purchased electricity, sold electricity, and loss and theft values in 2008

| No. | Regions | Purchased electricity (GWh) | Sold electricity (GWh) | Lost and theft (GWh) | Lost and theft (%) | Number of customers (million) |
|---|---|---|---|---|---|---|
| 1 | Dicle EDAŞ | 14,576 | 5,214 | 9,362 | 64.2 | 1.05 |
| 2 | Vangölü EDAŞ | 2,580 | 1,137 | 1,443 | 55.9 | 0.40 |
| 3 | Aras EDAŞ | 2,274 | 1,656 | 618 | 27.2 | 0.73 |
| 4 | Çoruh EDAŞ | 2,538 | 2,268 | 270 | 10.7 | 0.99 |
| 5 | Firat EDAŞ | 2,396 | 2,145 | 250 | 10.5 | 0.66 |
| 6 | Çamlıbel EDAŞ | 2,290 | 2,088 | 202 | 8.8 | 0.73 |
| 7 | Toroslar EDAŞ | 15,263 | 13,905 | 1,358 | 8.9 | 2.60 |
| 8 | Meram EDAŞ | 6,394 | 5,859 | 535 | 8.4 | 1.53 |
| 9 | Baskent EDAŞ | 12,167 | 11,161 | 1,005 | 8.3 | 3.08 |
| 10 | Akdeniz EDAŞ | 6,646 | 6,049 | 597 | 9.0 | 1.47 |
| 11 | Gediz EDAŞ | 14,797 | 13,862 | 935 | 6.3 | 2.34 |
| 12 | Uludağ EDAŞ | 11,643 | 10,941 | 702 | 6.0 | 2.28 |
| 13 | Trakya EDAŞ | 5,886 | 5,473 | 413 | 7.0 | 0.77 |
| 14 | Ayedaş | 9,491 | 8,672 | 819 | 8.6 | 2.10 |
| 15 | Sakarya EDAŞ | 9,349 | 8,760 | 588 | 6.3 | 1.31 |
| 16 | Osmangazi EDAŞ | 5,320 | 5,042 | 278 | 5.2 | 1.28 |
| 17 | Boğaziçi EDAŞ | 21,282 | 18,948 | 2,335 | 11.0 | 3.83 |
| 19 | Menderes EDAŞ | 3,982 | 3,815 | 167 | 4.2 | 1.51 |
| 20 | Göksu EDAŞ | 3,562 | 3,303 | 260 | 7.3 | 0.49 |
| 21 | Yeşilirmak EDAŞ | 4,467 | 4,063 | 405 | 9.1 | 1.48 |
| | Total | 156,901 | 134,360 | 22,542 | 14.4 | 30.62 |

*Source*: Privatization Administration (2010)

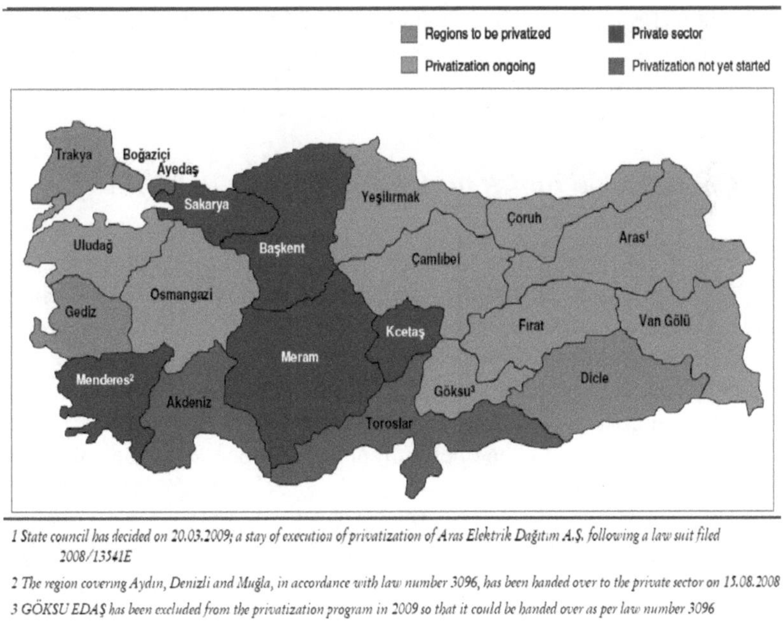


**Map 6.1** Current state of distribution companies (Privatization Administration 2010)

## 6.3 Regulatory Framework for the Turkish Electricity Industry

In addition to these investments, all other expenses and network losses will be covered by a cost reflective electricity tariff under the incentive-based regulation, as indicated in the Strategy Paper. However, the wide variations in network losses (Table 6.2) mean that this cost-based approach will unavoidably bring significantly different tariffs between distribution areas (Bağdadioğlu et al. 2009). To avoid the likely sudden price fluctuations and to ensure a smooth transition to the cost reflective tariff structure, the period between 2006 and 2010 was defined as the transition period. During this period, the existing national tariff scheme has been kept, and a tariff equalization scheme has been used to trim revenue imbalances between distribution areas. The end-user tariffs and revenue requirements of each distribution company were approved by EMRA for the first implementation period. In 2008, the transitory period and the implementation of tariff equalization scheme were extended to 2012 with the new Electricity Market Law No: 5784, which amended the Electricity Market Law 2001 (Higher Board of Planning 2009).

In any case, until the end of 2012, the distribution companies will be able to meet 85% of the electricity consumed by noneligible customers by signing energy sales agreements with TETAS and the EUAS portfolio companies based on regulated tariffs for the transition period. After the transition period terminates, each distribution company will be allowed to match its electricity demand by alternative sources, such as, spot market, bilateral contracts, and vertical integration. Meanwhile, TEIAS will handle daily market imbalances through the market balancing and settlement mechanism introduced at the beginning of the transition period in 2006 (Erdogdu 2010). For after 2012, EMRA will approve the new end-user tariffs for the distribution companies in line with the electricity market tariff communiqué and the related regulations.[1]

### *6.3.1 Composition and Regulation of End Users' Tariff*

As seen in Fig. 6.3, apart from taxes and other deduction components, the total end-user electricity tariff consists of four main components: the transmission tariff, the retail services tariff, the distribution system usage tariff, and the retail tariff. The taxes and deductions include the value-added tax, the municipality tax, and a share going to the energy and the Turkish Radio and Television Corporation fund. The transmission costs are directly reflected in the transmission tariff, which will be subject to a revenue cap. The operating and investment expenses of distribution

[1] The electricity market tariff regulations are determined by a series of communiqués, namely, the regulation of distribution system revenue, the regulation of retail service revenue and retail prices, the regulation of transmission system operation revenue, the regulation of transmission system revenue, and the determination of transmission and distribution connection charges; all communiqués are available at the Web site of EMRA (http://www.emra.gov.tr).

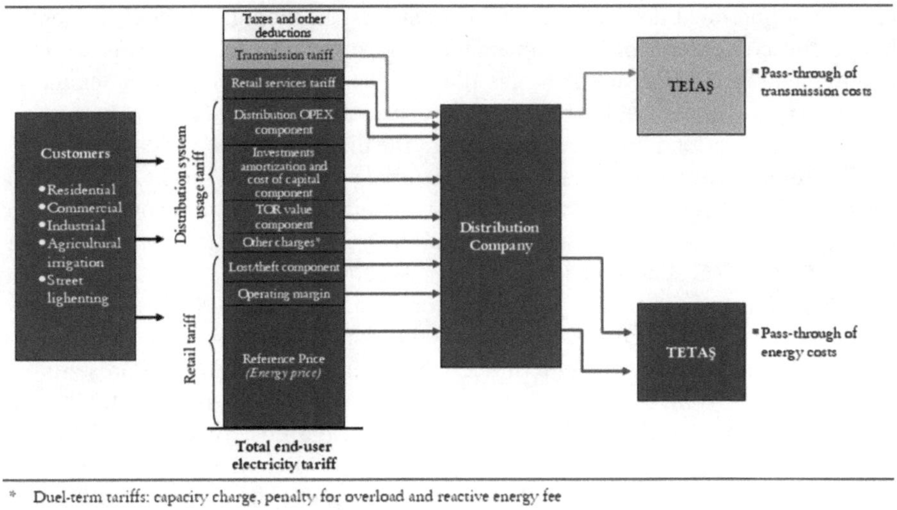


**Fig. 6.3** Decomposition of end-user tariff (Privatization Administration 2010)

and retail services will also be subject to a mixture of revenue cap/price cap, while the retail sales to noneligible customers will be price caped.

In addition to the total end-user tariff, customers will have to bear a distribution connection charge at the first time connection to the distribution network is established, a predetermined charge as a guarantee for nonpayment, and a disconnection/reconnection charge payable if a disconnection/reconnection occurs. The electricity generation and the supply to eligible customers are regarded as competitive; thus, apart from the entry into the market, which is by license from EMRA, the activities in generation market and in the aforementioned part of supply market will not be subject to direct regulation.

The revenue of distribution companies will be guaranteed regardless of the consumption levels in the distribution areas. That is, when a distribution company cannot earn enough revenue due to insufficient electricity demand, EMRA will adjust tariff for the next year. Additionally, the revenue caps valid until the end of 2012 will be adjusted by inflation according to the changes in the electricity market price index (EMPI) announced by EMRA. Meanwhile, the distribution company will be able to reflect any increases in its electricity costs to the retail price cap through a pass-through mechanism after EMRA's approval.

### *6.3.2 Determination of Revenue Requirements*[2]

The revenue requirements of each distribution company consist of the projected expenses for providing distribution and retail services and provide an allowance for the target level of network losses. The distribution company is expected to start the

[2] Necmi Odyakmaz's help at the writing stage of this subsection is gratefully acknowledged.

revenue requirement determination process at least 12 months, at most 18 months, before the completion of the implementation period and hand over its revenue requirements to EMRA until the last day of the last year of present regulatory period. The revenue requirements of the distribution system are determined for each implementation period and included in the distribution licenses.

The reference revenue is determined in three subsequent stages. At the first stage, the initial reference revenue (IRR) is determined. At the second stage, the revenue cap (RC) is defined, and the revenue is transformed into the tariff. And, at the third stage, RC is arranged and adjusted as required.

IRR is determined by the following formula: $\text{IRR} = Y + \text{OPEX} + P_{\text{new}}$, where $Y$ denotes the yield, OPEX stands for the forecasted operational costs for distribution activities at the end of account unbundling, and $P_{\text{new}}$ represents the payouts for new investments. $Y$ is calculated by multiplying the total asset value for yield (TAVY) with the weighted average cost of capital. TAVY is obtained by the formula: $\text{RAB} + I - P_{\text{old}}$, where, RAB corresponds to the total assets of company, which is called as stranded liabilities, $I$ refers to the new investments for capacity expansion, renewal and improvement during regulatory period, and $P_{\text{old}}$ symbolizes the payouts for old investments. At this stage, the demand forecast is very important since it will define the amounts of both $I$ and OPEX. The demand forecast is done by taking account of number of customers, total consumption of each customer groups, and capacity in terms of both MW and MWh.

The transformation of IRR into RC is one of the most essential parts of the foreseen incentive-based regulation. It involves determination of efficiency parameter $X$, quality indicators, network losses, and separation of fixed and variable costs. Only the efficiency parameter ($X$) is reflected to RC at the beginning of regulatory review period, while the quality indicators and targets for network losses are included into RC by 2 years delay according to their realizations. The predetermined $X$ parameter is calculated only for OPEX. The targets for network losses corresponds to realized (past 3 years), forecasted (present year), and planned (present regulatory period) targets. The quality indicators are taken as zero (0) for the first regulatory period in terms of network reliability and commercial quality. Lastly, the fixed and variable cost separation for distribution costs are used to protect distribution companies against demand fluctuations.

At the last stage of reference revenue determination process, RC is arranged and adjusted by the investment difference correction component (IDCC) and the revenue difference correction component (RDCC). IDCC is put into the system to prevent unfair yield stemming from unrealization of predetermined investments, or early realization of scheduled investment. RDCC is the correction component that aims to prevent distribution companies from unfair treat via reflection of unpredicted cost increases by EMPI to RC.

### 6.3.3 Incentive Regulation in Turkish Electricity Distribution

The aforementioned revenue/price cap regulation will be applied after 2012 in the new Turkish electricity industry. The price cap regulation is essentially the same as the revenue cap regulation, except that the company's price instead of revenue is capped by EMRA. This regulatory approach is regarded as superior to the traditional cost-based (rate of return) regulation, since under certain conditions it provides better incentives for network companies that are cost conscious (Joskow 2008).

In the cost-based regulation, the regulator sets the tariff for the network companies in such a way that they can cover all permitted production expenses, including a rate of return on capital invested, sufficient for the network companies to replace or expend electricity facilities. The tariff is adjusted as cost-level changes. Since the network companies know that they will be able to recover increasing costs with subsequent increase in tariff, they have essentially no incentive to operate efficiently. Moreover, they might overinvest in capital equipment to expend their rate base, as indicated by Averch and Johnson (1962). Since there is a positive correlation between capital and quality, the overinvestment in capital may lead to oversupply in quality.

In contrast, the revenue/price cap regulation determines the tariff for a predefined regulatory period, which is usually set from 3 to 5 years, and allow the network companies to benefit from any cost reduction they can achieve during that period. Thus, this regulatory approach gives strong incentive to the network companies to reduce costs. However, that may lead the network companies to reduce capital investments, and thus, undersupply quality. This necessitated the integration of specific quality of supply components into the incentive regulation scheme (Sappington 2005).

### 6.3.4 Service Quality Measures

The service quality in electricity distribution can be defined as ensuring continues supply of electricity at a required voltage level to customers. This is also known as network reliability or network quality[3] (Eurelectric 2006). The network reliability is closely related to network investments, and renewal and maintenance expenditures on network facilities. The level of investment and expenditures are

[3] Service quality has two other dimensions which are not examined in this paper. These are voltage quality, which is related to the quality of voltage waveform, and commercial quality, which is related to the contractual relationship between network company and customer. Detailed information about these service quality dimensions is given in CEER (2008).

critical for ensuring the long-term capacity for electricity delivery, as well as for the actual delivery of electricity in the short term. The network quality is usually measured by the number and duration of interruption in electricity delivery, and as Kueck et al. (2004) explain, it is commonly monitored by four indices, namely, the system average interruption frequency index (SAIFI), the system average interruption duration index (SAIDI), the customer average interruption duration index (CAIDI), and the momentary average interruption frequency index (MAIFI).

SAIFI is constructed by dividing the overall number of customer interruption in a particular service area by the total number of customers served. SAIDI is calculated by dividing the total duration of customer interruption experienced in distribution region by the total number of customers. CAIDI is computed by dividing the total duration of customer interruption by the total number of customer interruption. Lastly, MAIFI is determined by dividing the total number of customer momentary interruption by the total number of customers.

Practically, it is very difficult to have an uninterrupted delivery of electricity to customers. There will always be planned or unplanned interruptions. The crucial issue is to identify the level of service quality that the distributors can deliver and the customers are willing to accept. Theoretically, this mutually agreed service level by distributors and customers can be determined easily. What is needed for this is identifying the optimum service quality level at which the customers' willingness to pay matches the costs of delivering the required service level. However, the determination of such level can be troublesome, since, as indicated above, the distribution companies might not be interested in investing for better service quality when they are more concerned with cost minimization, or they might overinvest when they are allowed to pass their expenses to consumers. Furthermore, different customer groups might value service quality differently. For instance, industrial customers might favor a less frequently interrupted electricity delivery at a stable voltage level, while these might be valued less by residential customers.

Perhaps for these reasons it is usually observed that regulators set maximum levels or tolerable intervals of service quality measures for distribution companies. The regulators could set these service quality targets at system level or individual customer level, or both. The service quality at the system level could be monitored by observing the proportion of customers experiencing power cuts, the minutes lost by customers due to power cut, or the amount of energy not supplied. At individual customer level, the regulators link the service quality measures directly to individual customers. Customers receive automatic or on-demand compensation when the distribution company fails to meet the predetermined tolerable number and/or duration of unplanned (and/or planned) interruptions. Consequently, the distribution companies may be rewarded when they meet these service quality targets, or penalized if they fail to meet them.

### 6.3.5 *Reward/Penalty Schemes for Service Quality*

The regulators have a number of options in designing such a reward/penalty scheme, as illustrated by Ajodhia and Hakvoort (2005). Figure 6.4 shows in each approach how price adjustment is allowed depending on the performance of the distribution company in meeting the service quality target.

In Fig. 6.4, the horizontal axis represents the measured quality level of a company, while the vertical axis shows the adjustment in price. In the first approach, the link between price and quality is established as such that when the distribution company lowers its service quality below a predefined minimum level, it faces a predefined penalty. The second approach assumes a continuous adjustment between price and service quality, where the distribution company is allowed to keep more revenue with improved service quality, or might be obliged to compensate customers with deteriorated service quality. In the third approach the reward and penalty are capped, which means that, beyond these caps the distribution company is not rewarded for further improvement, or punished for worsened service quality. The last approach is establishing a dead band, where the distribution company does not face price adjustments while its service quality is between the predetermined lower and upper limits.

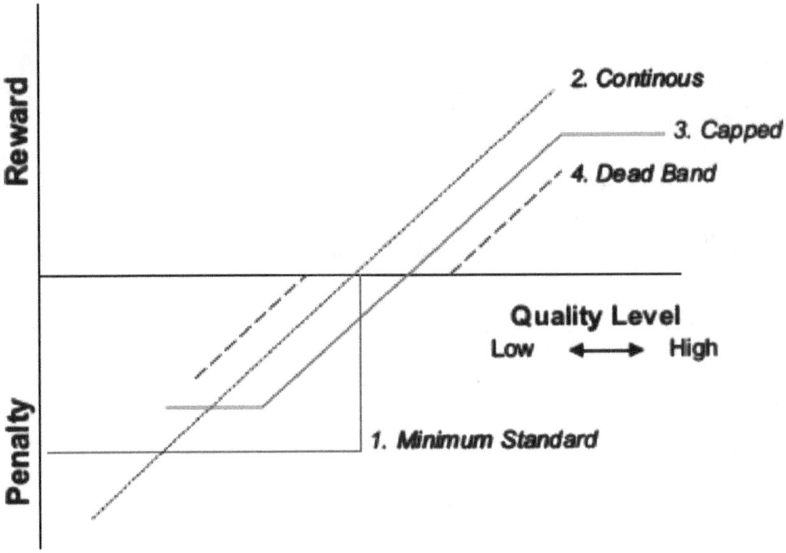


**Fig. 6.4** Examples of Quality Incentive Schemes. Source: Ajodhia and Hakvoort 2005: 215

## 6.4 An Application of DEA on the Turkish Electricity Distribution Industry

A recent survey by Haney and Pollitt (2009) exposes that the incentive-based benchmarking is widely employed by regulators in many reforming countries. Among them are several national sector regulators in the EU countries showing strong interest in implementing incentive/penalty schemes for network reliability at system level, to off-set the cost-cutting tendency of revenue/price cap regulation at the expense of reducing supply quality (CEER 2005; ECRB 2009). Haney and Pollitt (2009) also observe that DEA is the most frequently used methodology, among its alternatives, for such regulatory benchmarking.

### *6.4.1 DEA Methodology in a Nutshell*

DEA is a useful extension of efficiency measurement methodology proposed by Farrell (1957) for economic activities, particularly where price data is difficult to obtain. The methodology was refined in a series of papers, initiated by Charnes et al. (1978) and Banker et al. (1984) and contributed by others as reviewed in Cooper et al. (2004), allowing the technical efficiency measurement for the multiple input and output structures produced using various technological properties (constant as well as variable returns to scale). DEA is used to identify efficient decision making units (in our case distribution companies, but can be various entities as reviewed in Emrouznejad et al. (2008)), to construct a piece-wise best practice frontier, to which inefficient companies could aim to reach.

The direction of measurement is determined according to the nature of production process under consideration. Hence, it could be directed to compare companies in terms of their ability either to reduce input while holding output constant (the input-based efficiency measurement), or to produce more of output with given input (the output-based efficiency measurement). Since distribution companies are obliged to supply electricity, and has limited control on either number of customers or electricity demanded, the input-based efficiency measurement is more appropriate to employ in our study (Zhou et al. 2007).

Figure 6.5 is helpful to explain the input-based technical efficiency measurement graphically. The axes denote inputs ($x1$ and $x2$) used to produce output ($y$). ABCE represents the isoquant ($y$), where $D2$ is producing the same level of output as $D1$ but by consuming far more inputs than employed by $D1$. The rate of efficient to actual input usage gives the technical efficiency (TE). Thus, the excess amount of input usage (the rate of technical inefficiency) can be calculated as $0D1/0D2$, which by definition takes a value between 0 and 1 (or, 100). $(1-\text{TE})$ shows how much D2 is required to reduce its inputs to reach the efficiency frontier under the input-based approach.

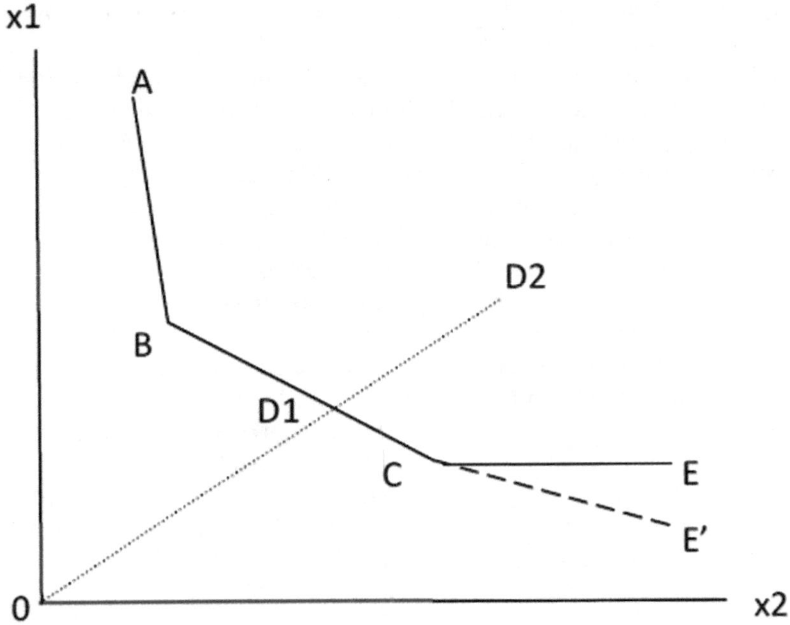


**Fig. 6.5** Input-based technical efficiency

$$\text{Minimize} \quad h_d = \theta_d - \varepsilon\left(\sum_r \sigma_r + \sum_i s_i\right)$$

$$\text{subject to} \quad \sum_j y_{rj}\lambda_j - \sigma_r = y_{rd} \qquad \sum_j x_{ij}\lambda_j - \theta_d x_{id} + s_i = 0 \tag{6.1}$$

In practice, the technical efficiency of each distribution company can be calculated by solving the linear programming problem as defined in (6.1). Here the definitions of notations are as follows. $\theta$ is the DEA efficiency score, $d$ is a specific distribution company to be evaluated ($1 \leq d \leq n$), $j$ is the subscript of distribution company ($j = 1, 2, \ldots, n$), $r$ is the subscript of outputs ($r = 1, 2, \ldots, s$), $i$ is the subscript of inputs ($i = 1, 2, \ldots, m$), $y_{rj}$ is the $r$th output of the $j$th distribution company, $x_{ij}$ is the $i$th input of the $j$th distribution company, $s_i$ is the slack variable for the $i$th input ($\geq 0$), $\sigma_r$ is the slack variable for the $r$th output ($\geq 0$), $\lambda_j$ is a nonnegative value related to the $j$th distribution company ($\geq 0$), and $\varepsilon$ is an arbitrarily small (non-Archimedean) positive number, such as $10^{-6}$.

The aim of this setting is to find nonnegative weights that will make the technical efficiency score of the distribution company under consideration minimum. This is done by comparing this company with distribution companies which use the same amount or less of input(s), while producing the same amount or more of output(s). The related values of $\lambda$ help to identify the most comparable companies, while the non-Archimedean disallows any company with extra potential to reduce input appearing on the efficiency frontier. For instance, in Fig. 6.5, C and E are producing the same amount of output, while E could still save on input 2. $\varepsilon$ resolves this problem by shifting the facet of efficiency frontier from CE to CE′.

Solving the linear programming problem (6.1) gives the technical efficiency score under the constant returns to scale technology (crste). Here, a company with 100% efficiency score is regarded as producing at the optimal scale under a competent management, while an efficiency score lower than 100% indicates inappropriate scale of operation as well as management incompetency. The part of inefficiency attributed to the management incompetency can be identified by solving the same linear programming problem with an additional restriction of $\sum \lambda_j = 1$. The new problem setting allows for the measurement of technical efficiency under the variable returns to scale technology (vrste). Meanwhile, the extent of diversion of the inefficient company from the optimal scale of production can be identified by simply dividing crste by vrste. This ratio gives the scale efficiency score (SE). As for crste, both vrste and SE can take value between 0 and 1 (or 100%).

### 6.4.2 *Data, Variables, and Findings*

The majority of benchmarking analyses on electricity distribution have used models that incorporated standard inputs, such as number of employees and total expenses (TOTEX, which consists of capital expenses (CAPEX) and operating expenses (OPEX)) with standard output characteristics, such as energy supplied, number of customers, and network size (e.g., service area or network length), as reviewed in Qassim et al. (2005). However, only few recent studies – for instance, Giannakis et al. (2005), Coelli et al. (2008), Bağdadioğlu (2009), Growitsch et al. (2009), Bagdadioglu and Senyücel (2010), and Weyman-Jones et al. (2010) – have included service quality measures, such as the number or/and duration of interruptions, into the usual benchmarking analysis.

The benchmarking is carried out against either calculated efficiency frontier (DEA) or its econometrically estimated counterpart known as the stochastic efficiency frontier, or both. DEA is usually found more convenient, since it easily accommodates multiple inputs and outputs feature of production structure. It also does not require imposition of any particular functional form on these inputs and outputs (Cooper et al. 2004).

The benchmarking with quality-based incentive scheme is not standard between countries and is usually shaped according to each country's specific conditions. In any case, the choice of variables is fundamentally important in a benchmarking analysis. In the Turkish case, the distribution companies are expected to meet the targets set for OPEX, network losses and quality measures for the regulatory period. Thus, these are included in our benchmarking study as inputs to be minimized by each distribution company, while supplying electricity to its service area.

The technical efficiency scores are calculated for 2006 to observe the situation of 20 distribution companies at the first year of the transition period. Data was not available for Kayseri EDAŞ, thus, it was not included in the study. Since the benchmarking is carried out only for 1 year, the short-run efficiency is calculated under the vrste. In fact, since CAPEX is a pass-through item, and may not reflect the actual amount of capital services consumed in a particular year, our choice of OPEX usage instead of CAPEX is appropriate.

Moreover, since the discriminatory power of DEA diminishes as the number of variables closes to the number of observations, the rule of thumb that the number of variables should not exceed one-third of the number of companies is usually sought in DEA applications (Golany and Roll 1989). To fulfill this requirement, instead of using customer number and network length as two separate output variables, they are converted into one variable as customer per network kilometer to represent customer density, as used in Coelli et al. (2008). The summary statistics of these variables are given in Table 6.3. The efficiency calculations are carried out by using DEAP Version 2.1 developed by Coelli (1996).

In 2006, the technical efficiency frontier is constructed by only 8 of 20 distribution companies, namely, Vangölü EDAŞ, Göksu EDAŞ, Ayedas, Çamlıbel EDAŞ, Gediz EDAŞ, Osmangazi EDAŞ, Menderes EDAŞ, and Bogaziçi EDAŞ. As seen in the first column of Table 6.4, 12 distribution companies are inefficient, that is, they lay away from the efficiency frontier at various degrees. The rate of input reduction required to shift each inefficient distribution company to the frontier is given in the second column of Table 6.4. As seen in the last column of Table 6.4, one or more of efficient distribution companies form a reference distribution company that could be imitated by the related inefficient distribution company to project its operation into the corresponding efficiency frontier. The average SE is very high suggesting that the scale inefficiency is not a serious problem in distribution companies in 2006. All inefficient distribution companies are operating with increasing returns to scale, and thus, they can eliminate the identified scale inefficiency by increasing their scale of operation.

In 2006, according to the DEA results, the largest rate of reduction in OPEX, network losses, number and duration of interruptions should be achieved by Dicle EDAŞ (about 55%) as shown in Table 6.5. The input reduction targets for the remaining inefficient distribution companies are somewhat less challenging, and

**Table 6.3** Summary statistics of variables for 20 distribution companies

| Inputs (I)/outputs (O) | Average | Maximum | Minimum | Standard deviation |
|---|---|---|---|---|
| I1: Operating expenses (TL) | 832,817,790 | 2,176,713,990 | 277,060,559 | 529,619,443 |
| I2: Network losses (MWh) | 1,097,091 | 8,157,822 | 189,315 | 1,754,828 |
| I3: Number of interruptions | 53,552 | 188,707 | 13,327 | 48,633 |
| I4: Duration of interruptions (h) | 51,452 | 122,271 | 6,723 | 33,122 |
| O1: Electricity supplied (MWh) | 6,304,309 | 17,986,651 | 1,004,028 | 4,515,620 |
| O2: Customer density | 37 | 120 | 15 | 30 |

**Table 6.4** Targeted input reduction under VRS for distribution companies in 2006

| EDAŞ | Input reduction | Comparable company |
|---|---|---|
| Dicle | 0.554 | Göksu (0.358), Gediz (0.268), Çamlıbel (0.374) |
| Baskent | 0.182 | Göksu (0.314), Gediz (0.686) |
| Aras | 0.158 | Çamlıbel (1.000) |
| Çoruh | 0.133 | Göksu (0.068), AyedaŞ (0.008), Çamlıbel (0.924) |
| Yesilirmak | 0.128 | Gediz (0.008), Göksu (0.698), Menderes (0.295) |
| Meram | 0.112 | Çamlıbel (0.689), Gediz (0.311) |
| Fırat | 0.062 | Çamlıbel (0.851), Göksu (0.149) |
| Uludağ | 0.060 | Gediz (0.476), AyedaŞ (0.063), Göksu (0.420), Çamlıbel (0.041) |
| Toroslar | 0.056 | Bogaziçi (0.174), Osmangazi (0.102), Gediz (0.724) |
| Akdeniz | 0.042 | Çamlıbel (0.141), Göksu (0.004), Osmangazi (0.747), Gediz (0.107) |
| Sakarya | 0.039 | Boğaziçi (0.081), Gediz (0.003), Osmangazi (0.916) |
| Trakya | 0.033 | Çamlıbel (0.402), Osmangazi (0.386), AyedaŞ (0.213) |

**Table 6.5** Actual and efficient values of inputs for Dicle EDAŞ

| Inputs | Actual value | Efficient value[a] |
|---|---|---|
| I1: Operating expenses (TL) | 1,182,402,155 | 527,728,729 |
| I2: Network losses (MWh) | 6,513,057 | 379,348 |
| I3: Number of interruptions | 164,688 | 27,498 |
| I4: Duration of interruptions (h) | 93,336 | 41,658 |

The same table is prepared for each inefficient distribution company and available from author

[a] Efficient value includes any further reduction indicated by slack variable ($s_i$), as well

thus, could be achieved with lesser effort. Then, under the incentive-based regulation, the distribution company can utilize any additional savings realized until the next regulatory review. Meanwhile, this synergy is expected to shift up the overall performance in the distribution market, as well. Therefore, EMRA may consider defining targets not only for the inefficient distribution companies but also for the efficient distribution companies, as well, so as to internalize the shift effect.

## 6.5 Conclusion

Essentially, the success of an electricity industry reform may be tested on the ground that whether the point is reached where the third party access to the networks is secured and the tariff is determined freely by the players in the market. Turkey has constructed a comprehensive framework to reach these theoretically sound and practically ambitious ends, however, making slow progress in implementation, as indicated in the Progress Report on Turkey published by the European Commission (2009), and identified in this chapter.

Indeed, the dominant public company EUAS, which was planned to be privatized by the end of 2009, has just been divided into 19 groups and offered to the private investors in 2010. Therefore, there are not sufficient numbers of private companies in the market yet, to test on whether the publicly owned TEIAS, the maestro of the electricity system and the controller of who will have link to the transmission network, is treating the access of private companies and public companies to the network in a nondiscriminatory manner. The privatization of distribution companies has been lagging behind the schedule, as well. Last but not least, the already deteriorated independence and power of EMRA has been weakened further, as the responsibility of security of supply was transferred to TEIAS, MENR, and the Council of Ministers with the new Electricity Market Law of 2008.

In spite of everything, considering the divide and slow progress in the implementation of energy directives and regulations in a number of European Countries, Turkey's commitment as an accession country, to the disintegrated industry structure and cost-based tariff mechanism is noticeable. Furthermore, the distribution companies will separate their generation and retail functions at least legally with the start of the new regulatory period in 01 January 2013. The full-scale implementation of the cost-based tariff mechanism initiated in 2008 will commence at the same date, as well. Nevertheless, whether the new electricity market structure will manage to bring more reliable, secure, high quality, and less costly electricity supply to customers is yet to be seen.

## References

Ajodhia V, Hakvoort R (2005) Economic regulation of quality in electricity distribution networks. Utilities Policy 13:211–221

Averch H, Johnson LL (1962) Behavior of the firm under regulatory constraint. American Economic Review 52(5):1052–1069

Bağdadioğlu N (2009) Türk elektrik dağıtım sektöründe hizmet kalitesine yönelik özendirici bir düzenleme uygulaması. Gazi Üniversitesi İktisadi ve İdari Bilimler Fakültesi Dergisi 11(1):23–44

Bağdadioğlu N, Basaran A, Kalaycıoğlu S, Pınar A (2009) Integrating poverty in utilities governance. UNDP-PEGEM. http://www.undp.org.tr/publicationsDocuments/Integrating_Poverty_in_Utilities_Governance_ES.pdf. Accessed 08 June 2010

Bagdadioglu N, Odyakmaz N (2009) Turkish electricity reform. Utilities Policy 17:144–152

Bagdadioglu N, Senyücel O (2010) Service quality regulation in electricity distribution. The 6th Conference: Business and Management, Vilnius Lithuania, May 13–14, 2010

Banker RD, Charnes RF, Cooper WW (1984) Some models for estimating technical and scale inefficiencies in data envelopment analysis. Management Science 30:1078–1092

CEER (2005) Third benchmarking report on quality of electricity supply. Council of European Energy Regulators (CEER) Electricity Working Group Quality of Supply Task Force. http://www.ceer-eu.org/portal/page/portal/CEER_HOME/CEER_PUBLICATIONS/CEER_DOCUMENTS/2005/CEER_3RDBR-QOES_2005-12-06.PDF. Accessed 28 May 2010

CEER (2008) 4th benchmarking report on quality of electricity supply – continuity of supply. Council of European Energy Regulators (CEER) Electricity Working Group Quality of Supply Task Force, Ref: C08-EQS-24-04, Brussels. http://www.energy-regulators.eu/portal/

page/portal/EER_HOME/EER_PUBLICATIONS/CEER_ERGEG_PAPERS/Electricity/2008/C08-EQS-24-04_4th%20Benchmarking%20Report%20EQS_10-Dec-2008_co.pdf. Accessed 28 May 2010

Cetin T, Oguz F (2007) The politics of regulation in the Turkish electricity market. Energy Policy 35(3):1761–1770

Charnes A, Cooper WW, Rhodes E (1978) Measuring the efficiency of decision-making units. European Journal of Operational Research 2:429–444

Coelli T (1996) A guide to deap version 2.1: a data envelopment analysis (computer) program. CEPA Working Paper 96/08

Coelli T, Crespo H, Paszukiewicz A, Perelman S, Plagnet MA, Romano E (2008) Incorporating quality of service in a benchmarking model: an application to French electricity distribution operators. http://www.gis-larsen.org/Pdf/Incorporating_quality_of_service_Zurich_0908.pdf. Accessed 28 May 2010

Cooper WW, Seiford LM, Zhu J (2004) Handbook on data envelopment analysis. Springer, Boston

Dubash NK (2003) Revisiting electricity reform: the case for a sustainable development approach. Utilities Policy 11:143–154

ECRB (2009) Standards and incentives in quality regulation. Energy Community Regulatory Board, Ref: R09-GA-11-06, 11th ECRB meeting, 9 July 2009

Electricity Market Law (2001) Official Journal of Turkey, Law No: 4628, Enactment Date: 03/03/2001. http://www.epdk.org.tr. Accessed 28 May 2010

Emrouznejad A, Parker B, Tavares G (2008) Evaluation of research in efficiency and productivity: a survey and analysis of the first 30 years of scholarly literature in DEA. Journal of Socio-Economic Planning Science 42(3):151–157

Erdogdu E (2010) A paper on the unsettled question of Turkish electricity market: balancing and settlement system (part I). Applied Energy 87:251–258

Eurelectric (2006) Security of supply – roles, responsibilities and experiences within the EU. Discussion Paper, Ref: 2006-180-0001. http://www.euroelectric.org. Accessed 18 May 2010

European Commission (2009) Turkey 2009 progress report. http://www.ec.europa.eu/enlargement/pdf/key_documents/2009/tr_rapport_2009_en.pdf. Accessed 28 May 2010

Farrell MJ (1957) The measurement of productive efficiency. Journal of the Royal Statistical Society 120:253–281

Giannakis D, Jamasb T, Pollitt M (2005) Benchmarking and incentive regulation of quality of service: an application to the UK electricity distribution networks. Energy Policy 33(17):2256–2271

Golany B, Roll Y (1989) An application procedure for dea. OMEGA 17(3):237–250

Growitsch C, Jamasb T, Pollitt M (2009) Quality of service, efficiency and scale in network industries: an analysis of European electricity distribution. Applied Economics 41(20):2555–2570

Haney AB, Pollitt M (2009) Efficiency analysis of energy networks: an international survey of regulators. Energy Policy 37:5814–5830

Higher Board of Planning (2009) Electricity energy market and supply security strategy paper. http://www.enerji.gov.tr/yayinlar_raporlar_EN/Arz_Guvenligi_Strateji_Belgesi_EN.pdf. Accessed 24 June 2010

International Monetary Fund (2008) World economic outlook: financial stress, downturns, and recoveries. http://www.imf.org/external/pubs/ft/weo/2008/02/pdf/text.pdf. Accessed 24 June 2010

Joskow PL (2008) Incentive regulation and its application to electricity networks. Review of Network Economics 7(4):547–560

Kueck JD, Kirby BJ, Overholt PN, Markel LC (2004) Measurement practices for reliability and power quality: a toolkit of reliability measurement practices. http://www.ornl.gov/sci/btc/apps/Restructuring/ORNLTM200491FINAL.pdf. Accessed 18 March 2009

Michaels RJ (2004) Vertical integration: the economics that electricity forgot. The Electricity Journal 17:11–23

Privatization Administration (2004) Electricity sector reform and privatization strategy paper. http://www.oib.gov.tr/program/2004_program/2004_electricity_strategy_paper.htm. Accessed 24 April 2009

Privatization Administration (2010) Teaser: privatization of Turkey's electricity distribution industry. http://www.oib.gov.tr. Accessed 28 May 2010

Qassim RY, Corso G, Lucena LDS, Thome ZD (2005) Application of data envelopment analysis in the performance evaluation of electricity distribution: a review. International Journal of Business Performance Management 7(1):60–70

Sappington DEM (2005) Regulatory service quality: a survey. Journal of Regulatory Economics 27(2):123–154

Weyman-Jones T, Boucinha JM, Inacio CF (2010) Quality of supply and efficiency: an analysis of Portuguese electricity distribution networks. Sosyoekonomi 6(12):177–209

World Bank (2005) The world bank in Turkey, 1993–2004: country assistance evaluation. Report No. 34783, December 20, 2005, Washington, USA

Zhang Y, Parker D, Kirkpatrick C (2005) Electricity sector reform in developing countries: does the sequencing matter? Quarterly Review of Economics and Finance 45:358–379

Zhou P, Ang BW, Poh KL (2007) A survey of data envelopment analysis in energy and environmental studies. European Journal of Operational Research 189(1):1–18

# Chapter 7
# The Regulation of Natural Gas Industry in Turkey*

**Erkan Erdoğdu**

## 7.1 Introduction

Natural gas came to Turkey quite late. It began to be used for residential and commercial purposes toward the end of 1980s. So, Turkish natural gas market is relatively immature, and most of the gas infrastructure in the country is either under construction or in planning phase. Besides, significant market reforms have recently been introduced in Turkish gas market. In short, Turkey is not so familiar with both gas markets and their regulation. This chapter focuses on the short story of Turkish gas market and associated issues of its reform and regulation. Before getting into the details of Turkish market, let me make some general comments on the structure of gas markets in general.

Before the reforms, natural gas industry was regarded as a natural monopoly in almost all countries and structured as a vertically integrated utility. The rationale for this includes some judgments about the industry. First of all, it was believed that in the natural gas sector one firm produces less expensively than if there were multiple firms in the market as average costs declined as output increased. Government ownership of the monopoly (or public regulation) was also justified on the grounds that the state was the guardian of the public interest and therefore would be the least likely to act in an opportunistic manner, as monopolists were likely to do. Besides, ownership by only one firm also helped to ensure the necessary coordination among the different segments of the industry (wholesale supply, transmission, distribution, and retail supply). Moreover, a general assumption was made about the strategic nature of the gas industry for economic development, which justified both vertical integration and public ownership. In short, prereform structure of the gas industry was primarily motivated by the existence of natural monopoly conditions,

* The views, findings, and conclusions expressed in this chapter are entirely those of the author and do not represent in any way the views of any institution he is affiliated with.

E. Erdoğdu (✉)
Judge Business School, University of Cambridge, Cambridge, UK
and
Energy Market Regulatory Authority, Ankara, Turkey
e-mail: erkan@erdogdu.net; ee243@cam.ac.uk

T. Çetin and F. Oğuz (eds.), *The Political Economy of Regulation in Turkey*,
DOI 10.1007/978-1-4419-7750-2_7, © Springer Science+Business Media, LLC 2011

externalities, and so-called "public good" characteristics.[1] Historically, therefore, gas industry as a whole was taken to be a natural monopoly, and legal monopoly model was adopted assuming that it is the most efficient one. Besides, the industry was organized and operated under one of the two basic structures: as state-owned enterprises under government control or as privately owned regulated monopolies.

By the 1980s, a number of political, financial, and technical factors converged and started to undermine the logic that gas industry should be handled via a vertically integrated (and usually state-owned) monopoly. Among these factors, there were ideological reasons,[2] improvement in information and communication technologies, questions about the efficiency of vertically integrated utilities (whether publicly owned or regulated by public), and poor performance of existing utilities especially in developing countries. However, gas market reform in most developing countries was a fundamentally different undertaking from the reform in developed countries in terms of motivations, sector conditions, and institutional context. In developed countries, the main targets of the reform have been the improvement in the economic efficiency of the sector, encouragement of inter-regional (or cross-border) trade, transferring investment risks to the private sector, and offering customer choice. Other subsidiary motives include the demonstration effects of some pioneering reforms of the gas sectors (especially in the UK) in the early 1990s, the desire to overcome what might be called suboptimal regulation, and the policy objective to eliminate the tendency to over-invest (so-called "gold-plating"). On the other hand, in developing countries, motivation for reform includes the poor performance of state-run gas operators in terms of high costs; inadequate expansion of access to gas services and unreliable supply; the inability of the public sector to meet the investment and maintenance costs of the gas industry associated with the increasing demands for gas resulting from economic development; the need to remove the burden of price subsidies (so as to release resources for other areas of public expenditure); low service quality, low collection rates, and the desire to raise immediate revenue for the government through the sale of state assets; the policy to attract foreign direct investment in gas sector; and encouragement of reform by international financial organizations and donor agencies such as the International Monetary Fund (IMF) and World Bank. Besides, gas reform in developed countries rested on the robust legal and institutional foundations of highly functional national political systems and aimed at optimizing the economic performance of an already well-developed industry. By contrast, in developing countries, reform took place

[1] In fact, gas industry has had these characteristics on the whole but some of its functional segments do not possess these features. Functionally, gas industry may be divided into wholesale supply, transmission, distribution, and retail supply. Transmission and distribution comprise natural monopoly segments of the industry because competition in these parts would result in duplication of the existing network. On the other hand, supply functions have nothing to do with monopoly characteristics and therefore may be open to competition.

[2] In the UK, for example, privatization of state-owned gas utility reinforced the ideology of the Thatcher government. Similar ideological and political explanations can be found in many other countries.

within problematic legal and institutional contexts. Even, definition of success differs between developed and developing countries. In developed countries, success of the reform depends mainly on how well the reformed gas markets function themselves, whereas in developing countries success usually means attracting capital from outside the country.

In addition to internal factors mentioned above, some factors external to the gas sector also played a major role. The most important of these factors was finance. The oil shocks of the 1970s caused serious economic crisis in developing countries and resulted in an increase in foreign debt, budget shortfalls, and inflation. These crises led governments to put into practice structural adjustment programs with the aim of reducing public spending and increasing private investment into the economy. In addition to other sectors, these reforms also focused on liberalizing the energy industries. State industries such as electricity, gas, oil, and mining were featured as having the greatest potential for revenue generation through commercialization and privatization. To sum up, both internal and external factors influenced the thinking of policy makers and economists, forcing them to question their long-held beliefs. In fact, this was a true paradigm shift. This shift has also been strongly encouraged by the World Bank, IMF, and other international financial institutions. In 1992, the World Bank officially changed its lending policy for energy development from traditional project lending to policy lending. That is, any country borrowing from the Bank on energy projects would have to agree to move away from a "single national gas utility as a public monopoly" and adopt ownership, structural, and regulatory reforms. Other international financial institutions, such as the Asian Development Bank, European Bank for Reconstruction and Development, and the Inter-American Development Bank, have followed suit.

Within this global framework and trend toward a liberal gas market, Turkey was not an exception. Before the reform process, she organized its gas industry as a vertically integrated entity. As part of an IMF loan program to help the country recover from an earlier recession in 2001, the Turkish government agreed to move forward with reforms to the country's gas sector, including the liberalization and the privatization. Turkey subsequently passed legislation to provide the basis for the development of competitive, transparent gas market in the country. The regulatory framework to realize these goals is still under development; however, despite repeated affirmations of the government's commitment to the reform program, progress to this effect has been slow. At present, in Turkey, the state-run gas company (BOTAS) retains a dominant position, although the government is trying to take steps to end its monopoly. Reform is proceeding through a number of tenders organized by Energy Market Regulatory Authority (EMRA) which issues licenses for the sector. A large number of new, regionally focused gas utilities have been formed as part of the reform process. Retail gas prices in Turkey remain regulated below-market rates, but after holding prices constant from 2002 to 2007, the government allowed domestic prices to increase sharply in 2008, in line with higher prices for gas imports. In approving the higher domestic prices, the Turkish government cited higher gas import prices. As a result, retail gas prices for Turkish industrial and residential consumers increased by approximately 70% in 2008 alone, although gas prices on the Turkish market are still below the European averages (IEA 2010a).

The literature on Turkey's natural gas market is very limited, with the exception of some International Energy Agency (IEA) and Organization for Economic Cooperation and Development (OECD) studies. To the best of our knowledge, so far, there have been very few studies on Turkish natural gas market and its regulation, which are usually discussed within the general context of energy markets. From a practical point of view, the lack of extensive discussions of the issue is one of the driving forces of this chapter. In this context, one of our goals is to provide a general picture of the Turkish gas market reform and draw attention to problems in this market. Besides, from an academic perspective, auctions in Turkish gas market are also appealing because the method (or auction model) developed to determine the tariffs in natural gas distribution regions of Turkey is unique and has never been employed before anywhere in the world. What is more is that the results of this specific model is also exceptional as in some regions firms accepted to set up all natural gas distribution infrastructure totally from their own sources and provide gas to consumers without any profit, challenging the very basic assumption of the science of economics, that is "firms are profit-seeking agents." Since it is obvious that these tenders will have important implications for the future of the country, the present chapter is expected to be an important contribution not only to the existing literature, but also to the energy policy formulation process in Turkey.

The chapter is organized as follows. The next section presents a short summary of the developments taking place in Turkish gas market since 1980s. Section 7.3 concentrates on the Turkish natural gas regulatory framework. Sections 7.4 and 7.5 are devoted to two important issues in Turkish gas market, namely, Turkish gas release program and the auctions in gas distribution market. Section 7.6 provides an overview of Turkish reforms within EU framework. In the following part, we touch upon some regulatory issues and provide policy guidelines to improve overall functioning of the gas market in Turkey.

## 7.2 Background to Turkish Natural Gas Market

In Turkey, natural gas began to be used for residential and commercial purposes in Ankara in 1988, and continued with Istanbul and Bursa in 1992, and then Eskisehir and Izmit in 1996. Turkey's natural gas consumption has increased rapidly for the last two decades. Economic growth and increasing use of natural gas in electricity generation, agriculture, and households have kept demand soaring. Turkey's natural gas consumption started with 0.04 bcm in 1982 and gradually reached 32.1 bcm in 2009. Table 7.1 presents the evolution of gas demand in Turkey by the consumer group (IEA 2010b). It is expected that this figure will be about 65 bcm in 2020 (Erdogdu 2010a). In line with this trend, the share of natural gas in total primary energy consumption has increased as well. It was 5.4% in 1990 and turned out to be 32% in 2008. Figure 7.1 shows the development of the share of natural gas in total primary energy supply since 1980.

**Table 7.1** Evolution of natural gas demand by sector, 1982–2009 (million cubic meters)

| Years | Electricity generation | Industry | Commercial and public services | Residential | Other | Total consumption |
|---|---|---|---|---|---|---|
| 1982 | 0 | 40 | 0 | 0 | 0 | 40 |
| 1983 | 0 | 71 | 0 | 0 | 0 | 71 |
| 1984 | 0 | 40 | 0 | 0 | 0 | 40 |
| 1985 | 18 | 49 | 0 | 0 | 0 | 67 |
| 1986 | 411 | 46 | 0 | 0 | 0 | 457 |
| 1987 | 674 | 53 | 0 | 0 | 0 | 727 |
| 1988 | 1,016 | 208 | 0 | 0 | 0 | 1,224 |
| 1989 | 2,712 | 494 | 0 | 7 | 6 | 3,219 |
| 1990 | 2,585 | 600 | 0 | 49 | 234 | 3,468 |
| 1991 | 2,877 | 675 | 0 | 184 | 501 | 4,237 |
| 1992 | 2,617 | 950 | 0 | 372 | 695 | 4,634 |
| 1993 | 2,585 | 1,167 | 0 | 540 | 858 | 5,150 |
| 1994 | 2,950 | 1,212 | 0 | 635 | 649 | 5,446 |
| 1995 | 3,600 | 1,264 | 0 | 1,364 | 801 | 7,029 |
| 1996 | 4,170 | 1,575 | 0 | 1,658 | 811 | 8,214 |
| 1997 | 4,913 | 1,849 | 0 | 2,157 | 881 | 9,800 |
| 1998 | 5,417 | 1,703 | 0 | 2,530 | 701 | 10,351 |
| 1999 | 7,574 | 1,819 | 0 | 2,834 | 301 | 12,528 |
| 2000 | 8,845 | 1,988 | 499 | 3,218 | 285 | 14,835 |
| 2001 | 9,569 | 1,708 | 838 | 3,577 | 252 | 15,944 |
| 2002 | 10,333 | 1,994 | 886 | 3,721 | 654 | 17,588 |
| 2003 | 11,907 | 2,692 | 1,477 | 4,455 | 650 | 21,181 |
| 2004 | 12,161 | 2,935 | 1,888 | 4,675 | 784 | 22,443 |
| 2005 | 15,157 | 3,255 | 2,359 | 5,747 | 857 | 27,375 |
| 2006 | 15,961 | 4,007 | 3,344 | 7,423 | 448 | 31,183 |
| 2007 | 19,019 | 4,473 | 3,689 | 8,304 | 1,114 | 36,599 |
| 2008 | – | – | – | – | – | 37,178 |
| 2009 | – | – | – | – | – | 32,134 |

*Source*: IEA (2010b)

In 2008, Turkey's gas production covered only 2.7% of the consumption due to very limited indigenous gas resources (IEA 2010c). Table 7.1 shows that more than half of the total gas consumption comes from electricity generation. Its share in total gas consumption was 52% in 2007. In the same year, industry sector consumed 12% of the gas while commercial and public services and residential consumers were responsible for 10 and 23% of all consumption, respectively.

Turkish natural gas industry was state-owned and vertically integrated through the 1980s and the 1990s. As a part of energy market restructuring, the legal structure of the gas market was reformed in 2001 with a new law, namely Natural Gas Market Law (NGML, Law No: 4646). The new law has been a first step toward gradual liberalization and vertical separation in the market. The law aims to establish a legal framework for developing a fair, transparent, and competitive natural gas market through unbundling market activities and eliminating the monopolistic structure. The new legal environment is projected to encourage privatization, establish a more competitive environment, and prepare the ground for the integration to

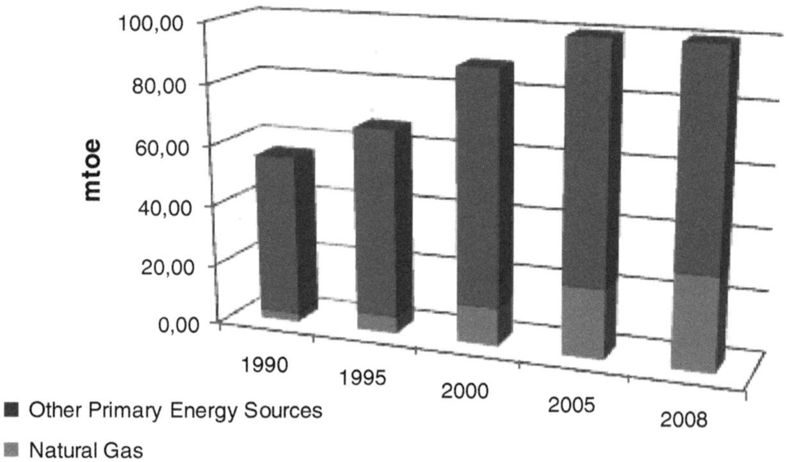


**Fig. 7.1** Share of natural gas in total primary energy supply (1980–2008). *Source*: IEA (2010c)

the EU natural gas market by harmonizing regulations. NGML designates EMRA as the market regulator and describes the procedures for regulations in the market.

BOTAS was established in 1974 by TPAO (Turkish Petroleum Corporation) for the purpose of transporting Iraqi crude oil to the Ceyhan (Yumurtalik) Marine Terminal, in accordance with the Iraq–Turkey Crude Oil Pipeline Agreement signed in 1973. Because of Turkey's increasing need for diversified energy sources, since 1987 BOTAS has expanded its original purpose of transporting crude oil through pipelines to cover natural gas transportation and trade activities, therefore becoming a gas trading company. BOTAS' monopoly rights on natural gas import, distribution, sales, and pricing were granted by the Decree of Natural Gas Utilization No. 397 on February 9, 1990. In February 1995, BOTAS was restructured as a corporation, and obtained the status of state economic enterprise. In June 1995, it was authorized to carry out all kinds of petroleum-related activities such as exploration, drilling, production, transportation, storage, and refining for the purpose of providing crude oil and natural gas from sources abroad. At present, BOTAS is the only gas transmission company in Turkey. Its monopoly in natural gas imports, exports, and wholesale trading was abolished with the enactment of the NGML in 2001, and its current de facto dominating position in the import activities is subject to change in the course of the gas market reform. The law requires BOTAS to transfer at least 10% of its total gas purchase quantity within the take-or-pay contracts every year to reach the 20% market share by 2009. Furthermore, the law also stipulates BOTAS to be legally unbundled after 2009 to form separate companies for transmission, storage, import, and trade. However, these last two requirements of the law have not been met so far.

In Turkey, distribution function is carried out by the local distribution companies. The major distribution companies are Baskentgaz (in Ankara), Igdas and

**Table 7.2** Gas import contracts of BOTAS

| Purchaser | Supplier | Start | End | Imports in 2008 (bcm/year) | Plateau volume (bcm/year) |
|---|---|---|---|---|---|
| BOTAS | Russia (through Bulgaria) | 1987 | 2012 | | 6 |
| BOTAS[a] | Russia (through Bulgaria) | 1998 | 2021 | 22.53 | 8 |
| BOTAS | Russia (Blue Stream) | 2002 | 2027 | | 16 |
| BOTAS | Algeria (LNG) | 1994 | 2014 | 4.15 | 4 |
| BOTAS | Nigeria (LNG) | 1999 | 2021 | 1.02 | 1.2 |
| BOTAS | Iran | 2001 | 2026 | 4.11 | 10 |
| BOTAS | Turkmenistan | – | 30 years from start | – | 16 |
| BOTAS | Azerbaijan | 2007 | 2021 | 4.58 | 6.6 |

[a] On November 30, 2005, 4 bcm of this contract was transferred to third parties within gas release program

*Source*: BOTAS (2010a) & IEA (2010b)

Bahcesehirgaz (in Istanbul), Izgaz (in Izmit), Agdas (in Adapazari), Bursagaz (in Bursa), and Esgaz (in Eskisehir). Igdas is owned by the municipality. Bahcesehirgaz, Agdas, Bursagaz, Esgaz, Izgaz, and Baskentgas were privatized. As the gas infrastructure is being expanded, new consumers are joining the networks. Tender procedures for gas distribution in 53 new regions have been completed. At present, 63 (out of 81) cities are supplied with natural gas. All cities are expected to have access to gas in the near future.

As of July 2010, BOTAS is still a dominant player in wholesale market and it still has a vertically integrated public monopoly structure. BOTAS' current gas import contracts are seen in Table 7.2 (BOTAS 2010a; IEA 2010b). In the table, it is seen that Turkey's main gas supplier is Russia, with whom she has signed three contracts. In 2008, Turkey imported 36.7 bcm natural gas and Russia supplied 61.4% of this volume. In order to limit its dependence on Russia, Turkey has turned to other suppliers (Azerbaijan, Algeria, Iran, Nigeria, and Turkmenistan). Turkey is able to get supplies from Azerbaijan. The construction of a gas pipeline connecting Azerbaijan (Shah Deniz field) to Turkey via Georgia (Baku-Tbilissi-Erzurum) was completed in April 2007. In 2008, Turkey imported 4.6 bcm of gas (12.5% of imports) from Azerbaijan and in the long-term it should reach 6.6 bcm/year. Algeria supplied 11.3% of Turkey's gas imports in 2008 under two long-term contracts: a first signed in 1988 for the supply of 2 bcm per year over 20 years [first deliveries in 1994 at the liquefied natural gas (LNG) terminal of Marmara] and a second signed in 1995 for the delivery of an additional 2 bcm over a 20-year period. In 2008, Iran supplied 11.2% of Turkey's gas imports (contract for 228 bcm over 23 years starting in January 2003, following the commissioning of the 325 km gas pipeline connecting Iran to Ankara). Nigeria is Turkey's fifth gas supplier, accounting for 2.8% of its gas imports in 2008 (contracts signed in October 1995 and May 1999, for a total supply of 1.2 bcm/year over 20 years starting in 2000).

The gas pipeline connecting Greece to Turkey was commissioned in December 2007. The purpose of this 296 km long pipeline is to diversify the EU's supply sources by transporting gas from Caucasus countries to Europe. It has an initial capacity of 0.75 bcm/year, with a projected capacity of 11.5 bcm/year by 2011. There are plans for an extension of this pipeline from Greece to Italy. This subsea line, which will be 800 km long, will supply 8 bcm/year to Italy.

## 7.3 General Regulatory Framework in Turkish Natural Gas Market

NGML requires companies to obtain licenses from EMRA for transmission, export, import, wholesale, distribution, and storage activities. Licenses are granted for a minimum of 10 and a maximum of 30 years. As of July 2010, EMRA issued a total of 198 licenses, of which 23 for import, 2 for export, 34 for wholesale, 4 for storage, 1 for transmission, 16 for LNG transmission, 58 for CNG, and 60 for distribution activities (EMRA 2010). EMRA also issued related secondary legislation, including nine regulations, six public notices, and numerous board decisions.

NGML stipulates that BOTAS is to be unbundled into separate transmission, storage, and trading units, with its import contracts transferred to private companies in order to end the company's monopoly. The law envisions that Turkey's gas transmission network will remain state-owned and operated. However, apart from transmission, all other functions are expected to be performed by private entrepreneurs in the near future. The plan to liberalize Turkey's gas market sets out requirements that would reduce BOTAS's share of Turkey's gas imports from 100% to 20% by 2009. As such, in 2005, Turkey offered a total of 16 bcm of its contracted-supply quantity of approximately 31 bcm, including four piped-gas contracts from Russia and Iran, as well as two LNG contracts from Algeria and Nigeria. However, the gas release program failed to attract much interest, as only a handful of the 64 lots on offer (0.25 bcm each) received bids. The vast majority of Turkey's contracted gas supplies remain under BOTAS's control, making targets for gas market liberalization unrealistic. We deal with this issue in depth in the following section.

It is the task of EMRA to determine the principles and procedures for setting the regulated prices and tariffs. At present, EMRA applies the price ceiling to storage, wholesale, and transmission tariffs. Before the enactment of the NGML, there were seven companies established in six cities. At the beginning of 2004, the two distribution companies owned by BOTAS were privatized, thus removing BOTAS from the distribution sector. Since then, four companies have also been privatized. Now, the only gas distribution company under public ownership is IGDAS in Istanbul, but it is also expected to be privatized in the near future. EMRA is responsible for organizing tenders for new natural gas distribution licenses in the cities. With the tenders for new distribution regions, the total number of distribution regions has reached 60 and is expected to increase. Prequalification to bid in tenders depends on the financial strength and experience of the potential licensees. Evaluation in the tenders is based on the unit service and depreciation charge (USDC) for supplying 1 kWh of natural gas to consumers (¢/kwh). So, for distribution zones tendered by EMRA, USDCs are determined as a result of auctions. In (public or privatized) distribution zones that were set up before the ratification of NGML, EMRA determines USDCs for the supply of natural gas. Licenses are granted for 30 years. So far (as of July 2010), the tender processes have been carried out in 53 cities and similar tenders are scheduled for three more regions. The regulation of distribution market and results of the tenders in more detail are dealt with in Sect. 7.5.

The law limits the amount an importer can buy from abroad to 20% of the national consumption. Similarly, importers, wholesalers, and distributors cannot have market shares more than 20% to ensure that competition will be institutionalized. Distribution companies cannot buy more than half of their gas from a single wholesaler or importer. The law gives discretion to EMRA to change these ratios.

Consumers whose annual consumption is above the threshold set by EMRA have the right to choose their own gas suppliers. These big gas users are called "eligible consumers." At present, the threshold for being an eligible consumer is 800,000 $m^3$/year (EMRA Board Decision, No: 2378, Dated December 29, 2009). Although eligible consumers have the right to choose their suppliers, this right cannot currently be exercised because of the de facto monopolistic position of BOTAS in import and trade.

Gas prices are regulated by EMRA, although a new automatic price-setting mechanism was put into effect on July 1, 2008. Under this mechanism, retail gas prices for both industrial and residential consumers are adjusted on a monthly basis. Residential gas prices are set higher than gas prices for industrial uses such as power generation and manufacturing. Retail gas prices increased dramatically in 2008 as the government moved to liberalize prices after holding rates constant from 2002 to 2007. Gas prices increased more than 70% over end-year 2007 prices as a result of five separate tariff increases. The government justified the price increases by citing higher gas import prices and the need to improve BOTAS's financial position after years of holding prices for domestic consumers at below-market rates. The government also argued that higher prices would help prepare the sector for privatization by making the gas market more attractive to investors. The fall in oil prices in the second half of 2008, however, translated to lower gas import prices for Turkey in 2009, prompting BOTAS to bring prices down for end-users in line with the automatic price-setting mechanism. Figure 7.2 shows trends in gas prices in Turkey since the late 1980s. Today, Turkish residential consumers subsidize an important portion of the cost of the gas consumed by industry and electricity generation plants. Unbundling of BOTAS' activities is of crucial importance to increase transparency and eliminate cross-subsidies seen in Fig. 7.2.

EMRA regulates third-party access (TPA) to the transmission system by importers and wholesalers. A network code has been in force since 2004 and it is amended frequently when needed. For the time being, apart from BOTAS, only few firms transport their gas through network, and volume of gas transported via TPA is quite limited. So, currently TPA does not seem to be a problem in the market. However, with the liberalization of the market and development

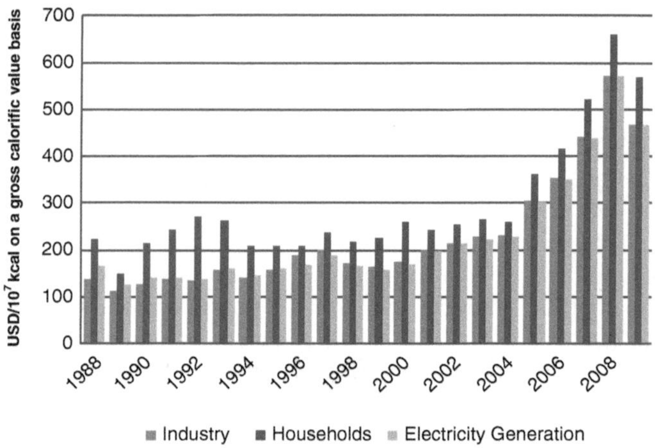


**Fig. 7.2** Evolution of end-user natural gas prices in Turkey since 1988. *Source*: IEA (2010a)

of competition, it is likely to be a source of trouble in the near future. The most crucial question then is how to prevent public monopoly company from discriminating against possible new entrants into the market. Discriminatory policies of incumbents have been one of the most important problems in many European countries that effectively impeded market development for a long time. Not to face with the same problems, Turkish regulatory authority has been granted the right to regulate TPA to networks and solve any conflicts arising from TPA-related issues. Efficiency and effectiveness of the EMRA in regulating TPA will most probably be one of the determinants of success in creation of a competitive gas market in Turkey.

As for the storage of natural gas, Turkey has very limited facilities. The natural gas storage and reproduction agreement was signed between TPAO and BOTAS on July 21, 1999 in order to establish the first storage facilities in Silivri (offshore) and Degirmenkoy (onshore). The northern Marmara region and Degirmenkoy natural gas underground storage facilities, having a storage capacity of 1.6 bcm, of which the surface facilities were also constructed at the same place, became operational in July 2007. Another project is the Salt Lake natural gas storage system. It is developed for the purpose of utilizing salt domes under the Salt Lake. Its capacity is 1 bcm/year. The latter project seeks to optimize the operation of the gas pipelines system during peak demand seasons in the central Anatolian region. When operationalized, facility in Salt Lake will be able to store a gas volume corresponding to 15-day consumption in Turkey. There are also two LNG terminals in Turkey to transform and supply imported liquefied gas to the main gas network. One is located in Marmara Ereglisi/Tekirdag and has been operated by BOTAS since 1994. The second LNG terminal is owned by EGEGAZ and operational since 2006 in Aliaga/Izmir. NGML requires both importers and wholesalers to store 10% of the gas they traded in storage facilities. The law also allows parties to determine the terms of the storage contract. That is, negotiated TPA regime is adopted for storage facilities. The number and capacity of storage facilities in Turkey should increase quickly; otherwise, lack of storage capacity will be another obstacle to the development of gas market in Turkey.

## 7.4 Turkish Gas Release Program

As we mentioned before, in April 2001, Turkish parliament passed NGML to liberalize the gas market, abolish the monopoly of state-owned BOTAS, and allow private firms to import, distribute, and sell natural gas. BOTAS will be split into units for natural gas import, transport, storage, and distribution. At that point, the company's various components (except for transmission) are to be privatized. Besides, according to the law, BOTAS was to sell off 10% of its market share every year, eventually getting down to 20%. But progress in this area has lagged. There have been parliamentary delays in approving an amendment easing restrictions on foreign players in Turkey's gas sector. Another law passed in 2005 had BOTAS focus on gas transmission and move away from purchasing gas. But the latter objective will only be attained beyond purchase contracts which BOTAS has signed with six different sources of supply. These involve a total of 67.8 bcm/year and the last contract, with Russia's Blue Stream venture, will expire in 2027 (see Table 7.2).

Turkey's gas release scheme has stalled mainly due to difficulties in re-negotiating contracts with existing suppliers. Under the terms of the 2001 Gas Law, BOTAS was required to sell off at least 10% of its supply contracts each year in order to reduce its share of total imports to 20% by 2009. In the late 2004, BOTAS finally agreed to initiate a gas release program to hand over six out of its eight existing contracts to new entrants. The amount of gas to be divested each year (16 bcm) via the gas release program corresponded to 60% of the demand in 2005. The bidding dates for gas release program were deferred many times on legal grounds and a new law had to be passed to amend the relevant article of the NGML of 2001. The new law enacted in June 2005 envisages separate tenders for contract and volume releases. The new mechanism requires that contract release tenders will be completed first and if some of the planned volumes are not transferred, then a new tender shall be held for the release of the remaining volumes. In addition, the new Law also requires companies to get the preliminary consent of sellers prior to the auction (Akcollu 2006). However, Gazprom, Turusgas, and the National Iranian Gas Export Company have all reportedly written to BOTAS expressing their opposition to transferring the contracts to third parties.

The first open contract release took place on November 30, 2005, when 4 bcm gas was offered to open bids. It was announced that the gas volumes would be released in 16 blocks of 0.25 bcm/year each and derive from natural gas imported from Russia under two contracts through the Trans-Balkan pipeline. Only four companies bid in the program, all of which secured gas volumes. Shell Energy bid \$2.1 million for one block of gas, Enerco Energy \$1.6 million each for ten blocks,

Avrasya Gaz $0.91 million each for two blocks, and Bosphorus Gaz $1.81 million each for three blocks. As a result of the first contract release, Shell Energy secured 0.25 bcm, Bosphorus Gaz 0.75 bcm, Enerco Energy 2.5 bcm, and Avrasya Gaz 0.5 bcm. This single sale, which only entered into effect on April 1, 2009, constitutes the only liberalized segment of the Turkish natural gas market.

Several factors deterred other new entrants from bidding for the gas, including confidential clauses in the import contracts, the requirement for sellers' consent prior to the tender, ambiguity as to how BOTAS would release its contracted customers, and the potential extra costs to companies arising from mandatory gas storage (Akcollu 2006). However, it is still no small achievement that the gas release program actually went ahead given the hurdles the winners must now overcome. After securing their shares in contract release process, the four buyers must negotiate terms directly with the seller, Russia's Gazprom, as well as obtaining permission to operate from Turkey's competition authority and securing import licenses from Turkey's energy regulator.

In the following process, all four companies were granted import licenses by EMRA. GazExport, the export arm of Gazprom, signed a contract with BOTAS and Shell Energy under which Gazprom was to supply 0.25 bcm/year of gas to Shell's Turkish market until 2021. Shell Energy was to assume the rights and obligations of BOTAS under the contract. A similar contract was also concluded between Gazprom, Bosphorus Gaz, and BOTAS under which Gazprom was to supply 0.75 bcm/year of gas to Bosphorus Gaz until 2021.

## 7.5 The Auctions in Turkish Gas Distribution Market

Having provided a general picture of the Turkish energy market, let me turn to the most interesting aspect of Turkish gas market reform experience, namely, application of auctions in the Turkish natural gas distribution zones. Before discussing the tenders in Turkey, I want to pay some attention to the literature that justifies the application of auctions in energy networks (Erdogdu 2010b).

### *7.5.1 Theoretical Foundations*

An industry is a natural monopoly if a single firm can produce more efficiently than two or more firms. Gas distribution networks are regarded to be natural monopolies. Left to the market, they will be undersupplied at prices which exceed marginal costs. The regulatory approach to the natural monopoly problem is based upon the establishment of agencies endowed with powers to control prices, entry, conditions of service and so on in a particular industry or group of industries. In principle, regulatory agencies could be set up to monitor the behavior of public corporations, but here we focus on their use in market environments characterized by private ownership.

All regulators are naturally skeptical of a utility's initial bid to invest and operate an energy network (or any network), given the incentives of the firms to "game" the periodic reviews. That is, one of the fundamental regulatory questions has been how to enjoy the cost benefits of single-firm production without suffering from monopolistic behavior. Franchising provides an answer to that question in the form of a competition for the market, where several firms competing to be one that actually operates in the market. That is to say, it provides a mechanism for regulators that enables them not to try to adjudicate on the "right" answer, but rather leave it to the market mechanisms.

Franchising involves conferring rights in the supply of a good or service to a sole producer for a specified period of time. It is regarded as an essential mechanism for introducing competition for the market where competition within the market is not feasible or desirable. Natural monopolies are, therefore, obvious candidates for franchising.

The concept of "franchising" was first pronounced by Chadwick (1859) and popularized by Demsetz (1968). In a so-called "Chadwick–Demsetz" auction, competition takes place through bidding for the franchise contract, and the winner is the one who bids the lowest price to supply the good or service, or more generally, who offers the best price-quality package.

At first sight, franchising appears to provide a very attractive way of combining competition and efficiency without any heavy burden for regulators. The competition for market appears to destroy the undesirable monopoly of information that hinders conventional regulation, and price is set by competition, not by bureaucrats. Provided bidding is competitive, a Chadwick–Demsetz auction will reduce the profits to the normal competitive level by inducing bid prices equal to unit costs of production.

Nevertheless, franchising is not without some difficulties. First of all, as mentioned above, bidding must be competitive and cases of collusive bidding need to be prevented. There exist mainly two reasons why bidding for the franchise might fail to be competitive. First of all, there is a danger of collusion between bidders, especially if they are few in number, or if the firms are in a repeated interaction (or, "game") with one another via frequent contracts. The second reason is that one firm might enjoy such strategic advantages in the competition for the franchise that other firms would be unwilling to compete with it. For instance, suppose that an incumbent firm is the holder of a franchise that is now up for renewal. Since, thanks to its past operation of the franchise, the incumbent has already reduced its costs; other firms will be unwilling to compete with the incumbent as they know that they are unlikely to win the competition. Also, another source of incumbent advantage may originate from asymmetries of information. The incumbent's knowledge of cost and demand conditions is likely superior to that of any other firm, which tends to deter others from competing with it for the future franchise.

The merits of franchising are further reduced by the issues related with asset handover. Unless sunk costs are zero (an extremely unlikely event), efficiency requires that the new operator of the franchise takes over the assets from the incumbent. Therefore, one needs to decide how the assets to be valued for this purpose.

In such a case, there is a problem of bilateral monopoly. If incumbent has no alternative, it has to accept as little as the scrap value of the assets. If the new operator firm has no alternative, it has to pay as much as their replacement value. The gap between replacement value and scrap value is likely to be large if the assets involve sunk costs.

The last difficulty with franchising is the question of specification, administration, and monitoring of franchise contract. The duration of franchise contract must also be considered. The difficulties of contract specification and administration perhaps suggest that short-term contracts have advantages, because fewer future unforeseeable events then need to be considered. Nevertheless, the organization of frequent contests for the franchise also involves major costs: all the problems of asset valuation and handover occur more often, and the industry would frequently be in a state of turmoil.

Actually, the Chadwick–Demsetz proposal is an ingenious scheme if the contract in question is simple. There are some economic activities where franchising would be an attractive scheme. But we are concerned with natural gas industries in which the difficulties of contract specification and administration would be immense. Therefore, regulation is an essential part of franchising. Far from being an alternative to regulation, franchising requires it.

In short, auctions are methods of revealing information in the context of the network operators' near-monopoly of information. They give some indications of firms' willingness to reduce their profit so as to invest in the specific gas industry in question. Clever auction design filters out some imperfections associated with auctions, and therefore the detail is extremely important.

But what is the focus of auctions? One clear role is to allocate network operation in predefined areas. In principle, auctions should be good at this. The property right is typically well defined so the bidders know what they are buying (Helm 2003). As long as auctions are confined in this way, there should be little controversy. Their use depends on the costs of design and implementation and the benefits of the information revealed, compared with other methods.

If regulators seriously want to rely on auctions for investment determination, there is a great deal to do to create some of the necessary conditions. Competition in auctions is required, and a series of structural measures would probably be necessary. In such a context, auctions require the support of a planning approach. They cannot be relied upon to determine investment in their pure form. It does not, however, follow that auctions are therefore irrelevant for investments. The information they create is not worthless. On the contrary, auctions provide a method to discover whether there are firms willing and able to invest in networks with at least profits as possible. That is, designing an auction provides a plan. The actual auction process tests the plan. However – and this is a crucial "however" – the determination of the investment level should rest with the regulator, not the auction. The notion of auctions as part of the planning process also raises the issue of the degree of regulation that auctions might require. Not only do investors in natural monopolies depend upon regulatory protection to finance their functions, but auctions also require regulators to determine the property rights and prevent the abuse of market power.

Auctions are, therefore, likely to require intensive regulation, as well as being placed within the planning context. Whether these costs are worth the expected benefits is an empirical question.

### 7.5.2 *Auctions in Practice*

Given the current natural gas market developments in Turkey and related literature, let us concentrate and analyze natural gas distribution tenders in Turkey and their current and expected effects on consumers. For the sake of simplicity and due to limited nature of the chapter, we focus only on residential consumers, not covering industry and electricity generation sectors.

Figure 7.3 shows the current stage of gas supply in Turkish cities. From the map, it is seen that 58 cities (out of 81) were supplied with natural gas and all remaining cities are planned for gas supply in the near future (BOTAS 2010b). According to NGML of 2001, in Turkey, EMRA is responsible for organizing tenders for natural gas distribution licenses in cities. So far, 53 tender processes were carried out. The main characteristics of these tenders may be summarized as follows. First of all, distribution licenses are granted through a tender process for 30 years. Prequalification to participate in the tenders requires financial strength and previous experience in the sector. Evaluation of bids is based on the "unit service and depreciation charge" (expressed in US cents) (USDC) for supplying 1 kWh of natural gas to consumers for the first 8 years. The firm with lowest USDC bid wins the tender and is qualified to set up natural gas distribution infrastructure and supply gas to all consumers in its predefined region. The distribution companies may charge consumers a one-time

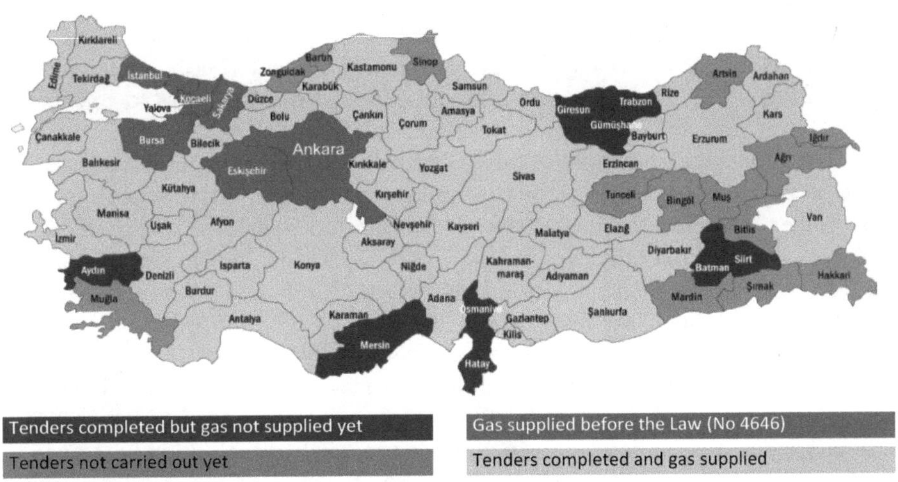


**Fig. 7.3** Gas supply in Turkey by cities (as of July 2010). *Source*: BOTAS (2010b)

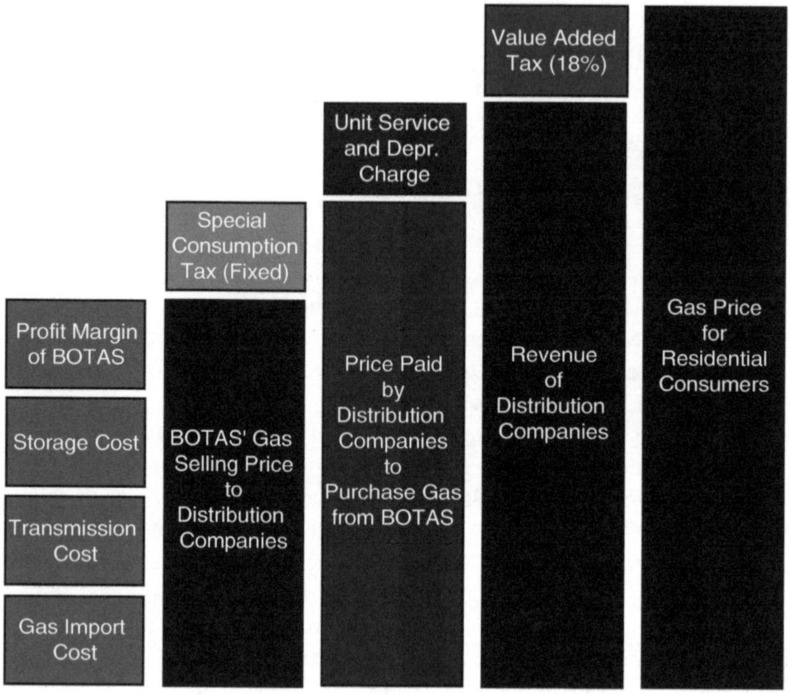


**Fig. 7.4** Components of natural gas price for households. *Source*: Prepared by the author

"connection fee" when they are connected to network for the first time. The upper limit of this charge is also determined by the EMRA. Apart from this, USDC is the sole source of winning firm for both profit and income to recover its investments for the first 8 years. After the first 8 years, the firm is expected to submit a tariff proposal to EMRA and new tariff is determined by EMRA. The winning firm is required to start investment within 6 months, to start providing gas to consumers within 18 months, and to cover all consumers in 5 years.

BOTAS' existing monopoly in the gas market does not allow distribution companies to purchase gas from competitive producers, wholesalers, or importers, even though they have de jure right to do so according to NGML. So, in practice, all distribution companies purchase gas from BOTAS. The main components of natural gas prices for households in Turkey are presented in Fig. 7.4. When we evaluate Fig. 7.4, we may easily see that USDC is the only source of distribution company for both recovering its investments and making a profit.

Table 7.3 shows the decomposition of gas price for residential users in 60 distribution zones in Turkey as of May 2010. Since the components of BOTAS' gas selling price to distribution companies are commercially sensitive and not open to public, Table 7.3 does not include them. Besides, total number of household equivalent customers reached to 8.3 million in Turkey at the end of 2009.

**Table 7.3** Residential natural gas prices in 60 cities of Turkey as of May 2010

| No | Distribution region and company | Tender date | Gas supplied | Cost of gas purchase from BOTAS (YTL/m$^3$) | As % of total price | Special consumption tax (YTL/m$^3$) | As % of total price | USDC (¢/kwh) | USDC (¢/m$^3$) | USDC (YTL/m$^3$) | As % of total price | Value added tax (18%) | As % of total price | Gas price for households (YTL/m$^3$) | Minimum price = 100 | Connection charge ($) |
|---|---|---|---|---|---|---|---|---|---|---|---|---|---|---|---|---|
| 1 | Kayseri – KAYSERIGAZ | June 19, 2003 | Yes | 0.505976 | 79.2 | 0.023 | 3.6 | 0.076 | 0.809 | 0.012173 | 1.9 | 0.097407 | 15.3 | 0.638556 | *102.30* | 180 |
| 2 | Konya – GAZNET | July 31, 2003 | Yes | 0.505976 | 79.5 | 0.023 | 3.6 | 0.064 | 0.681 | 0.010251 | 1.6 | 0.097061 | 15.3 | 0.636288 | *101.94* | 180 |
| 3 | Erzurum – PALEN | August 13, 2003 | Yes | 0.505976 | 79.9 | 0.023 | 3.6 | 0.046 | 0.489 | 0.007368 | 1.2 | 0.096542 | 15.3 | 0.632886 | *101.39* | 180 |
| 4 | Corlu – CORDAS | August 28, 2003 | Yes | 0.505976 | 80.2 | 0.023 | 3.6 | 0.036 | 0.383 | 0.005766 | 0.9 | 0.096254 | 15.3 | 0.630996 | *101.09* | 180 |
| 5 | Gebze – PALGAZ | September 11, 2003 | Yes | 0.505976 | 79.8 | 0.023 | 3.6 | 0.052 | 0.553 | 0.008329 | 1.3 | 0.096715 | 15.3 | 0.634020 | *101.57* | 180 |
| 6 | Inegol – INGAZ | September 18, 2003 | Yes | 0.505976 | 79.6 | 0.023 | 3.6 | 0.061 | 0.649 | 0.009771 | 1.5 | 0.096974 | 15.3 | 0.635721 | *101.85* | 180 |
| 7 | Catalca – TRAKYADAS | September 25, 2003 | Yes | 0.505976 | 80.0 | 0.023 | 3.6 | 0.044 | 0.468 | 0.007048 | 1.1 | 0.096484 | 15.3 | 0.632508 | *101.33* | 180 |
| 8 | Bandirma – BADAS | October 9, 2003 | Yes | 0.505976 | 77.0 | 0.023 | 3.5 | 0.174 | 1.851 | 0.027870 | 4.2 | 0.100232 | 15.3 | 0.657079 | *105.27* | 180 |
| 9 | Balikesir – BALGAZ | October 16, 2003 | Yes | 0.505976 | 78.4 | 0.023 | 3.6 | 0.112 | 1.192 | 0.017940 | 2.8 | 0.098445 | 15.3 | 0.645360 | *103.39* | 180 |
| 10 | Sivas – SIDAS | October 30, 2003 | Yes | 0.505976 | 77.2 | 0.023 | 3.5 | 0.164 | 1.745 | 0.026269 | 4.0 | 0.099944 | 15.3 | 0.655189 | *104.97* | 180 |
| 11 | Kutahya – CINIGAZ | November 6, 2003 | Yes | 0.505976 | 78.1 | 0.023 | 3.6 | 0.124 | 1.319 | 0.019862 | 3.1 | 0.098791 | 15.3 | 0.647628 | *103.75* | 180 |
| 12 | Eregli (Konya) – NETGAZ | December 4, 2003 | Yes | 0.505976 | 77.0 | 0.023 | 3.5 | 0.172 | 1.830 | 0.027550 | 4.2 | 0.100175 | 15.3 | 0.656701 | *105.21* | 180 |
| 13 | Corum – CORUMGAZ | December 18, 2003 | Yes | 0.505976 | 79.2 | 0.023 | 3.6 | 0.079 | 0.841 | 0.012654 | 2.0 | 0.097493 | 15.3 | 0.639123 | *102.39* | 180 |
| 14 | Kirikkale Kirsehir – KIRGAZ | January 8, 2004 | Yes | 0.505976 | 77.4 | 0.023 | 3.5 | 0.158 | 1.681 | 0.025308 | 3.9 | 0.099771 | 15.3 | 0.654055 | *104.78* | 180 |

(continued)

**Table 7.3** (continued)

| No | Distribution region and company | Tender date | Gas supplied | Cost of gas purchase from BOTAS (YTL/m³) | As % of total price | Special consumption tax (YTL/m³) | As % of total price | USDC (¢/kwh) | USDC (¢/m³) | USDC (YTL/m³) | As % of total price | Value added tax (18%) | As % of total price | Gas price for households (YTL/m³) | Minimum price = 100 | Connection charge ($) |
|---|---|---|---|---|---|---|---|---|---|---|---|---|---|---|---|---|
| 15 | Samsun – SAMGAZ | January 22, 2004 | Yes | 0.505976 | 79.7 | 0.023 | 3.6 | 0.055 | 0.585 | 0.008810 | 1.4 | 0.096801 | 15.3 | 0.634587 | *101.67* | 180 |
| 16 | Aksaray – AKSARAYGAZ | February 12, 2004 | Yes | 0.505976 | 75.7 | 0.023 | 3.4 | 0.236 | 2.511 | 0.037801 | 5.7 | 0.102020 | 15.3 | 0.668797 | *107.15* | 180 |
| 17 | Duzce Karadeniz Eregli – DERGAZ | April 8, 2004 | Yes | 0.505976 | 80.2 | 0.023 | 3.6 | 0.034 | 0.362 | 0.005446 | 0.9 | 0.096196 | 15.3 | 0.630618 | *101.03* | 180 |
| 18 | Gemlik – GEMDAS | April 22, 2004 | Yes | 0.505976 | 75.6 | 0.023 | 3.4 | 0.239 | 2.543 | 0.038282 | 5.7 | 0.102106 | 15.3 | 0.669364 | *107.24* | 180 |
| 19 | Yalova – ARMAGAZ | July 1, 2004 | Yes | 0.505976 | 80.3 | 0.023 | 3.7 | 0.031 | 0.330 | 0.004965 | 0.8 | 0.096109 | 15.3 | 0.630051 | *100.94* | 180 |
| 20 | Usak – UDAS | December 2, 2004 | Yes | 0.505976 | 79.7 | 0.023 | 3.6 | 0.055 | 0.585 | 0.008810 | 1.4 | 0.096801 | 15.3 | 0.634587 | *101.67* | 180 |
| 21 | Polatli – POLGAZ | January 13, 2005 | Yes | 0.505976 | 75.8 | 0.023 | 3.4 | 0.230 | 2.447 | 0.036840 | 5.5 | 0.101847 | 15.3 | 0.667663 | *106.96* | 180 |
| 22 | Izmir – IZMIRGAZ | January 27, 2005 | Yes | 0.505976 | 80.8 | 0.023 | 3.7 | 0.012 | 0.128 | 0.001922 | 0.3 | 0.095562 | 15.3 | 0.626460 | *100.36* | 180 |
| 23 | Manisa – MANISAGAZ | February 24, 2005 | Yes | 0.505976 | 80.7 | 0.023 | 3.7 | 0.016 | 0.170 | 0.002563 | 0.4 | 0.095677 | 15.3 | 0.627216 | *100.48* | 180 |
| 24 | Nigde Nevsehir – KAPADOKYAGAZ | March 17, 2005 | Yes | 0.505976 | 78.7 | 0.023 | 3.6 | 0.098 | 1.043 | 0.015697 | 2.4 | 0.098041 | 15.3 | 0.642714 | *102.97* | 180 |
| 25 | Bilecik Bolu – BEYGAZ | June 9, 2005 | Yes | 0.505976 | 80.7 | 0.023 | 3.7 | 0.016 | 0.170 | 0.002563 | 0.4 | 0.095677 | 15.3 | 0.627216 | *100.48* | 180 |
| 26 | Karabuk Kastamonu Cankiri – KARGAZ | June 16, 2005 | Yes | 0.505976 | 79.4 | 0.023 | 3.6 | 0.069 | 0.734 | 0.011052 | 1.7 | 0.097205 | 15.3 | 0.637233 | *102.09* | 180 |
| 27 | Edirne Kirklareli Tekirdag – TRAKYAGAZ | June 23, 2005 | Yes | 0.505976 | 81.1 | 0.023 | 3.7 | 0.000 | 0.000 | 0.000000 | 0.0 | 0.095216 | 15.3 | 0.624192 | *100.00* | 0 |
| 28 | Yozgat – SURMELIGAZ | June 30, 2005 | Yes | 0.505976 | 77.0 | 0.023 | 3.5 | 0.176 | 1.873 | 0.028191 | 4.3 | 0.100290 | 15.3 | 0.657457 | *105.33* | 180 |
| 29 | Malatya – PEGAZ | July 7, 2005 | Yes | 0.505976 | 80.2 | 0.023 | 3.6 | 0.037 | 0.394 | 0.005926 | 0.9 | 0.096282 | 15.3 | 0.631185 | *101.12* | 180 |

| | | | | | | | | | | | | | | | | |
|---|---|---|---|---|---|---|---|---|---|---|---|---|---|---|---|---|
| 30 | Kahramanmaras – ARMADAS | July 14, 2005 | Yes | 0.505976 | 80.8 | 0.023 | 3.7 | 0.009 | 0.096 | 0.001442 | 0.2 | 0.095475 | 15.3 | 0.625893 | *100.27* | 180 |
| 31 | Denizli – KENTGAZ | July 21, 2005 | Yes | 0.505976 | 81.1 | 0.023 | 3.7 | 0.000 | 0.000 | 0.000000 | 0.0 | 0.095216 | 15.3 | 0.624192 | *100.00* | 149 |
| 32 | Gaziantep Kilis – GAZDAS | July 28, 2005 | Yes | 0.505976 | 81.1 | 0.023 | 3.7 | 0.000 | 0.000 | 0.000000 | 0.0 | 0.095216 | 15.3 | 0.624192 | *100.00* | 30 |
| 33 | Sanli Urfa – GURGAZ | November 9, 2005 | Yes | 0.505976 | 78.8 | 0.023 | 3.6 | 0.095 | 1.011 | 0.015217 | 2.4 | 0.097955 | 15.3 | 0.642147 | *102.88* | 180 |
| 34 | Canakkale – CANAKKALEGAZ | December 16, 2005 | Yes | 0.505976 | 81.0 | 0.023 | 3.7 | 0.001 | 0.011 | 0.000160 | 0.0 | 0.095245 | 15.3 | 0.624381 | *100.03* | 180 |
| 35 | Isparta Burdur – TOROSGAZ | December 23, 2005 | Yes | 0.505976 | 80.7 | 0.023 | 3.7 | 0.015 | 0.160 | 0.002403 | 0.4 | 0.095648 | 15.3 | 0.627027 | *100.45* | 180 |
| 36 | Afyonkarahisar – AFYONGAZ | January 6, 2006 | Yes | 0.505976 | 81.1 | 0.023 | 3.7 | 0.000 | 0.000 | 0.000000 | 0.0 | 0.095216 | 15.3 | 0.624192 | *100.00* | 174 |
| 37 | Kars Ardahan – KARGAZ | January 20, 2006 | Yes | 0.505976 | 74.7 | 0.023 | 3.4 | 0.279 | 2.969 | 0.044689 | 6.6 | 0.103260 | 15.3 | 0.676924 | *108.45* | 180 |
| 38 | Erzincan – ERZINGAZ | January 27, 2006 | Yes | 0.505976 | 78.9 | 0.023 | 3.6 | 0.089 | 0.947 | 0.014256 | 2.2 | 0.097782 | 15.3 | 0.641013 | *102.69* | 180 |
| 39 | Karaman – DOGANGAZ | February 3, 2006 | Yes | 0.505976 | 77.7 | 0.023 | 3.5 | 0.144 | 1.532 | 0.023065 | 3.5 | 0.099367 | 15.3 | 0.651409 | *104.36* | 180 |
| 40 | Amasya Tokat Turhal – TAMDAS | February 10, 2006 | Yes | 0.505976 | 81.1 | 0.023 | 3.7 | 0.000 | 0.000 | 0.000000 | 0.0 | 0.095216 | 15.3 | 0.624192 | *100.00* | 163 |
| 41 | Antalya – OLIMPOSGAZ | February 17, 2006 | Yes | 0.505976 | 81.1 | 0.023 | 3.7 | 0.000 | 0.000 | 0.000000 | 0.0 | 0.095216 | 15.3 | 0.624192 | *100.00* | 5 |
| 42 | K.bey M. Kemalpasa Susurluk – OVAGAZ | February 24, 2006 | Yes | 0.505976 | 79.1 | 0.023 | 3.6 | 0.081 | 0.862 | 0.012974 | 2.0 | 0.097551 | 15.3 | 0.639501 | *102.45* | 180 |
| 43 | Elazig – ELAZIGGAZ | July 21, 2006 | Yes | 0.505976 | 81.1 | 0.023 | 3.7 | 0.000 | 0.000 | 0.000000 | 0.0 | 0.095216 | 15.3 | 0.624192 | *100.00* | 5 |
| 44 | Trabzon Rize – KARADENIZGAZ | September 15, 2006 | Yes | 0.505976 | 80.9 | 0.023 | 3.7 | 0.008 | 0.085 | 0.001281 | 0.2 | 0.095446 | 15.3 | 0.625704 | *100.24* | 180 |
| 45 | Gumushane Bayburt – ANADOLU | September 22, 2006 | Yes | 0.505976 | 75.4 | 0.023 | 3.4 | 0.250 | 2.660 | 0.040044 | 6.0 | 0.102424 | 15.3 | 0.671443 | *107.57* | 180 |

(continued)

**Table 7.3** (continued)

| No | Distribution region and company | Tender date | Gas supplied | Cost of gas purchase from BOTAS (YTL/m³) | As % of total price | Special consumption tax (YTL/m³) | As % of total price | USDC (¢/kwh) | USDC (¢/m³) | USDC (YTL/m³) | As % of total price | Value added tax (18%) | As % of total price | Gas price for households (YTL/m³) | Minimum price = 100 | Connection charge ($) |
|---|---|---|---|---|---|---|---|---|---|---|---|---|---|---|---|---|
| 46 | Diyarbakir – DIYARGAZ | November 3, 2006 | Yes | 0.505976 | 74.5 | 0.023 | 3.4 | 0.290 | 3.086 | 0.046451 | 6.8 | 0.103577 | 15.3 | 0.679003 | *108.78* | 180 |
| 47 | Adiyaman – AKMERCANGAZ | December 1, 2006 | Yes | 0.505976 | 80.8 | 0.023 | 3.7 | 0.010 | 0.106 | 0.001602 | 0.3 | 0.095504 | 15.3 | 0.626082 | *100.30* | 180 |
| 48 | Ordu Giresun – FINDIKGAZ | December 8, 2006 | Yes | 0.505976 | 81.1 | 0.023 | 3.7 | 0.000 | 0.000 | 0.000000 | 0.0 | 0.095216 | 15.3 | 0.624192 | *100.00* | 169 |
| 49 | Van – AKSA | March 16, 2007 | Yes | 0.505976 | 74.4 | 0.023 | 3.4 | 0.297 | 3.160 | 0.047572 | 7.0 | 0.103779 | 15.3 | 0.680326 | *108.99* | 180 |
| 50 | Seydisehir Cumra – CENGIZ | March 23, 2007 | Yes | 0.505976 | 79.5 | 0.023 | 3.6 | 0.063 | 0.670 | 0.010091 | 1.6 | 0.097032 | 15.3 | 0.636099 | *101.91* | 180 |
| 51 | Cukurova – AKSAGAZ | July 20, 2007 | Yes | 0.505976 | 81.1 | 0.023 | 3.7 | 0.000 | 0.000 | 0.000000 | 0.0 | 0.095216 | 15.3 | 0.624192 | *100.00* | 167 |
| 52 | Siirt Batman – ANADOLU | December 28, 2007 | No | 0.505976 | 75.7 | 0.023 | 3.4 | 0.235 | 2.500 | 0.037641 | 5.6 | 0.101991 | 15.3 | 0.668608 | *107.12* | 180 |
| 53 | Aydin – METANGAZ | February 8, 2008 | No | 0.505976 | 81.1 | 0.023 | 3.7 | 0.000 | 0.000 | 0.000000 | 0.0 | 0.095216 | 15.3 | 0.624192 | *100.00* | 165 |
| 54 | Istanbul – IGDAS | Public | Yes | 0.505976 | 68.8 | 0.023 | 3.1 | – | – | 0.093957 | 12.8 | 0.112128 | 15.3 | 0.735061 | *117.76* | 190 |
| 55 | Ankara – BASKENTGAZ | Privatized | Yes | 0.505976 | 70.0 | 0.023 | 3.2 | – | – | 0.083625 | 11.6 | 0.110268 | 15.3 | 0.722869 | *115.81* | 190 |
| 56 | Adapazari – AGDAS | Privatized | Yes | 0.505976 | 71.9 | 0.023 | 3.3 | – | – | 0.067640 | 9.6 | 0.107391 | 15.3 | 0.704007 | *112.79* | 290 |
| 57 | Izmit – IZGAZ | Privatized | Yes | 0.505976 | 70.2 | 0.023 | 3.2 | – | – | 0.082271 | 11.4 | 0.110024 | 15.3 | 0.721271 | *115.55* | 190 |
| 58 | Eskisehir – ESGAZ | Privatized | Yes | 0.505976 | 78.8 | 0.023 | 3.6 | – | – | 0.015434 | 2.4 | 0.097994 | 15.3 | 0.642404 | *102.92* | 190 |
| 59 | Bursa – BURSAGAZ | Privatized | Yes | 0.505976 | 75.7 | 0.023 | 3.4 | – | – | 0.037635 | 5.6 | 0.101990 | 15.3 | 0.668601 | *107.11* | 190 |
| 60 | Bahcesehir – BAHCESEHIRGAZ | Privatized | Yes | 0.505976 | 67.6 | 0.023 | 3.1 | – | – | 0.105233 | 14.1 | 0.114158 | 15.3 | 0.748367 | *119.89* | 190 |

*Notes*: $/YTL parity in May 2010 = 1.5054; m³/kwh = 10.64
*USDC*: unit service and depreciation charge
*Source*: The data are collected by the author from web sites of EMRA, BOTAS, and various regional natural gas distribution companies in Turkey

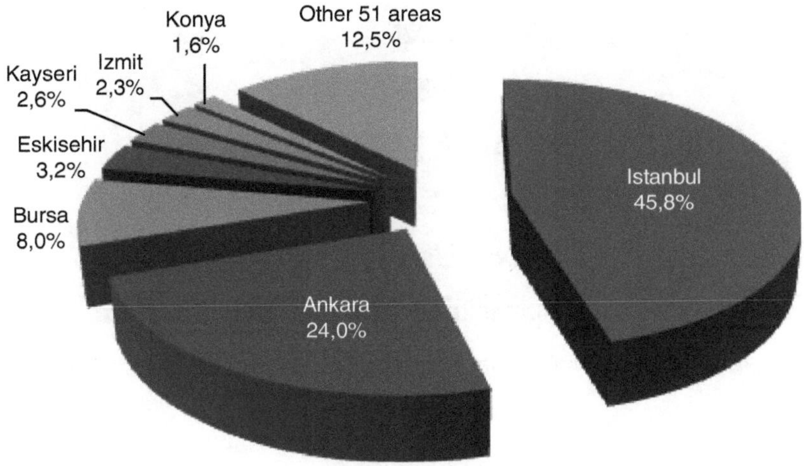


**Fig. 7.5** The distribution of household equivalent customers at the end of 2009. *Source*: The data are collected by the author from web sites of EMRA, BOTAS, and various regional natural gas distribution companies in Turkey

Figure 7.5 presents the share of each distribution area in total household equivalent customers. As clearly seen in Fig. 7.5, although IGDAS is the only publicly owned company in Turkish natural gas distribution market, it holds 45.8% of all customers, meaning that almost half of the natural gas consumers in Turkey depend on a public company for their gas supply. Moreover, the three largest companies (Igdas, Baskentgaz, and Bursagaz) control 78% of gas distribution market. The data in Table 7.3 and Fig. 7.5 are collected from various web sites of EMRA, BOTAS, and regional natural gas distribution companies in Turkey.

When we analyze Table 7.3 in more detail, some important points can be highlighted. First of all, the only price component that changes from one region to another is USDC. The share of USDC in total price fluctuates between 0 and 14.1%, meaning that in some regions (those with USDC is 0%) consumers pay about up to 20% less for natural gas than others living in other regions. Since USDC means investment recovery and profit for the distribution company, it is extremely striking to see that as a result of tenders in 11 regions, the bid of the winning firm for USDC was "0," meaning that in the first 8 years these firms agree that they will not recover their investment and will not make any profit! Even more striking example is the tender for Edirne–Kirklareli–Tekirdag distribution region. In this tender, after participating firms bid "0" for USDC, the tender continued on connection fee and it is announced that the firm with lowest connection fee proposal wins the tender. However, firms again reduced their bids up to "0." Then, the tender continued based on how much extra money to pay to operate in the region! At the end, the firm that agreed to pay an initial lump sum payment of 2,500,000 TL (about $1.6 million) won the tender. So, in this region, the winning firm accepted that for the first 8 years, it will invest into infrastructure and connect consumers without any cost recovery, will not make any profit, and, most remarkably, will pay even extra money to operate!

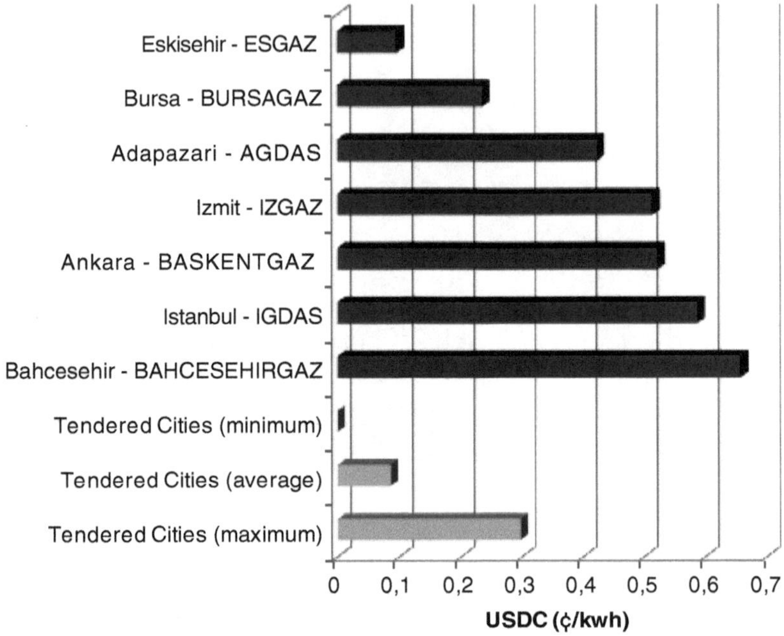


**Fig. 7.6** USDC in tendered and nontendered regions. *Source*: The data are collected by the author from web sites of EMRA, BOTAS, and various regional natural gas distribution companies in Turkey

The share of USDC in total price in tendered regions differs from that in privatized and publicly owned regions. The share of USDC is between 14.1% and 2.4% in privatized and public-owned regions while it is just between 7% and 0% in tendered regions. Figure 7.6 compares gas distribution regions in terms of USDC. On average, consumers in tendered regions pay about 10% less than those living in other six areas. However, a closer look to gas prices reveals that the main gas price components are the cost of gas purchase from BOTAS (between 68% and 81% of total price) and taxes (about 18%). The share of USDC in total price fluctuates between 0 and 14.1%. So any effective policy to reduce gas prices in Turkey should include a reduction in one of these, especially in gas purchase costs.

This unique tender process based upon USDC seems at first sight a clear success as it limits the profits of distribution companies and even in some cases reduces them to zero! However, a deeper analysis may reveal that it is actually not the case. Do we really expect firms to invest and operate without any cost recovery and profit? Are they charity organizations? Of course, answer is straightforward: "No!" So, why do they bid "0"? Actually, there are four explanations to this extraordinary situation. First of all, it is argued that although firms may incur a loss during the first 8 years, they expect a tariff from EMRA that allows them to recover their losses and have a huge profit in the second tariff period after the first 8 years. According to this explanation, in spite of some losses in the first 8 years, firms still bid "0" just to keep this region in their hands as they expect enormous returns in the following periods. Second explanation relates to the connection fees. Supporters of this argument point out that since almost all consumers will be connected for the first time in these regions, the total income from connection fees is enough to cover all investment cost and provide a reasonable return during the first 8 years. Advocates of the third explanation state that large gas consumers in some regions come together and bid "0" not to pay for USDC to any alternative distribution company. This explanation assumes that the gain from not paying USDC is more than the cost of setting up entire natural gas distribution infrastructure and supplying gas to consumers without any profit. Final possible answer to the question focuses on the future market policies of the firms. It states that firms bid "0" as they regard these distribution areas just as "markets" for the gas they are to import from abroad. The adherents of this view are in the opinion that when BOTAS' de facto monopoly on import is abolished in practice, current distribution firms will set up some sister companies, get import licenses from EMRA, import gas from other countries, and sell it in their distribution zones with huge profits. This view assumes that firms do not expect any profit from their distribution activities, but they expect enormous gains from their future import businesses as there exists no limit in Turkey on how much profit an importer can make as long as distribution company proves that it purchases gas from the most "economical" source.

The economic literature on auctions presumes tenders on a regular basis. However, Turkish version differs from the mainstream literature in that only one tender is projected for each distribution region. The tariff-setting process for the period after the first 8 years is not clear. After the first 8 years, there may be a tariff structure based on a rate-of-return-regulation (RoRR) or price cap (RPI-X) or another tender-based system may be put into practice. In short, Turkish regulatory system suffers from the problems of regulatory uncertainty and inconsistency. This largely stems from the fact that while licenses are granted for 30 years, the tenders fix USDCs for only 8 years. A logical solution to this problem may be the following strategy. Before 8-year period expires, EMRA receives proposals from distribution companies for the second-term USDCs and approves them if they are below the current USDC levels. If proposals are above the previous levels, EMRA organizes new tenders for the distribution zones. If EMRA employs such a strategy, the first answer to the question "why do firms bid '0' in tenders?" mentioned above may be falsified. As for second answer, it is not likely as it is very questionable whether the total revenue from connection fees is able to cover all investment and operation costs. In particular, this argument is totally displaced by the tender for Edirne–Kirklareli–Tekirdag distribution region in which even connection fees turned out to be "0." Third explanation is also not plausible as it is again very questionable whether gains from not paying USDC is more than the cost of setting up whole natural gas distribution infrastructure and supplying gas to consumers without any profit. Among four explanations, the final one is the one that sounds most convincing. However, there is nothing wrong with such a situation. If a distribution company sets up a sister importing company, purchases and distributes the gas imported by this company and, at the same time, proves that it is the most "economical" source; let it do so.

At the time of writing this chapter, EMRA published (on July 8, 2009) a draft regulation concerning the determination of gas distribution tariffs after the first 8 years in tendered cities. The draft regulation envisages that, after the first 8 years, the final gas sale price to consumers will consist of gas purchase cost, system utilization charge (SUC), and taxes. USDC and transportation charge form SUC, which is going to be determined by EMRA based on information about the cost structure of each distribution company.

## 7.6 Turkish Reforms Within EU Framework

The European Commission embarked on an ambitious program to reform natural gas markets of its member states in 1998. At the time, most of the 27 countries that now make up the EU had a single, vertically integrated gas supply firm, most of which were state-owned. In general, this company handled the purchase/extraction of gas, its transmission, storage, and supply to consumers or local distribution companies. The Commission's 1998 Gas Directive laid out a roadmap to achieve an open, competitive gas market across the EU. In 2003, a second Gas Directive introduced an accelerated timetable and more detailed regulatory rules.

The full opening-up of national gas markets, arrangements for which are set out in 2003 Directive, represents the completion of a competitive internal gas market within the European Union (EU). In practice, industrial clients and domestic customers have had the freedom to choose their gas supplier since July 1, 2004 and July 1, 2007, respectively. This directive also lays down the right of third parties to nondiscriminatory access to transmission and distribution systems and to LNG facilities. Access to storage facilities is covered by specific provisions by virtue of which access may be either negotiated or regulated. Besides, in each member state, system operators are appointed for the transmission, storage, LNG, and the distribution systems. They must guarantee nondiscriminatory and transparent access to the system for all users. Access must therefore be based on fair tariffs that are applied objectively. System operators may not favor certain companies, in particular, with which they are associated. In order to avoid any discrimination relating to network access and enable equal access for new entrants, when companies are vertically integrated, the transmission and distribution activities must be legally and functionally separate from other activities, such as production and supply. This separation does not, however, mean ownership unbundling. Moreover, independent regulators are expected to be responsible for monitoring, respect for the nondiscrimination principle, the level of transparency and competition, and the tariffs and methods for calculating them. The regulatory authorities also act as dispute settlement authorities.

Since enactment of 2003 directive, European gas markets have gradually liberalized. Today, with a few local exceptions, EU consumers can choose their gas supplier. Transmission networks have been unbundled from vertically integrated structures and are managed by separate operating companies. Most gas import, transmission, and storage infrastructure is open to TPA on an increasingly open and transparent basis. Controlled prices for end-users have largely been eliminated. Each national government has appointed a regulator to oversee liberalization process and competition. However, despite all these improvements, EU is far from achieving a fully liberal and competitive market. Although governments and companies eventually complied with the Directives, in many cases they have done so unwillingly. France delayed implementation until forced to do so by a European Court of Justice ruling. This allowed Gaz de France (GdF) to retain a near-monopoly on its home market until 2003, while moving into more rapidly liberalizing markets elsewhere in Europe. In Germany, the incumbent gas companies initially persuaded the government that they could implement an open, liberalized market through voluntary agreements, without formal market regulation. Their idea of an open market proved, predictably, to favor the status quo, in which a handful of vertically integrated suppliers dominated the market. Companies seeking to enter German market were effectively prevented by a system of long-term contracts and faced practical difficulties in using the complex TPA system to obtain transmission capacity. It was not until 2005 that a regulator was appointed and not until late 2006 that a workable system of TPA and customer access started to emerge in Germany. Besides, in several countries, including France, Spain, and Italy, governments maintained a system of controlled end-user prices to protect smaller consumers from competitive market prices. This created a two-tier market in which eligible customers were open to competitive supply offers, while tariff customers could be supplied only by incumbent companies, under protected terms. These and other distortions of the liberalization process allowed many incumbents to retain a favored position during the liberalization programs in EU member states.

On July 13, 2009, the European Parliament passed the third energy liberalization package that includes the third gas directive. However, the new package will be in effect after March 3, 2011. The package contains the following measures. First of all, member states will have to choose between the three "unbundling" options: (a) full ownership unbundling; (b) the independent system operator (ISO); and (c) the independent transmission operator (ITO). From March 3, 2012, member states are required to unbundle transmission systems and transmission system operators (TSOs). They must also designate distribution system operators that are independent in legal terms from other activities not relating to distribution. Moreover, new package also included regulations leading to a general improvement in consumer rights. For instance, the directive requires that all customers have the right to choose their gas supplier and to change supplier easily, with their operator's assistance, within 3 weeks. Another measure in the package is the introduction of the "Gazprom clause." It is agreed that a national regulator will have the right to refuse certification of a TSO controlled by "a person or persons from a third country" (meaning Russia!) if this company does not comply with the unbundling requirements, and its market entry would jeopardize the member states' or the EU's security of supply (EU 2009). In addition, an EU Agency for the Cooperation of Energy Regulators is created to set out nonbinding guidelines. Also, the new legislative package requires the establishment of European Networks of Transmission System Operators for Gas (ENTSOG), which is to implement the network codes. Finally, the new package also necessitates the implementation of measures to improve the regional cooperation between different national regulators, as well as measures to strengthen the independence of national regulators. After approval by national governments, states will have one and a half years to put the measures on unbundling and regulation in place, and 3 years to put into effect the Gazprom clause.

The new package has been criticized for not going far enough. Parliament had initially been strongly opposed to the "third way" option on unbundling (the ITO model). The national regulator is likely to face substantial additional responsibilities under such a model as it is largely based on greater monitoring and enforcement. The regulator would oversee activities including the appointment of senior staff, the appointment of a compliance officer, the drafting, and implementation of TPA arrangements, and the approval and ongoing monitoring and evaluation of a rolling investment plan. As such, the regulatory burden created by the ITO proposal is likely to be greater than under an ownership-unbundling model. However, the European Council refused to remove this option. It has also been criticized for the general lack of regional focus, illustrated not only by the supra-national ENTSOG, but also a lack of incentives for TSOs to maximize the availability of existing cross-border hubs and connections. The Parliament has demanded that regulators have extra power, with the creation of the EU Agency for the Cooperation of Energy Regulators, but there remains the concern that this is just another layer of bureaucracy in a package designed to free up the single market.

Within this context, Turkey is actually not required to implement any of the EU directives as she is not a member of the EU. However, the country has been very enthusiastic about following them and has put EU directives into practice as she regards them as a further step in its policy of becoming an EU member.[3] Therefore, NGML was prepared in line with 1998 Directive and has been modified to reflect changes introduced by 2003 Directive. It is expected that Turkey will again change NGML to incorporate new measures brought by new legislative package of 2009. However, within this framework, we need to mention two important points. First, EU legislation requires unbundling of transmission function from wholesale business. However, in Turkey, BOTAS currently perform these two activities within a vertically integrated structure. Also, new legislative package requires one of the three "unbundling" options: (a) full ownership unbundling; (b) the ISO; (c) the ITO. In Turkey, none is existent. Another, and probably more important, problem is Turkey's policy of blindly following EU directives. Today, in the European gas wholesale market, the concentration is great. The three largest wholesalers have a market share of 90% or more in 12 member states (European Commission 2009). Another particular problem in the EU is the lack of will among member states and the EU Commission to reduce the market power of dominant companies. They prefer to maintain or allow the emergence of "national champions" in the gas sector. This preference also explains why the EU gas reform model has not included priva-

[3] In October 2005, accession negotiations were opened with Turkey, who has been an associate member of the EU since 1963 and an official candidate since 1999. For a more detailed discussion of EU–Turkey relations, see Erdogdu (2002).

tization of any of the currently state-owned assets. In short, EU directives may not be the best guide to reform Turkey's gas market. They reflect a compromise among member states and definitely are the result of a political (not scientific) process that takes into account interests of specific EU countries. By implementing them without questioning, Turkey follows policies in the formation process of which her interests have not been taken into account.

## 7.7 Discussion and Guidelines for Policy Makers

After covering almost all main issues in Turkish gas market, let us make some comments on the developments so far. Our analysis will be made under five headings: (a) market structure, (b) gas release program, (c) gas distribution auctions, (d) regulatory environment, and (e) Turkey's position vis-à-vis EU framework.

The most important problem in Turkish gas market is the vertically integrated structure of BOTAS. Although NGML of 2001 includes many measures to limit and reduce its market power, in practice, little has been done to achieve this objective. At present, BOTAS controls about 90% of wholesale gas market while spot LNG importers and private import companies (emerged as a result of gas release program) are responsible for 8% of the market. The remaining 2% belongs to domestic gas producers. Two main reasons behind this failure are the unwillingness of BOTAS and inability of EMRA in enforcing the articles of the Law that aim at reducing BOTAS' influence in the market. Although the Law gives EMRA the right to impose large amounts of fines on market participants that violate the regulations, EMRA in practice has never applied any fines to BOTAS for violating articles of the Law. More importantly, in many occasions, BOTAS representatives never hesitated to claim that NGML is simply impracticable and there is a need for even further vertical integration in the industry. Although it is well understandable that BOTAS, like any other bureaucratic structure, wants to keep its sphere of influence intact and, therefore, opposes all initiatives aiming at reducing its power, no one can speak of a liberal competitive market without full disintegration in supply side of the sector. Without eliminating BOTAS's market dominance, reforms are destined to fail without producing any tangible benefits in practice.

Second topic is actually related to first one and focuses on the failure in contract release program. Turkey's official natural gas consumption projection for 2010 is 37 bcm (EMRA Board Decision, No: 2409/5, Dated January 28, 2010) and up to now BOTAS has released only 4 bcm of its contracted gas. That is, as of July 2010, BOTAS' market power in gas import/wholesale has only reduced by 10.8% and about 90% of the entire market is currently controlled by BOTAS. However, NGML still has an article that requires BOTAS to transfer at least 10% of its total gas purchase quantity within the take-or-pay contracts every year to reach the 20% market share by 2009! So, it is obvious that in import/wholesale segment of the market, reforms failed to a great extent. Now, the best policy to follow seems to unbundle and privatize BOTAS as soon as possible and develop new realistic targets with sensible timetables to transfer BOTAS' gas contracts. Besides, it should be kept in mind that so-called "volume transfer" is not a substitute for "contract transfer" and does not provide any benefits expected from a gas release program. So, Turkey should avoid any policies based on "volume transfer" option. What's more, Russia has not opened up its domestic natural gas market but developed a strategy for expanding into liberalized markets through Gazprom and its subsidiaries. In Turkey, Gazprom owns 40% share of Bosphorus Gaz and secured 0.75 bcm of gas in the first step of gas release program in Turkey through this company. Currently, its market share in Turkish wholesale gas market is only 2%, but it has a huge potential to increase this figure and have a dominant position in Turkish gas market. Since the main aim is not to replace a national public monopoly with a foreign private one, EMRA should monitor the developments in the market and never let any player (especially Gazprom) have a market share above 20% in wholesale supply market by taking necessary proactive measures.

Auctions in Turkish natural gas distribution market seems to be a clear success as they enabled the construction of gas infrastructure in many cities without being a burden on public finance and provided a relative reduction in end-user gas prices. Up to now, private distribution companies in tendered cities have invested about 2.1 billion TL (US$1.4 billion) in gas infrastructure. This shows that the reforms may work well in an environment where a vertically integrated monopolist is absent (*or* eliminated). Here, there are some points worth mentioning. First, EMRA should clarify and announce the tariff-setting process to be implemented after the first 8 years so as to eliminate regulatory uncertainty. In this context, current draft regulation on determination of distribution tariffs after the first 8 years seems to be in conflict with the basic logic of conducting auctions. Because of information asymmetries, like any other regulatory authority, EMRA could not determine optimum level of USDCs on its own and it may also be a target for "regulatory capture" if it tries to do so. Therefore, EMRA should not approve or determine USDC levels above current ones as such a policy may result in excessive profits. Instead, before the end of the first 8 year period, EMRA should receive proposals from distribution companies for the second-term USDCs and approve them if they are below the current USDC levels. If proposals turn out to be above the previous levels, EMRA should organize new tenders for these distribution zones. In 2011, the first tariff period based on auction results will end for some gas distribution companies and EMRA will have to specify and implement a new tariff structure for these distribution areas. The policy of EMRA on this issue will shape the future tariff structure of Turkish gas distribution market as most probably the same structure will apply all other distribution companies as the first tariff periods expire one by one. EMRA will decide, by its new tariff structure, whether the market will be based on a kind of RoRR[4] with all its deficiencies and risks or it will transform into an efficient market that limits excessive profits and reflects the true cost of supplying natural gas to consumers. Second, tariff-setting periods and duration of licenses should be

[4]For a discussion of RoRR regulation, see Erdogdu (2007).

equaled and preferably both may be set at 10 years. Third, the difference between tendered and nontendered regions in terms of USDC levels should gradually be eliminated. Tenders have showed that distribution service can be provided at much lower costs compared with those in nontendered regions. After expiration of current tariff periods in nontendered areas, tenders may be conducted for these regions as well. Finally, IGDAS should be privatized as soon as possible. If these issues are addressed satisfactorily, then Turkish gas distribution market model may serve well as a successful example that can be copied by other reforming countries.

As for regulatory structure, Turkey suffers from some deficiencies in regulatory design. The most important problem is regulator's inability and failure in enforcing the market rules against public monopolies. For example, although BOTAS did not implement any meaningful gas release program for a long time and has publicly opposed to it, EMRA did not take any action and simply ignored it. This inability originates to some extent from the fact that all board members of EMRA are appointed by Turkish Council of Ministers as a result of a political process. Since the main idea behind creating an autonomous regulatory agency is to prevent government intervention into gas market on political grounds and separate the regulation of gas sector from day-to-day politics, current appointment process looks irrelevant. Hence, some members of the board may be selected by the industry and consumer representatives, universities, and other related institutions. Moreover, another important reason for regulatory inability is the fact that EMRA devotes most of its human and material resources to regulate petroleum and LPG sectors. Actually, unlike electricity and gas markets, the petroleum and LPG markets in Turkey have been operating in a relatively liberalized manner for quite some time. In fact, recent reforms in petroleum and LPG markets have aimed at solving one of the most important problems of Turkish economy in general: large-scale fuel smuggling. Since fuel smuggling is a security-related issue and has nothing to do with economic regulation, EMRA's duties in these areas should be transferred to related institutions. Actually, from an academic point of view, there is no need for economic regulation in petroleum and LPG markets as these are not network industries. Besides, EMRA's responsibilities in these areas prevent it from effectively regulating gas and electricity industries.[5] For instance, up to now, EMRA has distributed 14,906 licenses for petroleum and 8,643 for LPG markets while it issued only 198 licenses for natural gas sector. When we take into account the fact that EMRA has about 400 employees to manage all these licenses, we can easily see the extent to which EMRA's resources are wasted for carrying out functions that are not supposed to be carried out by an economic regulator.

Another important topic relates to Turkey's position within EU legislative framework. Apart from some minor differences, on the whole, Turkish regulatory structure is in line with that of the EU. However, there are two important differences between EU and Turkish legal structures. First, current EU legislation requires that all consumers should be able to select their supplier. In Turkey, however, majority of the consumers are captive and do not have the right to determine who supplies the

[5]For a broad discussion of Turkish energy market reforms in general, see Erdogdu (2007).

gas they consume. Even if EMRA reduces the eligibility threshold to zero, it still does not meet EU standards as there exists no alternative supplier in Turkey to which consumers can switch. So without unbundling BOTAS and completing gas release program, it is impossible to realize EU norms in this area in the short run. Second, the new legislative package of 2009 requires the unbundling of BOTAS either in the form of complete ownership separation or in the form of establishment of an ISO or an ITO. For the time being, none of these options is available in Turkey. Therefore, Turkey needs to take measures to put into practice any of these models.

Overall, in Turkey, there exists a huge gap between expectations from the reform process and capabilities of institutions to realize these expectations. Although NGML of 2001 provides an ideal ground for reforms, the reform process fails largely due to this "capabilities-expectations gap." To close this gap, the targets set in the Law should be made more realistic, and the institutions and regulatory practices should be strengthened as much as possible. However, this does not mean that Turkey should give up her aim of creating a fully liberal gas market. Instead, this objective should be kept but the means to achieve it should be redefined.

## 7.8 Conclusion

In this chapter, we have tried to offer a glimpse of the Turkish natural gas market and various issues surrounding it. A functioning gas market can only become a reality if consumers play an active role and actually exercise their right to free choice of their gas supplier. Today, BOTAS' ongoing monopoly in Turkish natural gas market – such as its share in imports, long-term purchase contracts, and ownership of transmission network – prevents the establishment of a healthy structure in Turkish gas market. It is absolutely necessary to reduce BOTAS' dominant role in the market in order to successfully institutionalize competition and reduce prices to just and reasonable levels. However, despite failures in unbundling of BOTAS so far, there are still plenty of opportunities to create a competitive environment in Turkey. Just few years later, in 2015, BOTAS' contracted gas supply will reduce to 42 bcm while the demand is expected to be roughly 50 bcm at that time. In the following years, BOTAS' import contracts will gradually expire and demand will continue to grow. In short, it is possible to reduce BOTAS' market share by just preventing it from signing new import contracts and encouraging new players to import gas from various sources. Hence, even without gas release program, BOTAS' share will turn out to be <50% by 2020 and about 20% by 2030, provided that it is not allowed to conclude any new import contracts.

As before, BOTAS is expected to be very defensive about its position in Turkish gas market, and will not do its best to facilitate the implementation of reform measures. Therefore, the regulator should take a more active role in the future to prevent violation of market rules and policies aimed at slowing down reform process.

In Turkey, only about 3% of total gas consumption is produced domestically, the remaining 97% is imported. Then, more than half of this gas is used to produce electricity, and the remaining is consumed by households and industry. We agree that the encouragement of the expansion of the gas distribution networks to cities is an acceptable policy for various practical and environmental benefits; however, there is no logical justification for the utilization of an imported source in electricity production at such a gigantic scale. Turkey should take every necessary step to reduce natural gas consumption in electricity generation, including constructing nuclear power stations.

As we mentioned before, city natural gas distribution tenders constitute the most successful aspect of Turkish gas market reform experience. If this success in distribution side is combined with a potential success in import/wholesale side, then there is no reason for not creating a well-functioning natural gas market that may set an example to follow not only for various developing countries, but also for many European countries where most of the market is still controlled by a few integrated companies.

As no meaningful competition has developed in Turkish gas market so far, a significant amount of work still lies ahead. It should not be forgotten that the true test of regulatory success comes in the form of whether a structure in which suppliers, customers, and other actors in the market can all freely negotiate – each taking their own view of the prices, risks, opportunities, and threats that a competitive market offers – is created or not. As long as gas prices for end-users are determined by the government, no one can speak of a functioning gas market in Turkey.

## References


Akcollu, Y. (2006). Major Challenges to the Liberalization of the Turkish Natural Gas Market. Oxford Institute for Energy Studies, NG 16. Retrieved from http://www.oxfordenergy.org.

BOTAS (2010a). Gas Purchase Agreements. Retrieved on October 11, 2010, from http://www.botas.gov.tr.

BOTAS (2010b). Natural Gas Network. Retrieved on October 13, 2010, from http://www.botas.gov.tr.

Chadwick, E. (1859). Results of Different Principles of Legislation and Administration in Europe; Of Competition for the Field, as Compared with Competition Within the Field, of Service. Journal of the Statistical Society of London, 22(3), 381–420.

Demsetz, H. (1968). Why Regulate Utilities? The Journal of Law and Economics, 11(1), 55–65.

EMRA (2010). Natural Gas Market Statistics. Retrieved on October 12, 2010, from http://www.epdk.org.tr.

Erdogdu, E. (2002). Turkey and Europe: Undivided but Not United. Middle East Review of International Affairs (MERIA), 6(2), 40–51.

Erdogdu, E. (2007). Regulatory Reform in Turkish Energy Industry: An Analysis. Energy Policy, 35(2), 984–993.

Erdogdu, E. (2010a). Natural Gas Demand in Turkey. Applied Energy, 87(1), 211–219.

Erdogdu, E. (2010b). A Review of Turkish Natural Gas Distribution Market. Renewable and Sustainable Energy Reviews, 14(2), 806–813.

EU (2009). Directive 2009/73/EC of the European Parliament and of the Council of 13 July 2009 Concerning Common Rules for the Internal Market in Natural Gas and Repealing Directive 2003/55/EC. Retrieved on October 15, 2010, from http://ec.europa.eu/energy/gas_electricity.

European Commission (2009). Communication from the Commission to the Council and the European Parliament: Report on Progress in Creating the Internal Gas and Electricity Market. Retrieved from http://ec.europa.eu/energy/gas_electricity.
Helm, D. (2003). Auctions and Energy Networks. Utilities Policy, 11(1), 21–25.
IEA (2010a). Energy Prices and Taxes, End-use Prices (Edition: 2009, Quarter 4). International Energy Agency. Retrieved on May 13, 2010, from http://data.iea.org.
IEA (2010b). Natural Gas Information (Edition: 2009). International Energy Agency. Retrieved on May 11, 2010, from http://data.iea.org.
IEA (2010c). World Energy Balances. International Energy Agency. Retrieved on May 11, 2010, from http://data.iea.org.

# Chapter 8
# Regulation and Competition in the Turkish Telecommunications Industry

Izak Atiyas

## 8.1 Introduction

Liberalization in the Turkish telecommunications industry has a history of about 15 years in the mobile segments and at least 7 years in the fixed segments.[1] Developments in different sectors have been asymmetric with competition more prevalent in mobile than in fixed segments, where competition is seriously lagging behind. A new Electronic Communications Law (ECL) was enacted in 2008, and this was followed by the issuance of a large number of secondary legislation.

The purpose of this chapter is to provide an overview and update on the state of liberalization, regulation, and competition in the Turkish telecommunications industry. The chapter is organized as follows: the next section reviews the legal framework and discusses the new law. The developments in major segments are described in the subsequent sections. The final section concludes.

## 8.2 General Background and the New Legal Framework

Liberalization of telephony services started with the launch of mobile phone services in 1994 through operators Turkcell and Telsim, which had revenue sharing agreements with the incumbent fixed line operator, Türk Telekom. Turkcell and Telsim were awarded licenses in 1998, a move that rendered the two operators independent from Türk Telekom and which initiated genuine competition in the mobile segment. Liberalization in fixed line telephony started after the adoption of law No. 4502, which established an independent regulatory authority, the Telecommunications

[1] For the history and background of the Turkish telecommunications industry, see Atiyas (2005), Atiyas and Doğan (2007, 2010), Atiyas and Renda (2007), Renda et al. (2009), and Togan et al. (2010).

I. Atiyas (✉)
Sabancı University, Istanbul, Turkey
e-mail: izak@sabanciuniv.edu

T. Çetin and F. Oğuz (eds.), *The Political Economy of Regulation in Turkey*,
DOI 10.1007/978-1-4419-7750-2_8, © Springer Science+Business Media, LLC 2011

Authority (TA), with powers to regulate prices, interconnection, and access. Initially, the authority to issue licenses remained in the Ministry of Transport, but that was also subsequently delegated to the TA. Law No. 4502 also stated that monopoly rights of Türk Telekom would be terminated at the end of 2003.

The framework developed in Law No. 4502 was inspired by the 1998 regulatory framework in the European Union. It relied on an individual licenses regime and the identification of operators with significant market power (SMP), and the regulatory obligations that could be imposed on them were not designed as an exercise carried out on the basis of competition law, as was the case in the 2002 EU framework.[2] The TA itself moved in the direction of the 2002 framework in its efforts to define markets and identify operators with SMP. Finally, with the adoption of Law No. 5809 in 2008 (the ECL), the regulatory framework became much more compatible with the 2002 EU framework.

The ECL changed the name of the national regulatory authority to Information Technology and Communications Authority (ITCA).[3] Overall, the law brings the Turkish regulatory framework closer to the EU 2002 framework, especially in the area of authorizations. Some of the salient features of the law are as follows:

Art. 5 of the ECL lists the duties of the Ministry of Transport, which include determining strategy and policy for electronic communications services that use scarce resources such as numbering, satellite positions, and frequencies. It also authorizes the ministry to determine the principles and policies for the promotion of competition in the electronic communications industry and take supportive measures. This is in line with the general approach adopted in the liberalization of network industries where the ministry takes on responsibility for general formulation of policy and strategy for the industry, and an independent regulatory authority is given the responsibility for the formulation and implementation of regulations.

Indeed, the law mentions the following among the competencies of the ITCA (art. 6):

- To undertake regulations so as to install and protect competition and to prevent activities that prevent or distort competition, and to impose remedies on operators with SMP and on other operators if necessary
- To undertake market analysis and determine operators with SMP
- To undertake frequency, satellite position, and numbering planning and allocation
- To maintain Board decisions, along with justifications and procedures, on matters of interest to operators and consumers open to public
- To approve as necessary, tariffs and reference access offers

This list may deserve several comments: first, unlike in the previous regime, there is an explicit reference to market analyses to determine operators with SMP

[2]See Cave (2004) for a comparison of the 1998 and 2004 regulatory frameworks for electronic communications in the EU.

[3]Both TA and ITCA are used in this chapter, depending on the period under consideration.

but the link between obligations and market analyses is rather weak. Art. 7 states that "The Authority may identify the operators with SMP in the relevant markets as a result of conducting market analyses. The Authority may also impose obligations on operators with SMP with the aim of ensuring and promoting an effective competition environment." It is further stated that obligations can be differentiated across operators with SMP.

Second, the requirement that ITCA has to publish its decisions with justifications is a major improvement in terms the transparency and the accountability of the authority.

One of the most important features of the 2002 regime in Europe is that many regulatory obligations may only be imposed on operators with SMP, which are determined on the basis of market analyses. This is also the case in the ECL. For example, art. 13 states that in the case of operators with SMP, "the Authority shall be entitled to determine the procedures regarding the approval, monitoring and supervision of tariffs as well as the upper and lower limits of the tariffs and the procedures and principles for implementation" and also to take measures to prevent anticompetitive pricing behavior such as predatory pricing or price squeeze. Similarly art. 21 states that ITCA may impose accounting separation obligation on operators with SMP. However, there are also some divergences between the ECL and the EU. Art. 33 states that ITCA may impose carrier selection (CS) and preselection (CPS) on any operator, whereas under the EU regulations these remedies can only be imposed on operators with SMP (Renda et al. 2009: 33).[4]

Regarding ex-ante and ex-post regulation, art. 6/b states that the ITCA inspects and imposes enforcements against breaches of competition in the electronic communications industry in violation of this law (i.e., law No. 5809) or of regulations based on this law. This article seems to imply that violations of the competition law that are not at the same time violations of ECL are not under the authority of the ITCA. The same article also requires ITCA to seek the opinion of the Competition Authority (CA) "in situations envisaged by laws." It seems that the wording does not preclude the CA from investigating or adjudicating actions that are alleged to violate the competition law and ECL at the same time, though the practice of the CA so far has been not to investigate alleged infringements of competition if such actions are in an area regulated by the NRA. Art. 7, titled "Provision of Competition," uses a more general wording and states that the ITCA is authorized to investigate actions that restrict or prevent competition and impose remedies, suggesting a scope that may include anticompetitive activities that do not necessarily violate the ECL. Art. 7/b requires the CA to obtain the opinion of ITCA and take into consideration ITCA regulations in its cases in the electronic communications industry, including merger and acquisition cases. Art. 7/c states that ITCA, as a result of market analyses, may identify operators with SMP and may impose obligations on them in order to secure and protect an effective competition environment. In short, then, it can be said that the ECL does not provide for a clean divide

[4]Renda et al. discuss other instances of divergences from the EU legislation.

between the jurisdiction of ITCA on the one hand and the CA on the other. There have been instances where the degree of cooperation between the two agencies has been low and there has been some disputes regarding the respective scopes of the two agencies (Atiyas 2005; Ardıyok and Oğuz 2010).

The new law introduces two types of authorizations: notification and rights of use. According to art. 9 of the law, any operator who wishes to provide electronic communications service or establish and operate an electronic communications network or infrastructure notifies the ITCA. If the service in question does not require a resource such as a number, frequency, or satellite position, then authorization is provided through the notification. Otherwise authorization requires the provision of a right of use. The ITCA determines which services require a right of use and which among those requires a limited number of rights of use. The number of rights of use can only be limited in cases where resources need to be used by a limited number of operators and to achieve efficient use of resources. For those services which the ITCA has determined no limitation in number of authorization is required, the ITCA provides the right of use in 30 days. In case the number of rights of use will be limited, there are two cases: when the authorization entails a satellite opposition or a nationally designated bandwidth, then the conditions of authorization (such as starting date, duration, and number of operators) are determined by the Ministry of Transport, but the authorization is done by ITCA. In other cases, the ministry does not get involved in the authorization procedure (except for the determination of minimum fees, see below). Right of use that is limited in number is allocated through auctions.

Authorization fees consist of administrative fees and fees for right of use. The ITCA collects administrative fees from operators (not exceeding 0.5% previous year sales) in order to meet its administrative expenses. Minimum fees for rights of use are determined by the Cabinet of Ministers.

The new authorization regime is a major improvement over the previous regime, and possibly with the strongest practical implications. The previous regime was cumbersome in that the authority had to come up with quite narrow definitions of separate activities and authorize each through a separate license. The old regime also allowed Türk Telekom to delay liberalizations through legal challenges. One drawback of the current regime is that it still grants the ministry some leverage to delay authorizations by acting slowly on the determination of minimum fees as has occurred a number of times in the past (Atiyas 2005). Another drawback of the current regime is that it does not apply to existing concession agreements held by Türk Telekom and the three mobile operators.[5]

Regarding access, art. 16 states that ITCA may identify operators with access obligations and that in case the refusal of an operator to provide access prevents the development of competition or creates a situation that is against the consumers' interests, then the ITCA may force that operator to accept other operators' access

[5]This gap has also been identified in the latest progress report prepared by the European Commission (2009).

demands. On operators with access obligations, the ITCA may impose obligations of equality, nondiscrimination, transparency, clarity, orientation toward costs, and reasonable profit and the requirement that access service be provided on the same conditions and quality as provided to own partners, participations of partnerships. ITCA can also require the preparation of reference offers (art. 19). It can require operators to make changes in reference offers. Access agreements are established freely between interested parties; in case of disagreements, the ITCA engages in dispute resolution (art. 18). The ITCA may impose on operators with access obligations that access tariffs be cost-based. In case the ITCA determines that access tariffs are not cost-based, it can set the tariffs, if necessary, by taking into consideration the applications in other countries (art. 20). The ITCA may impose accounting separation on operators with SMP (art. 21).

To sum up, the primary legislation, although not perfect, and not completely aligned with that in the EU, presents a coherent framework on which to build measures to liberalize the telecommunications industry and enhance competition. Following the adoption of law no. 5809, the ITCA has been active in putting out or renewing the necessary secondary legislation. Such secondary legislation include ordinance on authorizations, ordinance on rights of way, ordinance on access and interconnection, ordinance on the determination of operators with SMP and obligations that can be imposed on them, tariff ordinance, and ordinance on number portability. Even though a detailed evaluation of the secondary legislation is beyond the scope of this chapter, overall, it can be said that most secondary legislation are consistent with their EU counterparts. Hence the legal gaps between the EU and the Turkish regime have been narrowed down. The implication is that the lack of progress in the development of competition will be due to weak implementation and enforcement rather than lack of legal instruments.

## 8.3 Developments in Major Segments

### *8.3.1 Competition and Regulation: Fixed Versus Mobile*

As discussed below, the development of competition in fixed telephony and internet/broadband has been extremely slow, primarily because the Ministry of Transport and the TA have been slow in adopting, implementing, and enforcing the necessary secondary legislation. Atiyas and Doğan (2010) argue that Türk Telekom's influence on the ministry and the TA's lack of independence from the ministry are to a large extent responsible for this state of affairs. The fact that the Turkish framework allowed some residual discretion to the ministry, especially in the area of authorizations, enhanced the scope for political influence. By contrast, the TA (and indeed the ministry) has been much more vigilant and procompetitive in the mobile communications segments, and has used its powers (albeit not always successfully) to encourage new entry (Atiyas and Doğan 2007). This difference in attitude, in turn,

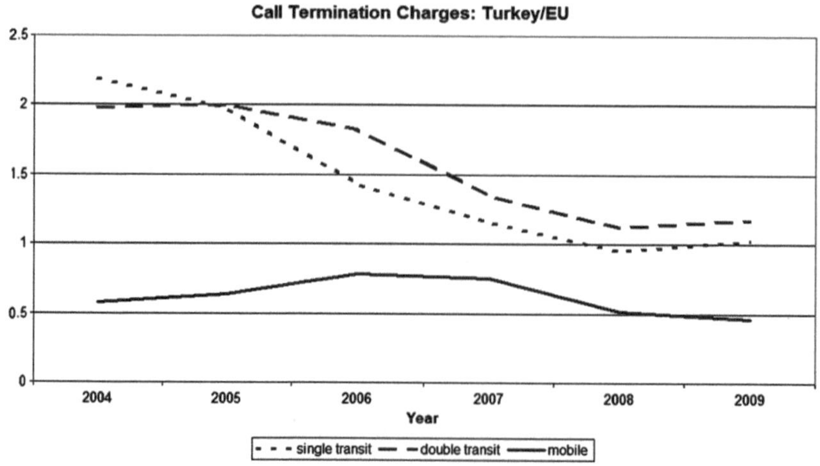


**Fig. 8.1** Call termination charges: Turkey/EU

is partly explained by the fact that Türk Telekom is actually a new entrant in the mobile segment through its subsidiary Avea (formerly Aycell).

The difference in the attitudes of the regulatory authority toward fixed and mobile segments is perhaps best reflected in the regulation of interconnection. There is general agreement that on the whole incumbents prefer higher termination charges and new entrants prefer lower termination charges. In Turkey, the access and interconnection regulation allows parties to reach their own interconnection agreements. If the parties cannot reach an agreement, the regulatory authority may intervene and impose an access charge on the parties. These default charges have been announced by the regulator on annual basis. Figure 8.1 compares the call termination rates in Turkey with EU average for mobile operators and single and double transit level for Türk Telekom. The figure shows that termination charges on calls ending on Türk Telekom's network were highly above EU averages until 2008, i.e., until 4 years after Türk Telekom's monopoly rights were terminated. This is an excessively gradual decline in termination rates. By contrast, termination rates for the largest operator in the mobile segment have always been lower than EU averages. Hence, if the EU charges can be taken as a benchmark, the figure shows that the regulatory authority has been more willing to encourage entry into the mobile segment relative to the fixed segment.

### 8.3.2 *Developments in Fixed Telephony*

The market for domestic long distance and international calls was liberalized a few months after the monopoly rights of Türk Telekom were terminated, but actual entry took much more time to materialize because of delays in interconnection agreements and the necessary infrastructure to allow new entrants to connect to Türk Telekom's network (Atiyas and Doğan 2010). Atiyas and Doğan (2010) also report that new entrants' capture of market share was much slower when compared with the experiences of OECD countries. In any case, competition in local calls remained impossible for a long time and was authorized 3.5 years after the monopoly rights of Türk Telekom were removed, in August 2007. The regulation that allowed competition in local calls actually was an amendment to the (now renewed) Authorization Regulation and covered the provision of telephony, data, internet, and value added services over the fixed terrestrial telecommunications networks. This regulation was canceled by the Council of State in January 2008 on the grounds that it was not possible to undertake more than one activity under a single license. The authorization was revised by the TA, and authorization for fixed telephony services (FTS) was finally published in November 2008. Licenses for FTS were issued in May 2009.

However, the mere granting of licenses is not sufficient to ensure the development of competition in fixed telephony. One way to speed-up service-based competition in fixed telephony is to oblige the incumbent operator to provide wholesale line rental (WLR) services. Through WLR, alternative operators can rent access lines on a wholesale basis from the incumbent operator and resell them to subscribers. That allows alternative operators to provide access services to subscribers. In combination with CPS, WLR enables the alternative operator to end the billing relationship between the incumbent operator and the customer, and allows the alternative operator to provide a single bill that covers both line rental and telephone calls. It has been used as a remedy widely in the EU member states to encourage service-based competition. In Turkey, it has been promoted by Telkoder, an organization of alternative telecommunications operators in Turkey. Telkoder's main argument was that operators' alternative means of developing access services, namely building their own access network or utilizing unbundled access to the local loop (UALL) provided by Türk Telekom (see below) would take a long time to develop (Telkoder 2008).

In November 2009, the ITCA has imposed WLR as a remedy on Türk Telekom as a result of analysis of the market for access to the fixed telephone network (ITCA 2009). As of July 2010, Türk Telekom has prepared a draft offer that has been made available for public consultation.

Another issue that has come up during implementation has to do with the assignment of call numbers. The ITCA decided in June 2009 that alternative FTS operators would be assigned area codes that are constructed by adding one to the existing 81 area codes (one for each province), and FTS operators would assign numbers to their subscribers under these area codes. According to Telkoder, that would have created the perception of dialing long distance calls among FTS subscribers and would have required them to memorize new area codes. Telkoder filed a petition with the Council of State to cancel these provisions of the ITCA decision. The Council of State decided to stop the execution of the decision in February 2010. A final decision is pending. The ITCA responded by announcing that it would start assigning available numbers under the current area codes. It seems there are still disputes between FTS operators and the ITCA about what numbers are available under the current area codes.

The degree of competition in fixed line telephony is still extremely low. According to market data provided by the ITCA (2010), as of first quarter of 2010, the share of FTS operators in total local calls was a mere 2.3%. The market share of FTS operators was 10% in domestic long distance (interprovince) calls, 18% in calls to mobile, and 26% in international calls. Overall, the share of FTS operators in total revenues is about 14% and the share in total telephone services revenues is about 7%. Needless to say, these figures do not point to much effective competition in the industry.

### *8.3.3 Developments in Broadband*

Until recently there have been two main technologies or platforms over which broadband services have been delivered to consumers (Bouckaert et al. 2008: 8–10). The first is digital subscriber line (DSL) which entails upgrading the legacy public switched telephone network (PSTN). The second platform consists of the cable-modem technology, which entails upgrading the cable-tv network.

In Turkey, as per a decision of the CA, the cable-tv network was separated from Türk Telekom when the latter was being privatized. The idea behind this separation was the hope that the cable-TV network would be privatized separately and sold to other buyers. That way the cable-TV network would also be used to provide broadband services and would serve as a basis of competition against Türk Telekom. Instead, the cable-TV network was placed under the state-owned satellite company. The ownership of the network itself became the subject of many legal disputes, and, effectively speaking, the network never became a serious competitor to Türk Telekom or its internet subsidiary, TTNet.

In most countries, incumbent operators such as Türk Telekom have been under the regulatory obligation of allowing new entrants to use the existing network to provide their own DSL services. This, in turn has taken three main forms, with varying degrees of infrastructure investment undertaken by the new entrant. Under *resale*, the new entrant buys the DSL product at wholesale prices from the incumbent operator and resells it at the retail level. This form of entry requires minimum level of investment from the new entrant. Under *bitstream access*, the incumbent installs a high-speed access link such as DSL to the customer premises and then makes this access link available to new entrants to enable them to provide broadband services. Under this form of access, the new entrant can provide its own value added services to consumers. This is different from pure resale because the latter "does not allow new entrants to differentiate their services from those of the incumbent."[6] UALL comes in two main forms: under *shared access,* the copper pairs are

---

[6]ERG (2004). The ERG statement continues to state: "In order to be able to differentiate their services (including such services as VoIP) from those of the incumbent, new entrants must have access at a point where they can control certain technical characteristics of the service to the end-user and/or make full use of their own network (or alternative network offerings), thus being in a position of altering the quality (e.g., the data rate or other features) supplied to the customer."

shared by the incumbent and the entrant. The incumbent provides telephone services to the subscriber and the new entrant uses the high-frequency channels to provide broadband service. Under full unbundling, the new entrant rents the full wire connection to the subscriber's premises. Under UALL, the incumbent provides the copper connection and the rest of the infrastructure is undertaken by the new entrant; hence this is the form in which the new entrant undertakes the highest level of investment. UALL also provides full control to the new entrant over the network.

In Turkey, Türk Telekom (through TTNet) started to provide ADSL services in the early 2000s. First attempts to promote new entry occurred when the regulatory authority mandated a resale arrangement in 2003 that allowed a margin of 18% to alternative operators. This was followed by a decision by the TA to mandate bitstream services in 2004, which through legal challenges and other delay efforts by Türk Telekom only became available in 2007–2008. Efforts to provide access through UALL started in 2005 but the product became available only in 2009.

Broadband penetration ratio is very low in Turkey: 9% in fixed broadband as opposed to an average of 23–24% in the OECD and EU (Köksal 2010). As of March 2010, there are 7.4 million broadband subscribers in Turkey, 86% of which are ADSL connections.[7] Mobile broadband over 3G has developed rapidly over the last year, reaching 8.6% of the total,[8] and cable-modem makes up only 2.4%. The share of TTNet in broadband subscribers is 81%, and the share of alternative internet service providers (ISPs) is only 6.1%. The most widespread means of access of the alternative operators is bitstream. The number of UALL is quite low, a total of 14.8 thousand as of March 2010 (only 75 fully unbundled access) and access through resale is about 43,000. UALL prices are not particularly high in Turkey, with wholesale shared access prices in Turkey almost the same as the EU average (€2.78 as of March 2010).[9] Alternative operators mention several important barriers, including high installation charges, high charges for backhaul services, and delay tactics by Türk Telekom with insufficient enforcement from the ITCA. In any case, the degree of competition in broadband is very low. TTNet share in fixed broadband is 89% and this is much higher than EU average, which in 2009 was only 46%!

Moreover, broadband prices in Turkey are also very high. According to OECD data,[10] average broadband monthly price per advertised megabits per second in Turkey ($14) is about 40% higher than the OECD average ($9.6). When prices are corrected for purchasing power parity, prices in Turkey are the third highest, after Mexico and Poland. OECD data also reveal that Turkey is really lagging behind in high-speed connections: prices in Turkey are relatively cheaper for low-speed connections and relatively more expensive for high-speed connections.[11]

---

[7]Data from ITCA (2010).

[8]3G licenses were awarded as a result of a tender held in November 2008. Concession agreements were signed in April 2009 and all three operators started to provide 3G services as of July 2009. The number of 3G subscribers increased quite rapidly, reaching 8.7 million as of March 2010.

[9]http://www.cullen-international.com.

[10]http://www.oecd.org/sti/ict/broadband.

[11]http://www.oecd.org/sti/ict/broadband. Compare Tables 4.1 and 4.n.

The low level of competition in broadband internet is also due to strategic behavior of Türk Telekom to prevent entry of alternative ISPs in Turkey. In a landmark decision[12] taken in November 2008, the CA has imposed a fine of 12.4 million TL (about €6.2 million) on Türk Telekom for abusing its dominance in the wholesale broadband internet market by price squeeze in the retail internet market. In its decision, the Competition Board stated that Türk Telekom and its internet subsidiary TTNet endured operating without profits for long periods of time and implemented campaigns that would not cover losses at reasonable amounts of time and that these strategies were executed in order to monopolize the sector.

In a recent decision,[13] the CA stated that Türk Telekom should provide naked DSL services. Provision of naked DSL means that Türk Telekom can no longer bundle voice and data services together and that the subscriber can subscribe to DSL services alone, without having to pay for voice services as well. This is important for alternative ISPs because as it stands, a consumer who wishes to obtain broadband internet services from an alternative ISP would still need to go to Türk Telekom to obtain a fixed line, and this reduces incentives to obtain services from the alternative ISP in the first place. The decision further states that unavailability of naked DSL also hurts mobile operators because it slows down consumer switches from fixed to mobile telephony services. Availability of naked DSL is expected to increase broadband penetration and also demand for VOIP services. The ITCA has specified naked DSL as a remedy in its latest analysis of the wholesale broadband market.[14] Türk Telekom provided a draft reference offer; however, as of June 2010, the ITCA has not finalized the offer and naked DSL is not yet commercially available.

### *8.3.4 Developments in the Mobile Segment*

The mobile communications market consists of three main mobile network operators (MNOs): Turkcell, Vodafone, and Avea, the subsidiary of Türk Telekom. The main problem faced by ITCA in the mobile segment was the continued dominance of Turkcell, the largest of the three operators. Turkcell has benefited from first mover advantages in the mobile market to establish its dominance, and is believed to maintain its dominance in the market by discriminating between on-net and off-net prices and thereby exploiting tariff-mediated network externalities to its advantage (Atiyas and Doğan 2007). Tariff-mediated network externalities are thought to work in the following way: When call termination charges are high, the cost of an off-net call increases. This makes it difficult for operators to lower the retail tariffs of off-net calls. On the other hand, since on-net calls are not subject to termination charges, on-net retail tariffs can be lower. In addition, most consumers face switching

[12] Decision no. 08-65/1055-411 dated November 19, 2008.

[13] Decision no. 09-07/127-38 dated February 18, 2009.

[14] http://www.tk.gov.tr/srth/dokumanlar/kgid/Toptangenisbantpiyasasi.pdf.

costs when they would like to switch to a new operator. One widespread form of switching costs emanate from the fact that the consumer would need to inform friends about her new phone number (unless, of course, there is number portability, see below). These provide a natural competitive advantage to operators with a large subscriber base: first, consumers who have not yet subscribed to an operator would choose an operator with a large subscriber base because everything else constant, that operator would contain a larger pool of people that this potential subscriber would call, so that a larger proportion of calls would be on-net. Second, if callers get utility not only from placing but also from receiving calls (i.e., if there are so-called call externalities), then again an operator with a larger subscriber base would be more attractive. Under call externalities, the incumbent would have an additional incentive to raise off-net prices in order to make the rival less attractive since that way the rival would receive less calls (Lopez and Rey 2009). In effect, the off-net price of an operator would be competing with the on-net tariff of the competitor (Atiyas and Doğan 2007: 511–512).

The ITCA used a number of measures to counter the dominance of Turkcell. These are explained below:

#### 8.3.4.1 Retail and Wholesale Tariff Controls

In 2007, the ITCA (then the TA) issued an "Evaluation of the Results of Monitoring Regarding Turkcell Tariffs." The monitoring was undertaken in response to complaints by Avea, Vodafone, Borusan Telekom, and Sabanci Telekom that Turkcell on-net tariffs were below interconnection charges and that differences between on-net and off-net prices were disproportionate. The report found that some Turkcell on-net tariffs were below the termination charges that Turkcell applies to the other competitors and required that Turkcell on-net tariffs should not be below the lowest termination charges (except for special packages designed for designated groups such as the disabled and the elderly). The report also imposed a cap of 0.66 TRY/min (about €39) on Turkcell off-net tariffs.

This decision of the authority was canceled by the Council of State on the grounds that the authority did not have the authority to establish floors on operators' prices. On March 26, 2009, ITCA published a new decision that imposed a new wholesale remedy upon Turkcell, as well as a symmetrical retail remedy upon all MNOs. Here again, ITCA was acting following an investigation into the complaints formulated by the two other MNOs, Vodafone and Avea, together with the fixed incumbent Türk Telekom, on alleged anticompetitive behavior of Turkcell. In its investigation, ITCA concluded that during 2007 and 2008, several retail offerings of Turkcell included on-net retail tariffs that were below the applicable mobile termination rates (MTR) and that this practice distorted competition in the retail market. The decision imposed two remedies: the first was that the weighted average of MTR charged by Turkcell to other operators cannot be higher than the retail on-net tariffs it uses in each of its retail packages. The second remedy was that MNOs are allowed to charge the maximum retail tariff of 0.64 TRY/min (€0.30) (including

VAT and the special telecommunications tax) for calls to other mobile networks. Even though the retail remedy was placed on all operators, the real target was presumably Turkcell: possibly, believing that call externalities do exist, the ITCA wanted to prevent Turkcell from harming rivals' profits or from rendering rival operators less attractive by raising off-net prices and thereby reducing the number of calls that rivals' subscribers would receive.

It can be said that ITCA was quite vigilant in the enforcement of these regulations. In April 2010, the ITCA imposed a fine of about €400,000 on Turkcell for violating the restriction on the termination charges and a fine of €25 million for violating the cap on retail tariffs.

#### 8.3.4.2 Mobile Number Portability

Number portability is seen as a major remedy to reduce switching costs (Atiyas and Doğan 2007). The number portability regulation was adopted in February 2007. Turkcell challenged the regulation and filed a petition at the Council of State for its cancelation, but the request was denied. Mobile number portability became effective in November 2008. An impact analysis carried out by ITCA (Güngör and Evren 2010) reported that by March 16, 2010 more than 11 million subscribers had transported their mobile numbers to rival operators. This amounted to 19% of prepaid and 15% of postpaid subscribers. Between November 2008 and January 2010, one operator lost a net of 1.7 million subscribers while the other two gained a net of 806,000 and 940,000 subscribers, respectively. Hence, according to the report, introduction of mobile number portability did reduce switching costs and increased the extent of competition in the market.

#### 8.3.4.3 Mobile Call Termination Rates

Another important remedy at the disposal of the ITCA was, of course, interconnection charges. It was mentioned above that termination charges in the mobile segment were among the lowest in Europe. This tendency continued and in March 2010 the ITCA further reduced MTRs by about 52–53%, to about €1.4–€1.7/min. They were already reduced by 30% in March 2009. As of March 2010, these were the lowest rates in Europe.[15]

While it is difficult to gauge the specific individual effects of these different measures, recent developments in the mobile markets do suggest that the measures may have had some impact. The most important impact seems to be a reduced incentive to discriminate between on-net and off-net calls. Atiyas et al. (2010) report that Turkcell launched in February 2009 a new package ("lemon reprieve") that entailed symmetric on-net and off-net prices. Interestingly, Turkcell started a major advertisement campaign for "lemon reprieve" possibly the first major ad

[15] Cullen International, Western Europe Cross Country Analysis http://www.cullen-international.com.

campaign in Turkcell history for a nondifferentiated package. This package was perhaps a response to Avea's launch of a nondiscriminating package on the eve of the implementation of number portability, but Avea's strategy itself possibly reflected the impact of both the introduction of number portability and reduction of call termination charges. The tendency of Turkcell to move away from discriminatory call packages and toward packages where on-net and off-net calls are priced symmetrically was evident in other instances as well. In April 2009, Turkcell introduced a package directed at public servants that included symmetric on-net and off-net prices, presumably as a replacement or extension of a popular package directed at the same group but where tariffs were differentiated. In addition, other popular discriminatory packages were changed so as to eliminate differences between on-net and off-net retail prices.

Güngör and Evren (2010) report other interesting price data that suggest that regulatory changes may have had significant impact on pricing strategies. On the basis of the retail prices of the most popular prepaid call packages, it is reported that Turkcell's prices declined by about 20% in 2008–2009 and that there was a significant convergence between the prices of the three operators, presumably reflecting a reduction in the premium that Turkcell could charge. Furthermore, between 2008 and 2009, there were significant increases in the volume of off-net calls per subscribers for all operators (Güngör and Evren 2010: 53).

First, it may be underlined that the number of subscriptions has actually declined over the last 2 years, from 65.8 million in 2008 to 61.6 million in 2010–2011. It seems that the primary reason for this decline has to do with the fact that many users are relinquishing multiple subscriptions with many operators to single subscriptions with a single operator. The main reasons for this, in turn, is that with the reduction in the degree of discrimination between on-net and off-net prices, users no longer need dual or triple subscriptions to avoid high off-net prices. Hence, according to that interpretation, the decline in the number of subscriptions is actually consistent with the view that these measures have been effective.

Turning to market shares, the market share of Turkcell (in terms of number of subscribers) did decline over the last decade from about 67% in 2001–2004 to about 55–56% in 2008–2010. However, there were no further declines in Turkcell's market share in terms of number of subscribers since 2008, but there was an increase in the market share of Aycell from 16.7 to 18.8 between 2008–2011 and 2010–2011 and a corresponding decrease in the market share of Vodafone (from about 27 to 25%). On the other hand, Turkcell's market share in terms of volume of traffic has declined from 49–50% in 2008–2012 to around 42–45% in 2009. It seems that there was a similar movement in market shares in terms of revenues. Güngör and Evren (2010: 42) interpret this as reflecting the impact of reduced prices and the consequent increase in number of call-minutes that has benefitted Avea and Vodafone more than Turkcell.

It is perhaps still too early to assess whether these are real trends or simply temporary changes, but at least one can tentatively conclude that market developments are not inconsistent with expectations about the likely impact of the regulatory interventions on the mobile markets.

## 8.4 Conclusion

The legal framework for regulation and competition in the telecommunications markets in Turkey has been improved considerably in the last 2 or 3 years. The new ECL, even though not perfect, provides a major improvement over the previous regime and establishes a coherent basis on which to push for the development of competition in the industry. Lack of or incoherence of legal instruments did play a role in the delays in the development of competition especially in the fixed telephony and broadband segments, but unwillingness or incomplete ownership of the liberalization agenda by the ministry and the ITCA also played a role. The ECL is also a major step toward improving the transparency and accountability of the ITCA, especially because the ITCA is now obliged to provide reasoning or justification for its decisions and make them available to the public. It remains to be seen whether the duality apparent in ITCA's approach to fixed versus mobile segments will continue in the near future or whether, as a result of these changes, it will give place to a more consistently procompetitive approach.

## References


Ardıyok, Ş. and Oğuz, F. (2010), Competition law and regulation in the Turkish telecommunications industry: Friends or foes? *Telecommunications Policy*, *34*(4), 233–243.

Atiyas, I. (2005). *Competition and Regulation in the Turkish Telecommunications Industry*. Ankara: TEPAV.

Atiyas, I. and Doğan, P. (2010) Glass half empty? Politics and institutions in the liberalization of the fixed line telecommunications industry in Turkey. In T. Çetin, F. Yilmaz (Eds.), *Understanding the Process of Economic Change in Turkey* (pp. 261–284). New York: Nova Science Publishers.

Atiyas, I. and Doğan, P. (2007). When good intentions are not enough: Sequential entry and competition in the Turkish mobile industry. *Telecommunications Policy*, *31*(8–9), 502–523.

Atiyas, I., Doğanoğlu, T. and Koç, M. (2010) Mobil elektronik haberleşme pazarında geçiş maliyetlerinin işletmecilerin fiyatlandırma Stratejileri üzerine etkileri ve etkin rekabetin tesis edilmesine yönelik regülasyon politikaları, *2. Rekabet ekonomisi ve politikası Sempozyumu* (pp. 99–134). Ankara: Rekabet Kurumu. http://www.rekabet.gov.tr/dosyalar/etkinlikkitap/etkinlikkitap26.pdf.

Atiyas, I. and Renda, A. (2007). Telecommunications, in S Ülgen (Ed.), *Second Generation Structural Reforms – De-regulation and Competition in Infrastructure Industries: The Evolution of the Turkish Telecommunications, Energy and Transport Sectors in Light of EU Harmonization* (pp. 25–78). Brussels: Center for European Policy Studies.

Bouckaert, J., van Dijk, T. and Verboven, F. (2008) Regulation and broadband penetration – what is required to regain speed in Belgium? http://www.ua.ac.be/download.aspx?c=jan.bouckaert&n=56483&ct=55018&e=184390.

Cave, M. (2004) Economic aspects of the new regulatory regime for electronic communications services. In P.A. Buigies and P. Rey (Eds.), *The Economics of Antitrust and Regulation in Telecommunications* (pp. 27–44). Cheltenham, UK: Edward Elgar.

ERG. (2004) Bitstream access – ERG common position – adopted on 2nd April 2004. http://www.berec.europa.eu/doc/whatsnew/erg_0333rev1_bitstream_access_common_position.pdf.

European Commission. (2009) Turkey progress report 2009, Commission Staff Working Document. http://www.ec.europa.eu/enlargement/pdf/key_documents/2009/tr_rapport_2009_en.pdf.

Güngör, M. and Evren, G. (2010) Mobil numara taşınabilirliği: Rekabete ve tüketicilere etkileri, Bilgi Teknolojileri ve İletişim Kurumu Sektörel Araştırma ve Stratejiler Dairesi Başkanlığı, Ankara. http://www.btk.gov.tr/Yayin/Raporlar/2010/DEA_MNT_v4.pdf.

ITCA. (2010) Türkiye elektronik haberleşme sektörü - Üç aylık pazar verileri raporu 2010 Yılı 1. Çeyrek, Ocak-Şubat-Mart. Bilgi Teknolojileri ve İletişim Kurumu Sektörel Araştırma ve Stratejiler Dairesi Başkanlığı.

ITCA. (2009) Piyasa analizi çalışmaları-IX: Sabit telefon şebekesine erişim piyasası, Kamuoyu görüşlerini içeren doküman. http://www.btk.gov.tr/srth/dokumanlar/kgid/sdenihaibelge.pdf.

Köksal, E. (2010) Genişbant internetin yaygınlaşması rekabetin gelişmesine bağlı. *Betam Araştırma Notu, 10*, 80.

Lopez, A.L. and Rey, P. (2009) Foreclosing competition through access charges and price discrimination. http://www.papers.ssrn.com/sol3/papers.cfm?abstract_id=1516207.

Renda, A., Guerin, S. and Arbak, E. (2009) EU-Turkey accession negotiations impact assessment of chapter 10 on information society and media, CEPS Special Report. http://www.ceps.eu/ceps/download/1690.

Telkoder. (2008) Toptan hat kiralama Telkoder görüşleri. http://www.telkoder.org.

Togan, S., Akdemir, E. and Başçı, E. (2010) Liberalization of telecommunications services. In S. Togan (Ed.), *Economic Liberalization and Turkey* (pp. 73–87). New York: Routledge.

# Chapter 9
# Regulation, Deregulation, and Competition in the Turkish Airline Industry

**Tamer Çetin and Serkan Benk**

## 9.1 Introduction

During the past two decades, the world has experienced a deregulation movement in the aviation industries. Governments have recognized the benefits of competition for the market and/or in the market. USA deregulated its airline industry. Since 1992, it has signed over 90 open skies agreements with other countries. The European Union (EU) recognized a single aviation industry in EU. From 1987 to 1993, EU introduced three packages for reforms that almost fully deregulated the EU air industry.

Turkey has also followed up this trend. In 2003, it opened the industry to competition by deregulating entry to market especially in the scheduled domestic flights. Before 2003, the Turkish airline industry had been dominated by Turkish Airlines (THY), a state-owned public enterprise. The deficiencies in the number of firms and the insufficiencies of the regulatory process in the industry impeded development of infrastructure and competition especially in the domestic flights. The deregulation movement of 2003 has differentiated the regulatory institutional environment and the monopolistic structure in the industry.

The focus of this chapter is on the structure of the pre-2003 industry and market developments after the deregulation movement. In this context, the chapter consists of four sections. Section 9.1 presents a statement of historical setting including legal endowment, the domestic and international regulatory structure, and institutions that are interested in regulation of the industry, privatization attempts, and the build-operate-transfer (BOT) model. Section 9.2 analyzes the pre-2003 industry structure. In Sect. 9.3, we focus on the impacts of the deregulation movement of 2003 over the industry. In this context, this section scrutinizes developments in entry to market, new route structure, passenger and cargo transportation, the number of firms and aircrafts, seat capacity, air traffic, and ground handling.

T. Çetin (✉)
Department of Economics, Yildiz Technical University, Besiktas,
Istanbul 34349, Turkey
e-mail: tcetin@yildiz.edu.tr

T. Çetin and F. Oğuz (eds.), *The Political Economy of Regulation in Turkey*, 
DOI 10.1007/978-1-4419-7750-2_9, 

This section also evaluates the alteration in the monopolistic structure of THY. Lastly, Sect. 9.4 concludes the chapter.

## 9.2 Historical Setting

The airline industry in Turkey has been subjected to many different national and international regulations. The institutional foundations of the industry were laid by the establishment of Turkish Airplane Association (Turk Teyyare Cemiyeti) in 1925, which was named Turkish Air Association (Turk Hava Kurumu) subsequently. The first civil air transportation begun with Turkish Airmails (Turk Hava Postaları) in 1933 with a small fleet of five aircrafts. Within the same year, Airlines Administration of Government Operation (Havayollari Devlet Isletme Idaresi) that was affiliated with the Ministry of National Defense was assigned to establish civil airlines and make transportation in Turkey.

In 1945, Turkey became one of the member countries to the International Civil Aviation Contract (ICAO) or the Chicago Agreement which determines international aviation rules. However, there was not yet a consensus regarding the trade rights on the contract as of 1945. Due to this situation, the countries around the world needed to contract bilateral and multilateral agreements each other. In this context, as of 2009, Turkey signed Mutual Aviation Transportation Contract with 90 countries. According to these agreements, 73 passengers and 6 cargo airline enterprises can enter Turkey via scheduled airline transportation. Scheduled flights are arranged upon 118 tracks into seven destinations throughout Turkey from 90 foreign places. Likewise, THY can arrange scheduled flights from six points in Turkey to 140 places in 69 countries (DGCA 2009: 67).

In parallel to developing technological and international conditions, the Administration of Civil Aviation (Sivil Havacilik Dairesi Baskanligi) as a new regulatory body was founded in 1954 within the Ministry to protect the national interests, to conduct the international relations, and to inspect the industry on a regular basis. In 1987, this institution was reshaped as one of the main regulatory institutions of the industry under the name of Directorate General of Civil Aviation (DGCA – Sivil Havacilik Genel Mudurlugu) in accordance with the current conditions (DGCA 2009).

In 2005, DGCA that performs a task to regulate and audit civil aviation activities in the industry and that holds a status as a Civil Aviation Authority in international platforms was restructured by the Law No. 5431 and its personnel structure was strengthened. This law directly reshapes DGCA and indirectly regulates the industry. Performing as the Main Service Unit of the Ministry of Transportation and Communication until November 18, 2005, DGCA started to become a financially autonomous public entity with a special budget and reached to its current management structure upon Law No. 5431 on the Organization and Tasks of Directorate of Civil Aviation which came into force on this date.[1]

---

[1] More information about DGCA can be found in the subsections.

As in many industries in Turkey during the post-1980 term, the Turkish airline industry was also restructured by various legal amendments. The main objective of the Law No. 2920 enacted in 1983 is to regulate activities in the Turkish airline industry by taking into account domestic and international relations. Currently, regulation of the activities of the airline industry in Turkey is implemented according to the provisions of the Law No. 2920 and Administrative and Technical Regulations and Aviation Instructions (Idari ve Teknik Yonetmelikler ve Havacilik Talimatlari) that are published in the scope of this law. Accordingly, the Law regulates:

- Using the Turkish aviation area
- Prohibitions and restrictions that will be applied to the aircrafts
- Aircraft accidents
- Aviation enterprises
- Airports
- Flight rules
- Rules concerning the civil aviation personnel
- Obligations for passenger transportation
- Conditions regarding liability and punishment

By the Civil Aviation Law, the industry has been experiencing increasing growth. Although the Civil Aviation Law de jure opened the door for liberalization in the industry, it had not been able to establish a competitive environment and this structure gave rise to THY's monopoly. After this term, the fleet owned by THY was modernized and THY tended to international aviation markets, rather than focusing on domestic flights and improving service quality. However, this enterprise as a state monopoly realized investments regarding air traffic control, navigation services, and ground handling. In particular, a regular increase occurred in the number of total passenger and aircrafts at Istanbul Ataturk Airport, Antalya, Ankara Esenboga, Izmir Adnan Menderes, and Dalaman Airports (TEPAV 2007).

The most important legal setting that has shaped the current structure of the industry was a decision taken by the Council of Ministers in 2003. This decision brought about a deregulation movement in the industry, which led to increased competition, especially in scheduled domestic flights. By affecting all other areas in the industry, this deregulation movement increased Turkey's total air traffic to 53% in 2005, which was foreseen by international organizations such as EUROCONTROL and IATA in 2015 (DGCA 2009: 26).

Currently, the industry is regulated by various national and international organizations and legal settings that reshape these organizations and the industry.

### *9.2.1 Regulatory Institutions in the Industry*

Regulatory institutions that are affiliated with the airline industry in Turkey are Ministry of Transportation and Communication, DGCA, and General Directorate of State Airports Authority (GDSAA). Moreover, some international organizations such as ICAO and EUROCONTROL are also responsible for regulations concerning international aviation relations.

#### 9.2.1.1 DGCA

DGCA is the main regulatory institution that is responsible for regulation of the industry. DGCA regulates the industry within the scope of the Civil Aviation Law, 15 secondary statutes, and 30 aviation documents that is interested in more technical subjects. The regulatory duties and responsibilities of DGCA are as follows:

- To follow up the basic points in a way to ensure sustainability and development of technological, economic, and social issues of civil aviation in line with public interest and national security purposes.
- To set the airworthiness terms of commercial aircrafts that operate in the air space of Turkey.
- To decide the relevant documents and keep their registers.
- To regulate and audit the license of licensee technical staff in accordance with the legislation.
- To determine the license terms of the personnel that are charged in Turkish civil aviation space as required by their specialization.
- To regulate the terms and conditions of licenses to be obtained by Turkish real or legal persons who seek to perform transport activities at home and abroad, and foreign real or legal persons who seek to perform transport activities at home, and to audit the development thereof.
- To regulate and audit the air navigation of commercial aircrafts in the air space of Turkey as well as traffic communication services by consulting with the related institutions and to take necessary precautions.
- To set the technical qualities and operating conditions of the airports for the sake of air navigation security and to inspect development thereof.
- To follow up developments in the field of international civil aviation and to take precautions to ensure that such activities are implemented in civil aviation activities in Turkey.
- To obtain collaboration with the related organizations for air search and rescue activities in Turkish space.
- To investigate civil aviation accidents and to take necessary precautions as per the investigation results.
- To take legal precautions against real and legal entities acting in contrary to legislations and rules that regulate civil aviation activities.
- To follow up with the further exercise of international bilateral and multilateral contracts regarding the air transport (DGCA 2009).

#### 9.2.1.2 GDSAA

On the other hand, GDSAA as another regulatory institution of the industry is responsible to conduct and inspect the borders of airports and air space in Turkey. GDSAA has performed under various names since 1933. In 1984, GDSAA was redefined as an autonomous state economic enterprise. GDSAA is obligated to carry out its own responsibilities as per the international civil aviation rules and regulations (TEPAV 2007). GDSAA that was established to produce and sell the monopolistic public utilities in the industry is a privileged state-owned enterprise and is affiliated with the Ministry of Transportation and Communication (GDSAA 2009a).

In terms of its audit, it is subject to the provisions of Law No. 3346 and Decree Laws with No. 71 and No. 233. In that context, Prime Ministry Supreme Audit Board (Basbakanlik Yuksek Denetleme Kurulu) audits and considers GDSAA in terms of administrative, technical, and fiscal. Because it is a related institution according to the relevant law, the Ministry of Transportation and Communication is also responsible to control the harmonization of GDSAA's activities with the relevant laws. The main activity field of the institution in the industry is the airport entrepreneurship and navigation services (GDSAA 2009a).

Moreover, GDSAA has mainly two strategic focuses. First, it wants to maintain its level of service performance and strives to continuously improve the quality of its services. Second, it aims to steadily develop its efficiency in Europe and to take over a leading role in the provision of air navigation services in the region. As a result, while the regulatory and policy-making institution in the industry is DGCA under the Ministry of Transportation and Communication, its affiliate GDSAA is the sole responsible institution for the provision of Air Navigation Services throughout Turkish airspace.

### *9.2.2 The Relevant International Institutions*

Because the airline industry required advanced technology and is characterized with unlimited qualities, in order to closely follow-up with developments in the international airline industries and to comply with the requirements of the age, Turkey is a member of different international (regulatory) organizations around the world. In this context, the Turkish airline industry is subject to regulations implemented by the two international aviation organizations, because Turkey signed the international agreements. These organizations are International Civil Aviation Organization (ICAO) and European Organization for the Safety of Air Navigation (EUROCONTROL).

#### 9.2.2.1 ICAO

With the Chicago Contract in 1945, Turkey became one of the founder members of ICAO. The airports, heliports, and helipads that are open to civil traffic in Turkey have been audited within the scope of Annexes which are published by ICAO and according to the Civil Aviation Law. In this context, while the number of audited airports[2] was 4 in 2002, all actively used airports were audited in 2008.

---

[2]This number was 41 in 2008.

As a result of audits carried out by ICAO in Turkey as of May 2007 in the scope of Universal Safety Oversight Audit Program (USOAP), it was concluded that Turkey had 50% better performance in efficient implementation of ICAO requirements in comparison to average of other 190 member states. According to the studies of ICAO, Turkey is in a much more advanced status in implementing ICAO requirements and standards in comparison to most other countries (DGCA 2009: 48, 52).

#### 9.2.2.2 EUROCONTROL

GDSAA which was subjected to the EUROCONTROL agreement in 1988 is one of the 38 members of EUROCONTROL since 1989. In this regard, Turkey is a member of Joint Aviation Authorities (JAA). According to a report published by JAA, the flight safety in Turkey is over high levels, and optimal operations are carried out for Technical Maintenance and Repair (DGCA 2009).

### *9.2.3 Privatization Attempts and the Build-Operate-Transfer Model*

Since 1986, privatization in Turkey has come to the forefront for all fields of the economy. The airline industry is not an exception to this trend. In that context, 70% of the shares of Ucak Servisi AS (USAŞ) as the first catering firm in the industry were privatized in 1989. The remaining share was privatized in 1993. A total of 60 and 40% of the shares of HAVAS, which is a ground handling enterprise, were privatized in 1995 and 1998, respectively. As a result, competition by privatization was introduced to the ground handling and catering segments of the industry.

On the other hand, 98.2% of the shares of THY as a state-owned enterprise were included within the scope of privatization by Law No. 3291 in September 1990. 1.8% of the shares of the enterprise was privatized within the same year (Özenen 2003: 97). Approximately 20 and 28% of the shares owned by the Privatization Administration were offered to public in 2004 and 2006, respectively. The share of state ownership in THY decreased below 50% as a result of a public offering in May 2006, and thus ended the enterprise's legal status as that of a state enterprise. As of December 31, 2009, the Privatization Administration owns 49.12% of the shares in the company and 50.88% of the shares are privatized by the public offering method (THY 2009).

Other privatization attempts in the industry occurred to renew and expand the airports in the airport entrepreneurship. In particular, terminals built and operated by the BOT model within the scope of Law No. 3996 introduce a crucial Turkish model as a global brand. With this model, which can be achieved without requiring any government investment, passenger terminals were constructed. Table 9.1 lists the airports constructed by the BOT model up to the end of 2009. Within the same scope, a tender for international terminal of Milas-Bodrum airport was realized as well.

**Table 9.1** The airport terminals constructed by the BOT model

| Airport | Starting date of operation |
|---|---|
| International terminal of Ataturk Airport | January 10, 2000 |
| First and second international terminals of Antalya Airport | April 7, 2005 |
| International terminal of Dalaman Airport | July 7, 2006 |
| Domestic and international terminals of Esenboğa Airport | October 16, 2006 |
| International terminal of Adnan Menderes Airport | May 27, 2007 |
| International terminal of Sabiha Gökçen Airport | October 29, 2009 |

*Source*: DGCA (2009: 107)

There are also many other impacts of the BOT model on the industry and the Turkish economy. So far, this model has provided employment for 8,500 people. Approximately $1.2 billion of investment was floated in the Turkish economy. Moreover, approximately revenue for $12 billion was brought in the treasury by means of privatization and transfer of rights for Domestic and International Terminals of Ataturk Airport, first and second International Terminal in Antalya Airport, and tenders for operational transfer of Sabiha Gokcen Airport. Only, the revenue that is gained by privatization of the airport terminals was $3.1 billion. In parallel to all of these developments, the passenger number reached 100 million people per year, the civil aviation grew very fast, and it arrived a very important destination. As a result, the airports in Turkey embraced a modern structure with the BOT model by prominent companies in aviation sector and without incurring a penny from the treasury (DGCA 2009: 106–107).

## 9.3 The Pre-2003 Industry Structure

Before 2003, the industry was not yet open to competition. THY was a legal and pure monopoly that carried out all the scheduled domestic flights. The necessary legal environment has not yet been established to ensure that private airline firms other than THY might also operate in the domestic flights and cargo transport segments of the industry. Thirteen firms along with THY that operated in the unscheduled flights were inadequate to trigger competition, to increase demand, and to attract investments in the industry.

### *9.3.1 Barriers to Entry*

In order to state the transition from regulation to competition in the industry, it is needed to make a distinction between international and domestic markets. They are needed to comply with the provisions of bilateral and multilateral agreements signed by Turkey, if the firms want to carry out a service in the scheduled international passenger and weight transportation segment of the Turkish airline industry. If a firm wants to enter into the unscheduled international flight market, it is sufficient to receive permission from the aviation authorities of two countries. The decisions of regulatory authorities are generally obligatory for other market conditions. Because regulatory rules in the scheduled international flights are determined by the bilateral contracts.

Accordingly, competition in the international flights in the Turkish airline industry has been in force especially since 1985. With the modernization of THY after 1985, the company tended to the international flights, and this situation gave rise to an increase in the number, the fleet capacity, and the market shares of private airline firms. In 1998, 45% of the international passengers were transported by the foreign airlines, 22% of them were transported by THY, and 33% of them were transported by the other private Turkish enterprises (DPT 2001: 42–44). In 2002, while the share of THY in the international transportation was 18%, it realized the flight to 78 points.

On the other hand, the case in the domestic flights is somewhat different. As per a decision of DGCA until deregulation in 2003, the scheduled domestic flights were only carried out by THY. Other enterprises were only able to carry out a flight, if THY does not have a scheduled flight on the related line and at the relevant time. Accordingly, it was granted permission to the private airline firms only in the following conditions as per the Civil Aviation Law and article 4 of the DGCA decision.

- In the lines that THY carry out no flight.
- In the lines that THY carry out a flight, but at the times that THY does not arrange a flight.
- In the conditions where THY cannot meet demand at the same time.

This regulation impeded competition in the industry and the scheduled domestic flights were carried out only by THY until 2003 (Hassu 2004). Accordingly, as depicted in Fig. 9.1, THY flew from 2 points to 25 destinations in 2002. Because there is no private airline firm in the industry, private-owned airline enterprises did not have the opportunity to make scheduled domestic flights. Because of the high-priced tickets that the monopolistic THY charged and a national bottleneck at the time, the number of passengers who preferred domestic air transportation did not reached nine million. Because of lower demands for air transportation, the unscheduled flights by 13 airline operators together with THY were inadequate.

During the pre-2003 term, the existing airports could not be utilized effectively due to the lack of private-owned firms, the inadequacy of demand, and the high ticket prices. Although quite a number of airports had been built, only eight of them were heavily used for the scheduled domestic flights and the remaining airports were unused. On the other hand, the economic and political setting in the country impacted the share of airlines transportation by and between transport modes and brought about a great impediment over deregulation and completion of the industry. In that context, the total seat capacity for 150 wide-body aircrafts, which were registered in Turkish registration office, was limited to 25,114. A total of 896,865 tons of cargos were being transported in domestic and international flights (DGCA 2009: 23).

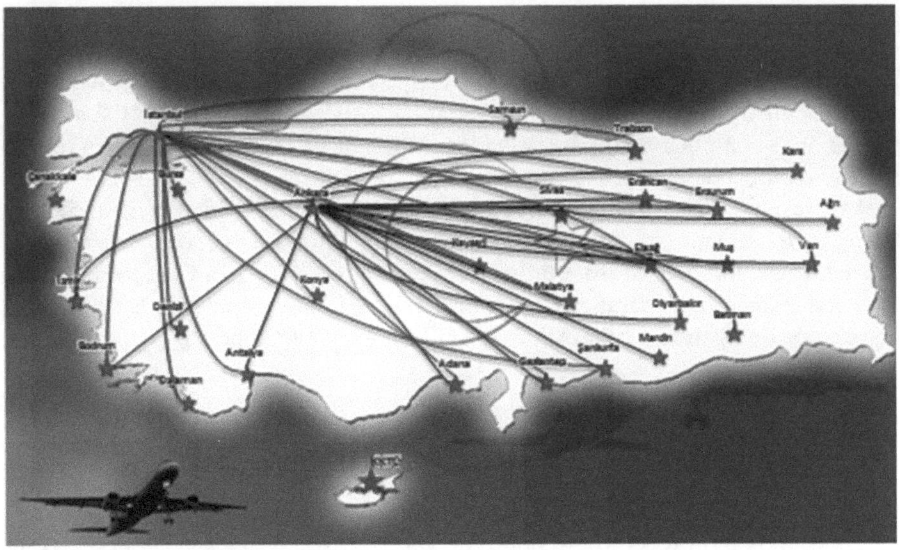


**Fig. 9.1** Domestic route structure in 2002. *Source*: DGCA (2009)

### *9.3.2 Pricing Policy and Potential Competition*

Price tariffs are essentially regulated by 25th article of Law No. 2920. Accordingly, "*a license owner cannot put in force flight and wage tariffs without receiving approval of Ministry of Transport and Communication and without declaring it maximum 15 days ago to third parties with the exception of rate of exchange.*" According to this first price regulation that is put in force in 1983, Ministry of Transport and Communication was the sole regulator body that regulates prices and wages in the industry. By taking into account the insufficiencies of this model, a new regulatory regime over price regulation was established. With Law No. 4647 enacted in 2001, it is adopted that "*a license owner determines wage tariffs and enforcement date as per fiscal and economical conditions and declares third parties before enforcement. Flight tariffs are determined by the license owner and they are enforced 7 days later than approval of Ministry of Transport and Communication.*" This amendment obtained an important incentive for firms to determine prices according to the competitive market conditions by decreasing the regulatory role of the Ministry over the tariffs.

On the other hand, according to EU Council Regulation No. 2409/92 accepted by Turkey, the private airlines enterprises should determine price tariffs under the competitive market conditions. By this regulation, the obligation that firms in the industry are needed to receive approval of the political or regulatory authority in their countries was removed. However, the political and/or regulatory bodies in the country would intervene in the tariffs that they deem as high or low as per the same regulation. In this context, according to a regulation put in force in Turkey in 2007, it was regulated that the flight rights over the relevant lines of the firms which determine their own prices under the operating costs will postpone for 1 year. This regulation is complied with the related legislation of EU and plays a crucial role in front of a probable destructive competition in the industry.

As a result, airline firms in Turkey can determine the price and wage tariffs by taking into account the competitive market conditions. However, this tariff is offered to the approval of the Ministry. Instead, in order to avoid loss of time and the cumbersome bureaucratic transactions, as in EU, it can only be established a notification obligation to the Ministry by removing the approval process of the Ministry.

## 9.4 The Post-2003 Market Structure: Results of Deregulation

The post-2003 term is a turning point for Turkish Airline Industry. Policy makers in the industry decided a new policy the so-called regional aviation policy. According to this new policy, it is aimed that "*every Turkish citizen will fly at least once in a lifetime.*" In this context, as a result of competitive environment in the industry, the quality of service introduced by the private airline firms has increasingly ameliorated, the passengers have been offered new opportunities, and the airlines transportation has become attractive for all who demand this service.

Moreover, there are many important impacts of deregulation movement attempted in the Turkish airlines industry in 2003. While some of these impacts are directly on the industry, some of them are catalytic[3] ones. According to a report prepared by InterVISTAS-EU Consulting on impacts of airlines liberalization in Turkey, deregulation movement increased competition, offered the means to protect profitability by expanding into new markets, increased international traffic to/from Turkey, provided considerable benefits for passengers, declined average prices[4] and thus increased consumer surplus, generated full-time job opportunities and increased employment, and caused increment in GDP (InterVISTAS-EU, 2009).

### *9.4.1 Entry and Route Restructure*

There are other important impacts of airline deregulation over the industry. These are the increment of demand in the domestic and international flights, the

[3] Catalytic impacts include the role of air transportation in facilitating growth and productivity in the general economy by increased trade, business activity, and greater personal productivity.

[4] Although it appears a decrease in the flight prices for passengers, a detailed analysis was not obtained in this chapter because there is not yet a healthy data concerning the development of prices in the industry.

**Table 9.2** The number of total annual passenger in domestic and international flights by years

| | The number of passengers | | |
|---|---|---|---|
| Year | Domestic | International | Total |
| 1995 | 10,347,528 | 17,419,851 | 27,767,379 |
| 1996 | 10,862,539 | 19,918,123 | 30,780,662 |
| 1997 | 12,413,720 | 21,982,614 | 34,396,334 |
| 1998 | 13,238,832 | 20,960,847 | 34,199,679 |
| 1999 | 12,931,771 | 17,079,887 | 30,011,658 |
| 2000 | 13,339,039 | 21,633,495 | 34,972,534 |
| 2001 | 10,057,808 | 23,562,640 | 33,620,448 |
| 2002 | 8,697,864 | 24,927,311 | 33,625,175 |
| 2003 | 9,125,298 | 25,141,870 | 34,267,168 |
| 2004 | 14,427,969 | 30,361,101 | 44,789,070 |
| 2005 | 19,942,692 | 34,583,035 | 54,525,727 |
| 2006 | 26,644,450 | 32,133,681 | 58,778,131 |
| 2007 | 29,310,333 | 37,152,953 | 66,463,286 |
| 2008 | 32,889,593 | 42,078,736 | 74,968,329 |
| 2009 | 36,510,588 | 42,231,487 | 78,742,075 |

*Source*: GDSAA (2005) and GDSAA (2009b)

*The figures that belong to the post-2005 term are taken from GDSAA (2009b). In particular, the figures of passengers concerning domestic flights in 2006 and after 2006 present a statistical discrepancy in terms of statistics between DGCA and GDSAA. In this study, it is used statistical yearbook of GDSAA (2009b) in statistics regarding the numbers of passenger

appearance of new flights from more points to more destinations in the domestic lines, and the elimination of the monopolistic power of THY especially in the domestic flights.

The most important impact is demand increment in the domestic flights. In 1995, as the number of total annual domestic passengers was 10.34 million, it reached 8.7 million in 2002 with the effect of the 2001 economic crisis as well, as shown in Table 9.2. With deregulation movement in 2003, more competitors entered into the industry and competition that occurs in the domestic flights increased the number of annual total passengers to 19.94 million in 2005 and 36.51 million in 2009. Accordingly, from 1995 to 2002, while the demand for domestic flights declined by 18.96%, from 2002 to 2005, it increased by 129.28%. At the end of 2009, the total increment in demand was 319.76%.

Competition that occurs in the domestic flights gave rise to remarkable increment in the number of international passengers as well because the same firms initiated the international passenger transportation. While the number of passengers in the international flights that was 17.42 million in 1995 reached 24.92 million in 2002, this number was 44.28 million as of 2009. As per these figures, while increment in demand between 1995 and 2002 was 43.09%, from 2002 to 2009, this increase was 77.64%. Consequently, the deregulation movement after 2003 brought about a great jump in the total demand increment for the domestic and international flights, as shown in Fig. 9.2. The number of total passengers in the domestic and international flights that was 33.62 million in 2002 reached 85.50 million with an increase of 154.30% in 2009.

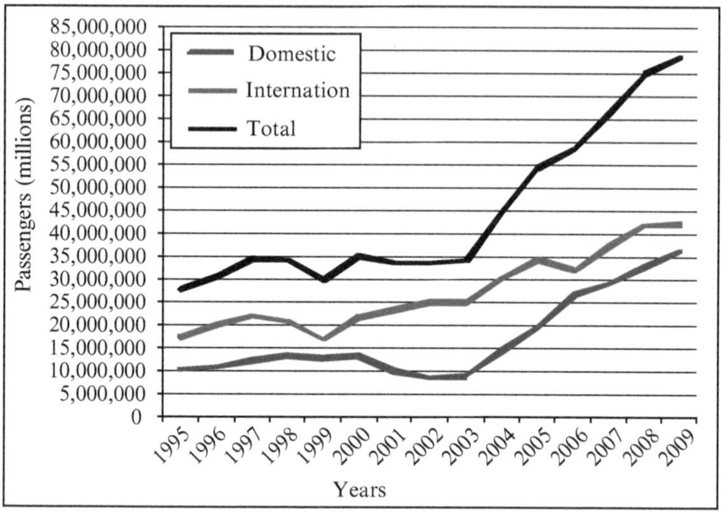


**Fig. 9.2** The number of domestic and international passengers. *Source*: GDSAA (2005) and GDSAA (2009b)

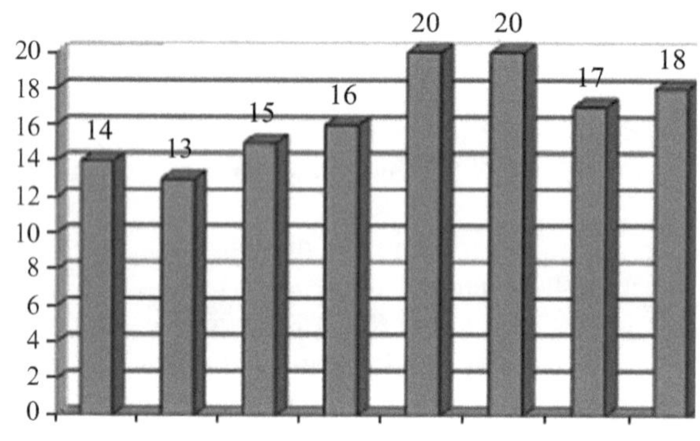


**Fig. 9.3** Number of air transport enterprises. *Source*: DGCA (2010)

With the deregulation movement, an important increment occurred in the number of private-owned firms that enter into the domestic flights market. Increment in the number of firms has brought about competition and thus more passengers begun to fly from different points to many different airports. As depicted in Fig. 9.3, while the number of firms that implement a flight in the domestic airlines was 13, it reached 18 at the end of 2009.

Table 9.3 summarizes the market activities of firms in the industry. Although the first three firms own a license to implement the passenger and cargo transport in the scheduled and unscheduled domestic and international flights, firms such as MNG,

**Table 9.3** The market activities of airline enterprises in the Turkish airlines industry, as of 2009

| Number | Name of enterprise | Scheduled domestic and international flights | Unscheduled domestic and international flights | Cargo transport | Mail and luggage transport |
|---|---|---|---|---|---|
| 1 | TYH | * | * | | * |
| 2 | Onur Air | * | * | | * |
| 3 | Atlas Jet | * | * | | * |
| 4 | Pegasus | * | * | | * |
| 5 | Sun Express | * | * | | * |
| 6 | Sky-Ay | * | * | | * |
| 7 | KTHY* | * | * | | * |
| 8 | Hurkus | * | * | | * |
| 9 | Borajet | * | * | | * |
| 10 | MNG | | | * | |
| 11 | ULS | | | * | |
| 12 | ACT | | | * | |
| 13 | Turistik Airlines | | * | | * |
| 14 | SAGA | | * | | * |
| 15 | Izmir Air Transport | | * | | * |
| 16 | Tunca | | * | | * |
| 17 | Turkuaz | | * | | * |
| 18 | Taiwild | | * | | * |

*Source*: DGCA, www.shgm.gov.tr.
*KTHY is sold by Pegasus, as of June 2010

ULS, and ACT have a license for the cargo transport in the scheduled and unscheduled flights. The remaining six firms own a license to implement the passenger and cargo transport only in the unscheduled domestic and international flights.

An important impact of deregulation is the effective utilization of airport infrastructure. Figure 9.4 illustrates the route structure for the domestic flights in 2008. Although the scheduled domestic flights were performed from 2 centers to 25 destinations by only THY in 2002, it is currently performed from 7 centers to 43 destinations by five airline firms. Likewise, the number of international destination increased from 78 in 2002 to 103 in 2007. In particular, the aircrafts of THY became available in various airports of the world by means of connecting services.

### *9.4.2 Other Developments*

In addition to the number of firms that carry out the passenger and cargo transport in the domestic and international flights in the industry, some other developments in the different segments of the industry have also occurred with the impact of competition after deregulation. Accordingly, as depicted in Fig. 9.5, while the number of air taxi

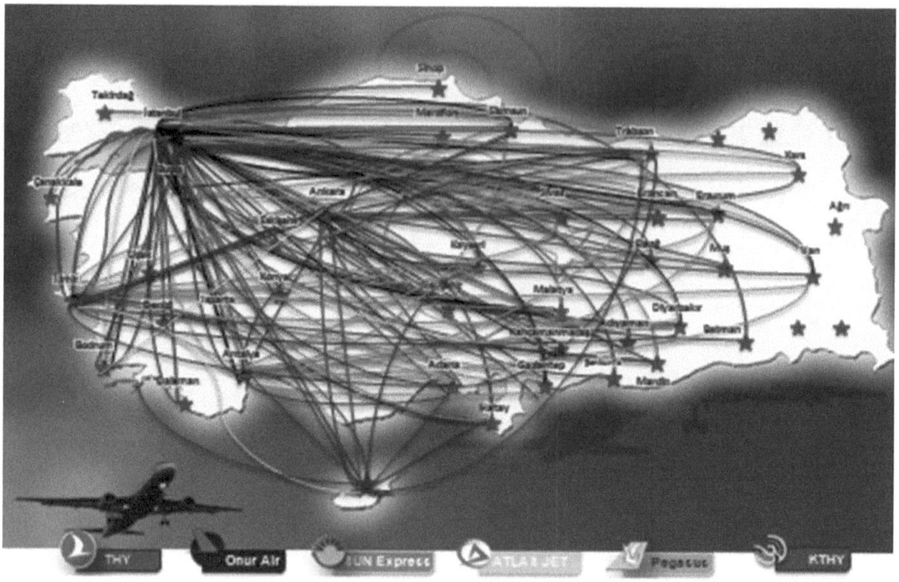


Fig. 9.4 Domestic route structure in 2008. *Source*: DGCA (2009)

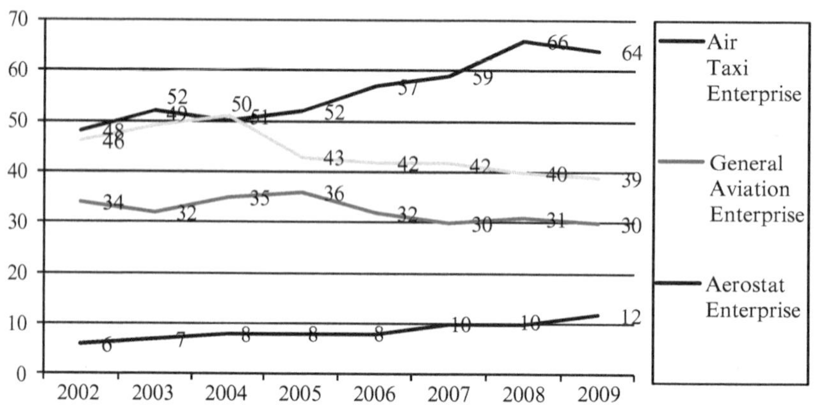


Fig. 9.5 The progress of enterprises in other segments of the industry. *Source*: DGCA (2009)

firms was 48 in 2002, it reached 64 in 2009. While the number of agricultural spraying firms was 6 in 2002, it reached 12 in 2009. However, the figure of aerostat and general aviation firms offered somewhat decline from 2002 to 2009.

On the other hand, due to the increased competition in the industry, the number of aircrafts has also increased rapidly. Figure 9.6 depicts the development in the number of aircrafts in the industry. Accordingly, while the number of wide-body aircrafts owned by airline firms was 150 in 2002, this number reached 290 with an increase of 93% in 2009. This number is above the total number of aircrafts available in most countries, which is rather important for probable emergency conditions

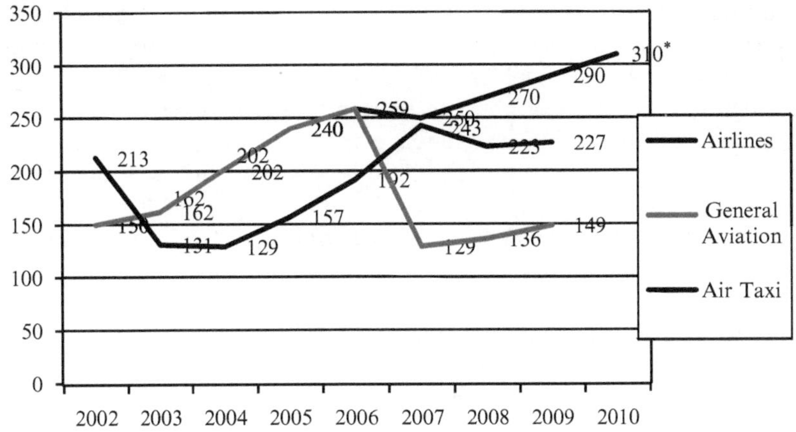


**Fig. 9.6** Developments in number of aircrafts in the industry. *Source*: DGCA (2009). *The number 310 for airlines aircrafts is valid as of March 2010

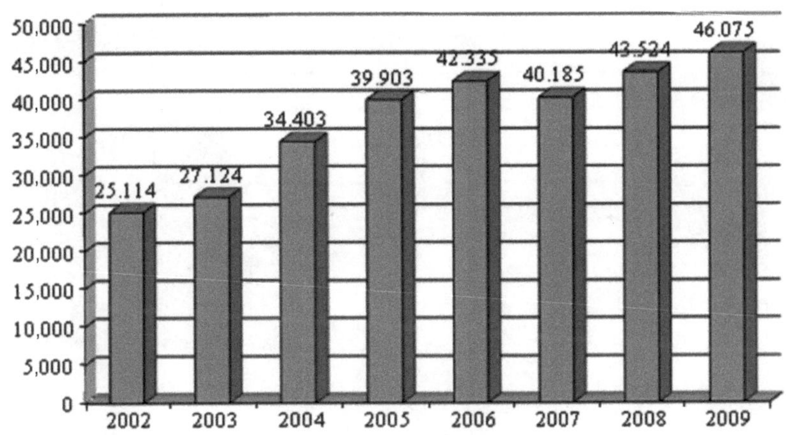


**Fig. 9.7** Seat capacity in the industry. *Source*: DGCA (2010)

in the country (DGCA 2009: 32). Likewise, the number of aircrafts owned by air taxi enterprises was 213 in 2002, it reached 227 in 2009. The number of aircrafts owned by general aviation firms was 150 in 2002 and 149 in 2009, respectively. Finally, the number of business jets, which disappeared during the economic crisis in 2001, went up to 55 in 2009 (DGCA 2009: 57).

Naturally, increment in the number of aircrafts has given rise to an increase in the seat capacity in the industry. In that context, as seen in Fig. 9.7, the seat capacity that was limited with 25,114 in 2002 reached 46,075 with an increase of 83.46%, as of 2009.

It is accepted that an increase in the cargo/freight transportation is one of the most significant indicators of economic growth in a country (DGCA 2009: 29). In the scope of regional aviation policy, Turkey enacted the necessary legal amendments to become a regional base in cargo transportation. In this context, Turkey initiated to construct a cargo village in a 1.2 million $m^2$ area within the borders of Ataturk Airport (DGCA 2007: 19). Turkey has also realized significant developments in this segment of the airlines industry. In Turkey, freight transportation including cargo, mail, and luggage increased to 100% in the period of 2002–2009 and exceeded 1.5 tones million in domestic and international flights on total, as shown in Fig. 9.8.

With the increase in the number of aircrafts in the industry, a significant increase occurred in the aircraft traffic numbers. Figure 9.9 summarizes the aircraft traffic domestic, international, and transit flights in 2002 and 2009. At the end of 2009, the aircraft traffic over Turkey exceeded one million. Between 2002 and 2009, the aircraft traffic was above 100% in domestic flights, as it was above 50% in international flights. In comparison of the flights at the most heavily used airports in 2001 with that of today, it is observed that Istanbul Ataturk Airport had an increase of 71%, whereas Antalya Airport had an increase of 106%.

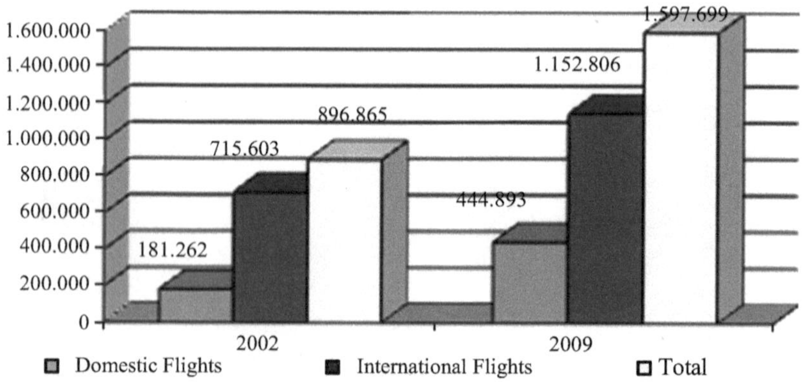


**Fig. 9.8** Freight transportation (cargo+mail+luggage) (ton). *Source*: DGCA (2009: 29) and GDSAA (2009b: 133)

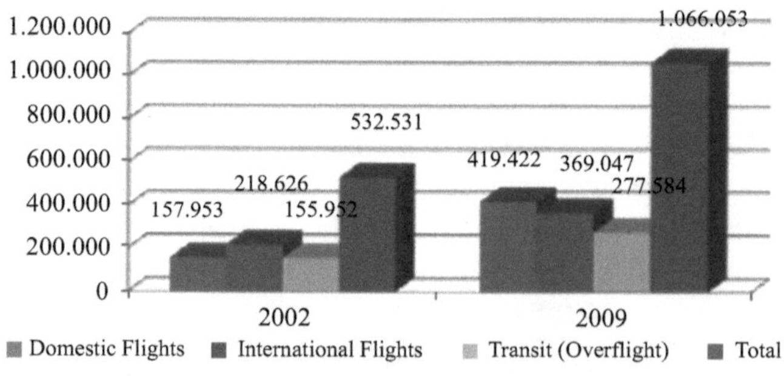


**Fig. 9.9** Aircraft traffic. *Source*: DGCA (2009: 29) and GDSAA (2009b: 12, 85)

### 9.4.3 Quality of Service and Ground Handling

At the airports in Turkey, there are many firms that have serviced concerning the ground handling including representation, passenger traffic, cargo control and communication, ramp (ramp, cargo and mail, aircraft cleansing, and checking of unit load device), aircraft line maintenance (including fuel and oil), flight operation, transportation, catering, supervising, administration and private security services, and inspection for aircrafts. In addition to HAVAS and USAS mentioned earlier, Celebi Aviation was founded as the first private-owned ground handling firm of Turkey in Ankara Esenboga Airport in 1958. Today, HAVAS and Celebi enterprises share the market over the ground handling. HEAS also carries out the ground handling activities in Sabiha Gokcen Airport. Other firms, which have serviced in representation, inspection, and administration, and private security also carry out a service at other airports in Turkey (Korul and Kucukonal 2004). As depicted in Fig. 9.10, the number of such firms with a work permit in 2002 was 261; however, this number reached 601 in 2009.

Since 2000, ground handling firms in the industry have offered a service as per a Ground Handling Statute for Airports (Havaalanlari Yer Hizmetleri Yonetmeligi) in full compliance with the related EU guidelines. Figure 9.11 illustrates ground handling licenses by groups. As of 2002, while the number of ground handling airports with group A work permit was 8, it reached 33 by the end of 2008 (DGCA 2009: 82). The total number of licenses granted by only DGCA was 13 in 2007. While one of these licenses was group A license on transportation, two group C licenses were granted for the enterprises that obtained e-service in catering. Ten group C licenses were also granted for supervising and administration (DGCA 2007: 43–44). As of 2009, there are 42 ground handling licenses in total. Twenty-eight of them are group C license. While 19 of group C licenses are on representation, inspection, and administration, 4 licenses are on catering and 5 licenses are also on private security services and inspection for aircrafts.

An important development occurred in the effectively utilization of airports. Deregulation movement has brought about the effective utilization of idle airports. In comparison of the flights at the most heavily used airports in 2002 with that of

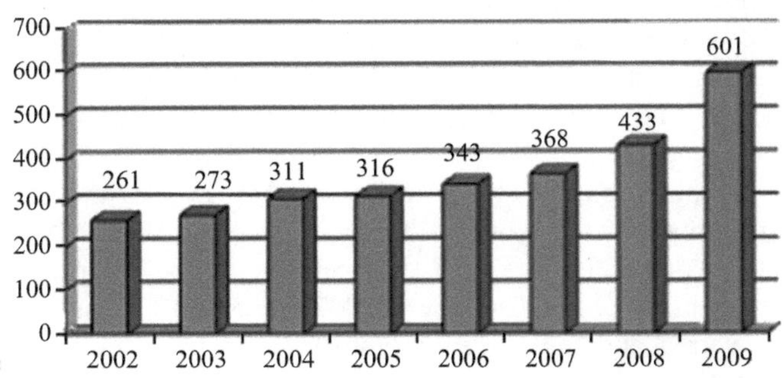


**Fig. 9.10** Total work permit (ground handling). *Source*: DGCA (2010)

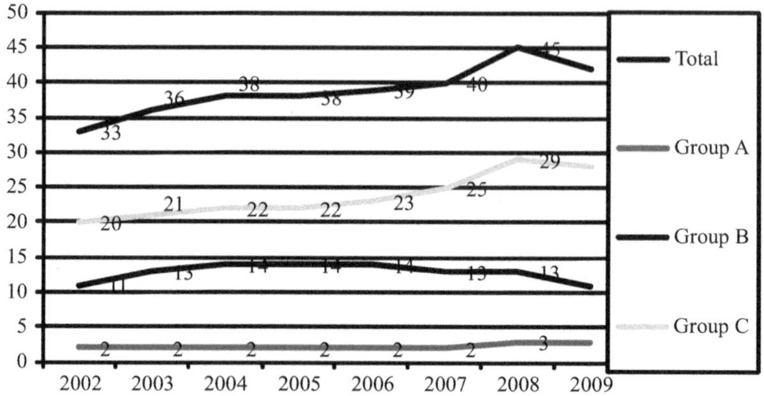


**Fig. 9.11** Ground handling licenses by groups. *Source*: DGCA (2007: 44) and DGCA (2009: 56)

today, it is observed that Istanbul Ataturk Airport had an increase of 71%, while Antalya Airport had an increment of 106%. This development has affected the utilization of all airports in Turkey. Accordingly, the daily average of air traffic grew 97% from 2002 to 2009 (DGCA 2009: 31). A significant increase in the number of airports that provide the ground handling services occurred in parallel to putting idle airports into service within the scope of deregulation movement.

### 9.4.4 Turkish Airlines as a Monopoly Power in the Industry

In order to state effectively the impacts of deregulation over the industry, it is needed to evaluate the change in the monopolistic power of THY. Although THY is a state-owned monopoly, it has been a profitable company for long time. At the end of 2008, its net profit was 1,134,226,211 TL (THY 2008). Although the Turkish airline industry was opened to competition by deregulation in 2003, THY has continued its monopoly power in the industry. The firm that transports 57.14% of total passengers in the scheduled and unscheduled domestic flights in 2002 goes on flying 32.04% of the total passenger as of 2009. Although this situation indicates a decrease in the monopoly power of THY, it is apparent that THY is still the leading firm in the industry. Figure 9.12 presents the development of the share of THY for the domestic passengers.

Likewise, another indicator is the share of THY in the total seat capacity. Although the number of seats owned by THY was 10,672 in 2002, it reached 23,549 in 2009, as depicted in Fig. 9.13. Accordingly, the share of THY which owned 42.49% of the total seat capacity in 2002 was 51.10% as of 2009. Again, in spite of deregulation and the presence of new competitors in the industry, the market share of THY has continued to increase in terms of seat capacity.

Undoubtedly, one of the most important impacts of deregulation is competition occurring in the domestic flights. There was no firm in the scheduled

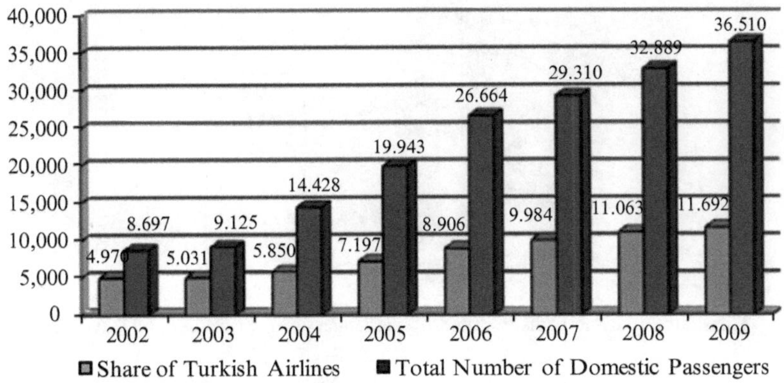


**Fig. 9.12** Share of Turkish airlines in the domestic passengers (million). *Source*: THY (2002, 2004, 2009) and DHMI (2009b)

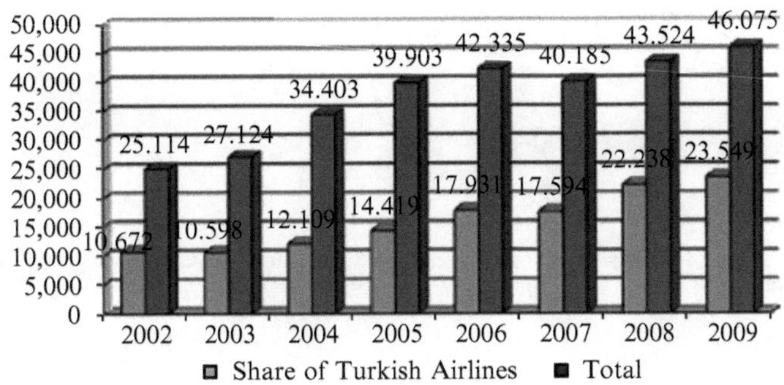


**Fig. 9.13** The share of Turkish airlines in the total seat capacity. *Source*: THY (2002, 2004, 2009) and DGCA (2010)

domestic flights in the industry as of 2002. Thus, it is possible to say that the share of THY in terms of the scheduled domestic flights was 100% in 2002. This rate was 62.2% at the end of 2009. Accordingly, it appears that the pure monopoly power of THY in the industry has disappeared or declined by means of deregulation in 2003. Figure 9.14 depicts the shares of other firms in the industry at the end of 2009. Accordingly, Pegasus (PGT) ranks second (with a share of 12.1%), Sun Express (SXS) ranks third (with a share of 11%), Onur Air (OHY) ranks fourth (with a share of 9.4%), and Atlas Jet (KKK) ranks fifth (with a share of 5%).

Figures 9.15 and 9.16 indicate the total and relative shares of firms in the international flights. As of September 2009, the share of THY in the international flights and domestic flights was 55 and 62.2%, respectively. Accordingly, it is possible to mention that the state-led THY has continued to protect its monopoly power in both domestic and international flights, in spite of deregulation movement in 2003.

The shares of firms which are registered in Turkish registration office in a share of 45% of the international flights are depicted in Fig. 9.16 as of 2009. Accordingly,

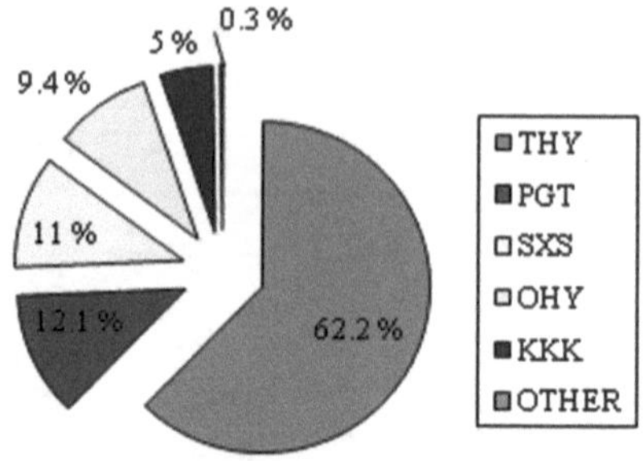


**Fig. 9.14** The share of airline firms in domestic passengers (2009). *Source*: GDSAA (2009b: 119)

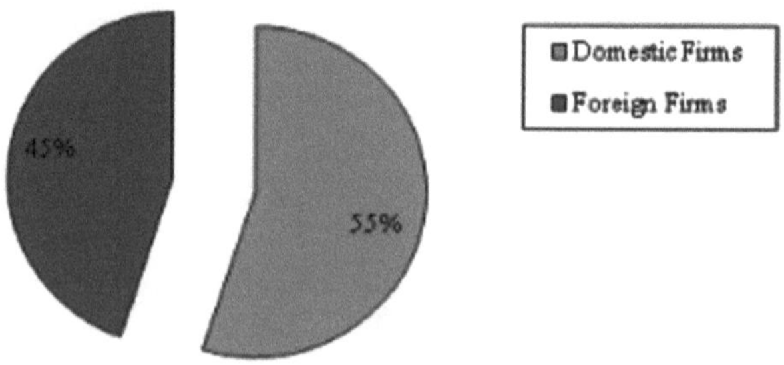


**Fig. 9.15** The share of Turkish and foreign enterprises in international passengers (2009). *Source*: GDSAA (2009b: 127)

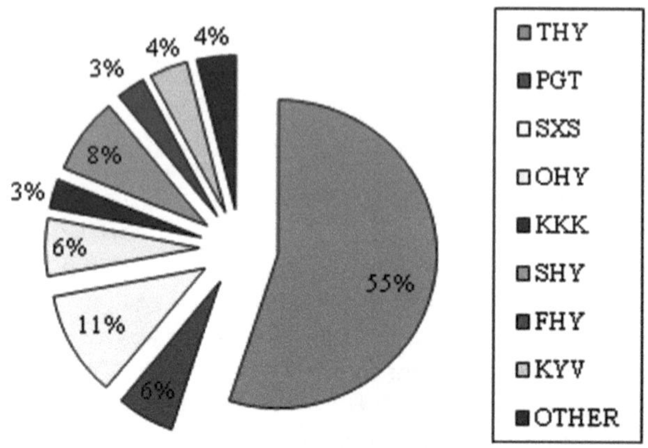


**Fig. 9.16** The share of airlines in international passengers (2009). *Source*: GDSAA (2009b: 120)

the share of Pegasus (PGT) is 6%, the share of Sun Express (SXS) is 11%, the share of Onur Air (OHY) is 6%, the share of Atlas Jet (KKK) is 3%, the share of Sky Airlines (SHY) is 8%, the share of Freebird Airlines (FHY) is 3%, the share of Cyprus THY (KYV) is 4%, and the share of other airline firms is 4%.

## 9.5 Conclusion

In 2003, Turkey has experienced a deregulation movement in the airline industry. It is possible to say that the deregulation movement has triggered the completion for all the fields of the industry. A new institutional structure was established for the regulation of the industry. The legal structure in the country complied with the EU aviation directions, and the relevant regulatory institutions in the country were restructured in compliance with the related international aviation organizations and legal environment. As a result of change in the regulatory legal framework entry, barriers into the industry were removed. The structure of pricing policy and tariffs was restructured. Demand for air transportation increased. New flight routes appeared. The monopoly power of THY has partly declined.

In parallel to the developments within the industry, deregulation increased international traffic to/from Turkey, presented the significant opportunities for airline passengers, declined the average ticket prices and thus increased consumer surplus, generated new job opportunities to thousands of people, and brought about somewhat increment in GDP. The world's most modern airport terminals were built all around the country. Deregulation triggered the effective utilization of airport infrastructure that remained unused before 2003.

However, THY has continued to dominate the industry, in spite of decrease in its market share. While it transported 57.14% of total passengers in the scheduled and unscheduled flights in 2002, this rate decreased 32.04% in 2009. On the other hand, while the seat capacity of THY was 10,672 in 2002, this number reached 23,549 in 2009. Finally, the share of THY in the scheduled domestic flights was 100% in 2002, this share was 62.2% at the end of 2009, although nine new firms entered into this segment of the industry.

Nevertheless, the deregulation movement of 2003 has brought about the significant positive impacts over the industry. The number of passengers which was 8.7 million in the domestic flights in 2002 reached 36.51 million in 2009. Although the number of total passengers in the domestic and international flights was 33.62 million in 2002, it reached 85.5 million in 2009, showing an increment of 154.3%. From 1995 to 2009 the total increment in demand was approximately 397%. As a result, the deregulation movement has succeeded in terms of the establishment and institutionalization of competition in the industry in comparison to the pre-deregulation industry structure.

## References

DGCA (2010); Statistics of 2010, www.sghm.gov.tr.

DGCA (2009); From 2002 to 2008: Turkish Civil Aviation, Republic of Turkey Ministry of Transport and Communication, Publications of Directorate General of Civil Aviation, No. 14, 2009, Ankara.

DGCA (2007); Annual Report: 2007, Publications of Directorate General of Civil Aviation, Ankara.

DPT (2001); 8.5 Yillik Kalkinma Plani: Havayolu Ulastirma Raporu (8th Five-Year Development Plan: Airline Transport Report), State Planning Organization, Ankara.

GDSAA (2009a); Annual Report: 2009, General Directorate of State Airports Authority, Ankara.
GDSAA (2009b); Statistical Yearbook: 2009, General Directorate of State Airports Authority, Ankara.
GDSAA (2005); Statistical Yearbook: 2005, General Directorate of State Airports Authority, Ankara.
Hassu, M. (2004); Rekabet Hukuku Ve Hava Taşımacılığı Sektörü, Unpublished Master Thesis, Competition Authority, Ankara.
InterVISTAS-EU Consulting (2009); Impact of International Air Service Liberalisation on Turkey, http://www.iata.org/SiteCollectionDocuments/Documents/TurkeyReport.pdf, July 2009.
Korul, V. and Kucukonal, H. (2004); Türk Siil Havacılık Sisteminin Yapısal Analizi, Anadolu Universitesi Sosyal Bilimler Dergisi, 24–38.
Özenen, C.G. (2003); Havaalanı Yatırımlarında Ozellestirme: Dunyadaki Uygulamalar ve Turkiye Icin Oneriler, Published DPT MA Thesis, Publication No. 2666, Ankara.
TEPAV (2007); *Turkiye'de Rekabetçilik ve Duzenleme,* in "Turkiye Ic Hat Yolcu Ucuslari Piyasasinda Duzenleme, Serbestlestirme ve Rekabet", Turkiye Ekonomi Politikaları Araştırma Vakfı, Ankara.
THY (2009); THY Annual Report, 2009, Turkish Airlines, www.thy.gov.tr.
THY (2008); THY Annual Report, 2008, Turkish Airlines, www.thy.gov.tr.
THY (2004); THY Annual Report, 2004, Turkish Airlines, www.thy.gov.tr.
THY (2002); THY Annual Report, 2002, Turkish Airlines, www.thy.gov.tr.

# Chapter 10
# Political Economy of Water Regulation and the Environment in Turkey

**Servet Mutlu**

## 10.1 Introduction

Water is life, but, more often than not, it is a scarce commodity. Hence, the degree of its scarcity and how it is allocated for competing uses is of paramount importance. In the absence of a market mechanism, as is often the case, allocation is through nonmarket institutions and by public policy implemented by public organizations at various levels of government.

Water is a renewable resource, but its use at sustainable levels is dependent upon the form it takes, i.e., whether it is surface or underground water. Underground waters are common, i.e., they are free-access resources unless access is limited by institutions developed over long periods of time and/or by public organizations. Their sustainable use often requires close monitoring, formal or informal, which is not necessary to the same extent in the use surface waters, which do not face the danger of unsustainable use.

Waters can be polluted by various users and hence may become unsuitable for some uses unless subjected to treatment, which may be quite expensive. Some uses of some waters may pollute other waters as in the case of irrigation drainage flowing into lakes and rivers. Close monitoring and enforcement of rules may be necessary to protect water resources from pollution by various sources. What matters more is that some uses of water may lead to irretrievable ecological damage and to destruction of unique environmental assets.

Water policies are not designed and implemented in a vacuum. They are context-dependent: on both the degree of scarcity of water and the political power of the various claimants. Hence, the chapter starts with an analysis of the context in its various dimensions and its change through time and then examines the various claims upon water and how public policy responded to these claims and why. Next comes the discussion of adverse environmental effects of the various water uses. Finally, a concluding section follows.

S. Mutlu (✉)
Department of Economics, Baskent University, Ankara, Turkey
e-mail: mservet@baskent.edu.tr

T. Çetin and F. Oğuz (eds.), *The Political Economy of Regulation in Turkey*,
DOI 10.1007/978-1-4419-7750-2_10, © Springer Science+Business Media, LLC 2011

## 10.2 Endowments

When one looks at the macro level, Turkey is not a water-rich country, but it is not a poor one either. Average annual rainfall over its land surface of 783.6 thousand square kilometers is 643 mm, which in aggregate amounts to 501 billion cubic meters of rain per year. Forty one billion cubic meters of this seeps underground, and 274 billion cubic meters evaporates, leaving a surface runoff of 186 billion cubic meters. However, only 98 billion cubic meters, or 52.69%, of this is usable. Adding to this an annual safe yield of 13.68 billion, roughly 14 billion, cubic meters from underground reserves, total usable water is 112 billion cubic meters per year (DSİ 2009, 50). As of 2010, this comes up to about 1,500 $m^3$ of water per person per year (Table 10.1).

This is not too bleak a picture, if not a very rosy one. However, Turkey is a relatively large country with quite a few climatic regimes, which divide the land into regions with quite large differences between them with respect to rainfall and usable water per person and per irrigable area. The country is a rectangular peninsula running east to west, with the Black Sea in the north, the Mediterranean in the south, and the Aegean Sea in the west. The mountains run parallel to the coast in the south and north, thus closing off the interior, and this geographical configuration broadly determines the regional climatic regimes. The Eastern Black Sea region gets almost thrice the rainfall of the Konya closed basin. Generally, the coastal lands facing the sea in the north and south get high rainfall. The Aegean plains lying between mountains that run perpendicular to the coast also get relatively high precipitation. But, the interior plateau and the southeastern steppes opening up to the Syrian Desert get low rainfall.

Not only the amount but also the distribution of precipitation and its form, whether mainly as rain or snow, is important from the standpoint of its beneficial use. In the northern coast, precipitation is more evenly divided over the months of the year, but along the Mediterranean and the Aegean, rainfall is mainly in winter and early spring, which leaves long, hot, and rainless months in between. In the interior and the southeast too, the summers are hot and dry. Thus, over much of the country, there is need for irrigation to increase land and labor productivity, and to achieve this, there is the need to build water impounding structures and transfer facilities.

From an agricultural viewpoint, the degree of coupling in each region between usable water and economically irrigable land is no less important than the amount of precipitation and its seasonal distribution. Table 10.1 makes it clear that where the amount of economically irrigable land is high as in the Konya closed basin and in the Büyük Menderes plain, the amount of usable water and hence water per irrigable hectare is low, and contrarily, where usable water is plenty, irrigable land is scarce, as in the Eastern Mediterranean region. In some regions such as the Eastern Black Sea, there is no need to irrigate as precipitation is high and it rains all year-round.

**Table 10.1** Precipitation and water resource by basin

| No | Basin | Average annual precipitation (mm) | Total surface runoff (km³) | Usable surface runoff (km³) | Usable underground water (km³) | Total usable water (km³) |
|---|---|---|---|---|---|---|
| 1 | Meriç-Ergene | 604.0 | 1.33 | 0.689 | 0.098 | 0.787 |
| 2 | Marmara | 728.7 | 8.33 | 4.315 | 0.613 | 4.928 |
| 3 | Susurluk | 711.6 | 5.43 | 2.813 | 0.399 | 3.212 |
| 4 | North Aegean | 624.0 | 2.09 | 1.083 | 0.154 | 1.236 |
| 5 | Gediz | 603.0 | 1.95 | 1.010 | 0.143 | 1.154 |
| 6 | Küçük Menderes | 727.4 | 1.19 | 0.616 | 0.088 | 0.704 |
| 7 | Büyük Menderes | 664.3 | 3.03 | 1.570 | 0.223 | 1.792 |
| 8 | Western Mediterranean | 857.8 | 8.93 | 4.626 | 0.657 | 5.283 |
| 9 | Antalya | 1,000.4 | 11.06 | 5.729 | 0.814 | 6.543 |
| 10 | Burdur, Lakes region | 446.3 | 0.50 | 0.259 | 0.037 | 0.296 |
| 11 | Akarçay | 451.8 | 0.49 | 0.254 | 0.036 | 0.290 |
| 12 | Sakarya | 524.7 | 6.40 | 3.315 | 0.471 | 3.786 |
| 13 | Western Black Sea | 811.0 | 9.93 | 5.144 | 0.730 | 5.874 |
| 14 | Yeşilırmak | 496.5 | 5.80 | 3.004 | 0.427 | 3.431 |
| 15 | Kızılırmak | 446.1 | 6.48 | 3.357 | 0.477 | 3.833 |
| 16 | Konya Closed Basin | 446.8 | 4.52 | 2.341 | 0.332 | 2.674 |
| 17 | Eastern Mediterranean | 745.0 | 11.07 | 5.734 | 0.814 | 6.549 |
| 18 | Seyhan | 624.0 | 8.01 | 4.149 | 0.589 | 4.738 |
| 19 | Asi | 815.6 | 1.17 | 0.606 | 0.086 | 0.692 |
| 20 | Ceyhan | 731.6 | 7.18 | 3.719 | 0.528 | 4.247 |
| 21 | The Euphrates | 540.1 | 31.61 | 16.374 | 2.325 | 18.699 |
| 22 | Eastern Black Sea | 1,198.2 | 14.90 | 7.718 | 1.096 | 8.814 |
| 23 | Çoruh | 629.4 | 6.30 | 3.263 | 0.463 | 3.727 |
| 24 | Aras | 432.4 | 4.63 | 2.398 | 0.341 | 2.739 |
| 25 | Van Closed Basin | 474.3 | 2.39 | 1.238 | 0.176 | 1.414 |
| 26 | Tigris | 807.2 | 21.33 | 11.049 | 1.569 | 12.618 |
| | Total | 642.6 | 186.05 | 96.374 | 13.685 | 110.059 |

*Source*: USIAD (2007, 51) and DPT (2001)

In the southeast, in the basin of the Euphrates and the Tigris, both the amount of usable water and the quantity of irrigable land are high (see Table 10.2). But, the two rivers run through deep beds, especially the Euphrates, and without building large impounding structures and transfer facilities, which Turkey began to build in the 1970s, it is impossible to make use of the water for agricultural purposes.

Just as in the case of water and irrigable land, population geography and water geography are decoupled and becoming increasingly so. For example, by 2006, 13.14 million people were living in the Marmara basin, and just 375 m³ usable water was available per person per year, whereas there were only 3.27 million people in the Tigris basin with 3,858.7 m³ of water per person. Altogether, 37.94 million people, 52.01% of the total population, were living in water-poor areas, in basins with a water availability of less than 1,000 m³ per person. Another 11.15 million, 15.2% of the total, were in water-short areas with an

**Table 10.2** Available water per irrigable area and per person

| No | Basin | Economically irrigable area (000 hectares) | Usable water per irrigable area (cubic meters per hectare) | Population (in 2006) (million persons) | Usable water per person (cubic meters per person) |
|---|---|---|---|---|---|
| 1 | Meriç-Ergene | 163.6 | 4,810 | 1.23 | 639.8 |
| 2 | Marmara | 123.2 | 40,000 | 13.14 | 375.0 |
| 3 | Susurluk | 183.8 | 17,475 | 3.10 | 1,036.1 |
| 4 | North Aegean | 90.9 | 13,597 | 0.72 | 1,716.7 |
| 5 | Gediz | 174.2 | 6,624 | 2.70 | 427.4 |
| 6 | Küçük Menderes | 45.7 | 15,400 | 2.29 | 307.4 |
| 7 | Büyük Menderes | 324.8 | 5,517 | 2.29 | 782.5 |
| 8 | Western Mediterranean | 133.7 | 39,514 | 1.03 | 5,129.1 |
| 9 | Antalya | 149.9 | 43,649 | 1.81 | 3,614.9 |
| 10 | Burdur, Lakes region | 43.0 | 6,884 | 0.23 | 1,286.9 |
| 11 | Akarçay | 33.4 | 8,683 | 0.77 | 376.6 |
| 12 | Sakarya | 377.5 | 10,029 | 6.62 | 571.9 |
| 13 | Western Black Sea | 101.9 | 57,645 | 2.20 | 2,670.0 |
| 14 | Yeßilırmak | 343.2 | 9,997 | 2.66 | 1,289.8 |
| 15 | Kızılırmak | 623.9 | 6,144 | 4.60 | 833.3 |
| 16 | Konya Closed Basin | 426.4 | 6,274 | 2.82 | 948.2 |
| 17 | Eastern Mediterranean | 99.9 | 65,556 | 2.39 | 2,740.2 |
| 18 | Seyhan | 310.9 | 15,239 | 1.97 | 2,405.1 |
| 19 | Asi | 97.9 | 7,068 | 1.48 | 467.6 |
| 20 | Ceyhan | 515.6 | 8,237 | 1.65 | 2,573.9 |
| 21 | The Euphrates | 1,869.7 | 10,001 | 8.35 | 2,239.4 |
| 22 | Eastern Black Sea | – | – | 2.89 | 3,049.8 |
| 23 | Çoruh | 42.5 | 87,694 | 0.54 | 6,901.9 |
| 24 | Aras | 279.2 | 9,810 | 1.03 | 2,659.2 |
| 25 | Van Closed Basin | 90.0 | 15,711 | 1.17 | 1,208.5 |
| 26 | Tigris | 609.2 | 20,712 | 3.27 | 3,858.7 |
| | Total | 7,254.7 | 15,171 | 72.94 | 1,508.9 |

*Source*: USIAD (2007, 51) and DPT (2001)

annual water availability of between 1,000 and 2,000 m$^3$ per person. Only 23.86 million people, 32.71% of the total, lived in areas that had between 2,000 and 7,000 m$^3$ of water per person per year. The aggregate picture, which indicates an annual water availability of 1,509 m$^3$ per person (Table 10.1), is quite misleading. Half a century ago when Turkey had only 40% of today's population, it was a moderately water-rich country as a whole. But now, it is a water-short country, with half of its people living in areas that are under severe water stress.

A feature of the various climatic regimes which has been of great importance for the development of water policy and for rural welfare is the high variability of precipitation from year to year and over the months within the same year (Mutlu 2002, 210). As most crops yield more if they get a more even distribution of water over their growth period, a high variability of precipitation over the year or during critical periods evinces a high need for irrigation and hence for development of irrigation works.

## 10.3 Forces Driving Water Policies

Water policies were fundamentally driven by three factors: (1) the growth of the population and its distribution by rural and urban, and by geographical region, (2) the growth and structural transformation of the economy, and (3) relations with riparian states in the south.

Population has grown by leaps and bounds since 1950 and has gone up from 20.95 million in that year to 72.56 million in 2009 (Table 10.3). It has grown at a rate of about 2.5% per year between 1950 and 1990, and the growth rate subsided to about 1.5% during the last decade. It was predominantly rural until the 1980s, but urban population has been increasing at a greater rate than rural population since 1950, and by 2009, the country had become 75.5% urban. Moreover, a greater part of the urban population, 33.1 million, has come to live in metropolitan areas, with roughly two thirds of the latter in just three agglomerations: Istanbul, Ankara, and İzmir. Population growth meant growth of water demand for domestic use. As urbanites use more water than ruralites, and that not just for cultural but also for hygienic reasons, urban growth signified a growth of water demand at a rate far higher than the rate of population growth.

Population growth also meant an increasingly higher demand for food. To increase food production in a predominantly arid land with a high frequency of droughts, besides implementing other measures such as increasing the application of fertilizers, developing and disseminating improved seeds suitable to ecological conditions, and fighting the growth of weeds and insects detrimental to crops, it was necessary to extend irrigation. Once the limits to the extension of cultivable area

**Table 10.3** Population by type of settlement

| Year | Total population (in millions) | City[a] population (in millions) | Village (rural) population[b, c] (in millions) | Metropolitan centers: Number | Metropolitan centers: Population (in millions) |
|---|---|---|---|---|---|
| 1927 | 13.65 | 3.31 | 10.34 | | |
| 1940 | 17.82 | 4.35 | 13.47 | | |
| 1950 | 20.95 | 5.24 | 15.70 | | |
| 1960 | 27.75 | 8.86 | 18.89 | | |
| 1970 | 35.61 | 13.69 | 21.91 | | |
| 1980 | 44.74 | 19.65 | 25.09 | | |
| 1990 | 56.47 | 33.33 | 23.15 | 8 | |
| 1997 | 62.87 | 40.88 | 21.98 | | |
| 2000 | 67.80 | 44.00 | 23.79 | 16 | 25.84 |
| 2009 | 72.56 | 54.81 | 17.74 | 16 | 33.10 |

*Source*: DIE (1996, 6), TUIK (2007), and TUIK (2009, 31)

[a] Province and district centers

[b] Settlements other then province and district centers

[c] Between the years 1980 and 1985, some villages were incorporated into province and district center's municipal boundaries. Their population was 2.35 million. During 1985–1990, 255 villages became district centers and some villages around these new district centers were incorporated into their municipal boundaries

were reached, which occurred during the late 1950s and early 1960s, depending upon the geographical area, development of more irrigation became necessary to increase rural incomes and welfare in the context of an increasing rural population (Table 10.3) and to check rural to urban migration, which started as a trickle in the 1950s and was transformed into a flood by the 1960s in some of the regions.

However, plans for the extension of irrigation and the implementation of these plans have been affected by ethnic disturbances and civil conflict in the southeastern region. Although plans for the development of the land and water resources of the southeast predated the start of the disturbances in July 1985, the implementation of these plans acquired further urgency, as much as it was argued by many circles including those in government that those joining the separatist and terrorist organization, the PKK, were poor and unemployed youth and that once employment and income possibilities were increased, the joiners of the PKK would become a trickle, if not cease completely. The joiners of the PKK are like mosquitoes in a swamp, it was argued, and draining the swamp would necessarily eliminate the mosquitoes. The master plan prepared for the development of the resources of the southeast, the so-called GAP Project (GAP is the acronym in Turkish for the Southeastern Anatolia Project), foresaw the construction of 22 dams, some of them huge such as the Atatürk dam on the Euphrates, which is the sixth highest earthfıll dam in the world, 19 hydroelectric plants, production of 27 billion kilowatt-hours of electricity, and the irrigation of 1.642 million hectares of land.

The concurrent increase of the urban and rural populations and the concentration of urban population in metropolitan areas has had the potential of conflict over the use of scarce water for irrigation and for domestic and industrial purposes. Also, pollution of water sources – rivers and lakes – by urban industrial discharges has been detrimental to the interests of users of contaminated water for irrigation purposes, and a source of enmity between them.

In the last 50 years or so, the country's population growth has been accompanied by structural transformation of its economy (Table 10.4). In the 1950s, 75% of its population resided in cities, and a similar percentage was occupied in agriculture, producing 41.7% of Gross Domestic Product (GDP). Industry's contribution was 14.7% and that of services 43.6%. By 1980, agriculture's share had dropped to 26.1%, and industry's and services' shares had gone up to 19.3 and 54.6% respectively. In 2005, agriculture's share in employment was down to 29.5%, while its

**Table 10.4** Sectorial shares in gross domestic product (% of GDP in current prices)

| Year | Agriculture | Industry | Services |
|---|---|---|---|
| 1950 | 41.7 | 14.7 | 43.6 |
| 1960 | 37.9 | 17.3 | 44.9 |
| 1970 | 37.3 | 17.2 | 45.5 |
| 1980 | 26.1 | 19.3 | 54.6 |
| 1990 | 17.5 | 25.5 | 57.0 |
| 2000 | 14.1 | 23.3 | 62.6 |
| 2005 | 10.3 | 25.4 | 64.3 |

*Source*: DPT (2007, 8) and DIE (1996, 410–411)

share in GDP had gone down to 10.3%. Meanwhile, 19.4% of the gainfully employed were working in industry and generating 25.4% of GDP. Services' share in employment was 51.1% and in GDP 64.3%.

These structural shifts in the economy were bound to effect demand for water in two respects, one directly and the other indirectly. Growing industry was bound to generate increasing demand for water directly and industry's increasing demand for electricity indirectly in as much as in the absence of domestic oil and high-quality coal resources, electricity generation had to rely on water power as much as possible.

The third factor driving water policy and plan implementation has been the issue of the use of the waters of the two transboundary rivers in the southeast. The Euphrates originates in Turkey and flows through Syria and Iraq, finally discharging into Shatt-al-Arab. Similarly, the Tigris originates in Turkey, forms a boundary between Turkey and Syria for a short while, and then flows through Iraq. There is no international agreement between the riparians over the division of the waters of these two rivers. Turkey and Iraq signed a protocol in 1946, but due to noncompliance on the Iraqi side, it became obsolete. Turkey proposed a three-stage plan for the development of an ultimate agreement, but despite several meetings since the 1980s, no agreement is in sight (Bilen 2000, 2009; Mutlu 1996, 2006; Bağış 1997; Öziş and Özdemir 2009).

Meanwhile, Turkey and Syria signed an economic cooperation protocol in 1987, by which Turkey pledged to release 500 $m^3$ of water per second from the Euphrates, with deficiencies in any month to be compensated the next month. Following this, Syria and Iraq agreed in 1990 to share the water released by Turkey in the ratio of 42 and 58% respectively (Bilen 1996). Iraq's position prior to the fall of Saddam had been that the Tigris was totally hers and that Turkey should increase the discharge from the Euphrates to 700 $m^3/s$ (Özißand Özdemir 2009, 37), a claim that is totally unrealistic in as much as Turkey's 1987 pledge of 500 $m^3/s$ flow on the Euphrates is only provisional and the long-term average allocation can only be in the order of 400 $m^3/s$. Iraq's new position after Saddam's fall is unknown.

Turkey's relations with Syria have greatly improved recently to the extent of lifting visa requirements between the two countries. Small-scale joint activities have been going on between Turkey's GAP Regional Development Administration and the Syrian's General Organization for Land Development since 2001. Syria might have come to realize that her claim to irrigate 640 thousand hectares in the Euphrates Basin is unrealistic and any investment to effect that would have been wasteful due to the soil structure in the region. (Mutlu 2004; Kolars and Mitchell 1991).

The Arabs, not just Syria and Iraq, have shown undue and unreasonable sensitivity over the Turkish plans for the development of land and water resources in the Euphrates–Tigris basin. During the impoundment of the Atatürk Reservoir on the Euphrates in 1990, the bottom outlet of the dam was closed for a month due to technical reasons, and this was effected after informing the downstream riparians of the plan and increasing the release to 830 $m^3/s$ to compensate for the temporary cut, 50 days in advance. Most of the Arab press was inundated with the charges that "The Turks have cut the water of Euphrates". There were cries of "water wars," which continued long after the regular release was resumed (Bilen 2000, 2009).

The Syrian and Iraqi response to the Turkish plans over the Euphrates and Tigris and the generally hostile Arab behavior over the issue have not affected the Turkish resolve to carry out the plan. However, the Arab pressure on potential foreign creditors and on international agencies has limited Turkey's access to credit, affecting the pace of development of irrigation in the basin. Though most of the dams and hydroelectric plants have been completed, the development of irrigation has been at snail's pace. The original plan was to finish the GAP Project by 2005. Only about one sixth of the planned irrigation is under operation. There is a new plan to finish it in 10 years. But it is only the latest of a number of plans with similar time horizons, and no one knows for certain when it will be completed.

Another factor that has come to affect the Tigris portion of the GAP Project is the environmental movement and the emergence of civil society organizations, which oppose the building of Ilisu dam, the reservoir of which will immerse the archeological sites and historical treasures in Hasankeyf under water. The opponents of the dam argue that it should be resisted to save Hasankeyf, and the DSİ (Turkish acronym for State Hydraulic Works) advances the view that resiting the dam or lowering its height will make it uneconomical. The block against the Ilisu Project has internationalized the issue, putting pressure on lending agencies, and so far, it has succeeded in blocking credits.

The environmentalists have become an increasingly powerful force especially in arousing public awareness on environmental issues (Atauz 2000). Concentration of people in metropolitan areas, where local administrations have given little thought to the development of healthy urban neighborhoods and aesthetical cityscapes, and to the preservation of historical and natural heritage, has provided a suitable seedbed for the development of the environmentalist movement. The environmentalists nowadays are especially active on the siting of new power plants, particularly where these plants are liable to irreversibly destroy natural and unique environments such as the valleys in the Eastern Black Sea region.

## 10.4 Institutions and Organizations

According to North, institutions are the rules of the game in a society. They are humanly designed constraints that shape human interaction and that structure incentives in political, social, and economic exchange. They can be formal such as rules human beings devise and informal such as conventions and codes of behavior that have evolved over time (North 1990, 4–5). Organizations on the other hand are groups of individuals bound by some common purpose to achieve certain objectives. Institutional framework affects how organizations come into being and how they evolve over time. In turn, organizations influence how institutions evolve (North 1990, 5).

We first take up the institutions, the laws and the rules, that have governed water policies and water uses. Then, we discuss the organizations that have devised and implemented water plans and policies within the framework of institutions.

The principal characteristic of the Islamic Law that governed the use of water in Ottoman times, and which still governs the outlook of many people is the belief that "water is the greatest blessing that God has granted His people" and hence it is everyone's right to use it without recompense. Water cannot be the subject of trade for profit, and if and when water is conveyed from its original source to another locality where it is needed, only the cost of storage, transfer structures, and administration can be charged.

Islamic Law was a jurist law. The judge ruled according to precedent, and opinions of jurisconsults compiled in books or obtained from a jurisconsult by any of the parties to a case. The first attempt at the codification of the law was undertaken in the second half of the nineteenth century. The code, known as Mecelle, was prepared during 1869–1876, by a commission headed by Ahmet Cevdet Paßa and came into force in 1877. According to article 1235 of the code, "underground waters are no one's property". By article 1268, people had the right to get water from a well located in someone's property for drinking and domestic use. However, the owner of the well had the right to forbid anyone entering his property, in which case when there was no alternative source nearby, he was obligated to give it to whomever needed it. The same provision applied in regard to water tanks and rivers which were in someone's absolute property.

Article 1234 of the code stated that "water, grass, and fire are free. The public are joint owners of these three things". Any person could make use of anything that is free provided that no injury is inflicted upon any other person while doing so (Article 1254). All seas and large lakes were free (Article 1237). Rivers belonged to the state, and were free (Article 1238), and no right of preemption applied (Article 1239). However, if a river passed through land belonging to a limited number of people, and disappeared at the limits of such land without flowing into vacant land, then the right of preemption applied (Paragraph 3 of Article 1239). Any person could irrigate his lands from rivers, and to do so and to build mills, he could open a canal or water channels, provided that he did not thereby inflict injury on any other person (Article 1265).

Mecelle was in force until February 17, 1926, when a new Civil Law was enacted. Article 641 of the law stated that all springs emanating from places unsuitable for agriculture such as mountains, hills, and rocks are no one's property and that the waters, the benefits of which are public, are under the authority and in disposition of the state. The rules under which the running waters and their beds were to be managed and used were to be the subject of a special law to be enacted. Article 679 considered a source, a spring, emanating from a piece of land as that land's complementary part and hence to be possessed together with the land's property right. However, by the same article, possessing the ground of the land did not also imply ownership of what is under. Underground water was treated like a spring. Later, Article 679 was modified, and underground waters were considered as public waters under the authority and in disposition of the state by Law no. 138. A special law, Law no. 167, was enacted in December 1960, 34 years after the enactment of the Civil Law, regulating the management and use of underground waters.

The issue of water as an implicit component of the wider concept of natural wealth and resources entered the constitution adopted in July 1961. Article 130 stated that "Natural wealth and resources are under the authority and disposition of the state". The right of exploration and management of these belong to the state. Article 168 of the new 1982 Constitution repeated the same principle word for word.

A new civil code, Law no 4721, was enacted on 8th December, 2001. Article 756 of the new Civil Law more or less reiterated article 679 of the old code but was more specific as to underground waters and explicitly stated that "underground waters are of those waters which are of public benefit". Articles 757–761 dwelled on further aspects on the use and management of water like compensation by the injurer of the injuries inflicted upon the user of a particular water, the rehabilitation of the water source in case of pollution, the use in privately held land of springs emanating from a common source, the applicability of local custom, and the obligatory provision of water by those having water in excess of their needs, on payment of its value, to those in need.

The Law on Underground Waters, Law no 167, enacted in December 1960, regulates the use and management of underground water. By Article 3 of the law, DSİ delineates underground water areas, and the related ministry approves and declares these as "Underground Water Management Areas". The exploitation of these areas is to be on the principle of safe yield (Article 21) and according to the technical byelaws prepared by the Ministry of Public Works (Article 4). Prospecting by individuals for underground water and its use once it is found are subject to the permission of DSİ (Articles 9 and 10).

There are also laws, byelaws, and directives the object of which is the preservation of the sources and the quality of waters. Article 237 of the General Hygiene Law, enacted in May 1930, obligates the delineation of protective areas around the water sources of cities and towns. The Law on Environment, Law no 2872, enacted in August 1983, puts down the fundamental framework for the preservation of the environment, and prevention of environmental pollution together with the "polluter pays" principle (Article 28). The byelaw on the control of water pollution, promulgated in December 2004, forbids the discharge of waste water into underground water reserves and decrees the enforcement of administrative penalties to the polluter.

The principal organization responsible for the issues related to the uses, regulation, and control of water is the DSİ. It was created by Law no. 6200, enacted in December 1953. By Article 2 of the law, DSİ is charged and authorized (1) to construct flood control works, (2) to build irrigation facilities, (3) to drain swamps and fens, (4) to examine, approve, and supervise water and sewerage projects of cities and towns, (5) to provide the technical organization and supervision of village drinking water, (6) to improve river and stream beds, and, where required, to make them suitable for navigation, (7) to produce energy from water, and (8) to operate, maintain, repair, and manage all the works and facilities related to functions enumerated in (1) to (7). By paragraph j of Article 2, DSİ can borrow long term domestically and internationally subject to the permission and guarantee of the

Ministry of Finance, and approval of the cabinet. The beneficiaries of the irrigation works are obligated to pay the operation and management costs (Article 28, paragraph c) and annual depreciation charges (Article 25, paragraph b).

DSI is also the organization charged and authorized by the Law on Underground Waters (Law no. 167) to prospect for underground waters, to determine safe yield for each reserve, and to grant permission to individuals for prospecting, drilling, and using underground water. No one can draw water from underground reserves, except from shallow wells, unless certified by DSİ. In each reserve area, DSİ determines the number, depth, and location of wells, and the amount of water that can be withdrawn (Article 4 of Law no 167).

The Law on the Provision of Domestic and Industrial Water to Settlements with Municipal Organization (Law no. 1053), enacted in July 1978, charges DSİ to construct dams, conveyance structures, and purification facilities to provide water to İstanbul, Ankara, Izmir, and to cities with a population of above a hundred thousand. Later, in April 2007, the law was modified, and DSİ was charged to perform the same functions for all settlements with municipal administration, which, as of April 2010, numbered 3228, of which 2266 were rural municipalities.

DSİ was created to undertake big water projects. By Law no. 7457, enacted in February 1960, General Directorate of Soil and Water (Toprak-Su, its Turkish acronym) was set up to implement small-scale irrigation projects using less than 500 l of water per second and generally covering less than 500 hectares, to provide water to rural settlements for doing soil analysis and effecting land consolidation. The functions of Toprak-Su were taken over by the General Directorate of Rural Affairs, created by Law no 3202, which was enacted in May 1985. Then, another change in law and organization was implemented in January 2005, by law no. 5286. By the new law, all the functions of this directorate, except in İstanbul and Kocaeli, were assumed by the provincial special administrations, which are elected bodies. In İstanbul and Kocaeli, the metropolitan municipality was the responsible body.

By Law no 5216, enacted in July 2004, each metropolitan municipality is charged with and authorized to protect the environment and water basins in accordance with the principle of sustainable development. By Paragraph 12 of Article 2 of the law, DSİ can propose to the Ministry of Public Works to form partnerships to manage and operate the facilities that it constructs or takes over, and to transfer the facilities when deemed necessary to natural and legal persons.

DSİ is organized on a regional basis. It has, as of 2010, 26 regional directorates. Each regional directorate may have one or more of the 81 province in its purview. In as much as the national space is divided into provinces on functional principles and the boundaries of the regional directorates have to follow the provincial boundaries, few of the 26 water basins – most of which are river basins – fall within the purview of only one regional directorate. The larger river basins encompass areas in the domain of several regional directorates. Each regional directorate has its headquarters in a province centre and may have several sections located in district centers. The decoupling of water basin boundaries of DSİ sometimes creates problems of coordination. The coordination problem may become acute when an underground water basin falls within more than one regional directorate or section's purview.

DSİ has been transferring, since 1993, operation, maintenance, and management of irrigation facilities to legal persons. The objectives sought are as follows: (1) to secure farmers' participation and to develop local – on the spot – administration, (2) to secure local self-supervision, and (3) to minimize maintenance and management costs.

Not all the components of irrigation networks are transferred. DSİ keeps the primary structures, dams, and primary and secondary canals under its control and transfers the maintenance of tertiary and auxiliary canals, and access roads, and the actual management of irrigation on the field. The bodies to which these responsibilities are transferred allocate water among farmers and collect the charges.

The transferees are the legal persons of villages, municipalities, irrigation associations, and cooperatives. The legal person of a village is constituted according to the village law, Law no. 442. An irrigation facility is transferred to the legal person of a village if that facility serves only to the lands of that village. The same principle applies in the case of a municipality. A municipality takes over the responsibilities of operation and management only if the facility serves the lands within the purview of that municipality constituted by Law no. 1580. When an irrigation facility serves the lands falling within the administrative boundaries of several municipalities, the responsibilities of operation and management are transferred to an "irrigation association" formed by those municipalities. Cooperatives, which are legal persons under private law, can take over operation and management responsibilities of irrigation facilities, only if their byelaws explicitly empower them to do so, and only if their boards approve the transfers.

Until the 1990s, DSİ not only built all the structures of irrigation networks but, with a few exceptions, also operated, maintained, and managed the system. In the 1990s, DSİ, partially under the influence of the World Bank, which financed many of the facilities, and in keeping with the principle of subsidiarity prevalent in the European Union, which Turkey hoped to join, transferred much of the field level activities to the various legal persons mentioned above. At first, some pilot projects were implemented and then, taking the lessons learnt from these into consideration, the transfers were generalized. The distribution of these transfers by type of legal person is given in Table 10.5. A similar policy was followed by the now defunct General Directorate of Rural Affairs and by the provincial special administrations. The principal structures were built by the General Directorate, and operation, maintenance, and management of the system was left to local bodies, except for large repair works.

Development of underground water resources by DSİ is conditional upon the formation of irrigation cooperatives by farmers. First, DSİ prospects, and upon finding an exploitable reserve requests the formation of an irrigation cooperative by the potential beneficiaries. Once the cooperative is formed, the parties, the cooperative, and DSİ sign a preliminary agreement in which the cooperative pledges to take over the facilities to be developed by DSİ and to operate, maintain, and manage them once they are completed. After completion of the works, a "Final Transfer Contract" is signed by the parties upon the approval by the Ministry of Public Works and the cabinet, and the irrigation cooperative takes over the facilities.

**Table 10.5** Irrigation by type of managing organization (as of 2008)

| Managing organization | Number | Net area irrigated (hectares) | Gross area irrigated (hectares) |
|---|---|---|---|
| 1. State hydraulic works (DSİ) | 60[a] | 88,054 | 101,914 |
| 2. Water user organizations | 682 | 2,090,330 | 2,419,364 |
| (a) Village legal person | 225 | 40,198 | |
| (b) Municipality | 154 | 70,612 | |
| (c) Irrigation association | 362 | 1,883,702 | |
| (d) Cooperatives | 100 | 94,148 | |
| (e) Other | | 1,670 | |
| 3. Other organizations | 6 | 16,066 | 18,595 |
| 4. Underground water cooperatives | 29[b] | 443,954 | 513,836 |
| Total | 1,319 | 2,638,404 | 3,053,709 |

*Source*: DSİ (2009, 75, 77, 163)

[a] Number of irrigation facilities managed by DSİ

[b] Number of irrigation facilities managed by other organizations

Prior to June 1997, by the final transfer contract, DSİ committed itself to renovate the wells once and to replace the pumps twice during the economic life of the project. The cooperative was obligated to pay the cost of development of the reserve in 25 annual installments, with a grace period of 5 years and no interest charge (Türker and Kaya 1994, 21–22). In June 1997, a Prime Ministerial decree reduced the grace period to 3 years, and payment to 12 equal annual installments (DSİ 2009, 83), again with no interest charged.

## 10.5 Environmental Laws and Organizations

Institutional arrangements relating to various aspects of the environment are almost 100 years old in Turkey. Article 78 paragraph 2 of the Provincial Special Administration Law enacted in 1913 decreed that every province should do whatever necessary to improve lakes and swamps within the limits of its ordinary and extraordinary revenues. Eleven different laws enacted between 1926 and 1971 had articles related to environment. The most important of them, insofar as their impact is concerned, were "The Law on the Draining of Swamps and Distribution of Land Gained" enacted in 1950, "The Law on Forests" enacted in 1956, and "The Law on Underground Waters" enacted in 1960 (Erim 2000, 177–193; Algan 2000, 221–234).

The real institutional and organizational developments on environmental issues started in the 1970s. Turkey took part in the 1972 Stockholm Conference on Environment, in which, after some interorganizational disputes between the State Planning Organization and the Foreign Ministry as to which side should be supported, Turkey sided with the block of developing countries which argued that environmental problems were the results of developments in advanced countries and hence they should meet the costs of solving these problems and amelioration of environmental issues. Environment as a specific sector to be addressed first appeared in the Third Five Year Development Plan (1973–1977) and in the 1973 Annual Program of that plan. The program decreed that environmental concerns should not hinder industrialization and development efforts. Although some policy makers looked at environmental issues with sympathy, these issues did not have priority. However, environmental consciousness was gaining ground in the 1970s as a result of both intellectual developments and deteriorating environmental conditions at some places, such as the progressively worsening air pollution in Ankara and sea pollution in İzmit Bay. In 1978, Environment Organization was created as a coordination and management agency for the development of environmental policies and their implementation. The organization was at the undersecretaryship level and had a High Committee on Environment. The organization had several changes in name and status in the 1980s, but finally in 1991, it was transformed into a Ministry, the Ministry of Environment, with regional environmental protection directorships (Arat 2000, 166–175). The name of the ministry was subsequently changed to the Ministry of Environment and Forestry.

The first Law, "The Law on Environment", specifically designed to address environmental issues was enacted in August 1983. The law was revised in April 2006. The objective of the law is stated as "the protection of environment, which is the common medium of all living things, within the framework of the principles of sustainable environment and sustainable development". The law has three fundamental components: (1) protection of the environment, (2) improvement of the environment, and (3) prevention of environmental pollution. It also embodies the principle that "the polluter pays". Environmental Impact Assessment Byelaw was promulgated in February 1993 and the Byelaw on the Control Medical Waste in July 1993. The Environmental Impact Assessment Byelaw was revised in 1996. The Byelaw on the Control of Water Pollution was issued in September 1988 and revised in December 2004. The byelaw seeks to determine the necessary legal and technical principles by which prevention of water pollution is reconciled with the objectives of sustainable development. Perhaps the most important article of the law is article 22, which states that "waste water cannot directly be discharged to underground waters even if it is treated". Moreover, the byelaw decrees the identification of the polluting source and the enforcement of administrative penalties whenever the quality of underground waters deteriorates.

Besides the development of institutional framework and the organizations related to the environment, another development, which has become increasingly vociferous, if not as yet very effective, is the emergence of civil society organizations on environmental issues. The number of nongovernmental oganizations (NGOs) focusing on environmental issues was 19 up till 1980; 35 new NGOs were added to this during 1981–1990 and 82 new ones during 1991–2000 so that there were 136 environmentalist NGOs by the latter period (Atauz 2000, 194–220).

## 10.6 Water Consumption and Irrigation Development

Development of water consumption by sector is given in Table 10.6. Total consumption increased by 175.6% between 1972 and 2005, and rose from 15.6 to 43 billion cubic meters. Paralleling the increase in urban population, The greatest percentage increase, paralleling the increase in urban population, was in the domestic sector whose consumption went up from 1.6 to 7.1 billion cubic meters. Industrial use increased moderately, but in absolute terms, it came to consume 60% more than the domestic sector.

The greatest consumer of water has been the agricultural, the irrigation, sector. Although its share in total consumption had fallen from 82.5% in 1972 to 72.1% in 2005, in absolute terms, the irrigation sector's use rose from 12.8 to 31.0 billion cubic meters during the period. Net irrigated area, developed by two public organizations, DSİ and KHGM, was only 275.4 thousand hectares in 1963; by 2008, it had risen to 3.78 million hectares (Table 10.7), which amounts to almost a 14-fold increase. To these, another one million hectares, the so-called "halk sulamaları," which the farmers have always been irrigating by their own means using nearby rivers and

**Table 10.6** Water consumption by different sectors

| Year | Total consumption (billion cubic meters) | Irrigation Amount (billion cubic meters) | Irrigation % of total | Domestic use Amount (billion cubic meters) | Domestic use % of total | Industry Amount (billion cubic meters) | Industry % of total |
|---|---|---|---|---|---|---|---|
| 1972 | 15.6 | 12.8 | 82.5 | 1.6 | 10.3 | 1.2 | 7.7 |
| 1977 | 21.6 | 17.5 | 81.0 | 2.0 | 9.3 | 2.1 | 9.7 |
| 1990 | 30.6 | 22.0 | 71.9 | 5.1 | 16.7 | 3.4 | 11.1 |
| 2000 | 42.0 | 31.5 | 75.0 | 6.4 | 15.2 | 4.1 | 9.8 |
| 2005 | 43.0 | 31.0 | 2.1 | 7.1 | 16.5 | 4.9 | 11.4 |

*Source*: DPT (1979, 343), DPT (2001, 39), and USIAD (2007, 48)

**Table 10.7** Irrigation development (cumulative net area in thousand hectares)

| | Developed by DSİ | Developed by KHGM | Total |
|---|---|---|---|
| Till 1963 | 264.2 | 11.3 | 275.4 |
| 1963 | 268.9 | 20.5 | 289.3 |
| 1970 | 597.7 | 205.6 | 803.3 |
| 1980 | 1,000.6 | 527.9 | 1,528.5 |
| 1990 | 1,626.2 | 827.5 | 2,453.7 |
| 1998 | 2,154.9 | 939.4 | 3,094.3 |
| 2008 Gross | 3,060.0 | 1,180.0 | 5,260.0 |
| Net[a] | 2,732.6 | 1,053.7 | 3,786.3 |

*Note*: Estimated by using the ratio of net to gross area obtained from the net and gross figures given for 1998 in DPT (2001, 42)
*Source*: DPT (2001) and DSİ(2009, 73–74)

streams, must be added. Thus, of the economically irrigable 8.5 million hectares, 36% has been brought under irrigation by the DSİ, and another 13.9% by KHGM. DSİ has plans to increase the irrigated area to 6.5 million hectares by 2023, by which date together with the areas developed by other public organizations and by private initiative, the full 8.5 million hectares will be under irrigation (DSİ 2009, 73).

As of the end of 2008, of the 3.79 million hectares brought under irrigation, 2.73 million hectares had been developed by DSİ, 2.19 million hectares using surface water, and the rest of the 543.5 thousand hectares, using underground water. Starting in 1993, to increase user participation in management efficiency in water use and to raise the level of cost recovery, and under the insistence of international creditor agencies like the World Bank, DSİ has transferred operation maintenance and management of surface water works, excepting primary structures, to various user organizations. The transfer was almost complete by 2008. Of the 2.19 million hectares, the management of 2.09 million hectares was transferred to user organizations, primarily to irrigation associations. There are indications that this transfer has not been entirely successful in fulfilling the sought after objectives (USİAD 2007, 113; Kibaroğlu 2002, 181–182).

Most of the 543.5 thousand hectares, 81.7%, developed for irrigation by DSİ using underground water reserves is managed by the "underground water cooperatives" specifically formed for this purpose in accordance with Law no. 167, and the rest, 18.3%, by DSİ itself and other public organizations. However, the area developed by DSİ is only a part, though no one knows how much of a part, of the total area under irrigation using underground water reserves. As of 2008, 156,103 well permits were given to individuals predominantly for irrigation purposes (DSİ 2009, 84), but this number does not exhaust the total number of wells drilled by individuals because not all of the wells have been drilled and operated in conformity with the law. It is one thing to enact laws and regulations and another thing to enforce them. The laws and regulations may be good but compliance and enforcement poor. The exploitation of underground water reserves exhibits a good example of low compliance and poor enforcement and the case of Konya closed basin a very good one.

As of 2008, according to a DSİ survey, there were 93,948 underground water wells in the Konya basin of which only 27,140 were legal and the rest illegal (İşçioğlu 2008, 136). Another study by OECD puts the total number of wells as substantially lower but still estimates that half of them are illegal (Sargın 2010, 6). Some of these illegal wells may have been drilled out of ignorance on the part of their owners who simply may not have known that a permit was necessary, but probably most were drilled knowing that a permit would be refused and that sooner or later a permit would be obtained in one way or another once the well is drilled and operating. Indeed, permits were later issued to illegally drilled wells so that these could have access to electricity, which has been a much cheaper source of power to pumps than diesel fuel (İşçioğlu 2008, 137; Çalışır 2008, 273; Acar et al. 2004, 53). Some of the illegal wells were drilled by farmers to get more water than they were allowed by the water user association and/or to get water in a timelier manner was possible under the association's timetable (Acar et al. 2004, 54).

The number of illegal wells clearly attests to the low level of enforcement of the related law. Part of the reason behind this may have been the insufficient number of monitoring personnel in the field. However, the more important reason may have been political, as a conversation between the author and a section chief at DSİ has revealed. Responding to my question as to why the illegal wells were not closed, the section chief expressed the view that most of the illegal drillers were small farmers who eked out a living out of small farms. If the wells were to be closed, he said, the alternative for the small farmer would be migration to towns, which would exacerbate urban and employment problems. So, in the present socioeconomic context, it was judged to be better, he continued, to let these small farmers continue using illegally drawn water and be self-employed than to have them join the potentially explosive mass of unemployed in the towns. It is needless to say that such a policy could not be implemented by DSİ or any other bureaucratic organization unless it were imposed from above as a general policy or were inferred by the bureaucrats from the actions and policies followed by political authorities.

Illegal wells are not the only problem in areas using underground water for irrigation. There are no meters at the pump heads, and more water is withdrawn than is allocated to each pump by DSİ. Underground water resources are being used at an unsustainable level, and alarm bells are ringing everywhere. A few examples would make the situation clear.

In Karaman, Ayrancı, Akçaşehir plain, the sustainable yield was calculated as 171 cubic hectometers per year, but actual withdrawal was 350 cubic hectometers in the early 2000s, and the water level was dropping fast (İşçioğlu 2008, 139). The minimum drop in the water table in 6 years between 2002 and 2007 in the 40 observation wells in the Konya closed basin was 0.38 m. However, the situation was much more drastic than this would suggest. The drop was between 0.3 and 4.99 m in 16 wells, between 5 and 9.99 m in 19 wells, and between 10 and 15 m in 6 wells (İşçioğlu 2008, 138). The water table in the basin has dropped by 1 m per year since 1970 (Bulduk et al. 2008, 128).

In Torbalı in the Küçük Menderes basin, the situation was no different, and the water table has been dropping by 1 m per year (Şimşek 2007, 86; Vliegenthart et al. 2007, 76). Safe yield in the Gediz Basin was estimated at 160 million cubic meters, but the actual withdrawal was 219 million cubic meters, and in the early 2000s, one third more than the sustainable yield (Harmancıoğlu et al. 2007, 142). So, overuse and withdrawal at unsustainable levels seem to be universal. The question is why.

In the absence of illegal wells, the amount of water withdrawn from a source for irrigation physically depends upon three things: (1) the delivery system, (2) the type of crops grown, and (3) the type of infield irrigation system used.

Water can be transferred from a source to the field either by open canals and canalets or by pipes. Forty-three percent of the area developed by DSİ is served by canals, 47% by canalets, and only 10% by pipes (DSİ 2009, 78). Water is lost in the open-canal and canalet system due to evaporation and leakage. Although the actual losses during transfer depend upon the length of the conveyance system and temperature, on the average, transfer losses estimated for one particular area, Konya plain, were found to be about one fourth of the withdrawal in the canal–canalet system and about one tenth in the pipe system (Kara et al. 2008, 54). There are also wide variations in the efficiency of the infield irrigation systems. Simple gravity flow irrigation wastes much of the water received at the field head, whereas drip irrigation wastes the least, again the actual percentages depending upon many parameters. Under the Konya plain conditions, it was estimated that simple gravity flow irrigation wastes 60% of the water received, sprinkler system 20%, and drip irrigation only 10%. It was also estimated that the available surface and underground water resources in the plain would irrigate only 377.5 thousand hectares if the transfer was through canals and infield irrigation by simple gravity. If the transfer system were to be of a more efficient one with losses only 10%, irrigated area would go up to 906 thousand hectares if thesprinkler system was used and to 1.02 million hectares if drip irrigation was employed (Kara et al. 2008, 54). Actual irrigation efficiency in the Konya plain ranged between 31 and 90% depending upon the soil type, the type of crop grown, and the type of transfer and infield irrigation system used (Kara et al. 2008, 53). Another study estimates that in the Konya closed basin, if a piped system were to be used along with drip irrigation, instead of the existing open canal system, 300 million cubic meters of underground water would be saved in the 4,000 wells managed by irrigation associations, and this is only about 30% less than the 414 million cubic meters to be transferred from the Göksu river by the so-called "Blue Tunnel," which is being drilled through the Taurus to the Konya basin (Sargın 2010, 7).

All the other parameters remaining the same, the second determinant of the amount of water used per area is the type of crop grown. In the Konya closed basin, where the problem of unsustainable withdrawal is at its most serious, 20.5% of the irrigated area on the average was planted with sugar beets, 6.1% with beans, 5.2% with corn, 7.8% with potatoes, 2.7% with sunflower, 8.1% with vegetables, and 5.8% with alfalfa during 2005–2007; altogether 62.4% of the irrigated area was planted with crops with high water use under the prevailing climatic and soil conditions . In the basin, in comparison with wheat, sugar beet requires 2.90 times more irrigation water, while beans, corn, potatoes, sunflower, and alfalfa require 1.95, 2.5, 2.20, 2.04, and 4.08 times more water, respectively (Topak et al. 2008, 71; see also Kara et al. 2008, 55). These figures relate to optimal irrigation levels, but the farmers in the basin, like most of the other farmers in the country, actually use considerably more water than what is required optimally in the mistaken belief that "more water, more crops". During the 2005–2007 period, the basin farmers used, on the average, 1.63 times more water than what is optimal for wheat. The ratio of what is actually used to what is required optimally was 1.49 for sugar beet, 1.56 for beans, 1.27 for corn, 1.30 for potatoes, and 1.20 for sunflower (Topak et al. 2008, 71).

The third determinant of water use is the infield irrigation system. Again, the relative efficiency of the various systems may vary according to temperature, wind, and porousness of the soil. Still, an example may be highly indicative. In the Konya plain, water loss is 10% in drip irrigation, 20% in sprinkler system, 25% in controlled long pan and furrow irrigation, and 40–45% in simple gravity irrigation (Kara et al. 2008, 54). This means that drip irrigation is at least four times and sprinklers at least two times more efficient than simple gravity irrigation in conserving water. Though highly variable among irrigation areas, irrigation efficiency has been about 40–45% in the country as a whole (DSİ 2009, 78; DSİ 2004, 27).

As has been pointed out earlier, the principal reason for the low level of irrigation efficiency, which is the ratio of the quantity of water used by the plant to the quantity released from the source to the system, is that the transfer system consists mainly of open canals and canalets. Besides having high leakages and evaporation, the system is unsuitable for the water-conserving sprinkler and drip irrigation methods unless additional costs such as installation of pumps are borne by the farmer. Currently, only about 200 thousand hectares are under sprinkler system. Despite the prevalence of gravity irrigation, farmers, especially in areas where the source is underground water, are shifting to sprinkler and drip methods. In the Okçu irrigation area in the Konya basin where a survey was conducted in 2007, for example, 33% of the farmers were using sprinklers, 23% drip irrigation, and 44% gravity methods. Moreover, 39% of the farmers in the Okçu area had changed irrigation methods in the face of climate change from gravity to sprinkler or drip methods. Sixty-six percent of the farmers were thinking of changing their current methods to more water-conserving irrigation methods then. However, it must be pointed out that Okçu area was atypical insofar as the education level of farmers is concerned. Ten percent of the farmers were university, 47% high-school, 24% middle-school, and 13% primary-school graduates. Only 6% were illiterate (Oğuz et al. 2008, 326).

The reason why the government has been developing transfer systems wasteful of water is cost. Piped system is much more expensive than open canal and canalet system. In the face of increasing rural population and rising demand for irrigation, which translated into political pressure, the implicit, if not explicit, objective has been to deliver water to as many farmers as possible. This may sound contradictory as more land could be brought under irrigation in a particular area using water conservation transfer systems. However, such a view disregards the geographic distribution of irrigable areas and the political implications of concentration. Using water-conserving methods could increase the acreage brought under irrigation in limited geographical areas, leaving few resources for irrigation development in others. This would have been politically infeasible; hence, the implemented policy has been to bring as much area under irrigation using the least-cost method of water transfer in as many regions or irrigable areas as possible. As the country has gotten richer and has become able to undertake more costly, but more efficient methods of water transfer, without necessarily sacrificing the interests of some in favor of others, it has shifted its policy toward piped systems.

At the farm level, together with the prevalent ignorance on the part of farmers as to the optimal use of water, it is the absence of incentives to conserve water that has led to inefficient and wasteful use of water. The ignorance of the farmers on efficient use of water emanates from their low level of education and from the absence of an efficient extension system. Extension has been the weak link in agricultural policies. Even a specially designed system such as the Agricultural Extension and Applied Research Project (TYUAP in its Turkish acronym), partially financed by the World Bank and implemented in the GAP region in the 1990s, has failed to make much of a difference principally due to the appropriation of the vehicles and other physical facilities dedicated for the use of the project personnel for other functions (Mutlu 2002, 149). The importance of agricultural extension is not appreciated enough even in the relevant circles as is indicated by absence of extension departments in most of the agricultural faculties at universities in the country.

Even if there were an efficient extension network, the water pricing policy would provide little incentive for water-conserving practices. In surface irrigation schemes developed by DSİ, farmers pay an area-based fee, which changes by type of crop and by irrigation scheme. The charge has two components. The first component covers the costs of operation and maintenance incurred by DSİ in the previous year without inflation adjustment, and the second component covers the capital recovery cost usually calculated at a low interest rate (Yavuz and Çakmak 1996, 35–36; DSİ 1994). In the context of high inflation, which has only recently subsided but which in some years exceeded 100%, such methods of calculation of operation and maintenance, and capital recovery meant heavy subsidization hardly conducive to water conservancy. Subsidization has been even more in the case of underground water development in as much as the cost of assets to be reimbursed to DSİ by the beneficiary water user associations was calculated at zero interest (DSİ 2009, 83). The extent of subsidy in all irrigation schemes was even higher than the method of calculation of operation, maintenance, and capital costs would suggest. Water charges incurred were almost never collected in full. Collection rates hardly ever exceeded 50% during years of high inflation, between 1976 and 2003, when the annual rise in wholesale prices ranged from 17.4 to 120.5%, the highest being in 1994 (DPT 2007, 116); yet, penalty for late payment remained around 10%.

Collection rates of water charges have improved after operation and management were transferred to water user associations, which set charges at lower rates than DSİ. This was as much due to lower overheads as to democratic control of management. The subsidy element in the recovery of the capital cost of fixed assets continues to help perpetuate the tendency to overuse water.

The lack of incentives to conserve water, the poor monitoring of the extent of withdrawal, and the absence of any policy of deterrence that might dissuade those who are much too liberal in the use of water have led to unsustainable exploitation of underground water reserves in many places (Harmancıoğlu et al. 2007, 144–146; Şimşek 2007), especially in the Konya closed basin (Bulduk et al. 2008, 128). The implicit policy seems to have been "in the long-run we are all dead, so don't bother too much with the present".

In urban-industrial use, water is not as much overused as it is wasted. The losses in the water distribution network vary between 30 and 40% depending upon the city and age of the network. Even in new and renovated networks, losses are about 20%. Besides network losses, another problem in urban areas is the illegal use or theft of water which sometimes may be as great as network losses (USİAD 2007, 124).

Water provision for urban-industrial use as well as for agricultural uses has been the responsibility of public sector. So far, there have been only two cases of privatization: one in İzmit and the other in Antalya. The operation and management of the Yuvacık Dam, which supplies water to the city of İzmit, was awarded to a foreign corporation for 16 years (Boztosun 2005, 237–238). The operation and management of Antalya Water Waste Project was given to a consortium of three firms, one French, the leading firm, and the others Turkish, under the urging of the World Bank, which partially financed the project. The concession was for 10 years, starting in 1996. However, the consortium, claiming that it was not making enough profits to meet the internal rate of return benchmark put down by the World Bank, pulled out of the project in 2002 and took the case to the arbitration court. Meanwhile, the water charges for domestic use rose by 357% between 2000 and 2004 (USİAD 2007, 126–127), whereas inflation, as measured by the wholesale price index, increased by only 216% during the same period (DPT 2007, 116). In the light of this experience, water provision for all types of uses is likely to be the responsibility of the public sector in the foreseeable future despite insistence by the World Bank and similar organizations to the contrary.

A third use of water, beside agricultural and urban-industrial uses, is hydropower generation, which is different from the other two sectors in that it generally does not compete with other uses. It is a rare case that more hydropower from a source means less water for other uses. One such case was Atatürk dam and power plant on the Euphrates where there was some tradeoff between more power and less irrigation and where the final decision went in favor of more irrigation.

Turkey's economically feasible hydropower potential is 127,623 GWh at an installed capacity of 36,950 MW (Yüksek et al. 2007, 727). Of this potential, 49,739 GWh has been realized with an installed capacity of 13,829 MW. As of 2008, a further 17,560 GWh with an installed capacity of 5,206 MW were being developed (DSİ 2009, 356). Some of these projects were being undertaken by the private sector then.

The electricity market was opened to the private sector by the Law on Energy Market (Law no. 4268) in 2003. As of 2008, the private sector had applied for permits to install 7,068 MWs in 1,192 different projects. Four hundred and twenty-six projects were approved and granted license by the Energy Market Regulatory Board (EPDK in its Turkish acronym), of which 150 were being implemented in 2008 (DSİ 2009, 142). Some of these projects are in ecologically sensitive areas such as the Eastern Black Sea valleys and Munzur National Park and are vehemently opposed by environmentalist groups.

## 10.7 Environmental Effects

Adverse environmental effects of water policy has emanated in the main from three fundamental factors: (1) increasing demand for water, especially for irrigation, (2) increasing demand for land, and (3) rising demand for electricity. The first two factors have affected lakes, rivers, and wetlands, and the third factor has impacted unique environmental assets such as river valleys, sometimes in unforeseen, unpredicted ways. Some examples make the state of things sufficiently clear.

### *10.7.1 Akşehir Gölü*

Akşehir Gölü is in the western periphery of Central Anatolia and lies south of the Eber Lake to which it is connected with a natural canal. The lake was classified as a class A wetland according to the Ramsar Convention in 1994 and was declared as a first-class area to be protected. It is fed by the Adıyan, Yağsuyan, and Dereçin streams, but the most important source is the Eber Lake whose waters being at a higher elevation, 963 m, flow through the natural canal to the lake, which is at an elevation of 959 m. In the 1970s, the natural canal was deepened and widened, and a regulator was built on it to provide irrigation water to the Akarçay basin. This was more or less the death blow to the Akşehir Lake because any excess water of Eber was now being diverted to irrigation (Okumuş 2007, 247–249; Kesici and Kesici 2008a, 9–14). Also, barrages were built on Kayabelen, Kırka, and Akdeğirmen streams, which used to feed the lake, to impound water for irrigation. To make matters worse, more than 200 wells were drilled by DSİ to provide irrigation water. Many illegal wells were also drilled. As a result of all these, surface area of the lake, including sedge areas, decreased from 360 km$^2$ in the early 1970s to 175 km$^2$ in 1995 and to 100 km$^2$ in 2001. Its depth during the same period went down from 7 m to 1–1.5 m. By 2006, its depth was down to a mere 50 cm at most (Kesici and Kesici 2008a, 11), with devastating consequences for its once rich ecology (TÇV 1993, 137–138).

### *10.7.2 Tuz Gölü*

Tuz Gölü was once the second largest lake in Turkey with an area of 1,942 km$^2$. It is fed by Peçenek, Bağlıca, Kırkdelik, Tersakan, and İnsuyu streams, most of which become dry and none of which reach the lake during summers. Mamasın stream, which was once an important source of fresh water for the lake, has no longer been so since it was impounded by a dam built for irrigation purposes. Eşmekaya springs were also a principal source. Another source has been the canal that discharges Konya's waste water and drains the Astım marshes since 1974 (TÇV 1993, 148–149). Tuz Gölü has not only been the principal source of salt for the country but also the principal breeding ground for a species of flamingos, *Phoenicopterus ruber*, besides other bird species (TÇV 1993, 149–150).

The lake reached the 1990s in a state in which more or less it has always been except for some pollution from the Konya canal. However, the situation started changing in the early 1990s with the damming of the Manasın stream and especially with the drilling of wells, legally and illegally, for irrigation. Although climatic change has also contributed to the change, the area of the lake has contracted from 92.6 thousand hectares in 1987 to 32.6 thousand hectares in 2005 in consequence of the diversion of the Mamasın and Peçenek streams waters for irrigation and especially because of the excessive withdrawal of underground water (Akpınar 2009; Sönmez 2010, 68–69; Kaya 2008).

### *10.7.3 Beyşehir Gölü*

Beyşehir Gölü is the largest freshwater lake in Turkey. Before recent changes, its area was 656 $km^2$. It was fed by the various streams rising from Sultandağları and Anamas Dağları and from the springs in Kabaklı marshes and at the bottom of the lake itself (TÇV 1993, 143). Four to five hundred million cubic meters of water has been taken from the lake since early in the twentieth century to irrigate Çumra Plain.

The conditions in the lake have changed during the last two decades. The streams have been dammed, and most of them no longer reach the lake. Many legal and illegal wells have been drilled to get water for irrigation. As a consequence of these developments, the surface area of the lake has decreased by one fifth, and its depth has gone down from 10 m, at its deepest, to 4–5 m by 2008 (Kesici and Kesici 2008b, 151–153; Mercan and Kardaşlı 2005, 274–278).

### *10.7.4 Seyfe Gölü*

Once there was a lake with such a name but no longer. The area of the lake was 3,400 hectares, excluding temporary lake and marsh areas; it was fed by Seyfe, Malya, and Horla streams and by the springs at its bottom in its eastern portion. It was 10 m deep at its deepest and was a breeding ground for flamingos and many other birds (TÇV 1993, 171–172). It was declared a Ramsar area to be protected in 1994 and a Natural Site of first degree back in 1989.

KHGM built a facility on Seyfe Stream to draw water for domestic use and a weir on Horla for irrigation with a capacity of 3.5 million cubic meters. But these were minor developments compared with what came later. A report was prepared in 1987, the so-called Seyfe–Mucur Improvement Planning Report, in which it was proposed to drain the temporary lake area to gain 23,168 hectares of land for agriculture. The plan was opposed by various organizations but finally approved in its modified form, which took the name "Mucur–Seyfe Basin Ecology Protection Plan," a mocking name change in retrospect (http://www.seyfegolu.org.seyfegolu.html). In accordance with the plan, DSİ built a canal draining the lake waters to Delice River. By December 2006, the lake was dry.

During winters, there is some water in the lake basin, but in summers it is completely dry, and a 20-cm thick salty layer is formed over the area that was once the lake. Whirlwinds carry the salty dust from the basin to agricultural areas causing material damage measured in millions of liras. Since 2004, DSİ has been trying to rectify its mistake but so far to no avail. A prominent columnist was still mourning over the lost beauty of the lake in January 2009 (Coşkun 2009).

### *10.7.5 Avlan Gölü*

Avlan Gölü high in the Elmalı Plain was drained through a canal to a swallet in 1978 to gain agricultural land. The environs of the lake were a primary apple-growing area then. However, once the lake was drained, the quality of the apples deteriorated, and production dropped from about 170 thousand tons in the early 1980s to negligible amounts. Deterioration was also observed in the junipers and 200–400-year-old cedars surrounding the lake basin. In the face of complaints from the farmers and pressure from environmentalist groups, the lake was rehabilitated in 1997. However, the lake dried up in summer in 2004 and 2005 due to leakage through the swallets. The leakages were subsequently checked, but a road was passed right through the lake bed which hinders the circulation of water and which hurts aesthetic sensibilities (Gündüz 2005; Çınar 2010, 15; Erdoğan and Aslan 2007, 55).

These are just a few examples of the environmental damage inflicted by developments occurring under the double pressure of rising demand for water and for agricultural land. Many more lakes and wetlands have disappeared. Of the 65 lakes in the lakes region, 25 have disappeared, and the surface areas of some, such as those of Burdur Lake, have contracted (Okumuş 2007, 244). Of the important wetlands in Central Anatolia, Hotamiş and Sazlıkları have completely dried up due to excessive withdrawal from underground water reserves. Ereğli Sazlığı has contracted so much that little remains of its former self. Sultansazlığı, which is one of the principal wetlands, has been suffering from insufficient water as a result of the canal, the so-called "Eastern Drainage Canal", which has drained off natural water sources in the Develi Plain (Ötegen 2007, 85; Gürer and Yıldız 2005, 489).

In the Konya closed basin alone, in addition to Hotamış and Ereğli sazlıkları, Güvenç Gölü, Eşmekaya Sazlıkları, Bolluk Gölü, Düden Gölü, Tersakan Gölü, Suğla Gölü, Yarma and Arapçayırı marshes have either partially or completely dried up (Sönmez 2010, 65). Yarma marshe, which had an area of 10 thousand hectares, was drained in the 1970s and early 1980s as a part of the Çumra Plain irrigation project.

Wetlands have been devastated by water policies. Turkey once had about 250 wetlands covering an area of over one million hectares. Although it is difficult to determine how much of it dried off due to excessive withdrawal of underground water and how much was drained for other reasons such as flood control and eradication of malaria, 405 thousand hectares of wetlands have disappeared since the mid-1950s, and half of this has been lost irretrievably (Demircan 2000, 113–114).

An increasingly important environmental problem in the last 30–40 years has been water pollution from agricultural, industrial, and domestic sources. There are very few rivers, lakes, and streams, especially in the western half of the country, which are not polluted to some degree. Sakarya, Gediz, Yeşilırmak, Kızılırmak, and Ergene rivers are heavily polluted, at least in some portions of their courses, especially because industrial waste water and sewerage of cities are discharged into these rivers either without any treatment or after only rudimentary treatment (Samsunlu 2007; DPT 2004, 5.1–5.12; USİAD 2007, 71–75; Cinokur 2008; Sarışen 2010; Harmancıoğlu et al. 2007, 144–146; Kaçan et al. 2007; Yüce et al. 2008).

The environmental law is weakly enforced. Some of the industrial establishments which have treatment plants do not operate them due to high operating cost emanating principally from high electricity price, except when they sense an inspection coming.

A very serious threat to the environment have been the dams and hydroelectric power plants. DSİ has built 656, and other public organizations 12 large dams, having a height of at least 15 m from the foundation and a reservoir capacity of 3 cubic hectometers or more. As of 2010, 83 large dams were under construction (DSİ 2009, 355–356). All of these dam projects were undertaken on economic criteria alone, disregarding almost everything else. Birecik Dam Lake submerged Zeugma, and Atatürk Dam Lake the old Samsat, both of which had great archaeological and historical value. The Ilısu Dam will submerge historic Hasankeyf. Anatolia being an ancient land that has served as the cradle of many civilizations, it was probably impossible to build water structures without damaging or submerging something of historical value. However, these water structures and the lakes formed upstream from them rarely destroyed or harmed any unique natural environmental asset. Some of the new water structures being built or planned will do just that. A couple of examples illustrate the extent of the danger.

The first example is of the valleys in the Eastern Black Sea, especially the Fırtına Vadisi. According to Derelerin Kardeşliği Platformu, an environmentalist group, close to 1,700 hydroelectric power plants and 2,000 micro (small) power plants are planned for the valleys in the region, all of them, except for some on Çoruh, to be undertaken under build–operate–transfer (BOT) principle (Fırtına Vadisi Web Portal). Despite some of the environmental impact studies (EIS), which argue to the contrary (http://www.kuzeymavi.com/firtina/f3.htm), it is certain that these plants will irretrievably damage the ecology of these valleys. Even if the EIS were entirely right with respect to other aspects, the visual beauty of these valleys will forever be lost, and this loss, for anyone with some consciousness of natural beauty, is immeasurably great.

The second example is of the Munzur Valley, which was declared a national park in 1971. The national park covers an area of 42 thousand hectares and is one of the largest of such parks in the country. Six dams and eight hydroelectric power plants are planned for the valley which if implemented will again irretrievably destroy the ecology and the natural beauty of the valley (Taş 2001, 131).

There are civil society organizations opposing these developments, but so far they have been unsuccessful. No project has yet been cancelled for ecological and aesthetical reasons. There are court cases pending, but some of the projects are being continued, nevertheless, without waiting for the court's verdict. The danger is that even if the court's verdict were to go against a project, by the time of the court's decision, the natural assets may already have been destroyed.

## 10.8 Conclusion

Turkey is not a water-rich country, even if it is not a poor one. Moreover, distribution of water resources differs greatly between regions, leading to a much more intensive competition for water in some regions such as the Konya closed basin than in others such as the Eastern Black Sea region.

Demand for water is mainly driven by (1) increasing population, (2) increasing demand for food, (3) rising demand for more land in the absence of accessible, low-cost, yield-increasing technologies, (4) increasing urbanization and industrialization, and (5) rising demand for power. Policies designed and implemented to meet demand have changed through time, though in not too radical a fashion, in response to the political weight of the various demand-generating groups.

Agricultural interests have always dominated the water policies. In the 1950s, when water projects began to be implemented in earnest with the creation of DSİ, Turkey was an agricultural country with about 80% of the population living in rural areas and mainly engaged in agriculture. The development problem was how to raise the living standards of this mass of population. One possible solution, besides taking other complementary measures, was to irrigate as much land as possible and this was the policy implemented. Dams were built to provide irrigation water as well as to generate electricity.

As population increased by leaps and bounds, at historically unseen rates, those who could not make a living in rural areas started migrating to towns. This outmigration could have reduced the rural mass as time went on, but high population growth rates continued to add to the rural mass, despite outmigration until the late 1990s. So, the need to raise the income and welfare level of an ever greater mass continued, which meant provision of more water for irrigation, besides provision of other services. When surface water was unavailable or when it was not enough, wells were drilled to provide water from underground water reserves.

As part of the income policy towards the rural mass whose productivity and per capita income stayed at a fraction of that of the urban population, water was provided at subsidized rates, sometimes greatly so. This policy coupled with lack of extension services to train farmers in the correct use of water led to overuse and wasteful use. Excessive use is such that in many places at least a third more water is used than optimal.

Increasing rural population meant more demand for land as well as water. Attempts to satisfy this double demand had especially devastating repercussions on wetlands and some lakes. Although some wetlands had been drained before the 1950s as part of the malaria eradication program, more and more wetlands were drained to gain agricultural land. The blocking of streams for irrigation sometimes completely cut off the flow to the wetlands and sometimes reduced it to a trickle with the consequent result that some wetlands completely dried up and some were reduced to a fraction of their former selves. In some places, excessive withdrawal from underground reserves led to the same outcome. A similar fate has befallen on some lakes for the same reasons.

Underground water reserves were exploited at unsustainable levels with the full knowledge of the authorities. Many wells were illegal. Both the illegal wells and excessive withdrawal were tolerated in the implicit belief that keeping more people on the land no matter at what environmental cost was a better policy for the time being than having more people in the cities where they have the potential of causing trouble. For the political authorities, which controlled the bureaucratic organizations in charge of implementation of water policy, the present is important. For them, the policy seems to have been "In the long run we are all dead".

No cooperative behavior has emerged in the exploitation of underground water reserves due to high rate of population increase and exploitation of the same reserve by people living in different villages, even though they may belong to the same water user association. This absence of cooperative behavior under these conditions is no surprise. Underground water reserves are commons, and the emergence of institutions and cooperative behavior in the sustainable management of commons are dependent upon small group size, clear boundaries, shared norms, homogeneity of interests, low poverty, low discount rates, and low levels of mobility (Kerr 2007; Ostrom 1990; Agrawal 2001). None of these conditions have been obtained in the water user associations, which have members from several villages. Even if all the other necessary conditions are present, the prevalence of historically high interest rates, which gives a much higher weight to a present benefit than to a future one of equal size, has not been conducive to development of cooperative behavior to exploit the commons, the underground water reserves, at sustainable levels.

Environmental consciousness in Turkey began to emerge only in the 1970s; until then, it was generally believed that less pollution could be only at the expense of development, and the choice was in favor of the latter. Things began to change with the air pollution experience in larger cities and water pollution in some bays, and an environmental movement and a higher environmental consciousness have emerged. However, despite these developments, there is hardly a lake or a river, which has not been polluted to some degree. There are laws and regulations, but they are poorly enforced. Purely economic objectives, and short-run economic objectives at that, still predominate. The danger is that some of the unique environmental assets, such as valleys of great visual beauty, may be lost forever if some changes in priorities are not effected in the near future.

## References

Acar, B. et al. (2004). Konya Çumra Çevresinde Yeraltı Sularının Tarımda Kullanımı. *1. Yeraltı Suları Ulusal Sempozyumu,* 23–24 Aralık (pp. 49–55). Konya.

Agrawal, A. (2001). Common Property Institutions and Sustainable Governance of Resources. *World Development*, 29(10), 1672–2001.

Akpınar, Z. (2009). *Tuz Gölü'nün Çölleşmesine 10 Yıl Kaldı.* http://www.radikal.com.tr/Radikal.aspx?aType= radikalDetay&article ID=938445&D... (26.03.2010).

Algan, N. (2000). Türkiye'de Devlet Politikaları Bağlamında Çevre ve Çevre Korumanın Tarihine Kısa Bir Bakış. In Z. Boratav (Ed.), *Türkiye'de Çevrenin ve Çevre Korumanın Tarihi Sempozyumu* (pp. 221–224). İstanbul: Türkiye Ekonomik ve Toplumsal Tarih Sempozyumu.

Alpaslan, A.H., Ataç, A., & Kimençe, T. (2007). Water Resources Management in Turkey and European Union. In *International Congress: River Basin Management: Vol. 1*, 22–24 March 2007, Antalya (pp. 228–244). Ankara: General Directorate of State Hydraulic Works.

Arat, Z. (2000). 1970'lerden Sonra Çevrede Kurumsal Yapının Değişimi. In Z. Boratav (Ed.), *Türkiye'de Çevrenin ve Çevre Korumanın Tarihi Sempozyumu* (pp. 166–176). İstanbul: Türkiye Ekonomik ve Toplumsal Tarih Vakfı.

Atauz, A. (2000). Çevreci Sivil Toplum Hareketinin Yakın Tarihi. In Z. Boratav (Ed.), *Türkiye'de Çevrenin ve Çevre Korumanın Tarihi Sempozyumu* (pp. 194–220). İstanbul: Türkiye Ekonomik ve Toplumsal Tarih Vakfı.

Bağış, A.İ. (1997). Turkey's Hydropolitics of the Euphrates-Tigris Basin. *Water Resources Development*, 13(4), 567–581.

Bilen, Ö. (1996). *Ortadoğu Su Sorunları ve Türkiye*. Ankara: TESAV.

Bilen, Ö. (2000). *Ortadoğu Su Sorunları ve Türkiye*, genişletilmiş 2. baskı. Ankara: TESAV Vakfı.

Bilen, Ö. (2009). *Türkiye'nin Su Gündemi: Su Yönetimi ve AB Su Politikaları*, 2. baskı. Ankara: özel basım.

Boztosun, A.O. (2005). Su Piyasasının Oluşturulması ve Denetimi. In *Uluslarası Sempozyum: Dünyada Kalkınma İçin Su*, 7–11 Eylül 2005 (pp. 231–246). Istanbul, 231–246.

Bulduk, A., et al. (2008). Konya Kapalı Havzası 16/2-a Alt Havzasında Yeraltı Suyu Seviye Değişimleri. In *Konya Kapalıhavzası Yeraltı Suyu ve Kuraklık Konferansı Bildiri Kitabı*, 11–12 Eylül 2008 (pp. 125–134). Konya: DSİ IV. Bölge Müdürlüğü.

Çalışır, S. (2008). Sulama Pompa Tesislerinde Etkinlik. In *Konya Kapalı Havzası Yeraltı Suyu ve Kuraklık Konferansı Bildiri Kitabı*, 11–12 Eylül 2008 (pp. 270–275). Konya: DSİ IV. Bölge Müdürlüğü.

Cihan Haber Ajansı (2009). Seyfe Gölüne Kovayla Su Taşıdılar, 20.06.2009, http://www.haberler.com/seyfe-golune-kovayla-sutasidilar-haberi/

Çınar, M. (2010). Göl Ortasındaki Karayoluna İtiraz. *Milliyet*, 18 Şubat 2010, p. 15.

Cinokur, R. (2008). Ergene Nehri Kirlendi, Tarım Durdu/Çevre/*Radikal Internet*. 16.12.2008, http://www.radikal.com.tr/Radikal.aspx?aType=radikalDetay&CategoryID=85&Arti..... (25.03.2010).

Coşkun, B. (2009). Seyfe Gölü Uzaktır, *Hürriyet*, 25 Ocak 2009, p. 3. http://www.seyfegolu.org/basınhurriyet.html. (23.03.2010).

Demircan, S. (2000). Tarih Boyunca Sulak Alanlar. In Z. Boratav (Ed.), *Türkiye'de Çevrenin ve Çevre Korumanın Tarihi Sempozyumu* (pp. 108–118). Istanbul: Türkiye Ekonomik ve Toplumsal Tarih Vakfı.

DİE: Devlet İstatistik Enstitüsü (1996). *Istatistik Göstergeler, 1923-1995*. Ankara: DİE.

DPT: Devlet Planlama Teşkilatı (1966). *İkinci Beş Yıllık Kalkınma Planı, Toprak ve Su Kaynaklarını Geliştirme Özel İhtisas Komisyonu Raporu (1968-1972)*. Ankara: DPT.

DPT: Devlet Planlama Teşkilatı (1973). *Yeni Strateji ve Kalkınma Planı: Üçüncü Beş Yıl, 1973–1973*. Ankara: DPT.

DPT: Devlet Planlama Teşkilatı (1979). *Dördüncü Beş Yıllık Kalkınma Planı, 1979–1983*. Ankara: DPT.

DPT: Devlet Planlama Teşkilatı (2001). *Sekizinci Beş Yıllık Kalkınma Planı, Su Havzaları, Kullanımı ve Yönetimi Özel İhtisas Komisyonu Raporu*. Ankara: DPT.

DPT: Devlet Planlama Teşkilatı (2004). *Yeşilırmak Havza Projesi: Mevcut Durum ve Analizi*. Ankara: DPT.

DPT: Devlet Planlama Teşkilatı (2007). *Ekonomik ve Sosyal Göstergeler (1950-2006)*. Ankara: DPT.

DSİ: Devlet Su İşleri (1994). *Statistical Bulletin with Maps*. Ankara: DSİ

DSİ: Devlet Su İşleri (2004). *2003 Yılı DSİ'ce İşletilen ve Devredilen Sulama Tesisleri Değerlendirme Raporu*. Ankara: DSİ.

DSİ: Devlet Su İşleri (2009). *2008 Yılı Faaliyet Raporu*. Ankara: DSİ.

Erdoğan, A. & Aslan, A. (2007). Antalya Yöresi Sulak Alanlarınının Kuş Faunası ve Sorunları: In S.V. Yerli, et al. (Eds.), *Göller Kongresi: Göller Yöresi, İç Anadolu Gölleri ve Sorunları, Bildiriler Kitabı, 09–10 Haziran 2007, Isparta* (pp. 50–51). Isparta: Isparta Valiliği İl Çevre ve Orman Müdürlüğü.

Erim, R. (2000). Çevre İle İlgili Hukuksal Düzenlemeler. In Z. Boratav (Ed.), *Türkiye'de Çevrenin ve Çevre Korumanın Tarihi Sempozyumu* (pp. 177–193). İstanbul: Türkiye Ekonomik ve Toplumsal Tarih Vakfı.

Fırtına Davası: Trabzon İdari Mahkemesi'ne Sunulan, Objektif ve Tarafsız Olması Gereken Bilirkişi Raporu'ndan Çarpıcı, Bilimsel Alıntılar. http://www.kuzeymavi.com/firtina/f3.htm (14.05.2010).

FırtınaVadisi Web Sitesi: (14.05.2010) http://www.firtinavadisi.net/modules.php?name=News &file=article&sid=96.

Gediz'de Sanayi Atıklarından Gelen Ağır Metal Birikintisi Bulundu (2008). http://www.tumgazeteler.com/?a=4105304. (25.03.2010)

Göçmez, G. & İşçioğlu, A. (2004). Konya Kapalı Havzasında Yeraltı Suyu Seviye Değişimleri. *1. Yeraltı Suları Ulusal Sempozyumu*, 23–24 Aralık 2004 (pp. 9–18). Konya.

Gündüz, H. (2005). *TTKD: Avlan Gölü'ne Dikkat*. http://www.agaclar.net/?id=showthread&t=13875. (09.02.2010).

Gürer, İ. & Yıldız, F.E. (2005). Develi Kapalı Havzasında Salma ve Damla Sulama Yöntemlerinin Karşılaştırılması. In *Uluslararası Sempozyum: Dünyada Kalkınma İçin Su*, 7–11 Eylül 2005 (pp. 499–492). İstanbul.

Harmancıoğlu, N. et al. (2007). Gediz Basin Management: Problems and Possible Remedies. In *International Congress: River Basin Management, Vol II*, 22–24 March 2007, Antalya (pp. 138–153). Ankara: General Directorate of State Hydraulic Works.

HES'e Kan Bulaştı, *Cumhuriyet*, 12 Mayıs 2010, p. 3.

İşçioğlu, A. (2008). Konya Kapalı Havzasındaki Su Tahsisi ve Kullanımına Genel Bir Bakış. In *Konya Kapalı Havzası Yeraltı Suyu ve Kuraklık Konferansı Bildiri Kitabı*, 11–12 Eylül 2008 (pp. 135–142). Konya: DSİ IV. Bölge Müdürlüğü.

İzmir'in İçme Suyunu Gediz Nehri Zehirliyormuş (2009). http://www.tumgazeteler.com/?a=4550460 (25.03.2010).

Kaçan, E., Ülkü, G., & Turan, F. (2007). Total Pollution Load Discharged to Creeks and River Büyük Menderes Near Denizli City. In *International Congress: River Basin Management: Vol. 1*, 22–24 March 2007, Antalya (pp. 54–63). Ankara: General Directorate of State Hydraulic Works.

Kara, M., et al. (2008). Konya Ovasında Sulamada Yeraltı Suyu Tüketimi Azaltma Çareleri. In *Konya Kapalı Havzası Yeraltı Suyu ve Kuraklık Konferansı Bildiri Kitabı*, 11–12 Eylül 2008 (pp. 51–56). Konya: DSİ IV. Bölge Müdürlüğü.

Kaya, A. (2008). Konya Kapalı Havzası Altınekin Bölgesindeki Sulama Durumu ve Su İsrafı. In *Konya Kapalı Havzası Yeraltı Suyu ve Kuraklık Konferansı Bildiri Kitabı*, 11–12 Eylül 2008 (pp. 278–281). Konya: DSİ IV. Bölge Müdürlüğü.

Kerr, J (2007). Watershed Management: Lessons from Common Property Theory. *International Journal of the Commons*, 1(1), 89–109.

Kesici, E. & Kesici, C. (2008a). Akşehir Gölü Su Dengesinin Phragmites (Kamış)-Typha (Saz) vb. Makrohidrofitlerin Dağılımına Olan Etkileri. *Tabiat ve İnsan*, Sayı 1 (Mart), 9–16.

Kesici, E. & Kesici, C. (2008b) Beyşehir Gölü'nün Ekolojik Yapısının Kuraklığa Olan Etkisi. In *Konya Kapalı Havzası Yeraltı Suyu ve Kuraklık Konferansı Bildiri Kitabı*, 11–12 Eylül 2008 (pp. 149–155). Konya: DSİ IV. Bölge Müdürlüğü.

Kibaroğlu, A. (2002). Building Bridges Between Key Stakeholders in the Irrigation Sector. GAP-RDA's Management, Operation and Maintenance Model. In İ.H. Olcay Ünver & R.K. Gupta (Eds.), *Water Resources Management. Cross Cutting Issues* (pp. 172–192). Ankara: METU Press.

Kolars, J.F. & Mitchell, W.A. (1991). *The Euphrates River and the Southeast Anatolia Development Project*. Carbondale, IL: Southern Illinois University Press.

Mercan, D.E. & Kardaşlı, S. (2005). Göl Yönetimi: Beyşehir Gölü Uygulaması. In *Uluslararası Sempozyum: Dünyada Kalkınma İçin Su*, 7–11 Eylül 2005 (pp. 270–282). İstanbul.
Mutlu, S. (1996). The Southeastern Anatolia Project (GAP) of Turkey: Its Context, Objectives and Prospects. *Orients: Zeitschrift Des Deutschen Orient-Instituts*, 37 (März), 59–86.
Mutlu, S. (2002). *Doğu Sorununun Kökenleri: Ekonomik Açıdan*. İstanbul: Ötüken.
Mutlu, S. (2006). Güneydoğu Anadolu Projesi (GAP) ve Uluslararası Hukuk ve Ortadoğu'daki Gelişmeler Bağlamında Geleceği. *Türkiye Günlüğü,* Sayı 78 (Güz), 58–82.
North, D.C. (1990). *Institutions, Institutional Change and Economic Performance*. Cambridge: Cambridge University Press.
Oğuz, C., Evli, G., & Karaçayır, F. (2008). Konya İli Çumra İlçesi Okçu Kasabasında Tarım İşletmelerinin Toprak Kullanım Durumları Üzerinde Bir Çalışma. In *Konya Kapalı Havzası Yeraltı Suyu ve Kuraklık Konferansı Bildiri Kitabı*, 11–12 Eylül 2008 (pp. 324–330). Konya: DSİ IV. Bölge Müdürlüğü.
Oğuztüzün, C. (2008). Kuşların Dönüşü: Sultan Sazlığı. *Atlas, 184* (Temmuz), 44–60.
Okumuş, E. (2007). Türkiye'deki Sulak Alanlar ve İç Anadolu Örneği. In S.V. Yerli, et al. (Eds.), *Göller Kongresi: Göller Yöresi İç Anadolu Gölleri ve Sorunları, Bildiriler Kitabı*, 09–10 Haziran 2007, Isparta (pp. 241–250). Isparta: Isparta Valiliği, İl Çevre ve Orman Müdürlüğü.
Önder, S. & Önder, D. (2007). Evaluation of Water Resources On the Basis of River Basins and the Probable Changes to Occur in Basin Management in the Future Due to Global Climate Change. In *International Congress: River Basin Management*: Vol. 1, 22–24 March, 2007, Antalya (pp. 777–786). Ankara: General Directorate of State Hydraulic Works.
Ordu, Ş., et al. (2005). Endüstriyel Atıksularının Geri Kazanılması ve Tekrar Kullanılması. In *Uluslararası Sempozyum: Dünyada Kalkınma İçin Su*, 7–11 Eylül 2005 (pp. 415–427). İstanbul.
Ostrom, E. (1990). *Governing the Commons*. Cambridge: Cambridge University Press.
Ötegen, N. (2007). Develi Ovasındaki Sultan Sazlığı Milli Parkını Yeniden Canlandırmanın Yolları. In S.V. Yerli, et al. (Eds.), *Göller Kongresi: Göller Yöresi, İç Anadolu Gölleri ve Sorunları, Bildiriler Kitabı*, 09–10 Haziran, 2007, Isparta (p. 85). Isparta: Isparta Valiliği, İl Çevre ve Orman Müdürlüğü.
Özdemir, F.Y. (2004). Su Kaynaklarının Sürdürülebilirliği Kapsamında Sulak Alanların Değerlendirilmesi: Beyşehir Gölü Örneği. *1. Yeraltı Suları Ulusal Sempozyumu*, 23–24 Aralık 2004 (pp. 75–84). Konya.
Öziş, Ü. & Özdemir, Y. (2009). Turkey's Transboundary Watercourses and The Euphrates- Tigris Basin. In M. Karpuzcu, M.D. Gürol, S. Bayer (Eds.), T*ransboundary Waters and Turkey* (pp. 21–60). Gebze: Gebze Institute of Technology.
Ergene Nehri İnsan Sağlığını Tehdit Ediyor 2007.11.07, *Yenişafak* http://www.tumgazateler.com/?a=2347949. (25.03.2010).
Samsunlu, A. (2007). Ruhr-Yeşilırmak Watersheds: Infrastructure Management and Implementations. In *International Congress: Water Basin Management, Vol. II*, 22–24 March 2007, Antalya (pp. 372–385). Ankara: General Directorate of State Hydraulic Works.
Sargın, A.H. (2008). Ülkemizdeki Yeraltı Suları Mevzuatı ve AB Mevzuatına Uyumlaştırılma Süreci. In *Konya Kapalı HavzasıYeraltı Suyu ve Kuraklık Konferansı Bildiri Kitabı*, 11–12 Eylül 2008 (pp. 256–261). Konya: DSİ IV. Bölge Müdürlüğü.
Sargın, A.H. (2010). *Konya Kapalı Havzası: Sorunlar ve Çözüm Önerileri*, mimeo Ankara: DSİ.
Sarışen, U. (2010). *Eber Gölü: Sazların Dönüşü, 206* (Mayıs), 114–130.
Seyfe Gölü Kurudu (2005). http://arsiv.ntvmsnbc.com/news/34247.asp Sönmez, Y. (2010).
Seyfe Gölü. http://www.seyfegolu.org/seyfegolu.html (23.03.2010).
Şimşek, C. (2007). The GIS-Integrated Surfacial Aquifer Potential Mapping and Its Importance for Aquifer Protection, Küçük Menderes Basin/West Turkey. In *International Congress: River Basin Management, Vol. II*, 22–24 March 2007, Antalya (pp. 78–94). Ankara: General Directorate of State Hydraulic Works.
Sönmez, Y. (2010). Türkiye'nin Suyu. *National Geographic Türkiye*, no 108 (Nisan), 60–81.
Tahmiscioğlu, M.S., San, E.Ö., & Kimençe, T. (2005). Çevre Kirliliğinin Su kaynaklarına Etkileri ve Çubuk -1 Barajı Örneği. In *Uluslararası Sempozyum: Dünyada Kalkınma İçin Su,* 7–11 Eylül 2005 (pp. 348–355). İstanbul.

Taş, T. (2001). Ak Munzur Ak. *Atlas, 101* (Ağustos), 112–132.
Taşdemir, N. et al. (2008). Konya Yöresindeki Sulama Tesislerinden Faydalanan İşletmelerin Bazı Özellikleri. I. In *Konya Kapalı Havzası Yeraltı Suyu ve Kuraklık Konferansı Bildiri Kitabı*, 11–12 Eylül 2008 (pp. 282–288). Konya: DSİ IV. Bölge Müdürlüğü.
TÇV: Türkiye Çevre Vakfı (1993). *Türkiye'nin Sulak Alanları*. Ankara: TÇV.
TÜİK: Türkiye İstatistik Kurumu (2007). *Türkiye İstatistik Yıllığı, 2006*. Ankara: TUİK.
TÜİK: Türkiye İstatistik Kurumu (2009). *Türkiye İstatistik Yıllığı, 2008*. Ankara: TUİK.
Türker, M. & Kaya, A. (1994). *Türkiye'de Yeraltı Suyu Sulama Kooperatiflerinin Kuruluşu, Yatırım ve Devir İşlemleri*. Ankara: DSİ.
USİAD: Ulusal Sanayici ve İşadamları Derneği (2007). *Su Raporu: Ulusal Su Politikası İhtiyacımız*, 2. baskı. Ankara: USİAD.
Vliegenthart, F.J.L., et al. (2007). A New Approach for Groundwater Management in Turkey. In *International Congress: River Basin Management: Vol. I*, 22–24 March 2007, Antalya (pp. 64–79). Ankara: General Directorate of State Hydraulic Works.
Yavuz, H. & Çakmak, E.N. (1996). *Water Policy Reform in Turkey*, mimeo (June). Ankara: DSİ.
Yüce, G., Özçelik, Ş., & Yasin, D.U. (2008). Eskişehir Ovası (Aşağı Porsuk Havzası) Yüzey ve Yeraltı Su Kaynaklarındaki Kirliliğin Nedenleri ve Zamansal Değişimi. In *Konya Kapalı Havzası Yeraltı Suyu ve Kuraklık Konferansı Bildiri Kitabı*, 11–12 Eylül 2008 (pp. 192–202). Konya: DSİ IV. Bölge Müdürlüğü.
Yüksek, Ö., et al. (2007). The Importance of Hydropower Plants in Turkeys Energy Planning. In *International Congress: River Basin Management. Vol. 1*, 22–24 March 2007, Antalya (pp. 720–732). Ankara: General Directorate of State Hydraulic Works.

# Index



T. Çetin and F. Oğuz (eds.), *The Political Economy of Regulation in Turkey*,
DOI 10.1007/978-1-4419-7750-2, 

Kolibri 360 GmbH
Ferdinand-Jühlke-Straße 7
99095 Erfurt, Deutschland
produktsicherheit@kolibri360.de